The Asian Economic Catharsis

How Asian Firms Bounce Back from Crisis

EDITED BY
Frank-Jürgen Richter

QUORUM BOOKS
Westport, Connecticut • London

Library of Congress Cataloging-in-Publication Data

The Asian economic catharsis : how Asian firms bounce back from crisis / edited by
Frank-Jürgen Richter.
p. cm.
Includes bibliographical references and index.
ISBN 1–56720–377–9 (alk. paper)
1. Industrial management—Asia. 2. Corporations—Asia. I. Richter, Frank-Jürgen.
HD70.A7A75 2000
338.5'43'095—dc21 99–056364

British Library Cataloguing in Publication Data is available.

Library of Congress Catalog Card Number: 99–056364
ISBN: 1–56720–377–9

First published in 2000

Quorum Books, 88 Post Road West, Westport, CT 06881
An imprint of Greenwood Publishing Group, Inc.
www.quorumbooks.com

Printed in the United States of America

The paper used in this book complies with the
Permanent Paper Standard issued by the National
Information Standards Organization (Z39.48–1984).

10 9 8 7 6 5 4 3 2 1

Contents

Figures and Tables

FIGURES

TABLES

Preface

This book provides an analysis of the strategic responses of Asian firms to the Asian economic crisis. It discusses up-to-date developments in both the theory and practice of Asian ways of management.

The contributors examine the ongoing organizational restructuring of Asian firms, analyze emerging cooperation strategies, and search for an Asian "post-crisis" management paradigm. While each author looks at the topic of the "Asian Economic Catharsis" differently, a common perspective is being put forward. There are plenty of new opportunities in Asia which have to be grasped and channeled.

The contributors to this volume are from industry, management consultancies, and academia. They use case studies to illustrate the long journey back of Asian firms.

This book offers insights to management practitioners and scholars seeking to understand Asian firms, and the issue of strategic reorientation and catharsis in the aftermath of the Asian economic crisis.

The Asian Economic Catharsis

Chapter 1

A Perspective on Asian Management

Frank-Jürgen Richter

INTRODUCTION

Recent dramatic changes in the global and national economic environment have presented Asian firms with a series of complex problems. Until a few years ago, Asia's vigorously growing companies were rapidly expanding, contributing to the so-called "Asian miracle" (Arogyaswamy, 1999; World Bank, 1993). Thus the Asian managers, seduced by the strength of their economies, became convinced that the long-term growth of their economies would continue, and they were sure of the superiority of *their* "Asian style of management." Their thoughts were congruent with values widespread in Asia, wherein relationships usually count more than market efficiency; conglomerates and networks often matter more than individual firms; and wealth creation for society as a whole, over the long term, takes priority over short-term profit taking.

Meanwhile, in the Western literature, some authors praised Asian management methods (Fallows, 1996; Phongpaichit and Baker, 1996; Richter, 1999; Womack, Jones, and Roos, 1990), some harbored envy (Witley, 1992), and others warned of an economic threat from Japan, South Korea, and the Asian Newly Industrializing Countries (NICs) (Harland, 1997; Rowher, 1996). Only a few, like Yoshihara (1988) and Krugman (1994), warned about the coming crisis of the Asian economic system and the regression of the so-called Asian style of management.

Until the mid-1990s, however, there was widespread confidence that the "Asian miracle" of rapid growth would continue and that Asia would maintain its role as the chief powerhouse for growth in the world economy. Real per capita incomes in Asian economies had grown at an average rate of 4 to 6 percent per annum since the 1960s. Asia performed well above the world average for some three decades. Asian firms, which have grown increasingly global, not only challenged Western firms in terms of market share, but also questioned the fundamental assumptions about economic rationality which guide Western firms' behavior. Although there is no common definition of "Asian management," there are some common features among the countries in how they perceive and do business:

- The crucial economic player in Asian societies is typically not the individual but rather the network in which the individual is embedded. Asians believe that social relations between economic actors do not impede market functioning but rather promote it. Just as Western economies have institutionalized ways of maintaining autonomy between actors, Asian economies are rooted institutions that encourage and maintain ties.
- The emphasis in Asia on pragmatism stands in contrast to "Western" rationality. The decision-making process of Asian firms, known as *nemawashi* in Japan, *noonchi* in Korea, *musjawara* in Malaysia, or *tonguo houmen* in China, is not well understood and may lead—in Western eyes—to biased and noncomprehensible decisions.
- The management practice is based on social arrangements peculiar to the employment system which assure acceptance of authority and the cooperative and diligent participation of all employees in corporate activities.
- Asian firms focus more on creating growth—and less on shareholder value as perceived within the framework of Western capitalism. Business groups proliferate across a wide range of industrial activities, hindering a clear focus on core competencies.

In mid-1997, the belief that Asian management was superior to Western forms of organizing was shattered as currencies plunged, financial institutions closed their doors, and rapid growth turned to recession, resulting in the failure of Asian firms and conglomerates. The Asian economic crisis destroyed businesses and reputations. Quite often, organizational orthodoxy survived the events of the crisis more or less intact. Throughout Asia, many firms have been worrying about the external factors of the economic crisis and are rightly concerned about these factors. Many, however, have become overly distressed over these and forgotten about internal ones within their own organizations. External factors like the foundations of economic policy and the efficiency of the finance sector are almost beyond their own control. Internal factors, on the other hand, such as their general ways of doing business are well within their power to change.

When Asian economies were growing rapidly, governments and firms paid little attention to returns on capital investment. Similarly, as long as labor was cheap and export markets were widely receptive, labor efficiency was not an issue. Today, improved labor efficiency is a priority in every part of any business, from research and development to sales. The steps Asian firms need to take are standard practices in most multinationals. For Asian firms, however, the extent of the improvements they must make represents a massive challenge.

This is not just another book on the Asian economic crisis. There are many excellent analyses available which trace the history of economic default with all its side-effects (see, e.g., Backman, 1999; Delhaise, 1999; Godement, 1999;

Jomo, 1998; McLeod and Garnaut, 1998). Instead, this book explores the impact of the crisis and the implications for business. How are Asian firms adjusting to the new economic realities? How have they developed their management style? Does "Asian management" have to be adjusted to the world's current dominant form of economic organization—American capitalism? Or are Asian firms developing hybrid forms of management that combine elements of both Western and Asian thinking?

With regard to these open questions, it seems that talk about the term *Asian economic catharsis* is preferable to *Asian economic crisis*, for Asian firms *must* develop a new organizational dynamism simply to survive. And many economists are certain that they will (Bhagwati, 1999; Cheah, 2000; Zahra, George, and Garvis 1999). The region has developed many efforts to overcome the emergency at hand through sweeping restructuring. With more positive economic signals appearing every day, many Asian managers assume that all will be well.

This book is not the last word in understanding the crisis and the resulting loss in confidence. The chapters seek to represent a wide range of perspectives, as viewed by academics, consultants, and businesspeople.

CRISIS AND CATHARSIS: AN OVERVIEW

Part I presents overviews of the subject. The likely length and severity of the Asian catharsis, the prospects for the future, and the implications and opportunities for firms in the years ahead are being considered, distilling lessons learned from entrepreneurs and managers that see the current situation as an opportunity to build, or even strengthen, their positions in the region through the pursuit of new game opportunities. Chapter 2 provides a forward look at the recovering nexus of Asian business. Chapter 3 reflects the decline of Japanese economic leadership in Asia. Apparently, there are serious questions about the Japanese economic model, both for Japan and its continued application to the emerging Asian economies. Chapter 4 explores the various dimensions of the crisis and discusses the implications for international business.

The remaining chapters in this book examine themes related to organizational restructuring, allying and venturing, and new Asian management paradigms.

ORGANIZATIONAL RESTRUCTURING AND THE MANAGEMENT OF THE FIRM

Asian firms will have an increasingly tough time sustaining growth through exports as they did in the past. It is not just that everyone is trying to export their way out of the crisis. Asia's economic collapse was largely triggered by overinvestment in production capacity that exceeded the various countries' domestic demand. The conviction that exports would absorb the overcapacity obviously proved wrong. Now, Asian firms have to make real changes within their businesses to stay competitive.

The pace of restructuring has varied considerably within Asia. Southeast Asian firms, in particular, are finally getting down to the painful task of restructuring their businesses. Japan and South Korea, however, may be seen as lagging behind their neighbors. The accelerating pace of restructuring throughout most of Asia may help cushion the region from Japan's and Korea's problems.

How can Asian firms maneuver through the storms of the crisis? First, they can embark on a fast turnaround program, which may comprise typical elements as short-term adjustments and operational improvement. The approach Asian firms adopt to manage turnaround programs should not be so very different from that taken by any multinational in similar straits, although Asian firms face a tougher challenge. Many Asian firms are unprepared.

For many Asian firms, debt has been a dead weight around their necks. They have either been at risk of defaulting on their loans, or they have already stopped making debt repayments. These firms have little choice but to take the drastic measures needed to avoid extinction. At the same time, Asian firms need to release cash by, for example, selling nonessential assets, limiting capital spending to the bare minimum, and cutting back on inventories and accounts receivable. They must also reassure lenders if loans are to continue, or even increase. Promoting early retirement and negotiating salary reductions are further options. Reducing purchasing costs and improving marketing and pricing capabilities are essential.

The chapters in this section highlight the organizational responses of Thai construction firms, Indian banks, and Chinese state-owned enterprises. Although all the firms analyzed show some kind of organizational response, they vary substantially in terms of direction, magnitude, and timing of response. The case of Chinese state-owned firms is of particular interest: China's surprising stability—until now—amidst the economic turmoil of other Asian countries led to delays in the restructuring efforts of the state sector. In the near future, with China's entry into the World Trade Organization (WTO), limitations to foreign investment might be further reduced, since China's state-run enterprises, which in the past used to be off-limits for foreign investors, are expected to be transformed into market-driven corporations. This policy will provide China's economy and foreign companies with new opportunities. However, as the recent Asian crisis suggests, it will probably add risk as well.

ALLYING AND VENTURING: THE UNFOLDING OF A NEW INTERFIRM RATIONALITY

Some Asian management practices proved to work out until recently. By carefully combining resources located within and outside the organization, Asian firms have steadily made innovations across the spectrum of industry and have formed alliances and conglomerates. Until the economic crisis occurred, this way of organizing in Asia efficiently facilitated the supply chain, flexible production, and forceful research and development (R&D) activities by emphasizing process innovations. Like the Japanese vertical production networks—where there are several suppliers of parts all of whom are competing with each other and where a 20 percent attrition rate holds—this is competition actually. Whereas if IBM is making all its chips within the organization through vertical integration, or if General Motors is buying 75 percent of parts from within its own system rather from outside, it may be argued that Japanese vertical production networks have been more efficient. The oriental concept of cooperation always comprehends elements of competition, whereas the basic relationship is based on trust and interdependence. However, the risk of Asian cooperation practices is that the pooling of resources may be worn out to expand in unrelated businesses.

Most of the reforms being championed by the International Monetary Fund (IMF) and Western economists have been aimed at unraveling the tight networks of collaboration among government agencies, financial institutions, firms, and distributors. The concern, however, is that the region's conglomerates are being dismantled, with little concern about what might replace them as engines of growth able to hold their own in the global economy.

The chapters in this section provide some fresh thoughts on how to transcend traditional forms of cooperative arrangement in Asia, taking advantage of both occidental and oriental perspectives. The reader can witness Sony's bold experiments in reorganizing its business network and new kinds of alliances in the Japanese finance sector, and read some strategic advice on how to increase the competitiveness of joint ventures in India.

On one issue, above all, the chapters agree. The major aim of reforming business networks should be to identify risks that might threaten survival by separating healthy businesses from ailing ones. Diversification at any cost is no longer tenable. Asian firms do not have the capacity to manage all of their businesses well, nor are the domestic markets big enough to support them. Firms have to give up their inclination with growth, but they have to generate profits.

IN SEARCH OF AN ASIAN "POST-CRISIS" MANAGEMENT PARADIGM

Restructuring so far has focused on fixing the organization's short-term problems, not generating new business models. For its long-term prosperity, Asian firms still face plenty of tough challenges. In the long term they have to rethink their way of doing business by changing their organizational layout, modes of knowledge creating, or their corporate culture. High growth may not resume for years, so firms need to focus on highly efficient organizations and cultures.

The pace of change, however, may be rather slow. Despite the strength of the crisis, "Asian capitalism" will continue to exist in most Asian economies. In many cases, however, management systems with hybrid characteristics are emerging, whether in Southeast Asia, Japan, South Korea, India, or even China. The future could bring a hybrid of Asian and Western capitalism and management styles rather than the domination of one system. The best of both worlds may be merged in post-crisis management practices. As Asian firms are in the midst of change, the business models–or paradigms–also are subject to change and developments. Hence, there is the hope that management practices and academic discussion around a new Asian management paradigm will be advanced.

Part IV provides a glimpse of models that seek to describe a new Asian management paradigm. Asian management, as it existed before the crisis in 1997, was instrumental in propelling Asia's dynamic growth. The old mechanisms of relying on fast growth, however, have become counterproductive. It is suggested that Asian firms need to induce creative learning to be rewarded with a proactive management system. Creative learning is seen as a new mechanism for reflecting on culturally bound behavior and for providing an avenue through which new models of perception may emerge. The creation of knowledge may also provide a platform for increasing the value of products and services. Chinese network management as an alternative strategic management model, in particular, may be best suited to situations that resemble the scarce business environments in which it was developed—environments generally found in emerging economies—and in unstable situations like those that have developed in the midst of the Asian economic crisis.

Another suggestion centers around the assumption that, in foreign transplants, Asian—and more particular—Japanese management was successfully transferred by introducing a set of changes in its original structure, due to the need to cope with different environments. This ''hybrid model'' can be used as a benchmark for Japanese parent companies willing to change their management systems.

In the end, the Asian economic crisis may well be a blessing for the region because it has provided an opportunity for a fundamental review of practices, models, and assumptions. Like the entrepreneurs who built the Asian economies, today's firms have the opportunity to lead a revival providing they can redirect their businesses. Today, those willing to forgo rapid expansion in favor of building focused businesses that create value for shareholders may be those that can look forward to a bright future.

Asian firms may move beyond manufacturing and toward knowledge industries. The region's relative backwardness in knowledge industries means it can take a path of growth by developing the Internet, e-business, and computer software.

Asia still offers one of the most important contexts for business and management in the world today. Understanding Asian management practices presents a daunting intellectual challenge. Managers, academics, and policy scientists are presently only just beginning to work toward a more mature handling of the Asian economic crisis and its consequences for the management of Asian firms. Whether this volume provides a fully comprehensive view of the challenges faced by Asian firms, only time will tell. Asian firms have now started their long way into recovery. They need inputs along the way, together with a willingness to challenge their own understanding in light of new evidence. This book should provide a step in that direction.

REFERENCES

Arogyaswamy, B. (1999). *The Asian Miracle, Myth, and Mirage*. Westport, CT: Quorum.

Backman, M. (1999). *Asian Eclipse: Exposing the Dark Side of Business in Asia*. New York: Wiley.

Bhagwati, J. (1999). *A Stream of Windows: Unsetting Reflections on Trade, Immigration, and Democracy*. Boston: MIT Press.

Cheah, H. B. (2000). The Asian Crisis? Three Perspectives on the Unfolding Problems in the Global Economy. In F. J. Richter (ed.), *The East Asian Development Model*. London: Macmillan.

Delhaise, P. (1999). *Asia in Crisis: The Implosion of the Banking and Finance Systems*. Singapore: Wiley.

Fallows, J. (1996). *Looking at the Sun: The Rise of the New East Asian Economic and Political System*. New York: Vintage Books.

Godement, F. (1999). *The Downsizing of Asia*. London: Routledge.

Harland, B. (1997). *Collision Course: America and East Asia in the Past and the Future*. New York: St. Martin's Press.

Jomo, K. S. (ed.) (1998). *Tigers in Trouble: Financial Governance, Liberalisation and Crises in East Asia*. London: Zed Books.

Krugman, P. (1994). The Myth of Asia's Miracle. *Foreign Affairs*, 73(6), November–December, pp. 62–78.

McLeod, R. H., and Garnaut, R. (eds.) (1998). *East Asia in Crisis: From Being a Miracle to Needing One?* London: Routledge.

Phongpaichit, P., and Baker, C. (1996). *Thailand's Boom!* New York: Allen & Unwin.

Richter, F. J. (1999). *Strategic Networks: The Art of Japanese Interfirm Cooperation*. Binghamton, NY: International Business Press.

Rohwer, J. (1996). *Asia Rising*. New York: Touchstone Books.

Whitley, R. D. (1992). *Business Systems in East Asia: Firms, Markets, and Societies*. London: Sage.

Womack, J. P, Jones, D. T., and Roos, D. (1990). *The Machine That Changed the World*. New York: Rawson Associates.

World Bank (1993). *The East Asian Miracle: Economic Growth and Public Policy*. New York: Oxford University Press.

Yoshihara, K. (1988). *The Rise of Ersatz Capitalism in South East Asia*. Singapore: Oxford University Press.

Zahra, S. A., George, G., and Garvis, D. M. (1999). Networks and Entrepreneurship in Southeast Asia: The Role of Social Capital and Membership Commitment. In F. J. Richter (ed.), *Business Networks in Asia: Promises, Doubts, and Perspectives*. Westport, CT: Quorum, pp. 39–60.

Part I

Crisis and Catharsis: An Overview

Chapter 2

Recovering from the Crisis: New Game Opportunities in Asia

Ian C. Buchanan, Chipper Boulas, and Babu Raj Gopi

ASIAN GROWTH: MYTH OR MIRACLE?

Any balanced assessment of Asia's prospects must first explode the myth of the Asian "miracle." In reality, there never was any miracle, nor was there even an Asia (Arogyaswamy, 1999; Buchanan, 1999; Krugman, 1999)! The so-called Asia is a colonial legacy, a region so vast and complex that it contains 60 percent of the world's population and defies any attempt at precise definition. It consists of some 24 of the world's most diverse economies and over 2,000 language groups. Populations range from under 300,000 in Brunei to over 1.2 billion in China. Gross national product per capita extends from U.S.$200 in Nepal to U.S.$39,640 in Japan, and gross domestic product growth rates range from under 1 percent in Brunei to more than 11 percent in China (see Figure 2.1). While the geographically co-located portfolio of countries which, for lack of a better term, we will refer to as "Asia," has not experienced a miracle, the region has outpaced the rest of the world with its sustained high growth.

Explaining why so many Asian-based economies all managed to transform, modernize, and industrialize their economies faster than anywhere else in the world, or at any other time in history, requires a new perspective. The crucial issue is to understand the changes in the global geopolitical, technological, and economic environment in the years following World War II, as well as their impact on the internal political economies in Asia, specifically how different countries shaped their domestic policies in response to the global and regional geopolitical circumstances of the period.

The External Growth Drivers

Following the end of World War II, the world began to split into two ideological camps centered around Moscow and Washington. This bipolar, nuclear-

Figure 2.1
Growth in Real GDP Per Capita

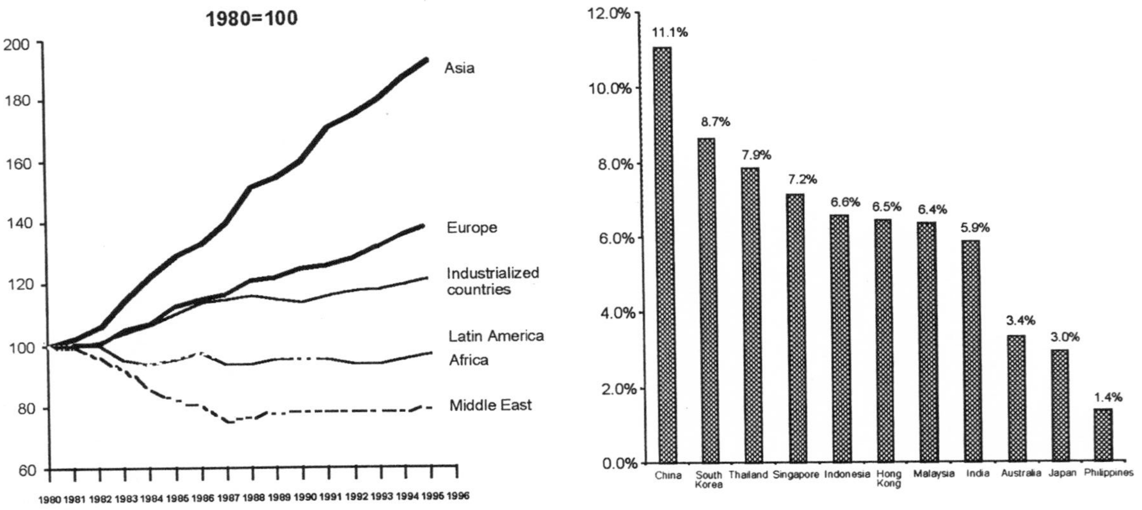

Source: Booz-Allen & Hamilton.

equipped world redefined the rules of military—and ultimately economic—competition. The Cold War contributed to dramatic increases in defense spending, with both powers investing heavily in new technologies. Though primarily directed into military programs, this spending produced commercial benefits by revolutionizing computing, communications, and transportation technologies. Together, the exponential improvement in price-to-performance ratios in these key areas effectively "shrank" the globe. This opened up a period of global economic competition, which initially resulted in manufacturing relocating to take advantage of factor cost differentials.

The beginning of Asia's 40 years of prosperity can be traced back to a series of events that took place in the four years following the end of World War II. These events, which occurred in three world regions—Europe, the United States, and Asia—created strong growth drivers that uniquely benefited developing Asia.

The first critical event took place in 1948 in post-war Europe. Following the Allied response to the Soviet isolation of Berlin, the Berlin airlift, a nuclear-tipped Iron Curtain divided East from West, and no further Soviet expansion was possible. In the United States during the 1940s three new key global institutions—the IMF, the World Bank, and the General Agreement on Tariffs and Trade (GATT)—were created. These institutions contributed to a steep fall in global tariffs and, ultimately, to the globalization of capital flows. In Asia, the two critical events were the accelerating wave of newly independent states emerging from colonial rule, and in 1949 the creation of a Communist People's Republic in the world's most populous nation, China.

The communist victory in China signaled the opening of a new battle front in the Cold War as a Bamboo Curtain began to descend across the region. Unlike Europe's Iron Curtain, this Bamboo Curtain did not yet have a precisely defined frontier, and the two superpowers and their allies fought to bring emerging independent states to their side of the curtain. Over the years following the end of World War II, the new leaders of over a dozen countries were confronted with tough political, security, and economic choices in post-colonial Asia.

The Domestic Response

The newly independent nations of Asia looked at the post-war bipolar world and recognized that their first choice had to be which of the global ideological camps to join, a decision influenced in part by their proximity to China, their powerful new communist neighbor. The outcome of this first—ideological and pragmatic—decision was the emergence of three broad political groups within post-war Asia: the communist command economies, the stuck-in-the middle socialists, and the democratic market economies.

The communist command economies resisted the global wave of economic integration, recreating the Soviet political and economic model, which was based on top-down, centrally planned, command-and-control systems that emphasized self-reliance and import substitution. The outcome was a set of closed "autarchic" economies that were insulated from accelerating global economic and technological change, and relied on directed, public sector investment as their primary growth driver. This was the model in China before 1977, in Vietnam before 1987, in the Soviet Far East before 1988, and in North Korea today. This group missed out on the globalization wave and Asia's rapid growth.

The stuck-in-the-middle socialists sought to follow a nonaligned political middle ground between the two global superpowers. They elected hybrid, but mainly import substituting, economic policies and in many ways missed out on the high-growth "miracle" (see, e.g., World Bank, 1993).

The democratic market economies broadly embraced market economics and more-or-less democratic political systems. This small group of resource-poor NIEs came closest to being economic "miracles" in that they defied conventional economic wisdom, overcame a lack of natural resources, and embarked on a true high-speed industrial revolution based on labor-intensive, export-oriented policies.

While the countries in this third group were all more open to investment, technology, and pricing/resource allocation signals from the global economy than either the communist or socialist economies, their economic policies varied, depending on their population and resources.

The economies that were relatively resource rich, had large populations, and had potentially large domestic markets tended to adopt import-substituting policies. These nations—Indonesia, Malaysia, the Philippines, and Thailand—believed that their raw materials would be in ever-increasing ("Malthusian") demand and should be protected from foreign exploitation. This strategy depended on ever improving terms of trade and the acquisition of capital goods, which could then be employed in protected domestic "infant industries" until they advanced up the scale curve. Unfortunately, many industrial infants remained in need of perpetual protection. Economic growth in these nations depended on rising commodity prices alone, and until the mid-1980s, most failed to fully capitalize on the rapid rise in global integration, transfer of technology, and global division of labor.

The remaining Asian developing market economies were mostly small and resource-poor nations with strong political leadership facing poverty-stricken populations. These nations experimented with different policy models and became early adopters of the then radical option of opening up to international trade and investment flows. In these "option-poor" countries, low-cost labor—their only resource—became the basis of economic success, and they exported it by adding value to imported commodities for re-export. These nations, along with the four NIEs and Japan, grew rapidly on the back of the global division of labor and ultimately capital. This globalization was in turn facilitated by declines in the cost of global transport, communication, and information processing, which were the by-product of the Cold War technology explosion.

Over the next four decades, global trade in manufactured goods grew three times faster than global output and the terms of trade shifted away from primary products toward the labor-intensive manufactured goods exporters of Japan, the NIEs, and—after 1977—coastal China. Their unfashionable domestic policies, with their emphasis on labor-intensive, export-oriented industrialization, coincided with external growth drivers of globalization, producing, if not a miracle, then certainly an unprecedented high-speed industrial revolution. Thus, these economies' apparent limitations proved their fortunes: with no resources except people, and no policy options except to open up to inward and export-creating investment, they grew by integrating into a global economy growing faster than at any earlier time.

THE FOUR PHASES OF GROWTH

Recognizing that the individual growth strategies of the newly decolonized Asian nations that adopted market-based economies were a function of the uniquely attractive external environment and country-specific domestic political and economic forces, we can distinguish four distinct stages of growth in the region's pre-crisis history (see Figure 2.2).

Phase 1: Post-Colonial Transition (Pre-1960s)

In the first phase, the pre- and trans-colonial period, growth for both groups of market-oriented economies was slow.

Phase 2: "Win-Win" (1960–1980)

This second phase, from 1960 to 1980, coincided with an era of tremendous growth in the world economy, when the global growth rate was over 5 percent per annum, faster than at any other time in history. During this win-win phase, world commodity prices temporarily broke out of their long downward trend, achieving a short but dramatic price increase. This increase followed a dramatic increase in the world money supply as G7 finance ministers sought to offset the deflationary impact of the 1973 tripling of oil prices by the OPEC cartel. As a direct consequence of this money supply–driven global inflation, the commodity-based economies grew at record rates during this period.

Meanwhile, the globally integrating economies (GIEs) grew on the back of an unprecedented decline in tariffs; rapid growth in world trade; and falling transport and communication costs. These economies grew at over 9 percent per annum, almost twice the rate of growth of the global economy and substantially faster than the commodity-based economies. However, this period of growth was not specific to Asia. It was a win-win period for the majority of developing countries, most of whom benefited from rising commodity prices and accelerating global division of labor.

Figure 2.2
Phases of Growth of Asia's "Democractic Market" Economies

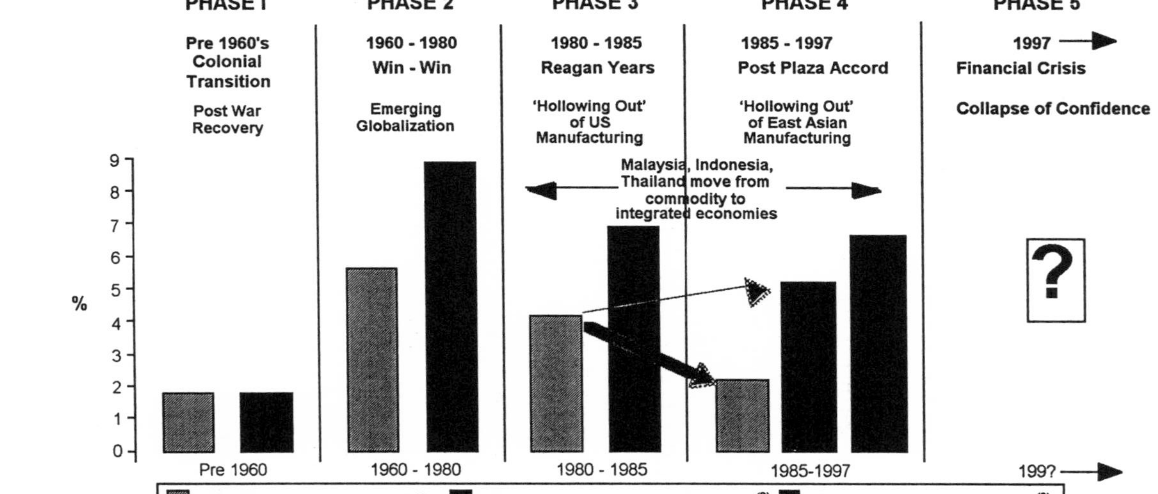

(1) Australia, New Zealand, India, Sri Lanka, Philippines, Indonesia, Malaysia, and Thailand; (through 1985).
(2) Hong Kong, Singapore, South Korea, and Taiwan.
(3) Indonesia, Malaysia, and Thailand.
Source: Booz-Allen & Hamilton.

Phase 3: The Reagan Years (1980–1985)

Between 1980 and 1985, the global growth drivers were influenced by the Reagan administration's policies of supply-side economics. U.S. domestic policies led to high interest rates and an overvalued dollar. The consequences in such an open and competitive domestic economy were predictable: major U.S. manufacturers moved production out of the country. Virtually all of the dramatic growth in outward foreign investment of labor-intensive jobs went to just four economies—the four Asian NIEs that had followed outward-oriented development strategies. The commodity-based economies suffered from a worldwide recession triggered by a quadrupling of oil prices in 1979, the global tight money policies that followed, and the consequential steep decline in commodity prices. This caused the economic performance of the commodity-based economies to decline by half to 2.5 to 3 percent per annum.

During this period, the globally integrated economies benefited from an overvalued U.S. dollar. The U.S. economy exported manufacturing jobs and sucked in an unprecedented incremental U.S.$122 billion of manufactured imports. The four NIEs plus Japan captured 46 percent of this increase, relative to a historical share of around 20 percent. This was sufficient to sustain their growth rates at just slightly less than during the "win-win" years and resulted in 7 percent per annum average real growth.

Phase 4: Post–Plaza Accord (1985–1997)

In the second half of the 1980s, Asia's growth was driven by the results of a meeting in New York's Plaza Hotel in 1985. This resulted in concerted action to push down the value of the dollar.

The dramatic increase in the value of the yen and other East Asian currencies against the dollar came at a time when labor was becoming more expensive and less flexible in the GIEs. This led to an explosive outflow of labor-intensive investment from Northeast Asia to the low-labor-cost countries of Southeast Asia. In the 18 months that followed the Plaza Accord, Thailand received more inward investment from Japan alone than it had in the entire preceding 25 years.

Commodity prices continued to fall, and the growth rates of commodity-based economies dropped to 2 percent per annum. GIE growth also slowed to 6 percent per annum. However, fueled by the dramatic influx of foreign investment and sustained by rapid shifts in government policy, including a shift away from import substitution toward labor-intensive, export-oriented industrialization, Malaysia, Indonesia, and Thailand experienced a growth surge.

Thus, the combination of the Cold War and its by-products—access to new markets and U.S. technology; rapid growth in world trade and investment flows; and an accelerating global division of labor—created a global surf wave. The group of Asian economic superstars that rode this wave were christened by the

World Bank as HPAEs (High-Performance Asian Economies)—and created a new global paradigm that will influence policymakers long into the future.

ASIAN MELTDOWN: WHAT WENT WRONG?

In 1997, after over four decades of strong growth driven mostly by foreign direct investment and integration with a rapidly growing global economy, the Asian "miracle" was already well on its way to becoming an Asian "bubble" (Henderson, 1998; Soros, 1998). The principal causes were the gradual shift from productive direct investment to portfolio investment that occurred between 1993 and 1996 and the sticky exchange rates of many Southeast Asian nations, which contributed to growing current account deficits. The economies most at risk of a financial crisis were the latecomers: the three Emerging Asian Newly Industrializing Economies (EANIEs) and South Korea, the one NIE which had, in line with the Japanese model, created a bloated bureaucratic superstructure to "direct" economic activity.

The financial avalanche began on July 2, 1997, in Bangkok, when the Bank of Thailand floated the baht. Over the next six months, the currencies and stock markets of the most vulnerable economies fell like dominoes (see Figure 2.3).

What went wrong with the Asian miracle? Why did this sudden avalanche occur? And why did it begin in Bangkok?

While the trigger event of the July 1997 baht crisis had many uniquely Thai political, cultural, and institutional elements, most of the underlying political, economic, and institutional weaknesses surfaced by the currency and banking crisis were common also to Indonesia, Malaysia, Korea, and—to a lesser extent—the Philippines.

The specifically Thai aspects that contributed to this, the first avalanche site, included a post-war political system based on a pragmatic alliance between the military and foreign educated-technocrats that granted the technocrats a free hand in running the economy, provided that the growing economy would fund a large and growing military budget. In 1992, a bloody repression of peaceful civilian protestors destroyed the trust in, and prestige of, the military and opened the way for a strengthened parliamentary democracy and a reduction in the technocrats' authority.

The emergence of a pluralistic democratic system and a multiplicity of new parties bred rampant vote buying, and the combination of increasingly expensive elections and governments with an average life span of one year created the worst kind of short-term, "pork-barrel" money politics. Major infrastructure projects were forced through and awarded to crony capitalists rather than justified on economic terms. Though the economy was booming, the demands of foreign direct investors and increasingly wealthy Thais for better public infrastructure—roads, public transport, telecommunications, power, water, and airports—were not being satisfied. Accelerating corruption and mismanagement began eroding Thailand's underlying competitiveness.

Figure 2.3
The Asian "Miracle"

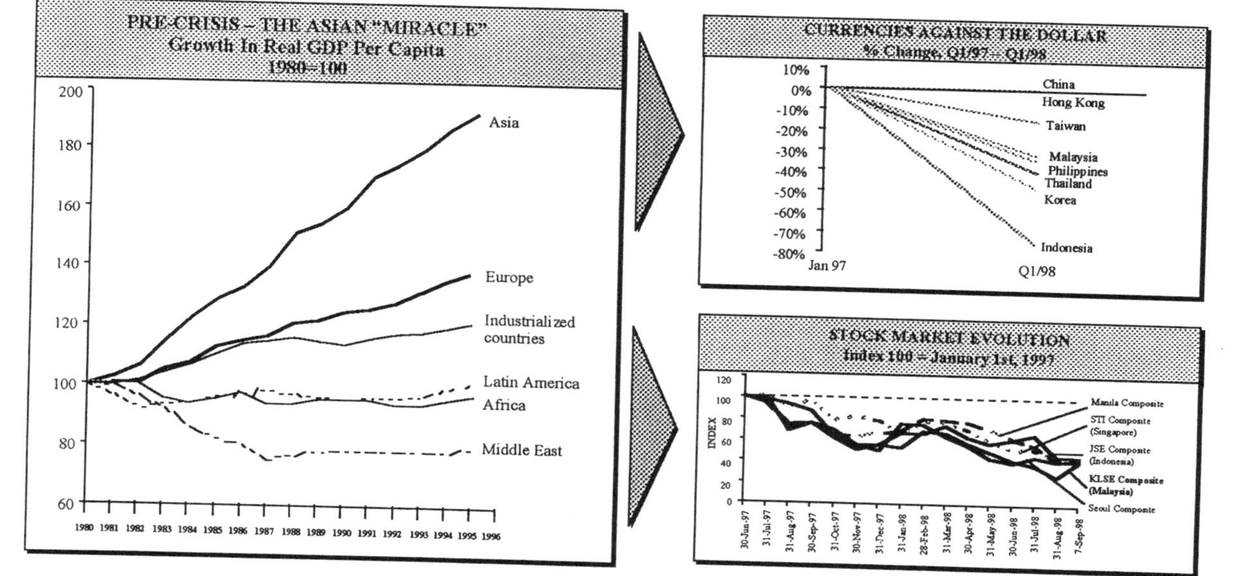

Source: Booz-Allen & Hamilton.

As frustrated foreign direct investors pulled back, the gap was filled by hot money. Portfolio investors attracted by the media hype of Thailand's "miracle"; bid up stock prices. In a parallel frenzy, international banks sought a slice of the action. As a result, rapidly expanding, cash-hungry, frequently family-controlled companies raised funds on the strength of less than transparent accounts. They were able to do so in U.S. dollars at interest rates significantly lower than those prevailing in baht because of the government's moves to liberalize the capital account.

The baht had been stable against the U.S. dollar since 1985. However, the influx of hot money, combined with limited facilities for forward foreign exchange cover; unsophisticated company treasurers; overanxious lenders; weak domestic financial institutions, and corrupt, or politically directed, lending—reflected in the increasingly public scandal around Bangkok Bank of Commerce—provided all the ingredients for an avalanche. As the U.S. dollar began to strengthen, Thailand's export growth slowed, and its current account deficit climbed, the bubble economy party was about to end for Thailand, the other EANIEs, and South Korea.

The end came swiftly. Following the float of the baht on July 2, and its ensuing rapid decline, there was a sharp reversal of funding flows throughout the region. Panic replaced euphoria, laying the foundation for a prolonged crisis.

While the reasons for the baht crisis hitting the rest of East Asia with such severity are complex, seven factors account for the bulk of the meltdown: declining relative competitiveness; an asset bubble; crony capitalism; currencies tied to a strengthening U.S. dollar, a weak and insufficiently regulated financial system; overreaction as euphoria turned to panic; and a compounding effect as Asian leaders went into denial and sought foreign scapegoats.

While the first symptoms of the crisis were in the financial economy, in the real goods economy the late industrializing EANIEs, such as Malaysia, were lagging in key sectoral productivity indices even against the best in Southeast Asia.

As a consequence, Malaysia, South Korea, and much of Southeast Asia were trapped between increasingly productive developed countries and lower cost, less developed countries, especially China. This reduced competitiveness masked the emerging asset bubble and translated into declining relative shares of U.S. and EU export markets for much of the region.

With foreign capital increasingly going into portfolio investment rather than direct investment in export-oriented manufacturing, an asset bubble emerged as stock markets grew faster than GNP. And in many countries new property supply outstripped demand.

The next factor—crony capitalism—has its roots in two separate political domains. In the domain of national development, ambitious politicians sought to cut the costs and time of infrastructure development by by-passing the civil service and harnessing the private sector. In the domain of party politics, politicians struggling to fund increasingly expensive elections sought access to the "monopoly rents" accruing to these new infrastructure capitalists by means of "black money" contributions to election funds. In turn, the new political blue-chip conglomerates used their political connections to seek rapid expansion in other areas, lobbying to reduce domestic economic competition and gain preferential access to other, noninfrastructure deals. They then embarked on ambitious investments in underperforming assets as their inexperienced executives directed cash flow away from their protected core toward new businesses where their organizations lacked the ability to compete.

A lack of transparency combined with a herd mentality among investors and lenders assured these high-profile political blue chips easy access to cash. This in turn perpetuated expansion long after cash-flow deficits should have put on the brakes.

Meanwhile, the combination of foreign and domestic investment continued to drive domestic growth throughout the region. This in turn meant that a growing proportion of the domestic population moved into a disposable income bracket where consumption of imported branded and luxury products took off, contributing to a persistent trade deficit.

In the financial sector, a pawnbroker mentality prevailed. This translated into a tendency to lend against asset value rather than cash flow. When combined with an asset bubble, this contributed to a rapid expansion of bank assets, with some smaller banks in countries such as Malaysia expanding 700 percent in just two years.

Finally, the combination of the hot-money bubble and domestic overconfidence turned what could have been an overdue correction into a panic. Poorly informed investors became a panicking herd, their stampede urged on by indecisive and ill-informed statements from several long-serving Asian leaders blaming "foreign conspirators" for what were in reality domestic policy, political, and institutional weaknesses.

THE POST-CRISIS OUTLOOK

With currencies stabilizing and stock markets recovering, the panic seems to be nearing its end. However, tremendous challenges remain, from low intra-Asian exports and declining consumer spending to an overstretched U.S. economy and an inward-looking European one. At the regional level, the long-term outlook is for a return to a growth rate that exceeds world averages, due to the region's large, comparatively young population and its relatively low share of global output. Subject to continued globalization, we believe that Asia will continue to "catch up," provided regional governments continue to take a pragmatic approach to reforms (see Figure 2.4). In the near term, the outlook varies considerably across the region, depending both on how hard a particular country was hit by the crisis (see Figure 2.5) and the extent, speed, and effectiveness of

Figure 2.4
Phase 5: Crisis-Driven Reforms

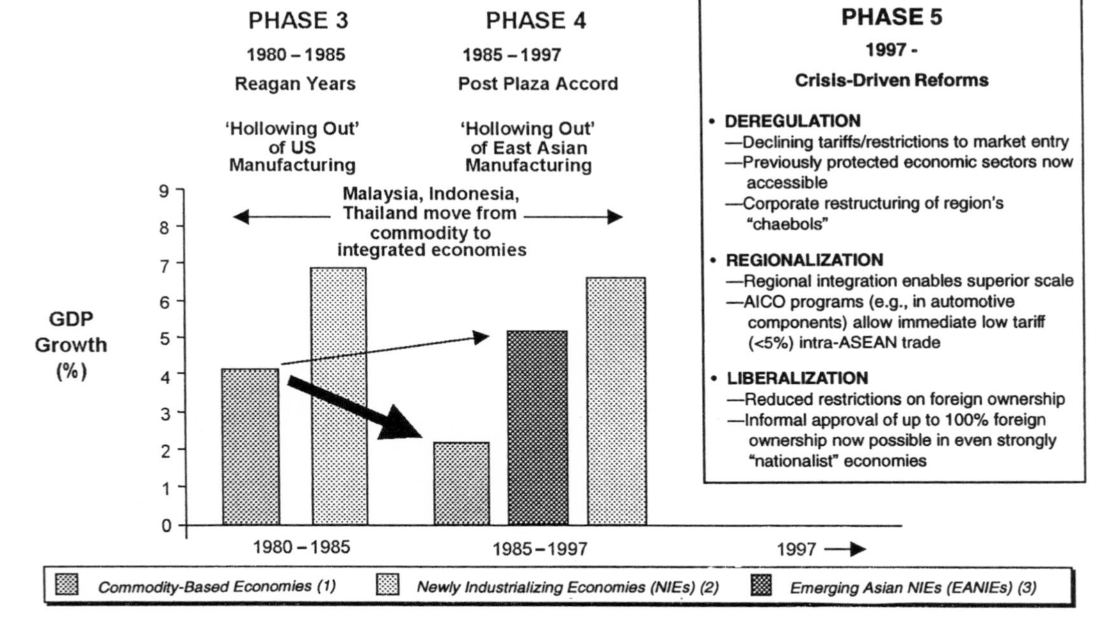

(1) Australia, New Zealand, India, Sri Lanka, Philippines PWS, Indonesia, Malaysia, and Thailand (through 1985).
(2) Hong Kong, Singapore, South Korea, and Taiwan.
(3) Indonesia, Malaysia, and Thailand (post-1985).

Figure 2.5
Dominant Themes in Crisis-Hit Countries

Country/Group	DOMINANT THEME Regionalization	Liberalization	Deregulation	Comments
Japan	1	3	4	• Corporate restructuring, fuelled by financial sector crisis • Investment, alliance and acquisition opportunities for foreigners
Korea	2	4	3	• Liberalizing foreign direct investment, trade and financial services • Potential for acquiring high-quality manufacturing assets
China	2	4	4	• Imminent entry into WTO will create discontinuity in liberalization and deregulation • Especially in automotive and financial services
India	0	3	4	• Increased openness of domestic market through lower tariff protection and lower investment barriers for foreign investors • De-licensing of economy • "Cautious" privatization process
ASEAN	4	4	4	• Implementation of ASEAN free trade area accelerated to 2003, 90% of total tariff fines will be 0–5% by the year 2000 • 30% national equity requirement for AICO scheme waived for the period 1999–2000 • Recent approval for 100% foreign ownership in restricted sectors in several countries

reforms not only in the "financial" economy, but also in the "real" and the "political" economy.

Emerging/Improving Opportunities

Although many firms have been hard hit by the crisis, for some—and especially for those MNCs who missed out on the region's boom years—this crisis spells opportunity, with cheap assets, more flexible government policies on foreign ownership, and more receptive local partners (Boulas, 1998; Faustino, 1999). As the old Asian expression goes, "empty rice bowl improves the hearing," and those multinationals that move quickly can potentially achieve permanently advantaged positions in key economies as the hearing of those policymakers previously advocating restrictions on foreign ownership is improved by the crisis.

The degree of impact—and opportunity—that domestic firms and established MNCs face is a function of their export orientation and their funding position when the crisis hit, with cash-rich exporters looking at the world very differently from heavily geared importers and distributors of consumer durables or luxury goods (see Figure 2.6). For multinationals, those that are "seizing the moment" fall into different categories, depending on their experiences in the region. While this downturn does provide a second chance for companies that missed out on Asia's high growth, in our view the biggest potential opportunity is for those multinationals that have had a long-term presence in Asia and have built a good understanding of the region's cultures and governments. These companies are now well-positioned to consolidate their lead, provided they carefully analyze whether the impact on sectors, and companies, of interest is "temporary shock" or "mortal wound" and provided they are in a position to move quickly when attractive opportunities arise.

NEW GAME OPPORTUNITIES

In the following pages, we will consider the different types of opportunities available to multinationals in three key regions—the ASEAN bloc, Korea, and China—highlighting examples of MNCs that are exploiting the volatile market and "new game opportunities" to translate regional discontinuity into a chance to re-shape the rules of competition.

New Game Opportunities: ASEAN

The ASEAN bloc (Brunei, Burma, Indonesia, Laos, Malaysia, the Philippines, Singapore, Thailand, and Vietnam, plus Cambodia) currently contributes 9 percent of Asia's population and accounts for 17 percent of the region's GDP. With its commitment to economic integration, ASEAN is emerging as a significant

Figure 2.6
Differential Impact of the Crisis

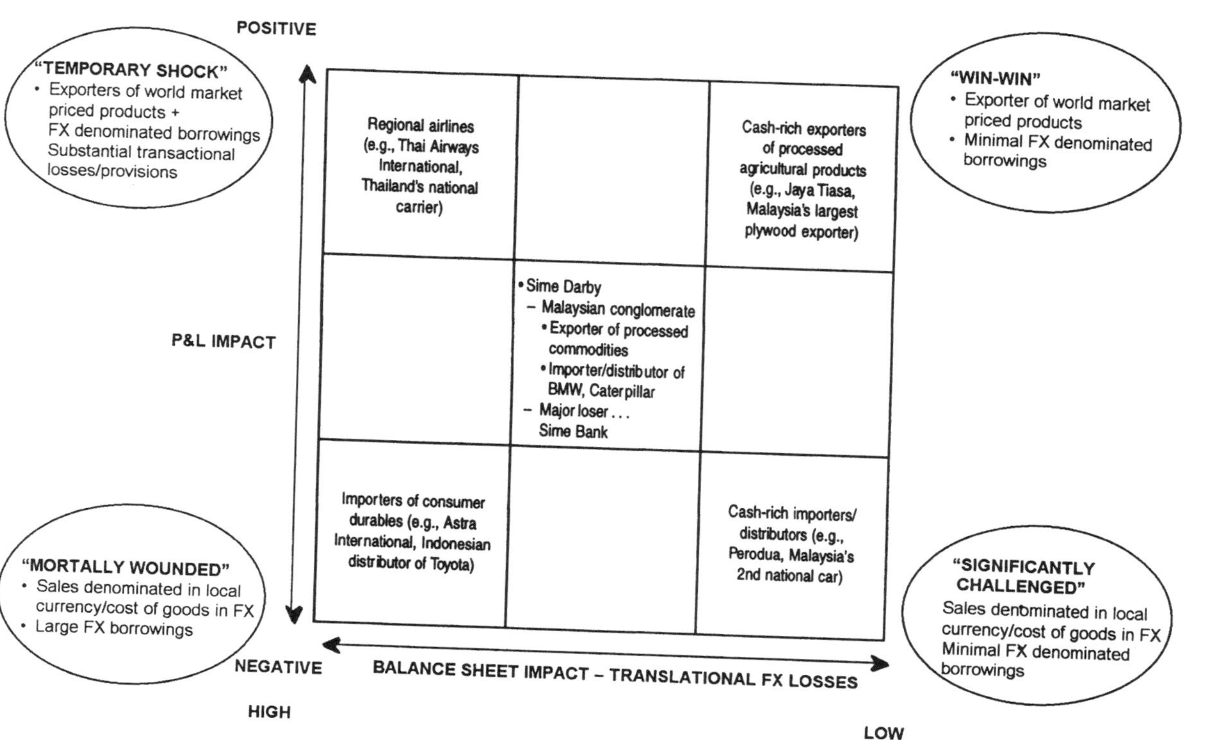

new regional market, although the pace of integration will be constrained by national and intraregional politics.

Discontinuities in the form of deregulation, liberalization, and regionalization have created a range of opportunities for companies to enhance their margins and market positions. Deregulation, for example, is underway in banking and is accelerating in the oil, gas, and power generation sectors, as well as state airlines. The implementation of the ASEAN Free Trade Area has also been moved up to 2003, and 90 percent of total tariff lines will be under 5 percent by the year 2000. In addition, the 30 percent national equity requirement for the AICO scheme has been waived through 2000. Further opportunities stem from liberalization, as foreign equity ownership limits have been officially lifted in sectors from banking and insurance to telecommunications.

Companies throughout the region have begun leveraging the discontinuities of deregulation, regionalization, and liberalization to re-shape the rules of competition in their industries. Examples include:

- Having received approval for up to 100 percent ownership, a leading automotive company is taking advantage of deregulation and liberalization to acquire its distributors in Malaysia, Thailand, and Singapore. Their primary objective: to capture the growing share of "post-manufacturing" value and to enhance their margins by focusing on the highest value customer segments.
- A global automotive and heavy equipment company is taking advantage of regionalization to merge all ASEAN assembly under a "one-factory" concept in an effort to capture scale economies with an NPV potentially in excess of U.S.$100 million. The company has already received approval for licenses, as well as an increase in factory ownership from 50 to 100 percent.
- A European telco is taking advantage of deregulation, regionalization, and liberalization by buying significant stakes in telecommunication firms in different ASEAN countries in order to create an integrated "one-stop" service offering for its global MNC clients, as well as regional mobile business users.
- A Japanese vehicle manufacturer is exploiting the potential deregulation of a "National Car" project to acquire 100 percent of a modern manufacturing facility at low cost, while simultaneously creating nontariff barriers to entry, plus leading the consolidation of distribution facilities around four existing government-linked companies.

New Game Opportunities: China

The most significant discontinuities in China stem from the aggressive measures that have been introduced to gain entry into the World Trade Organization (WTO). To this end, priority areas for 1999 will include driving economic growth through increased domestic investment and industry restructuring; achieving breakthroughs in state enterprise reform; addressing financial sector problems and managing financial risks; developing the suburban and rural economy; and attracting direct investment to drive the technology sector.

Specific terms under negotiation in the most recent WTO proposal include granting of trade and distribution rights across many industries, as well as tariff reductions for a wide range of goods including high-tech, wood, paper, auto parts, chemicals, fish, and spirits. In addition, various markets are being opened, from commodity agricultural products to professional services, insurance and banking, and travel and tourism. Proposed concessions in telecommunications—one of the largest growth sectors in the world—will enhance the market's appeal for MNCs. With the opening up of the service sector and the introduction of real competition (both foreign and domestic), real opportunities will emerge for capability-based competition.

Focusing on a single industry—automotive—the potential impact of these lifted or eased restrictions becomes clear. In the current WTO proposal, by 2005, import tariffs for automotive and auto parts are slated to be lowered to 25 and 10 percent, respectively. Quotas on auto imports will also be relaxed and then phased out by 2005. Similarly, all restriction on distribution and auxiliary services such as rental and leasing and freight forwarding will be phased out within three to four years. Local content, technology transfer, and research and development requirements will also be removed upon accession and, though not specifically addressed in the latest WTO proposal, restrictions on foreign ownership are expected to relax over time.

New Game Opportunities: Korea

In Korea, discontinuities are centered primarily around increased competition from market liberalization and corporate-driven restructuring. Ongoing deregulation measures encompassing foreign direct investments, trade, and the financial services sector are creating opportunities for multinationals across a wide range of industries.

Key regulatory initiatives include

- Full liberalization of eleven industries, including investment, petrochemical refining, and land development; partial liberalization of gambling and tobacco; and further liberalization of electric power and telecommunications to 50 and 49 percent foreign ownership, respectively
- Privatization of many government owned companies, including POSCO, KT, Korea Heavy Industry, and Korea General Chemical
- Lowering of average tariff rates on manufactured goods to approximately 6 percent
- Complete elimination of restrictive import licensing by January 2000
- Tax benefits for foreign direct investments
- General raising of foreign ownership limits to 30 percent; foreign direct ownership of commercial banks and life insurance companies (Korea First and Seoul Bank)

Simultaneously, the Korean government is forcing corporate restructuring, creating an environment for freer action for both domestic and foreign companies. The key corporate restructuring objectives include: enhanced financial transparency (for example, consolidation of financial statements and application of international accounting principles); resolution of cross-chaebol (Korean conglomerates) debt guarantees; improvements in financial structure (working toward a 200 percent debt/equity ratio); streamlining business activities, selling noncore assets to focus on the core business; and strengthening management accountability to shareholders.

To date, government-mandated mergers have affected key industries such as the aerospace, automotive, semiconductor, petrochemical, and power generation industries. Hyundai, for example, was able to purchase Kia Motors, LG Semicon, and Hanwha (petrochemicals). In addition, the forced ''workout'' of chaebols by commercial banks through operational and financial restructuring has made the market more attractive to foreign investors.

These measures have created opportunities for multinationals with limited market presence to gain market access. Korea has traditionally been closed to multinationals, but the financial crisis has prompted the government to deregulate and liberalize investment regulations and simplify historically esoteric legal procedures, giving multinationals a significant opportunity to gain market access. Creation of special tax incentives, in conjunction with the deregulation of key industries, is also helping to attract passive and active foreign investments.

Multinationals with an existing Korean market presence can also take the initiative to aggressively expand their domestic market share while their Korean competitors are significantly weakened by the financial crisis. Many local companies are in a vulnerable state with government-forced restructuring, heavily geared with little hope of financial relief. Multinationals can also take advantage of the current environment to purchase key manufacturing assets in Korea, gaining market share and access, as well as export products. Multinational buy-out of joint ventures (JVs) is the most prevalent, but there has also been a rise in the number of multinationals with Korean market presence buying out their largest domestic competitors.

The case of a multinational automotive component demonstrates the potential benefit of these discontinuities for multinationals in the Korean market. Prior to the crisis, the multinational had a technology-based relationship with an automotive components supplier but given market restrictions, was limited to a JV relationship with the local supplier. The primary objective of this JV was to support Korean automakers, with the longer-term possibility of sourcing key components for U.S. makers. The impact of the crisis reduced growth in the Korean economy, leading to a sharp decline in automobile demand. The highly geared local supplier was unable to meet its financial obligations, creating an opportunity for a buy-out of the manufacturing base and the creation of a customer relationship with one of the surviving Korean automakers. Under this new arrangement, the multinational is able to source components globally for this automaker and develop the manufacturing base in Korea for domestic as well as export markets.

CONCLUSION: THE CHALLENGE FOR RECOVERY

> The real action is increasingly going to be in the developing and emerging markets. Business should not be so mesmerized by the current economic difficulties in these markets that companies ignore the enormous long-term economic potential. However, realizing that potential will not be easy. It will not only require a greater emphasis on understanding what are the needs of the consumer, but a radically different way of approaching them.
>
> —Niall W.W. Fitzgerald, Chairman, Unilever Plc, 1998

The opportunities for multinationals in Asia are not simply there for the taking. Those who desire to be major emerging market players are well advised to carefully reflect on the uniqueness of these markets and how their Westernized strategies and business models need to be redesigned for the emerging world. The experiences of Unilever and other multinationals that have pioneered the approach into emerging markets provide key lessons for success.

Lesson 1: Reach the Masses . . . Manage Affordability

The ''middle-class'' family income in the strategic emerging markets is U.S.$3,000–10,000. However, as markets open up, the right price/value equation can rapidly tap latent demand. For example, television penetration in urban coastal China is close to 100 percent.

Reaching deeper into the real mass market often requires a revolutionary vision. Consumer goods multinationals can build big businesses in emerging markets only if they manage affordability in a way that makes their products accessible to the masses. Roberto Goizueta, the late chief executive officer of Coca-Cola, captured this strategy when he observed that Coke should be the same price as tea in China.

Reaching the masses frequently means that consumer goods companies need to rethink their product lines with a sharp eye on the price/performance equation. Unilever learned this lesson in India, where it was ambushed by a local detergent maker, Nirma, which captured a substantial portion of the market with a low-cost alternative to Unilever's premium brands. Only after Unilever completely revised its product, price point, marketing strategy, and distribution system was it able to come up with a viable low-cost competitor, called Wheel, priced at nearly one-quarter the price of premium brands. Today, Unilever has regained control of nearly half of the Indian market, and its sales of Wheel exceed the sales of its leading premium brand.

Lesson 2: Be Ubiquitous . . . Invest in Distribution

Distribution is one of the most challenging problems for consumer-products businesses in emerging markets. While supermarket and hypermarket retailers are increasingly present in major capital cities, consumers living on the peripheries of these cities and in the countryside continue to purchase the large majority of goods through local shops. New multinational entrants tend to focus initially on large chains in major cities, seeking to build volume quickly, without having to invest in costly sales and distribution systems.

There are several difficulties with this strategy, however. The most obvious is that these manufacturers are walking away from what is typically 50 to 90 percent of the market. The strategy also puts them in an extremely vulnerable negotiating position with the major retailers. Failing to build quickly a broad distribution base also allows competitors to more readily combat new entrants.

Finding cost-effective ways to build broad and deep sales and distribution coverage in the emerging markets is one of the most critical challenges facing consumer products companies. This can rarely be done on the cheap and often requires creative alternatives. For example, several consumer products companies have patiently developed a network of exclusive distributors to service small accounts in selected countries. These exclusive distributors can operate at as little as half the cost of broader-line wholesalers, with greater effectiveness. Even when companies serve smaller shops directly, there may be creative ways to do so less expensively. In several countries, Coca-Cola, which usually visits its smallest retailers once or twice weekly, has proposed that they receive three to four weeks of consigned inventory in return for exclusivity. When Coca-Cola returns at the end of the period, the retailers pay only for the product sold during that time. For small cash-strapped shop owners, this is extremely attractive. Coca-Cola wins increased sales at the expense of displaced competition and a much lower cost-to-serve, with delivery visits cut by a factor of three or more.

Lesson 3: Create Desirability . . . Build Strong Brands

Despite the limited financial means of the emerging market consumer, branding could well be more important in these markets than in markets such as the United States or Western Europe. In part, this is due to the aspirational attraction that strong brands have for lower-income consumers, particularly in "badge" categories. For instance, the number of lower-income consumers on the streets of Shanghai wearing $100 jeans, a price that represents a month's wages, is striking.

Because the investment required to build and support a brand in these markets is high compared with the small size of many categories, companies should carefully weigh using umbrella brands in emerging markets as a means to create scale, particularly when exploring new categories. Often the best strategy is to invest behind local brands that already have some degree of consumer loyalty, especially when targeting middle-income consumers. For example, Danone has built a significant business in China largely through strong local brands such as Haomen Amoy, just as Coca-Cola reversed course in India, investing behind the local Thumbs Up brand.

Lesson 4: Play to Win . . . Pick Your Fights Well

Many multinationals try to play the white space game in Asia, harvesting the high end of markets, remaining timid about investment, and not playing to win. Rather than shielding these companies from losses, this flag-planting strategy only exacerbates them. Dabblers in these markets should either get serious or get out.

Asia's emerging markets are no different in this respect from those in the United States or Western Europe. The challenge is getting the value proposition right to reach critical mass and then gaining and holding the number one or two position to capture adequate returns. To do this, a clear overarching vision must be supported by well-timed entry into key categories—consumer purchase patterns are fairly predictable and, when used with industry structure analysis, can allow correct sequencing and prioritization of market entry and investment. Scale and the demonstration of long-term commitment are also critical elements of this strategy, creating a virtuous cycle that attracts the best and brightest local talent to leverage local understanding.

Lesson 5: Be Local . . . Foster Emerging Market Entrepreneurs

In volatile emerging markets, the prevalent attitude—"constant change is here to stay"—may not be compatible with corporate processes or people. Asia's "crisis" has caused dramatic shifts in consumption patterns and distribution systems, as evidenced by the rise of "micro-shops" and the "van man" (or enhanced "kaki lima"). These can require rapid local adaptation of product, package size, and price point to reach consumers seeking new values, for example, selling margarine in single scoops, not blocks.

Creating this level of agility may require that multinationals retool their traditional planning and budgeting systems. Coca-Cola's chief executive officer, Douglas Ivester, for one, is hoping to eventually do away with annual business plans and move to a system of continuous planning that will allow Coke's executives to respond more quickly to changing conditions.

For emerging market participants, the coming years will not be a smooth ride. In many cases, the rapid growth in the economies of the emerging nations has outpaced the required improvements in their financial and government institutions. There will undoubtedly be more bumps in the road, as the most recent rumblings in China suggest. Nevertheless, for consumer businesses that aspire to grow, these markets represent an opportunity that cannot be ignored.

NOTE

Some of the material in this chapter was first published in the *Monash Mt. Eliza Business Review*, 1(2), pp. 24–45. Reprinted with permission.

REFERENCES

Arogyaswamy, B. (1999). *The Asian Miracle, Myth, and Mirage*. Westport, CT: Quorum.

Boulas, C. (1998). The Long Journey Back. *Asian Business*, December, pp. 2–3.

Buchanan, I. (1999). Asian Paradox: Miracle, Myth and Financial Crisis. *Monash MT Eliza Business Review*, 1(2), pp. 24–45.

Faustino, J. M. (1999). Lessons from an Asian Company: Beating the Global Competitor. *Monash MT Eliza Business Review*, 1(2), pp. 99–107.

Henderson, C. (1998). *Asia Falling: Making Sense of the Asian Currency Crisis and Its Aftermath*. Singapore: McGraw-Hill.

Krugman, P. (1999). *The Return of the Depression Economics*. New York: W. W. Norton.

Soros, G. (1998). *The Crisis of Global Capitalism*. New York: Public Affairs.

World Bank. (1993). *The East Asian Miracle: Economic Growth and Public Policy*. New York: Oxford University Press.

Chapter 3

The Asian Economic Crisis and the Decline of Japanese Economic Leadership in Asia

Harold R. Kerbo and Robert Slagter

INTRODUCTION

In the concluding chapter to his best-selling book of 1987, *The Rise and Fall of the Great Powers*, Paul Kennedy shows agreement with those who have "argued that Japan will be 'number one' economically in the early twenty-first century" (Kennedy, 1987: 467). In the context of fear about permanent U.S. economic decline, there was something of a growth industry during the 1980s for books explaining how and why Japan had become such an economic power. In Asia during the second half of the 1980s, the Japanese foreign direct investment (FDI) began to soar above that of all other nations, accounting for some $80 billion and 80 percent of all the Japanese FDI by the mid-1990s (Hatch and Yamamura, 1996: 5–7). Few questioned that something like the "Greater East Asian Co-Prosperity Sphere" the Japanese attempted to force upon other Asian nations during World War II would finally become a reality during the early twenty-first century.

How quickly things seem to change. Almost no one, of course, predicted that Japan would fall into long economic stagnation for virtually all of the 1990s, or that the booming Asian NICs would follow before the end of the twentieth century. In contrast to President George Bush's trip to Japan during 1992 to plead for more open markets to help the still faltering U.S. economy, President Clinton visited Japan during November of 1998 to lecture Japan about how they must reform their economy (i.e., become more like the United States) to keep themselves and all of Asia from falling further into economic depression. And in another dramatic change of events, during this 1998 meeting, the Japanese were complaining that the United States had begun catering to China as the next political and economic leader of Asia.

The Japanese economy will most likely recover in the early twenty-first century, but predictions of ''Japan as Number One'' in the world economy, and particularly throughout Asia, are not likely to rebound as quickly, if at all. To begin with, there are serious questions about the future of the ''Japanese economic model,'' for Japan as well as its continued application to the emerging Asian economies. But there are other reasons to question the ability of the Japanese to sustain their drive as the economic leader of East Asian and Southeast Asian nations. As the relative economic muscle of Japan falters, there are old cracks in Japan's relationships with other Asian nations which are becoming more evident.

Much, of course, depends on future events, such as how quickly the Japanese are able to reform their political and economic institutions to regain economic momentum, and whether or not China can continue to remain less affected by the Asian economic crisis that began in July of 1997 and continue developing its regional leadership qualities. And of course, there are questions about how and when the other East Asian and Southeast Asian economies are able to shake off the crisis and return to their earlier paths of rapid economic growth.

In the face of all these unpredictable future events, however, we can take a fresh look at Japan and some of the *underlying problems that brought on economic stagnation* in Japan by the early 1990s, as well as *the roots of Japan's often uneasy relations with other nations of East and Southeast Asia.*

In the present chapter we briefly examine (1) some of the internal contradictions of the ''Japanese model'' of rapid economic development and then (2) focus on problems for Japan in relations with its Asian neighbors. In the second part of this analysis, we present research findings from our recently completed study of relations between Thai employees of Japanese and American corporations in Thailand and their foreign managers. In contrast to the view often held by Westerners, East and Southeast Asia is not a sea of cultural homogeneity ready for easy cooperation between Asian employees and Japanese bosses. In fact, as we will suggest, the underlying conflicts run deep, and many Asians would prefer working for Western multinational corporations rather than Japanese multinationals. They would also prefer Western nations to step up their investments to prevent the Japanese from dominating foreign investments within their countries.

THE JAPANESE ECONOMIC MODEL: FROM ECONOMIC MIRACLE TO DECLINE

There is broad agreement that Japan's rapid industrialization in the twentieth century, and especially Japan's rise from the ashes of World War II, was made possible by a form of political economy in which the state (or more specifically, government ministry elites) guided and directed the economy (Johnson, 1982; Fallows, 1994; Vogel, 1991). Following dominant Western economic theory, this Japanese economic development through a ''capitalist development state'' should have been impossible, and in fact, it led to economic doom. But such Western economic theory neglects the realities of the modern world system today in which nations that have already achieved economic dominance can easily create unintentional blocks against economic development in poorer nations (Chase-Dunn, 1975; Chirot, 1986; Kerbo, 1996: 415). In sharp contrast to the logic of such Western economic theory, studies have consistently found that extensive outside investments in poorer countries actually tend to reduce the rate of long-term economic development (Chase-Dunn, 1989; Bornschier and Chase-Dunn, 1985; Snyder and Kick, 1979; Stokes and Jaffee, 1982). To overcome the negative factors of this outside interference and other barriers to economic development faced by poorer countries today, there is need for what Myrdal (1970) in his famous work on the subject called a "hard state." In brief, he argues that there must be a state with the power to coordinate economic policy and enforce the hard decisions that, for the short term at least, can harm the interests of many sectors of the rich and middle class in developing nations. It is this kind of "hard state" that is behind the Japanese or Asian development model that Japan first introduced to the world and that several other Asian nations, in one form or another, took up to create the rapid economic expansion of East Asia and Southeast Asia in the 1980s and much of the 1990s (Vogel, 1989; Kim, 1994; Barrett and Whyte, 1982; Gold, 1986; Pasuk and Baker, 1998; Kulick and Wilson, 1992; Muscat, 1994).

In Japan, behind the capitalist development state since World War II has been what is often referred to as the "iron triangle" of elites—the top managers of the biggest corporations, the top government ministry officials, and to a lesser extent, the top Japanese politicians (Kerbo and McKinstry, 1995; Kerbo, 1996: 449–456). These are the elites who led Japan up from the ashes of World War II to status as the second largest economy in the world by the 1970s. And the government ministry elite in particular (the elite officials in bureaucracies such as the Ministry of Finance and the Ministry of International Trade and Industry) represents the "hard state" Myrdal (1970) referred to as necessary for rapid economic development today.

As shown in detail elsewhere (Kerbo and McKinstry, 1995), it is also important to note that the "iron triangle" of elites in Japan have had more unity, cross-cooperation, and interchange of personnel than are found in any other advanced industrial nation in this century. A majority of the top ministry officials and top corporate officials in Japan graduated from the same university (Tokyo University), and many were even together in the *same academic department* at the *same time* when they were students. There is a system of extensive exchange of personnel from the top ministry to the most powerful corporations, called *amakudari*, that would be considered illegal in Western industrial nations (Koh, 1989). The largest Japanese corporations are united into roughly ten large groupings of corporations, called *keiretsu*, wherein they control large blocks of each others' corporate stock and coordinate common economic interests through such devices as a "president's council" (Gerlach, 1992). This Japanese corporate elite also cooperates to influence government policies through *Keidanren*, sometimes referred to as "the parliament of big business" and perhaps the most powerful single organization in Japan.

Through most of the post–World War II period, this big business organization contributed some 90 percent of the campaign funds to the Liberal Democratic Party (LDP), the political party that held power from 1955 through the 1990s, with the exception of only one year in the early 1990s (Kerbo and McKinstry, 1995: 103; *Japan Times*, September 3, 1993). Finally, Japanese social scientists have detailed the existence of several family alliances actively formed through intermarriage among the sons and daughters of powerful figures in the government ministry, *keiretsu* corporate groups, and leading politicians (Kerbo and McKinstry, 1995: Chapter 7; Jin, 1989; Hayakawa, 1983). These *keibatsu* family alliances, it is argued, help create unity and cooperation between *keiretsu* corporate interests and the coordinating interests of the government ministry officials, as well as politicians.

During the post–World War II period, the Japanese people held great respect for members of the "iron triangle," or at least the top ministry officials, and to a lesser extent the corporate executives running the mighty *keiretsu* corporate groupings. By all indications, these elites were a true meritocracy, dedicated to their country and to rebuilding Japan, as well as remarkably free of corruption (Koh, 1989: 227–229; Kerbo and McKinstry, 1995: 79–85). And finally, it is hard to deny that during the post–World War II period, this system of political and economic elites worked well in bringing Japan out of the ashes of World War II to prosperity in a remarkably short period of time.

Cracks in Japan's Capitalist Development State

What may be needed to achieve rapid economic development, however, may not necessarily be what is needed to continue prosperity. When a newly developed nation moves into a more open world economy, a world economy today of rapid change and deadly competition, the Japanese "capitalist development state" (at least as originally created in Japan) may no longer be what the Japanese (or any other nation) require to *continue* building a strong economy. Moreover, once prosperity has been achieved, and a new generation of elites takes over, the dedication and self-sacrifice originally shaped in the context of wartime defeat and destruction is difficult to maintain.

With relatively little accountability from below, an elite can become shortsighted and greedy, which clearly describes the popular attitude of the Japanese people today toward their elites. Since the late 1980s, there have been massive scandals involving political, corporate, and finally even the highly respected ministry elites. Particularly the ministry elites are now resisting basic change that most people know is needed, but that is against the narrow thinking and interests of many among the current generation of the "iron triangle." For example, in the face of massive losses to major Japanese banks, there has been extensive criticism of Ministry of Finance officials, and of course, the bank executives themselves, for achieving no progress toward basic reform, as well as for propping up banks that should be allowed to fall. But what this criticism has neglected to note is that many of these major banks are central members of the powerful *keiretsu*; Toyota, Mitsubishi, Sony, and all the other major corporations generally have 20 to 25 percent stakes in these major banks, and their executives are board members of these banks and sit on the ''presidents' councils'' with the bank presidents. These elites do not want their banks to fail, and if they do, in contrast to other capitalist economies, the large holdings in these banks by other major corporations are likely to endanger the whole Japanese economy even further.

Outside of Japan, in much of the rest of Asia, there were problems similar to those of Japan when the Asian economic crisis hit in July 1997. The Asian nations, which to a large degree had adopted major parts of the Japanese capitalist development state, also found themselves in sharp economic reversal with elites embroiled in scandal. Some have argued that it was the growth of the Japanese markets and investments that pulled other Asian nations up in economic prosperity (Fallows, 1994), and thus a long-term Japanese decline would bring the other Asian Tigers down as well. But it can also be argued that it was the Japanese development model, the ''capitalist development state'' adopted by these Asian Tigers, that also helped bring about their economic crisis. Like Japan a few years earlier, they also hit a wall as this Japanese development model brought them about as far as it could. In countries from Korea to Thailand, Malaysia, and Indonesia, relatively protected economies had been able to develop with outside investment and export-based industries. But when a relative level of wealth and capital accumulation was achieved, rather unaccountable ministry, corporate, and political elites began turning toward quick investment schemes in particular in real estate (the ''golf course capitalism''), which enriched elites but added little to sustainable economic development. Whatever harm had been done by outside agencies such as the IMF, one could argue that at least one result of IMF intervention has been some new accountability for these domestic elites.

Whichever has been more responsible for the broader Asian economic crisis beginning in 1997—economic stagnation in Japan, bringing less Japanese investment and a reduced market for Asian exports, or a borrowed Japanese development model that reached its limits—in the eyes of their Asian neighbors, the Japanese lost considerable respect in the later 1990s. Japan is less likely seen as the Asian big brother showing them the way to take in the Western nations in economic competition. And the old negative views and even antagonisms directed toward the Japanese by their Asian neighbors seem to be coming more to the surface. In order to understand these old antagonisms, as well as new ones, it is necessary to examine more closely some of the characteristics of Japanese society and culture which affect relations between Japan and its Asian neighbors.

JAPANESE RELATIONS IN ASIA

Western people have long assumed, in the old saying, that east is east and west is west, assuming also that all Asian nations are basically alike with respect to cultural characteristics. Recent empirical studies are showing even more clearly what "old Asia hands" from the West have known all along; There is extensive diversity in cultural values and forms of social organization among Asian nations (e.g., Hofstede, 1991). Further, there is increasing agreement that among Asian nations it is the Japanese who are most different or unique, adding further to the current problems of the Japanese in Asia.

Japanese Uniqueness

The question of Japanese uniqueness has been the subject of debate for most of the twentieth century, if not longer, and needs some clarification because of the importance of the issue. Early claims of uniqueness by noted Japan scholars in the West such as Edwin Reischauer (1988) and others brought counterclaims that the uniqueness was overstated. But most of the counterclaims against Japanese uniqueness have been stimulated by the sometimes wild claims of the *Nihonjinron* literature among the Japanese themselves. Japanese brains, biological functions, geographical forces, and even some biological characteristics of animals in Japan have been described as basically different from those in the West in this *Nihonjinron* literature. The reaction against such claims (sometimes claims of superiority, sometimes claims of need for special sympathetic treatment) have led to politically related reactions from so-called revisionists in the West that Japan was taking advantage of naive Western nations for special advantages (van Wolferen, 1989; Prestowitz, 1989; Choate, 1990). Among social scientists, even some counterclaims emerged that Japanese society and culture were no different from those of any modern nation (Mouer and Sugimoto, 1986).

More recently, however, scholars have returned to themes of Japanese uniqueness, with a focus on how Japanese society and culture are not only different from those of Western nations, but also relatively unique among Asian nations. The most extensive of these new works by Eisenstadt (1995) picks up a theme that Japan is the only "non-Axial" modern civilization, and therefore remains culturally distinct even among Asians. All other modern industrial nations (as well as most other nations of all levels of development) are members of Axial civilizations, which means they have come from a broader community of nations that share many cultural traditions, particularly found among the major Axial grouping of Christian, Islamic, Orthodox, Buddhist, and Hindu civilizations (Eisenstadt, 1995: 13–17). Samuel Huntington (1996) has picked up this theme of Japan as the only economic power from a non-Axial civilization in trying to explain future political and economic alinements with the fall of the Cold War. In his view, the Japanese inability to understand and identify with its Asian neighbors will give the Chinese an edge in becoming the leader of Asian nations in the twenty-first century.

Added to this condition of Japanese cultural uniqueness is the homogeneous nature of Japanese society. Again, such claims can be taken too far; there are indigenous Inu peoples native to northern Japan, as well as longstanding regional differences within Japan. However, when we compare Japan to the other developed nations around the world, we must agree with the description of a homogeneous Japanese society. The nation was almost completely closed for 250 years beginning in the early 1600s, and 97 percent of the Japanese people today are racially, ethnically, and in every other way Japanese, and have been for many generations. The 3 percent of people living in the country today who are not Japanese are almost all of Korean or Chinese origin.

Often the claims of homogeneity have implied a unified people without significant internal conflicts, as well as an obedient and cooperative people. However, it is easy to show that "likeness" does not imply the absence of internal conflict. For example, family members are more likely to kill each other all over the world than nonrelatives. It is important to recognize that Japanese history has been full of conflict (Pharr, 1990; Bowen, 1980; Hane, 1982, 1988; Apter and Sawa, 1984). Such conflict, in fact, can be explained in part by the strong sense of "in-group" loyalty historically demanded of Japanese people (Kerbo and McKinstry, 1995: 26–27). As the abundance of sociological theory and research suggests, strong in-group loyalty breeds strong conflict with an out-group (Simmel, 1955; Coser, 1956, 1967; Collins, 1975; Sherif, 1966). What is interesting about the Japanese society is that such in-group/out-group conflict *occurs on varying levels*—conflicts between families, conflicts between classes at times, conflicts between corporations and divisions within corporations, and ultimately in-group versus out-group conflict focused on Japanese versus non-Japanese. What this means, according to Japan scholars, is that Japanese people have a particularly strong sense of *in-group* when interacting with foreigners, which places foreigners in the sharply separated category of *out-group* in the Japanese mind.

The key point of all this for our present subject is that (1) a rather unique non-Axial civilization and culture, (2) a homogeneous and historically closed society, and (3) a society with a strong sense of in-group versus out-group, creates problems for Japanese people when they must interact with non-Japanese. Huntington (1996: 134–135) suggests that their non-Axial civilization will make the Japanese a lonely people in an increasingly global network of nations. Furthermore, following the extensive use of the Japanese term *gaijin* to refer to foreigners (usually Western foreigners but increasingly all foreigners), many scholars and businesspeople have cited a "gaijin complex" among the Japanese that makes them uncomfortable among foreigners. A small, informal survey by March (1992: 41) has led him to suggest that over 60 percent of Japanese would prefer to avoid foreigners. Indeed, larger national surveys in Japan have shown repeatedly that about 70 percent of the Japanese people would prefer not to interact with foreigners if given the choice (*Japan Times*, May, 1992; Taylor, 1983: 258).

A final aspect of the sense of Japanese uniqueness is important. In its original meaning, the ''gaijin complex'' was said to involve a feeling of inferiority on the part of Japanese among Westerners (March 1992: 41–47). In interaction among other Asians, however, this ''foreigner complex'' falls more toward the side of feeling superior. It has long been noted that Japanese people have tended to feel superior to other Asians, particularly Koreans and Southeast Asians (Fallows, 1994: 103). In her classic cultural analysis of Japan, Ruth Benedict (1947) argued that the rigid sense of ranking that permeates most aspects of the Japanese society leads them to rank nations and peoples, along with almost everything else, from superior to inferior. Through most of history, the Japanese tendency was to rank Japanese as superior and all others as inferior, but after World War II there was a tendency to judge Western people (and particularly Americans) to be superior, while other Asians remained in an inferior position in the Japanese conception of world order.

These descriptions of Japan and Japanese society are generalizations. As in any country, Japanese people are not all alike. During our interviews of Japanese executives in Asia and Europe we found many who did not fit the generalizations, and many who preferred living outside Japan and among foreigners. But as the data indicate, these descriptions of Japan and Japanese society are generally accurate, and, as we will show in more detail later in this chapter, have a significant impact on interactions between Japanese people and foreigners.

JAPANESE CORPORATIONS IN ASIA: CO-PROSPERITY ALLIANCE OR CULTURE CLASH?

Even if the Japanese economic model is less respected among Japan's neighbors in the 1990s, and despite what we have described earlier, many people would no doubt suggest that a common ''Asian-ness'' (however it might be defined) would give Japan and Japanese corporations an edge when working with other peoples in Asia. Recent research, however, questions such a possibility: At the managerial level Japanese executives tend to have several problems working with other Asians (Hatch and Yamamura, 1996: 146–157). Such research has been limited to small samples of foreign middle managers in Japanese corporations throughout Asia, and it could still be suggested that with Asian employees below the top managerial level, Japanese corporations and their managers are able to work well with other Asians. It is time we turn to recently completed research in Thailand which suggests the contrary—Japanese corporations in Thailand have significant labor problems.

Research Methods and Data

The primary data used in this second part of our chapter were obtained in Japanese and American transplant corporations in the Bangkok area during several months in 1995 and 1996. Detailed interviews with Japanese, American, and Thai managers were obtained from 24 corporations—17 Japanese and 7 American—during the summer months of 1995 and 1996, with follow-up interviews with some of these managers again in the summer of 1997 and early 1998.[1] Additional interviews were conducted with Thai government officials, personnel from several NGOs in Thailand, and faculty members from several universities in Thailand. Detailed questionnaire[2] data were obtained from 959 Thai employees in 11 Japanese and 4 large American transplants,[3] including 549 employees from Japanese companies and 410 from U.S. transplant corporations.[4]

Following our questions about the ability of Japanese managers to work with other Asians, and considering previous research on transplant corporations and employee relations, we were particularly interested in *employee commitment* to the foreign corporation and *identification with the organization*. Organizational commitment is the relative strength of an individual's identification with and involvement in a particular organization (Porter and Smith, 1970). At least three factors characterize organizational commitment; (1) a strong belief in and acceptance of the organization's goals and values; (2) a willingness to exert considerable effort on behalf of the organization; and (3) a strong desire to maintain membership in the organization. Organizational commitment is then comprised of both affective (attitudinal) and behavioral components. The affective component has generally been operationalized as identification with the organization. Identification means that the individual worker perceives that the organization's goals and values are congruent with his or her own and derives a sense of pride from being a member of the organization. Although not measured in this study, identification can focus not only on the organization as a whole but on the specific workgroup or supervisor. Behavioral aspects of commitment are found in the lower rates of absenteeism and tardiness, as well as continuance commitment—the greater probability of remaining with an organization. The willingness of workers to exert effort on the job greater than that demanded by the organization, in order to help the organization succeed, is another behavioral manifestation of commitment and the one addressed in this chapter.[5]

The importance of commitment in the organizational context is well established. Continuance commitment has long been recognized as significantly reducing recruitment and training costs for firms as well as keeping employees from transferring skills to competing organizations. A number of studies have demonstrated that more committed employees are less likely to leave an organization than the uncommitted (Angle and Perry, 1981; Porter et al., 1974; Lincoln and Kalleberg, 1996). Recent research has demonstrated that affective commitment is positively related to job performance and negatively correlated with continuance commitment (Meyer et al., 1989). O'Reilly and Chatman (1986) found a relationship between identification with the organization and prosocial organizational behaviors which involved going beyond job-mandated activities in order to help an organization succeed. Benkhoff (1997), also has found a significant relationship between commitment and the performance of bank employees in the United States.

Another set of scales was created from a range of items measuring the employees' perceptions of the workplace. A scale comprised of six items was created measuring attitudes toward the foreign management combining items measuring the managers' perceived *distance and aloofness from the employees.* Other scales measured perceptions of the availability of organizational resources, reliance on standard operating procedures, and the degree of variability in workers' jobs. Unlike many organizational studies, these scales measure *employees' perceptions* of the company and organization of the workplace rather than the more usual measurement of the formal organizational structure.

Included in our analysis are three measures of *job satisfaction* pertaining to satisfaction with superiors, tasks, and the organization as a whole. We also include the employees' perceptions of pay and benefits relative to those working in other companies in similar positions. Finally, our analysis also included as variables several personal characteristics of the workers—sex, years of formal education, and tenure with the organization.

A main strength of our analysis is that it holds the national culture of the workers constant while the home nationality of the transplant enterprises varies. We can therefore access the differential impact of Japanese versus American management on the Thai workers in terms of the level of organizational commitment each elicits.

Findings from Worker Questionnaires

Thai Employee Perceptions of the American and Japanese Workplace

Scores and significant differences in the Thai workers' perceptions of the workplace in Japanese and American firms, measures of job satisfaction, ratings of pay and benefits compared to workers in other firms (a relative, not absolute measure), and characteristics of the workers have been investigated. On three of the measures—years employed with the company, satisfaction with superiors and tasks, and availability of organizational resources—there is no significant difference between the Thais in Japanese and American corporations.

However, the two types of workplaces defined by the home country management do appear to differ significantly in the eyes of Thai workers. *Management Distance* refers to the social distance of the home country management from the workers, approachable or aloof, sticking to themselves or blending with the workers. Clearly in line with descriptions of the Japanese society and culture in the first half of this chapter, the Thai workers in American companies see American management as closer, more approachable, and less likely to stick together in a social sense. The American managed workplace also provides more variety on the job than does the Japanese managed workplace. In contrast, however, the

Japanese workplace exhibits greater reliance on standard operating procedures than does the American.

Overall, the Thai workers from the American firms are more satisfied with their organizations and think their pay is higher compared to workers with similar jobs in other organizations. However, the workers in the Japanese firms think that their benefits are better than workers at other firms.

Identification Commitment

The following presents an analysis of the relative degree of identification commitment of the workers in Japanese and American firms. This analysis identifies workplace and individual characteristics that are related to levels of commitment. Relevant to this analysis is the central question of the effect of home country management on organizational commitment. The zero order analysis establishes that there is a difference in that the *Thai workers in American firms identify more strongly with these firms* than do the Thai workers from the Japanese firms. An important finding of the regression and partial correlation analysis is that the effect of the firm's home country remains significant, though slightly diminished after controlling for the effects of the other independent variables in the regression model.

The findings help us understand some of the reasons why Thai employee commitment is higher in the U.S. corporations. Both management distance and job variety are fairly strongly related to identification commitment. Thai employees perceive less distance between managers and employees in American companies, and greater variety in the work environment, both of which contribute to the greater identification of the workers from the American companies. Conversely, greater reliance on standard operating procedures found related to commitment is characteristic of the Japanese managed workplace and is associated with greater identification. Although all three measures of satisfaction are related to identification commitment, there was a significant difference between Thai employees in American and Japanese corporations only with regard to satisfaction with the organization, which no doubt contributes to the greater identification of the workers in U.S. firms. Relative perception of pay (compare pay) and benefits (compare benefits) have the expected relationship with identification: As workers perceive their pay and benefits to be greater than others, their identification with the organization increases. In this regard, however, American and Japanese firms are divided on these characteristics. Quite surprisingly, years of education and tenure with the company are shown not to be related to identification.

To summarize the findings, identification commitment is higher in American corporations largely because of differences in perceived management distance, job variety, and satisfaction with the organization. The only factor found important for employee identification commitment that gives Japanese firms an advantage is the employees' perceptions that standard operating procedures are clearer in Japanese firms. However, controlling for all the other variables, a significant difference still exists in employee identification between the employees of Japanese and American corporations, *to the advantage of the American corporations.*

Effort Commitment

The analysis of the workers' willingness to exert effort on the company's behalf in order to help it succeed, a more behavioral component of commitment, is further discussed. Once again, the most salient point of the analysis is that there is a difference by home country of management, with *workers from the American companies indicating a greater willingness to expend effort.*

Unlike the analysis of identification, the only workplace characteristic that is significantly related to effort is reliance on standard operating procedures, which is shown to be higher for Japanese corporations. This would increase commitment in the Japanese managed workplace. Two of the satisfaction items remain significant in the partial correlations, but in one (satisfaction with superiors) there is no difference between the American and Japanese firms, and in the other (satisfaction with the organization) the advantage goes to American companies again. Unlike identification commitment to the company, years with the company and years of education are significantly associated with the effort variable, and their relationship is strengthened in the control analysis with the partial correlations. Sex, which was significantly associated with identification (women identified more strongly then men), is not associated with willingness to exert effort on behalf of the organization.

In summary, we find that our independent variables explain less of effort commitment among Thai employees than these variables did with respect to identification commitment. However, we again find that satisfaction with the organization gives American companies an advantage, while clear standard procedures give Japanese firms an advantage. But again, when controlling for all of these variables, a significant difference remains in effort commitment between Japanese and American firms, *with effort higher among Thai employees in American firms.*

Analysis of Management Interviews

Among the many themes relevant to employee relations uncovered in our detailed interviews with Thai managers in Japanese and American firms, two help us understand the above findings of greater employee identification commitment and effort commitment in American firms, as well as the greater distance and coldness of management perceived by Thai employees in Japanese corporations.

Thai managers told us repeatedly that whereas American firms are ''results oriented,'' Japanese firms are ''process oriented,'' One Thai middle manager put it this way: ''The Japanese are overly systematized. There must be a system that all will follow without deviation. In U.S. corporations they are much more results oriented. They don't care so much how you do it as long as it gets done well. They can have an advantage of being more flexible in a U.S. corporation.'' Another Thai manager in an American company stated: ''An advantage in U.S. corporations is the flexibility of U.S. managers. There is no set formula, and they can change to what works best.'' Also, ''they give Thais much more authority to make decisions on their own than in Thai and Japanese corporations.'' But, he added as an afterthought, ''a disadvantage of U.S. corporations is too much flexibility and change: Sometimes there is too much change and we don't know what to expect, and we are not told enough about changes.'' It is this statement, heard in different words by other Thai managers, that seems to get at the heart of Thai employees' perceptions of variety on the job and clear standard operating procedures: The greater freedom given Thai employees to use different work approaches in American companies may contribute to greater commitment among employees. At the same time, it seems that American managers can be too flexible for Thais, giving them some uncertainty over operating procedures.

Another important difference between the Japanese and American management approaches in Thailand related to the above affects worker commitment and seems to indicate broader problems for Japanese corporations in Thailand as well as all over Asian. This second theme we found stressed much more often and with greater emotion and emphasis by Thai middle managers in Japanese corporations. The theme can be best summarized as *''trust'' for foreign employees*. Our interviews suggest that one of the most significant problems among Japanese companies in Thailand (and elsewhere) is the *inability of Japanese managers to give complete trust to foreign employees.*

In a subtle but telling cut by a Thai manager in a Japanese company, when the top Thai manager in the company and the top Japanese manager were being interviewed together, the Japanese manager referred to his company's joint venture with the Thai company as being like a marriage, to which the Thai manager quickly added, ''If it is like a marriage I wonder sometimes what side of the family is still being represented and protected.'' Further discussion showed she clearly felt that the Japanese would not completely trust the Thais or allow them to be equal partners. In other companies, Thai as well as Japanese managers told us that there are often two important managerial meetings, one with both top Thai and Japanese managers, and later another one with only Japanese managers present. One Japanese manager even admitted to us that they hold ''Japanese only'' meetings on the weekends, hoping the Thais will not find out about them. Another Thai manager of a big U.S. firm who had previous employment in a Japanese company put it this way: ''When Japanese delegate they don't really delegate. The Japanese are still going to monitor very closely. Americans just say what needs to be done and when it has to be accomplished and expect results.[6]

This greater trust given to employees by American managers may explain the Thai employees' perceptions of less distance between American managers and Thai employees, as well as greater satisfaction with the organization in American companies, both shown related to more identification commitment and the latter shown to be related to effort commitment. It is somewhat puzzling that Thais did not express less satisfaction with their bosses when compared to American companies, but we suspect that the less satisfaction among the Thais with the Japanese company as an organization places this lack of trust for foreign employees on a general level rather than on the level of specific Japanese managers they work with individually in the company.

JAPANESE CORPORATIONS IN THAILAND, ASIA, AND THE WORLD

An abundance of evidence suggests that the negative views of Japan, views that they are arrogant and do not trust foreigners, are not confined to the corporations within which we conducted interviews, or even Thailand. In fact, the views of Japan may be less negative in Thailand than elsewhere in Asia. Unlike almost all of the rest of Asia, Japan never forcefully occupied Thailand or committed war atrocities against Thais. Our interviews with Thai people outside of the corporate world suggest that during the 1970s there were significant protests against Japan when the Japanese government was one of the first to recognize a new military government after a coup. But there have been other public outrages over what is perceived as Japanese arrogance over Japanese aid which requires Thailand to build such things as concert halls and art museums to Japanese specifications.[7]

More recently, however, the wider Thai criticism of Japan has focused on the economy. News articles in the *Bangkok Post* (e.g., January 25, 1997; September 18, 1998) have noted how Japanese corporations do not promote foreign managers into top positions or how transplant corporations from the United States do so. In the context of this criticism of Japanese corporations, some of the Japanese executives in our interview sample complained that the Thai government's Bureau of Investments (BoI, the agency that regulates foreign investments into Thailand) has been favoring U.S. corporations over Japanese corporations. Although BoI officials denied this charge when asked about it during our interviews, a later article in the local press seemed to confirm it (see *Bangkok Post*, October 2, 1998).

Perhaps more importantly, labor tensions in Japanese corporations in Thailand seem to be rising. The biggest case concerned the Sanyo plant near Bangkok where a large strike involving 2,000 Thai employees led to injuries and destroyed buildings in December 1996. Japanese managers we interviewed since, however, told us that other such cases (though smaller) have occurred in Japanese factories around Bangkok which have not been reported in the press. And perhaps equally important, Japanese executives in some of the factories where we conducted interviews expressed fear of labor sabotage and other acts of violence by Thai employees. Follow-up interviews with some of the Japanese managers since the economic crisis began in July 1997 indicate that concern about strikes and violence among their Thai employees has increased substantially. When we posed the same questions to American managers in our sample of corporations in the Bangkok area, none of them expressed any knowledge of labor violence or tensions in American companies in Thailand, or any concern or fear about labor problems in their factories.

In other Southeast Asian countries, the criticism of Japanese transplant corporations has been stronger. In countries such as Malaysia, Indonesia, the Philippines, Singapore, and Taiwan, there are complaints that the Japanese managers do not trust the foreign employees and do not promote them into positions of authority as American corporations do (Hatch and Yamamura, 1996: 153–157; Kawabe, 1991; Beechler, 1992).

This is a problem not just for Japanese transplant corporations in Asia, but for firms all over the world (Fallows, 1994: 234; Rinehart et al., 1994; Dedoussis and Littler, 1994: Taylor et al., 1994; Milkman, 1991). Indeed, in earlier research on 31 large Japanese corporations in Germany which followed the same procedures as reported earlier in our Thai research, we heard most of the same complaints from German middle managers in these corporations (Kerbo, Wittenhagen, and Nakao, 1994a, 1994b; Lincoln, Kerbo, and Wittenhagen, 1995). German blue-collar employees of Japanese corporations in Germany are in a far different situation when compared to Asian employees. German labor laws and strong German unions mandate that German employees in Japanese transplants have the same extensive influence and legal protection as employees of German corporations. German middle managers, however, are in a much different position. We heard the same complaints from German middle managers in Japanese transplant corporations that the Japanese ''don't trust'' them, will not allow them to participate in important decisions, and do not promote them to higher positions in the company.

CONCLUSION

Japan, of course, has other problems that make it difficult for it to take a leadership position in Asia. For example, Japan has seldom been able to act decisively and quickly as is required of a world leader. Nor is Japan known for leaders who are able to display such qualities (van Wolferen, 1989; Pye, 1985). But equally important, as a number of scholars have pointed out, other Asians tend to dislike the Japanese and find them difficult to work with (Fallows, 1994: 248; Bartu, 1992). While the situation may be worse in Asia, such problems are found to some degree wherever Japanese transplants are located.

At the beginning this chapter, we attempted to explain why Japanese culture and social organization are at the root of these problems for the Japanese. Beginning in the late 1980s, the Japanese government mounted a campaign to ''internationalize'' Japan and the Japanese people so that they would feel less uncomfortable with foreigners and learn to work with them better. By all indications, as many Japan scholars at the time predicted, these government efforts have been quite ineffective. For example, national polls in the early 1980s and before indicated that some 70 percent of Japanese people would prefer not to interact with foreigners if it could be avoided (Taylor, 1983: 258). In 1992 a national poll asked similar questions, with a result that some 70 percent of Japanese people said they would prefer not to interact with foreigners if it could be avoided (*Japan Times*, May 1992). Japanese people, it is often said, know more about other people and accept foreign intrusions into their society far more than most people; Still, it seems there is that inability to overcome the ''gaijin complex'' and discomfort when interacting with foreigners. The long history of isolation, a homogeneous society, and the experience of being a lone non-Axial civilization among the world of nations makes any campaign for ''internationalization'' difficult to advance. During the 1990s and no doubt beyond, in conjunction with the long-term problem of a ''gaijin complex'' for Japan, the Japanese must now face declining respect for the Japanese economic model due to recent economic crises in Japan and now throughout Asia.

Added to all of this are the rise of the Chinese economy and a strong potential for Chinese leadership in the region. There have been long-festering problems between the native peoples and Overseas Chinese in Indonesia, Malaysia, and to a lesser extent in Vietnam, but in most other Asian nations the Chinese immigrants have experienced good relations and extensive assimilation (Osborne, 1995: 108). The ethnic Chinese in these Asian nations tend to be very important economic participants. For example, in Thailand they own about 80 percent of private capital, along with 80 percent in Indonesia, 65 percent in Malaysia, and 40 percent in the Philippines (Hatch and Yamamura, 1996: 82; Huntington, 1996: 169). And in Taiwan and Singapore (not to mention Hong Kong), almost all private capital is in the hands of ethnic Chinese. Several books have been published in recent years about these Overseas Chinese, their new investments, and their business deals back on the mainland, all creating a vast Chinese economic network throughout the northern part of the Pacific Rim. If Samuel Huntington (1996) is correct, the ''Greater China'' with the Han Chinese Axial civilization at its core will increasingly come to dominate all of Asia as we move through the twenty-first century.

The future can take unforseen turns, and Chinese internal problems, if not managed well, could create severe setbacks for China in the twenty-first century. In the absence of such setbacks for China, however, the problems for Japan outlined in this chapter suggest that Japan's future in Asia may be much less positive than it looked just a decade ago. Japan, as a ''distant cousin'' of Asian nations that is becoming less rich, will likely find it difficult to compete with the reemergence of China, which will be more of ''a rich uncle'' than a ''distant cousin'' to most Asians—or we might even say, Chinese relatives versus Japan Inc.

NOTES

1. Of this total, thirteen had manufacturing operations in Thailand, two were trading companies, three were banks, and six were sales/distribution offices. Among the Japanese corporations in the sample, ten were manufacturing, two were trading companies, one was a bank, and four were sales/distribution offices. Among the American corporations, three were manufacturing, two were banks, and two involved only sales/distribution. Because every company was assured complete privacy for the information it provided, we will not further identify particular corporations or individuals involved in this research.

2. The employee questionnaire was taken primarily from Lincoln's research on Japanese transplants in the United States (Lincoln, Hanada, and McBride, 1986; Lincoln, Hanada, and Olson, 1981; Lincoln, Olson, and Hanada, 1978) and consisted of ten pages of items ranging from personal data to the employees' perceptions of workplace organization, job satisfaction, and standard measures of organizational commitment. The questionnaire was translated from English to Thai, back translated, and then the final Thai version was produced.

3. Of the 24 companies where management interviews were obtained, 13 provided us with employee questionnaires, 9 Japanese, and 4 American. This is not to say, however, that the other 11 all refused to allow employee questionnaires to be distributed. In fact, we were denied employee questionnaires at only six corporations, all of them Japanese. We did not obtain employee questionnaires from the other five companies either because there was no time to distribute and pick up questionnaires in the Bangkok traffic, or the company had so few employees we chose not to spend our time trying to distribute and pick up the questionnaires.

Our method of distributing questionnaires in the eleven companies was to leave the agreed upon number (in terms of number of employees in the immediate location) with the personnel manager for distribution to employees who filled out the questionnaire at home. Each questionnaire had an envelope attached, which was then sealed and dropped in a box by each employee to be picked up by the researchers. A total of 2,650 questionnaires were left in such a manner for the employees to fill out at home and returned. With approximately 1,000 questionnaires picked up, our return rate was under 50 percent but still in the normal range for this type of research procedure, especially considering each questionnaire was ten pages in length.

4. Our sample was drawn from the lists of corporations in the booklets published by the Japanese Chamber of Commerce (1994) and the American Chamber of Commerce (1995). Our sample of American and Japanese corporations was not exactly random in that we had to assure selection of companies that were likely to have a significant number of Thai employees and were in the general area of Bangkok. Within these guidelines, however, the sample was randomly selected with letters of introduction sent from California to 100 Japanese corporations and 25 American corporations. Once in Bangkok during the summer months of 1995 and 1996, we began making calls to these corporations in Bangkok to ask for interviews with some of these managers.

Brief mention of our acceptance rate in these corporations is necessary and perhaps interesting. To our surprise, we were directly refused interviews by only four of the Japanese corporations and one of the American corporations. With almost all of the corporations, several phone calls were required to finally reach the correct manager and gain approval, often sending several faxes with information about the research project and questionnaires in the process. Our main limitations in doing this research in the Bangkok area involved time—time to make calls with limited phone lines and especially time involved in getting from one place to another in Bangkok for interviews. Some of the corporations we were working with to obtain permission for interviews had to be dropped for consideration due to the time limitations. It is possible some of these would have been added to the list of rejections for interviews. However, several more than the 24 corporations had granted us personal interviews but had to be canceled owing to our time limitations in Bangkok.

In each corporation where interviews with management were obtained, we tried to interview both the American or Japanese manager or managers as well as Thai managers. This was not always possible, however, and our qualitative interviews with managers involved an approximately equal mixture of Japanese or American managers alone, Japanese or American and Thai managers together, and Thai managers alone.

5. The following three items were the measures of organizational commitment: Measuring the identification component of commitment were the items, "I feel a sense of pride working for this company" and "My values and the values of this company are similar." Commitment as willingness to expend effort for the organization was measured by the item, "I am willing to work harder than I have to in order to help this company succeed." The two items measuring identification were summed to create a single identification scale, while the other item was analyzed separately.

6. We did find at least one exception. At one of the more famous Japanese corporations around the world, we found no Japanese managers present in the main plant, and the two top Thai managers claimed they had the complete confidence of the Japanese managers and extensive autonomy. We were told that despite the fact that a famous Thai corporation had 40 percent of the investment, for the first five years the Japanese managers were heavily involved with management and did not seem to trust them. However, once they proved themselves, they were given almost complete authority. We tend to believe much of this because when we asked if we could distribute employee questionnaires, this Thai manager made the instant decision that they would be done without asking any Japanese manager. This did not happen in any other Japanese corporation, and the return rate of questionnaires at this particular plant was quite high.

7. Thai academic informants told us that many Thai academics and artists are still boycotting a new large concert hall financed by the Japanese because the Japanese required the almost exclusive use of Japanese design and art in the complex.

REFERENCES

Angle, H., and Perry, J. (1981). An Empirical Assessment of Organizational Commitment and Organizational Effectiveness. *Administrative Science Quarterly*, 26(1), pp. 1–14.

Apter, D. E., and Sawa, N. (1984). *Against the State: Politics and Social Protest in Japan*. Cambridge, MA: Harvard University Press.

Barrett, R., and Whyte, M. K. (1982). Dependency Theory and Taiwan: Analysis of a Deviant Case. *American Journal of Sociology*, 87, pp. 1064–1089.

Bartu, F. (1992). *The Ugly Japanese: Nippon's Economic Empire in Asia*. Singapore: Longman.

Beechler, S. (1992). International Management Control in Multinational Corporations: The Case of Japanese Consumer Electronics Firms in Asia. *ASEAN Economic Bulletin*, November.

Benedict, R. (1947). *The Chrysanthemum and the Sword: Patterns of Japanese Culture*. New York: Houghton Mifflin.

Benkhoff, B. (1997). Ignoring Commitment Is Costly: New Approaches Establish the Missing Link Between Commitment and Performance. *Human Relations*, 50(6), pp. 701–726.

Bornschier, V., and Chase-Dunn, C. (1985). *Transnational Corporations and Underdevelopment*. New York: Praeger.

Bowen, R. W. (1980). *Rebellion and Democracy in Meiji Japan*. Berkeley: University of California Press.

Chase-Dunn, C. (1975). The Effects of International Economic Dependence on Development and Inequality: A Cross-National Study. *American Sociological Review*, 40, pp. 720–738.

Chase-Dunn, C. (1989). *Global Formation: Structures of the World-Economy*. Oxford: Basil Blackwell.

Chirot, D. (1986). *Social Change in the Modern Era*. New York: Harcourt Brace Jovanovich.

Choate, P. (1990). *Agents of Influence: How Japan Manipulates America's Political and Economic System*. New York: Simon and Schuster.

Collins, R. (1975). *Conflict Sociology*. New York: Academic Press.

Coser, L. (1956). *The Function of Social Conflict*. New York: Free Press.

Coser, L. (1967). *Continuities in the Study of Social Conflict*. New York: Free Press.

Dedoussis, V., and Littler, C. R. (1994). Understanding the Transfer of Japanese Management Practices: The Australian Case. In T. Elger and C. Smith (eds.), *Global Japanization? The Transnational Transformation of the Labour Process*. London: Routledge, pp. 175–194.

Eisenstadt, S. N. (1995). *Japanese Civilization*. Chicago: University of Chicago Press.

Fallows, J. (1994). *Looking at the Sun: The Rise of the New East Asian Economic and Political System*. New York: Pantheon.

Gerlach, M. L. (1992). *Alliance Capitalism: The Social Organization of Japanese Business*. Berkeley: University of California Press.

Gold, T. B. (1986). *State and Society in the Taiwan Miracle*. Armonk, NY: M. E. Sharpe.

Hane, M. (1982). *Peasants, Rebels, and Outcasts: The Underside of Modern Japan*. New York: Pantheon.

Hane, M. (1988). *Reflections on the Way to the Gallows: Voices of Japanese Rebel Women*. New York: Pantheon.

Hatch, W., and Yamamura, K. (1996). *Asia in Japan's Embrace: Building a Regional Production Alliance*. Cambridge: Cambridge University Press.

Hayakawa, T. (1983). *Nihon no Shakai to Keibatsu* (Japan's upper strata social groups and their family connections). Tokyo: Kadokawa Shoten.

Hofstede, G. (1991). *Cultures and Organization: Software of the Mind*. New York: McGraw-Hill.

Huntington, S. (1996). *The Clash of Civilizations and the Remaking of World Order*. New York: Simon and Schuster.

Jin, I. (1981). *Nihon Eriito Gundan* (Japan's elite corps). Tokyo: Guriin Aroo Shuppansha.

Jin, I. (1989). *Keibatsu—Shin Tokuken Kaikyu no Keifu* (Genealogy of the new privileged class). Tokyo: Mainishi Shimbunsha.

Johnson, C. (1982). *MITI and the Japanese Miracle*. Stanford, CA: Stanford University Press.

Kawabe, N. (1991). Problems of and Perspectives on Japanese Management in Malaysia. In S. Yamashita (ed.), *Transfer of Japanese Technology and Management*. Tokyo: University of Tokyo Press.

Kennedy, P. (1987). *The Rise and Fall of the Great Powers*. New York: Random House.

Kerbo, H. R. (1996). *Social Stratification and Inequality: Class Conflict in Historical and Comparative Perspective* (3rd ed.). New York: McGraw-Hill.

Kerbo, H. R., and McKinstry, J. (1995). *Who Rules Japan? The Inner Circles of Economic and Political Power*. Westport, CT: Praeger.

Kerbo, H. R., Wittenhagen E., and Nakao, K. (1994a). *Japanische Unternehmen in Deutschland: Unternehmenstruktur und Arbeitsverhältnis*. Gelsenkirchen, Germany: Veröffentlichungsliste des Instituts für Arbeit und Technik.

Kerbo, H. R., Wittenhagen, E., and Nakao, K. (1994b). *Japanese Transplant Corporations, Foreign Employees, and the German Economy: A Comparative analysis of Germany and the United States*. Duisburg, Germany: Duisburger Beiträge zur Soziologischen Forschung.

Kim, E. M. (1994). *Big Business, Strong State: Collusion and Conflict in South Korean Development, 1960–1990*. Albany: State University of New York Press.

Koh, B. C. (1989). *Japan's Administrative Elite*. Berkeley: University of California Press.

Kulick, E., and Wilson, D. (1996). *Time for Thailand: Profile of a New Success*. Bangkok: White Lotus.

Lincoln, J. R., Hanada, M., and McBride, K. (1986). Organizational Structures in Japanese and U.S. Manufacturing. *Administrative Science Quarterly*, 31, pp. 338–364.

Lincoln, J. R., Hanada, M., and Olson, J. (1981). Cultural Orientations and Individual Reactions to Organizations: A Study of Employees of Japanese Owned Firms. *Administrative Science Quarterly*, 26, pp. 93–115.

Lincoln, J. R., and Kalleberg, A. L. (1985). Work Organization and Work Force Commitment: A Study of Plants and Employees in the U.S. and Japan. *American Sociological Review*, 50, pp. 738–760.

Lincoln, J. R., and Kalleberg, A. L. (1996). Commitment, Quits, and Work Organization in Japanese and U.S. Plants. *Industrial and Labor Relations Review*, 50(1), pp. 39–59.

Lincoln, J. R., and Kalleberg, A. L. (1990). *Culture, Control, and Commitment: A Study of Work Organization and Work Attitudes in the United States and Japan*. Cambridge: Cambridge University Press.

Lincoln, J. R., Kerbo, H. R., and Wittenhagen, E. (1995). Japanese Companies in Germany: A Case Study in Cross-Cultural Management. *Journal of Industrial Relations* (Spring), pp. 17–29.

Lincoln, J. R., Olson, J., and Hanada, M. (1978). Cultural Effects on Organizational Structure: The Case of Japanese Firms in the United States. *American Sociological Review*, 43, pp. 829–847.

March, R. M. (1992). *Working for a Japanese Company: Insights into the Multicultural Workplace*. Tokyo: Kodansha.

Meyer, J. P. et al. (1989). Organizational Commitment and Job Performance: It's the

Nature of the Commitment That Counts. *Journal of Applied Psychology*, 74(1), pp. 152–156.

Milkman, R. (1992). *Japan's California Factories: Labor Relations and Economic Globalization*. Los Angeles: Institute of Industrial Relations, UCLA.

Mouer, R., and Sugimoto, Y. (1986). *Images of Japanese Society*. London: Kegan Paul International.

Muscat, R. J. (1994). *The Fifth Tiger: A Study of Thai Development*. Armonk, NY: M. E. Sharpe.

Myrdal, G. (1970). *The Challenge of World Poverty*. New York: Pantheon.

O'Reilly, C., III, and Chatman, J. (1986). Organizational Commitment and Psychological Attachment: The Effect of Compliance, Identification, and Internalization on Prosocial Behavior, *Journal of Applied Psychology*, 71(3), pp. 492–499.

Osborne, M. (1995). *Southeast Asia: An Introductory History*. St. Leonard's, NSW, Australia: Allen and Unwin.

Pasuk, P., and Baker, C. (1996a). *Thailand's Boom*. Chaing Mai, Thailand: Silkworm Books.

Pasuk, P., and Baker, C. (1996b). *Thailand: Economy and Politics*. Kuala Lumpur: Oxford University Press.

Pasuk, P., and Baker, C. (1998). *Thailand's Boom and Bust*. Chiang Mai, Thailand: Silkworm Books.

Pharr, S. J. (1990). *Losing Face: Status Politics in Japan*. Berkeley: University of California Press.

Porter, L. W., and Smith, F. J. (1970). The Etiology of Organizational Commitment. Unpublished Paper, University of California, Irvine.

Porter, L. W. et al. (1974). Organizational Commitment, Job Satisfaction, and Turnover among Psychiatric Technicians. *Journal of Applied Psychology*, 59, pp. 603–609.

Prestowitz, C. V. (1989). *Trading Places: How We Are Giving Our Future to Japan and How to Reclaim It*. New York: Basic Books.

Pye, L. W. (1985). *Asian Power and Politics: The Cultural Dimensions of Authority*. Cambridge, MA: Belknap Press/Harvard University Press.

Reischauer, E. O. (1988). *The Japanese*. Cambridge, MA: Harvard University Press.

Rinehart, J., Robertson, D., Huxley, C., and Wareham, J. (1994). Reunifying Conception and and Execution of Work under Japanese Production Management? A Canadian Case Study. In T. Elger and C. Smith (eds.), *Global Japanization? The Transnational Transformation of the Labour Process*. London: Routledge, pp. 152–174.

Sherif, M. (1966). *In Common Predicament: Social Psychology of Intergroup Conflict and Cooperation*. Boston: Houghton Mifflin.

Simmel, G. (1955). *Conflict and the Web of Group Affiliations*, ed. Kurt Wolff and Reinhard Bendix. New York: Free Press.

Snyder, D., and Kick, E. (1979). Structural Position in the World System and Economic Growth, 1955–1970: A Multiple Analysis of Transnational Interactions. *American Journal of Sociology*, 84, pp. 1096–1128.

Stokes, R., and Jaffee, D. (1982). Another Look at the Export of Raw Materials and Economic Growth. *American Sociological Review*, 47, pp. 402–407.

Taylor, B., Elger, T., and Fairbrother, P. (1994). Transplants and Emulators: The Fate of the Japanese Model in British Electronics. In T. Elger and C. Smith (eds.),

Global Japanization? The Transnational Transformation of the Labour Process. London: Routledge, pp. 196–228.

Taylor, J. (1983). *Shadows of the Rising Sun: A Critical View of the "Japanese Miracle."* Tokyo: Tuttle.

van Wolferen, K. (1989). *The Enigma of Japanese Power.* New York: Alfred A. Knopf.

Vogel, E. (1989). *One Step Ahead in China: Guangdong under Reform.* Cambridge, MA: Harvard University Press.

Vogel, E. (1991). *The Four Little Dragons: The Spread of Industrialization in East Asia.* Cambridge, MA: Harvard University Press.

Chapter 4

The Asian Economic Crisis: A Forward Look at Issues and Implications for International Business

Frank L. Bartels and Hafiz R. Mirza

INTRODUCTION

The perturbations that began as "a little local difficulty" in Thailand with the failure of Finance One (a nonbank financial intermediary) in early 1997 has become so amplified and intense as to make painfully raw the nerves of the global financial system, even though at the time of writing signs of a frail recovery are emergent.[1] East Asia conveniently categorized in terms of the High-Performance Asian Economies (HPAEs—Hong Kong, Singapore, South Korea, and Taiwan) and Newly Industrializing Economies (NIEs—Indonesia, Malaysia, the Philippines, and Thailand) has suffered a precipitous decline in its economic fortunes since mid-1997.[2] The attendant social losses, which are relatively mild in Singapore but devastating in Indonesia, where some 34 percent of key industries have been closed, carry the threat of isolationalism.[3] The present view is punctuated on the one hand by a stubborn belief in a regional renaissance and, on the other, by a pessimism that the regional political will is emaciated.[4]

Nonetheless, since the early 1990s, the East Asian economic performance has been seen retrospectively as "miraculous" (World Bank, 1993). It has been the subject of interesting academic analysis but unbalanced commentary from the more popular business press. What made the region's growth remarkable was, first, the fact that there were few Cassandras (Krugman, 1994). Second, the debate has been circumscribed almost exclusively by neoclassical arguments on the advantages of the free-market approach to economics and its management (Fallows, 1993, 1994) on the one hand, and the so-called Asian development model on the other. Commentators willing to publish penetrating analysis were severely criticized and dismissed as incapable of appreciating the "miracle." However, observations on Asia's developmental model have generally occurred with insufficient reference to theoretical foundations provided by List (1837/1983) and Reich (1991). To the discerning, the serious systemic risks associated with endogenous policy developments in some Asian economies could not be dismissed so easily. According to one highly respected regional observer, the policies adopted during the years of "miraculous" growth, on the back of a weak U.S. dollar, were neither well developed nor well understood.[5] When faced, in mid-1997, with rapid and uncontrollable exogenous pressures, the policies failed at both country and regional level. In the event, the pressures, uncorked by finance capital, demanded almost too much from the Bretton Woods institutions—the only facility able to sanction Asian responses.

At the annual meetings of the International Monetary Fund and World Bank in Hong Kong in late 1997, instead of the expected tributes to the "miracle" economies, in the glare of worldwide publicity, the corroded state of Asia's development model was exposed cruelly. Fundamental systemic flaws and managerial shortcomings were apparent. In debating the dynamics of the startling demise of regional economies, observers witnessed the undiplomatic behavior of one prominent statesman (Dr. Mahathir Mohamad) and a powerful financier (George Soros) insulting each other. In the circumstances, and given the prize at stake—control of world markets—this confrontation should not have been unexpected (Stopford et al., 1991).

In 1998, "The Year of the Tiger," the Asian crisis, in its six differentiated phases (currency, banking, economic, social, political, and psychological) became a full-blown slump.[6] The crisis is the first and most significant one of finance capital in globalization and world economic interdependency (Soros, 1998). It is not an exaggeration to state that its coverage in academic, business, economic, and socioeconomic publications that detail the gut-wrenching descriptive statistics is intellectually sensational. The velocity and dimensions of its regional and global shock-waves have surprised all but the most prescient observers.[7] The abnormal indices of growth posted by the miracle economies coupled with capital from inward foreign portfolio investment (FPI) and long-term private foreign direct investment (FDI) flows presaged the development of a classic speculative economy. In 1997, FDI inflows to developing countries totaled U.S.$256 billion, of which U.S.$90 billion (70%) went to Southeast Asia.[8] To all intents and purposes, the crisis has reversed this flow[9] and has resulted in an IMF projected regional output growth of a depressing −10.4% (for ASEAN) and −2.5% (for Japan) in 1998.[10]

Why another article on the Asian crisis? The lateral dimensions of the crisis—currency, banking economic, socioeconomic, political, and now psychological (as the crisis matures, a detectable identity crisis in Asia is unsettling fragile social cohesion)[11] in the international, regional, and national contexts—deserve scrutiny. In light of a long-term view of international business and the rampant globalization of the last decade,[12] six arguments are unassailable.

1. During the past 25 years, since the collapse of the Bretton Woods system of fixed exchange rates, capital markets and financial operations have become pervasively deregulated and extensively liberalized to an unprecedented degree. As a consequence, not only have the frequency and amplitude of financial crises increased but also there has been a "domain shift." Subsequent crises have moved from the public (i.e., government) to the private arena. The Asian crisis is the first genuine crisis of the private sector (notwithstanding the interventionist role played by Asian governments in their respective economies).
2. Despite the economic shallowness of individual emerging markets,[13] neither national nor collateral (regional) effects have been contained, nor has damage been limited by the conventional "Washington consensus." The crisis is global and is encapsulating all emerging markets as well as the Triad economies.[14]
3. The crisis has been exacerbated by the impact of oil and commodity prices slumping to pre-1973 levels.[15]
4. The fundamental problems of the unfolding crisis are the dislocations of social norms in the last 30 to 40 years of Asian urban development.[16]
5. Both the laissez-faire posture of Hong Kong and the developmental state of "soft authoritarianism"[17] reveal the following as explanatory factors for the Asian crisis: (a) asymmetric urbanization and industrialization; (b) incapacitated institutional structures of Japan[18] (Drucker, 1998; Sayle, 1998); (c) corrosive antipathies toward the Chinese diaspora and its capital (both the international variety and the domestic entrepreneurial type); and (d) unwillingness to render efficient and effective the separation between the economic interests of domestic policy and the strategies of individual businesses.
6. The sheer magnitude of regional losses—since mid-1997, nonperforming loans amounting to over U.S.$1 trillion, equity assets write-downs of over U.S.$2 trillion (at the height of the crisis), over U.S.$3 trillion decrease in regional GDP, and the resulting absolute collapse of not only FPI activity (from U.S.$103 billion in 1996 to less than U.S.$15 billion in 1998)[19] but also FDI (from U.S.$93.8 billion in 1996 to a 1999 forecast of −U.S.$15.1 billion for Indonesia, Malaysia, the Philippines, South Korea, and Thailand). At the broader regional level, the 1996 U.S.$161 billion FDI was forecast to drop to U.S.$23.4 billion in 1999.[20] Furthermore, Japan–ASEAN 3 (Indonesia, Malaysia, and Thailand) trade in terms of exports to Japan is set for an average of −23.5 percent decline in 1999.[21]

These facts are giving rise to tensions of strategic security and potentially could produce conflagration in Asia. From the perspective of the political economy of international business, Asia's crisis, no longer its own, deserves attention.

The regional consequences are grim. Japan has astonishing problems—its economy, according to some, has been in recession since 1991 and is falling out of control—and holds 40 percent of Asia's external liabilities.[22] There is the alarming possibility that China will crack because of mounting, and ultimately intolerable, speculative pressures on its currency as well as from its own internal stresses and wider regional tensions. Indonesia alone could take more than a decade to recover to pre-crash indices. The notion of ''Asia's lost decade'' similar to Africa's lost 1980s is no longer fanciful. From the perspective of finance capital, the Asian crisis represents the contest for, and control of, the integrated global economy by public institutions concerned with welfare and private forces concerned with shareholder value (Harman, 1996).

ASIA'S HEXAGRAMIC CRISIS—A RETROSPECTIVE

Given its currency, banking, economic, socioeconomic, political, and psychological dimensions, it is becoming increasingly difficult to delineate unambiguously the technical and social causations for the contagious reach of the Asian crisis. Technical arguments articulate the interrelationships of increased macroeconomic pressures for globalization, liberalization, and deregulation in financially immature emerging markets, asymmetric accumulation and distribution of FPI and FDI, as well as excess global liquidity.[23] This led ultimately to unmanageable economic output that, at the dawn of the crisis, featured rapid import growth.[24] The social causes encapsulate a distorted analysis of Asian values[25] by Asian nations that led invariably to investment choices on the basis of cronyism and grandeur.[26]

The World Bank Report (1993), *The East Asian Miracle*, which implicitly trumpeted Asian values, has been interpreted by many in terms of Asian values being anchored in the category—valid for all time and all places. However, in response to the question posed by *Time* Magazine, ''Do you regret the prominence that has been given to Asian values?'' Singapore's senior minister, Lee Kuan Yew, replied in a manner that, on balance, placed Asian values in a second category—valid for one place and not another.[27] Asian values, at least those pertinent to the economic ''miracle,'' like all values, are in contention and in a dynamic flux; they are plainly in a third category—valid at one time but no longer so. Values drive human endeavor and enterprise. Had Asian economic actors in particular, and Asians in general, understood their values at a more intimate level, the hubris that contributed to the collapse of the ''miracle economies'' might well have been avoided.

The crisis that touched off the regional contagion was manifest by the crisis of confidence in the Thai government's ability to maintain a U.S. dollar-pegged currency in the face of deteriorating macroeconomic fundamentals, especially in the balance-of-payments. The apparent regional overreliance on debt and capital inflows that at the time averaged 13 percent and 17 percent of capital formation for Thailand and Malaysia, respectively (Zhang, 1998) raised dramatically the risk associated with Asian emerging markets. Furthermore, inadequate banking supervision policies, corporate corruption, and government–corporate collusion contributed to the eventual erosion of confidence.

The rigidly pegged exchange rates, together with deteriorating macroeconomic indices and current account deficits averaging −5.2 percent of GDP, assisted currency volatility for NIEs. At first glance, the regional GDP growth rates masked decreasing competitiveness. Negative current account balances above −5 percent of GDP are unsustainable, especially when investment in nonproductive sectors is excessive (evidenced by property asset inflation).

The indebtedness and poor quality of bank intermediation in Southeast Asia have been analyzed further. The history of input factor growth (Krugman, 1994) enabled regional short-term external debts to grow without due diligence. The credit available to Asia (and in contrast—the extent of the present credit crunch) is indicated by Triad banking assets in the region at the end of 1997. European banks held U.S.$320 billion, Japanese banks held on-balance sheet assets of U.S.$260 billion, and U.S. banks held U.S.$46 billion.[28] The actual figures (and concomitant nonperforming loans) are likely to be much higher (taking a cue from the 1994 Mexican crisis) in the explosive growth of private sector bank lending in the latter part of the economic boom from the second half of 1980s until the collapse of investor confidence in mid-1997.[29] Between 1994 and 1996, expansion of bank assets in Asian emerging markets averaged 22.4 percent in Indonesia, 23.9 percent in Malaysia, 30.20 percent in the Philippines, 22.0 percent in Thailand, and even 15.8 percent in even conservative Singapore. The extent of Asia's banking problems is a measure of the seriousness of the Asian crisis that these ratios are on average three to seven times those posted at the height of the 1994–1995 Mexican currency crisis. However, these assets were collateralized by relatively low productive input factor structures, namely, realty rather than factories; leverage rather than equity; speculation in stock markets rather than long-term equity stakes; overcapacity in services investments and other overambitious asset ventures rather than competitive investment positions.[30] Asia's private sector companies may be charged with profligacy, but so too may the governments for policy failings.[31] The principal indicators of the scale of "overheating" in the emerging markets and subsequent distress are several[32] but the following examples capture the nuances:

- The taken-for-granted sustainability of double-digit growth in loan portfolios and avoiding the implications of growing imbalances between the growth of loans relative to GDP growth. This led to unsustainable growth of high credit-to-GDP ratios.
- The hitherto unquestioned commitment to peg local currencies to the U.S. dollar under conditions of high interest rates, unfavorable current account imbalances, and an appreciating U.S. dollar in the 1990s. Thus, the propensity to increase imports and loss of export competitiveness rendered Asian emerging markets vulnerable to exogenous shocks.
- The long-term pressures for capital account and financial deregulation to which regional governments had succumbed without either adequate banking regulations or supervisory structures. This enabled companies to oversubstitute equity with debt and so create high returns-on-equity balance sheets that obscured unstable underlying capital structures. South Korea's leading 30 conglomerates had average debt-to-equity ratios of approximately 400 percent in 1996.[33] Similarly, Japanese firms show a debt-to-equity ratio of 4 to 1 and carry unserviceable burdens.

- The greatly expanded range of investors coupled with excess global liquidity in the 1990s, which enabled the companies and banks of emerging markets to borrow U.S. dollars short term in response to low U.S. interest rates for long-term investments confident in the continued growth of the Southeast Asian ''miracle.'' In the light of poor or insignificant Total Factor Productivity Growth (Rodrik, 1997), when regional export competitiveness declined precipitously in 1996, current account deficits as far as foreign investors were concerned became unsustainable without currency realignments. The erosion of investor confidence subsequently began the ''flight'' from Asia, and other emerging markets, toward quality.
- In retrospect, the misunderstanding of the transaction dynamics of foreign exchange derivatives, financial instruments, and their intermediation by locals which indicated the immaturity of institutional arrangements in Asia's emerging markets. The *Financial Times* (January 12, 1998) provides an exposé that is absolutely staggering. The respected paper states: ''With the blessing of his superiors, the central bank's young and inexperienced chief currency trader, Paiboon Kittisrikangwan, had locked up most of Thailand's foreign exchange reserves in forward contracts. Thailand's reported foreign reserves of over $30bn were a myth—in fact they had dwindled to $1.4bn, equal to just two days of imports.''[34]
- The little-publicized but explosive increase in the derivative class of financial intermediation instruments by retail and investment banks to increase returns in the light of poor lending performance and by governments to hedge. The estimate of U.S.$10 trillion worth of maturing derivative contracts due from Asia in 1998 exacerbates the regional problem of indebtedness.[35]
- The ''miracle'' as inherently unstable and untenable. In contrast, the regional governments failed to recognize that the disciplines (or herd instincts) of the market that compelled the global financial machine to bring vast investment in-flows to the region in search of high yields could cause massive outflows in search of lower risk.

The evidence suggests that inadequate policies for bank asset management were highly significant in the crisis (Delhaise, 1999). A typical example is provided by Peregrine Investment Holdings. It risked over two and one-half times its asset base to a then well-connected taxi company in Indonesia with scant regard for due diligence and was promptly bankrupted. Loan decisions tended to be directed (South Korea) (Galbraith and Kim, 1998) or at best based on dubious collateral or at worst on cronyism (Indonesia). Consequently, in the presence of a regional credit crunch, industrial strategies were bound to suffer.

The perilous descent from a currency crisis into a combined crisis of financial, economic, socioeconomic, and psychological proportions belies the sentiment that ''money'' and ''real'' economies are separate (Drucker, 1989). Currency and asset devaluations erode collateral, promote greater margin calls, and stampede investors into the classic ''flight to quality.'' This in turn forces an overzealous reexamination of a widening range of asset qualities that exposes a more painfully realistic evaluation of economic fundamentals. In the case of Asia, this scrutiny continues to expose the poor quality of industrial linkages and national banking sectors.[36] The regional economic contagion (rising inflation, liquidity traps, rising indebtedness and associated involuntary lending, increasing unemployment, and erosion of living standards) that ensues manifests itself in an extraordinary social crisis as citizens become intolerant and demand "unreasonable" changes in the social rubric. The more disaffected begin agitating for wholesale change that is difficult to mange even at the best of times. This is clearly evident in Indonesia and is increasingly so in Malaysia.[37]

INTRAREGIONAL AND INTERREGIONAL DIMENSIONS OF THE CRISIS

The ensuing banking crisis in Thailand in mid-1997 quickly spread throughout the region as investors questioned the quality of other regional investments. The episodal event was the attempted recapitalization of Finance One, followed by the crucial realization that Thailand's financial sector companies were distressed.[38] The ensuing suspension, by the Bank of Thailand, of sixteen finance companies tore away any remaining consensus on the viability of the "miracle" economies' financial health and caused widespread panic among local and international investors. Subsequent international (and domestic) speculative attacks on Thailand's currency resulted in a precipitous fall in its value. The abandoning of the U.S. dollar pegging of the Thai baht then touched off the intraregional currency crisis. At the nadir of the crisis, regional currencies declined relative to the U.S. dollar by between 15 and 60 percent. Regional stock market indices declined by about 60 percent relative to world markets. The depreciation of regional currencies continued relentlessly from mid-1997, but at the time of writing the currencies show signs of recovery.[39]

The state of GDP growth in selected Asian countries may reveal the regional dimensions of the crisis. Ominously, apart from China and Singapore, the Asian region including Japan (accounting for 40% of pre-crisis regional GDP) is set for a massive and unprecedented contraction of GDP wrought by the corrosive combination of NPLs, falling collateral values, and a vicious credit contraction, as well as a sharp reduction in private capital in-flows.[40] The loss of national purchasing power has led to import contractions and may, however, cause an eventual rebalancing of the regional capital accounts, at the expense of import-intense manufacturing output. Having become the region for Japanese FDI, multinational enterprises (MNEs), and sourcing activities (Ozawa, 1992), the high levels of intraregional exchange imply structural intermediation arrangements and directions of trade that will be difficult to adjust in the shortterm.[41] Ironically, this high degree of intraregional FDI and trade that, pre-crisis, gave rise to a virtuous circle of growth, in the context of weak banking and financial sectors, has become the Achilles heel of Asia's recovery. The Japanese-led FDI has shifted into reverse, and the dynamics of associated IISPM have come to a standstill.[42] Asia simply cannot export, import, or perform economic intermediation effectively, and it will be unable to do so to a significant extent until debt is swapped for equity and the destructive forces of capitalism are enabled to work to clear markets. The export and import business that is occurring at a fraction of the efficiencies of pre-crisis levels (perhaps with the exception of Singapore) testifies to the inefficiencies of Asian markets. The collapse of distribution logistics to a great extent in Indonesia and imposition of capital controls by Malaysia are cases in point.

Asia's pre-1997 near double-digit GDP growth indices encouraged the view that consumption and demand booms fueled by exports from the Triad were on the horizon for Asia's rapidly expanding middle classes. It is important to remember that a number of factors articulate the links between the Pacific and Atlantic economies. The first and most obvious is the electronic nervous system of globalized capital markets that allows the instantaneous transmission of investor sentiment (good or ill). The depression of the more significant Latin American stock markets by about 60 percent since mid-1997 is evidence of this mechanism. The second mechanism through bank panics (a feature of the 1930s depression)[43] is so far limited to the region. The Japanese lack of trust in their banks is not reflected in either the United States or Europe. The third mechanism, although FDI and trade have begun to affect the United States and Europe, is that without Japan's import capacity, the manufacturing plants of the region cannot function to enable Japanese MNEs (predominantly smaller sized in employment terms in comparison to their U.S. and uropean counterparts) to benefit from the advantages of offshore production and economies of scale in Asian domestic markets. The termination of all but the most strategic infrastructure projects, the catastrophic drop in domestic consumption, and the slow but eventual restructuring of industrial and service sectors represent a dramatic shrinkage of overseas market shares of Japanese, U.S., and European MNEs. Without Asia buying and producing, activity in input factor markets is declining and is exacerbated by the long-term decline in commodity prices. The regional credit crunch, as banks readjust their portfolio risks and loan profiles, is being transmitted to financial capitals in the United States and Europe (Chote, 1998). Significant losses have been posted by European banks. They evidence that the U.S. corporate sector is suffering directly from the Asian crisis and that contagion effects are increasingly interregional, effect that are no longer anecdotal or confined to the operations of capital markets. The profitability of U.S. MNEs in 1998 was the worst of the decade.[44]

IMPLICATIONS FOR INTERNATIONAL BUSINESS

Beyond the second anniversary of Asia's economic heart attack, there is, in general, an emerging consensus regarding the causes and contagious effects. However, the debate over the required surgical solution is intensely convoluted and involves institutional responses to private sector initiatives and vice versa. The Sachs argument (you do not solve bank panics by calling the IMF)[45] is opposed by Linda Lim (Asia would need to show maturity in accepting its share of responsibility).[46] The currency board solution advanced by Steve Hanke is dismissed by Paul Krugman.[47] The Western perspective is qualified by competitive exigencies. Similarly, implications for international business and MNEs are contradictory—it depends on who they are, the structure of their production, and for whom they produce.

The Asian crisis not only has become a regional socioeconomic crisis but also has exposed the systemic frailties of the global financial architecture, with obviously serious consequences. According to one respected observer, its dimensions (if they are to be believed) are truly staggering: "in the last two years, Indonesia's economy has shrunk by almost 80 per cent, Thailand's by 50 per cent, South Korea's by 45 per cent, Malaysia's by 25 per cent" (Zakaria, 1998). Resolution of the crisis is being contested in ideological, political-economy, and psychological terms. First, the crisis highlights the Hilferding analysis of the global operations of finance capital (McLelland, 1979: 59–71). Second, it evokes the contention over Asia's economic ascendancy (Huntington, 1996). Two observations about the latter are apposite. In the tensions created up by the crisis, Asia has released an ambivalent voice evident in nationalism, displayed, for example, by South Korea resentfully opening its economy to foreign participation,[48] and fervently championed, for example, by Dr. Mahathir Mohamad—the prime minister of Malaysia. In the case of Malaysia, this has become a vigilant posture toward foreign ownership, resulting ultimately in the imposition of capital controls and a shift toward autarky.[49] In reaction, the regional lobbying efforts by MNEs (already extensive and costly) will require complete reappraisal and consequently will lead to a reduced emphasis on favoritism in business strategies.

The confusion in the managerial ranks of MNEs is apparent. Just as the financial crisis has thrown Asia into turmoil, MNEs have experienced the negation of many of their cherished operational and strategic assumptions about Asia—getting close to power and its brokers, *guanxi*, reciprocity as a key to doing business, and so on. How should they now adapt[50] not only to economic conditions but also in the light of regional press coverage which, to those unfamiliar with the diversity of Asia, must seem a discomfiting blend of the bizarre, macabre, and surreal.[51]

At the level of MNE operations, the Asian crisis and its global ramifications permit factor markets to engage with increased interdependency and diminishing trade barriers of international business. The perception of MNEs as partners in Asia's development and "sharing Asia's dynamism" (UNCTAD, 1996a) is bound to be viewed increasingly as rapacious and self-serving, especially so in the absence of localization efforts.[52] It is entirely reasonable to argue that as a result, issues of personnel and organizational security, as well as corporate social responsibilities and what it means to be a global company, will be at the forefront of the MNEs' resource deployment decisions.

Negative tentacular multiplier, accelerator effects and socially corrosive outcomes of the crisis are likely to permeate the entire region. The story is one of a great leap backwards[53] into an uncertain world of increased graft and corruption.[54] MNEs will have to change their regional foreign market servicing strategies from reliance on domestic factors to a more proactive search for profitable market re-segmentations that are location specific but that avoid the perils of incumbency in places like Indonesia, Malaysia, and Indochina. The merging view of post-crisis Asia is that MNEs will ''need to *re-learn* the art of doing business in Asia'' (Lim Chon-Phung, general manager with Hewlett-Packard[55]) but are unlikely to alter fundamentally their long-term FDI view on Asia's potential (UNCTAD-ICC, 1998). In the short term, however, FDI from Japan will diminish if only because its economy is mired in recession and its *keiretsu* are bleeding from huge losses.[56] Others, investors like George Soros, are abandoning whole countries altogether.[57]

Internationally, latent stagflationary pressures are prompting MNEs to reappraise their strategic postures for global competitiveness.[58] Denials of disinvestment by MNEs are a sure sign that this process is well underway.[59] MNEs in export-oriented sectors are selectively investing. In a wider context, U.S. MNEs led acquisitions activity, with 1998 purchases totaling some U.S.$8.8 billion, while European (mostly UK and German) MNEs followed with some U.S.$3 billion.[60] However, not only is the pattern of mergers and acquisitions asymmetric—favoring entry into Japan, South Korea, Hong Kong, and Thailand but neither Malaysia, Indonesia, China, the Philippines, nor even India and Australia—but also the speed of merger activity is slowing. This is a measure of the spreading lack of confidence that, in the face of the challenges of due diligence, confirms the restrategizing priorities of MNEs. This is especially so for German MNEs which are (traditionally reluctant to internationalize aggressively, with very few exceptions) of whom 84 percent, in a 1999 survey of 1,500 senior managers in ten Asian countries, indicated that despite the obstacles to FDI, they would increase their Asian presence. Singapore's concerns in this context are real notwithstanding the view of German MNEs.[61]

Many MNEs with FDI servicing domestic markets and infrastructure developments are divesting and shrinking regional representation. Others are exploiting low asset prices.[62] The process will create substantial staffing movements as MNEs reconfigure their IISPM networks and reposition logistics and profit centers. A prominent example is provided by Caltex which has reorganized its global operations into knowledge and capability centers dispersed across Asia and headquartered in Singapore. In this large-scale rearrangement, there will not only be initial write-offs but also the idling and ''moth-balling'' of productive capacity. These plants, even upon the eventual regional economic recovery (which is at present doubtful or is ambiguously supported by contradictory evidence), might not be useful. Months, possibly years, of inactivity will render useless the corroded and unsafe electromechanical structures of production. Consequently, international business will have to be acutely aware of the hidden costs involved in delayed acquisitions. The crisis therefore carries the promise of what Asia may fear—few choices in economic ''assistance'' by U.S. and European capital.

Ultimately, the Asian crisis allows a comparative examination of the neoclassical and dirigiste ideologies for economic development (Fallows, 1993, 1994). It also exposes the ideological contention between West and East and, if one believes in conspiracies, the battle for dominance between Western and Eastern hegemons. In this battle, firms and MNEs are not, and cannot be, neutral. For example, Malaysia's leading conglomerates have been at the leading edge of the competition to realize the country's vision of industrialization. In addition, Singapore's regionalization policy has been enacted in part by, and through, government-linked firms.[63] The fact that the vast majority of the world's leading MNEs are American and European, not Asian, implies that Asia's recovery (which is still fragile[64]), will be in no small way assisted by these same MNEs soliciting Western governments to help the stricken economies directly, even if this soliciting occurs after a lag that assists in the emasculation of Asian industrial competitiveness.[65] The political dimensions of the MNEs' behavior and operations, usually studied in terms of political economy, are likely to come to the fore as a major international business research issue (Boddewyn and Brewer, 1994) in terms of headquarter-subsidiary organization and strategic management of globally dispersed centers of core competencies.

CONCLUDING REMARKS

The Asian crisis demonstrates the fallibility of markets in the present state of globalization, at least as far as the Triad, their MNEs, and "clusters" are concerned. It also illustrates how volatilities of FDI within factor markets, and FPI within financial markets, together with deregulation and liberalization, translate into industrial instability.[66] There is a need for restructuring the industrial and financial landscapes of Asia as well as industrial consolidation in Europe and the United States (UNCTAD-ICC, 1998). How will MNEs, and international small and medium-sized enterprises map, and navigate through, the unfamiliar terrain of protected bankrupts, absent clients, new owners, and either new or disrupted supply chain relationships? More importantly, how are international businesses going to cope with the "tooth-and-claw" competition that the corporate struggle to survive will unleash once the psychological acceptance of the new reality is embedded regionally?

Nobel laureate Gary S. Becker concisely articulated the concept of the advance in globalization being framed by a world political economy characterized increasingly by centripetal forces in the contemporaneous fusion of markets and fission in nation-states.[67] At first, one may conclude that Asia's troubles may reverse market agglomeration; a deeper examination, however, points perversely to increasing pressures for globalization (talk of a regional currency has been seriously mooted) but a real acceleration of the centripeted forces. The essential features of Southeast Asia revolve about the vast diversity in its socio-ethnographic archipelago, which is dominated by the Indonesian and Philippine "jig-saws" (2,000 islands and 1,000 dialects). For convenience these were downplayed during the "miracle" years. Regional geo-economic disintegration would multiply many times the "sovereign" boundaries across which MNEs do business. This is an emergent feature in Asia. Concomitantly, the degrees of difficulty in doing business would increase to an extent that is not readily quantifiable. Thus has the Asian crisis given the discipline of international business a new reality for reexamining key concepts and corroborating research findings.

From the international business perspective, and in the light of the now widely accepted view that Asia's full recovery is a long way off,[68] the major question now is how attractive to FDI does Asia remain? Bartels et al. (1997) and Mirza et al. (1998) strongly suggest that particular locations in the region have a significant selective attractiveness. UNCTAD-ICC (1998) reported that this sentiment, as far as MNEs are concerned and despite the crisis, is unchanged in the long term. However, great pressures inherent in managing credit risk and domestic factors are increasing and are demanding that businesses differentiate between location-specific advantages much more effectively in terms of the correspondence with their own firm-specific advantages. This said, there is, however, conflicting evidence from the sentiment toward Asia within the international investing community. Some investors are beginning to differentiate carefully within the region. At the same time, "funds aren't expected to return to Asia."[69] Although Asia is far from homogeneous even in the crisis contagion,[70] South Korea and Thailand have taken progressive initiatives.[71] Indonesia on the other hand, has exhibited contrariness and xenophobia since the fall of Suharto. Although a more conciliatory mood is now evident in Jakarta, the economy is still living dangerously.[72] As an aside, the crisis has far-reaching, very unexpected consequences that affect the entire environment.[73] Malaysia has turned its back on capitalism in order to indulge itself in self-reliance (with some success according to some) and has rejected economic imperialism—the Third World's revisit of the anxieties first exposed at the Conference of the Non-aligned States held at Bandung, Indonesia, in 1955. At that time, while MNEs' concerns focused on the threats of appropriation and nationalization, developing country governments were concerned about being integrated more fairly into the global economy. The issue now is that the concerns have been almost reverse.[74]

Clearly, in Asia's brittle path to recovery MNEs face contradictions, conflicting advice, and uncertainties. In addition to the usual business uncertainties, there are issues not only of ideology, politics and political economy. The process of establishing the new rules for the business of FDI (further liberalizations) is fraught with problems of statutory coherence and consistency in interpretation. (Witness Malaysia's twists and turns and the vagaries of Indonesia's laws.)[75] At a time when Asian domestic markets are contracting (any indications to the contrary may be explained by the deleveraging that is occurring in Asian capital markets,[76] the pullout from the steep dive of the crisis requires a radical solution: substitution of "export-led growth strategy with an import-accommodating one" (Buchman and Wolf, 1998: 8). This presents a serious challenge for emaciated domestic economies as well as MNEs, which may have concluded that prospects for regional domestic markets are poor. Critical articles increasingly denote the kind of regional policies that will help in restore some of the lost confidence of MNEs. Among these are policies aimed at increasing the transparency of market transactions in order to enable competitive decisions based more on the realistic assessment of risk rather than on insider status.[77]

The location of production in Asia during the past 20 years has been rationalized through the relative productivity of low-cost labor. The volatile regional currency depreciations have created more complexity in the assessment of location-relative productivities. By definition, FDI is location bound (Rugman and Verbeke, 1992), and relocation decisions are correlated with longer term changes in relative factor efficiencies rather than volatility in exchange rates. The anxiety that the volatile of regional currencies are showing few signs of stabilizing renders locational decisions difficult (in addition to problems posed by incumbency).

Two years into Asia's economic ordeal, industrial output and GDP remain negative in general. International portfolio investors continue to be guarded with the stock of localized firms amid persistent fears of competitive devaluations, starting with China.[78] Japan, as the region's most significant investor, lender, and trading partner, has the potential to alter substantially the attractiveness of the region but is stagnant. Perceptions of regional attractiveness (Jackson and Markowski, 1995) or unattractiveness (Bartels and Freeman, 1995) can have far more importance in reinforcing Asian economies. However, it seems that every week regional developments expose more unexpected flaws in the governance of Asia's capitalism. This stems from a fundamentally unstable economic morphology (Sayle, 1998). In addition, increasing attention to calls for (market-distorting) capital controls might constrict further FDI ventures. This raises profoundly serious questions about the strength of commitment by European and North American MNEs to Asia in the short and medium term, as well as about the future of Asia's intermediation in the world economy.

Among the several regional challenges facing Atlantic MNEs, one of the most severe concerns public charges of manipulation—asset bargains at the expense of local businesses at a time when there is a general invitation to foreign investors to recapitalize local enterprises. This possibility should be weighed with the empirical finding (Mirza et al., 1998) that Triad MNEs are looking to the ASEAN component of Asia as "a single market." The implications for Asia are enormous.[79] As one of the central pieces of regional stability, ASEAN must simultaneously contain the pressures for geopolitical fragmentation; manage the civil forces set against the negative impacts of structural adjustment; and change the qualitative character of the intra-ASEAN dialogue,[80] as well as enhance its attractiveness as a free trade area. Under intense global scrutiny this is a tall order. It is tempting to conclude that policy responses have been less than adequate.[81]

In the light of the crisis becoming even more disproportionately gravitational,[82] what are the possibilities for the endgame? Prediction can be hazardous. Those who announced that the twenty-first century would be the Asian century may well be correct. At present, however, the studied slogans—''miracle'' economies, ''Asia rising,'' and ''Pacific Shift'' are misplaced—in the face of evidence that the health of the world economy depends increasingly on America and Europe.[83] According to economic orthodoxy, open systems tend toward dynamic equilibrium, and although the region is no more immune to the rational or irrational behavior of market operations than other locations, the crisis may test such conventional wisdom. Three regional scenarios invite close and continued research attention: (1) equilibrium recovery in the long term through increased regional and global integration (Barrell and Pain, 1998; McKibbin, 1998); (2) re-emergent nationalism favoring autarky and isolationalism;[84] and (3) massive geo-economic displacement resulting in continued economic stress and fission of national entities.

NOTES

1. See Walter Fernandez, Asian Crisis ''to Bottom Out Soon,'' *The Straits Times*, 22 February 1999, p. 50; William Choong, Capital Inflows May Slow Asia's Rebound, *The Straits Times*, 15 May 1999, p. 76; and Michael Schuman, Korea's Recovery Suggests Reform Isn't the Only Key, *The Asian Wall Street Journal*, 17 May 1999, p. 1.

2. See Reuters, OECD Paints Grim Outlook for Asia, *The Straits Times*, 18 November 1998, p. 59.

3. See *Newsweek*, Global Meltdown Is the West's Fault, cited in *The Sunday Times*, 22 November 1998, p. 39.

4. See Tommy Koh, East Asian Miracle Is Not Over, *The Sunday Times*, 20 December 1998, p. 38; Jusuf Wanandi, Is ASEAN Dead? *The Sunday Times*, 20 December 1998, p. 41 for the contrasting views.

5. See Lee Siew Hua, Liberalisation of Capital Accounts Left Economies Exposed, *The Straits Times*, 22 October 1998, p. 2.

6. According to the OECD, South Korea, the world's tenth-largest economy, will suffer a decline in real GDP of minus 4.7 percent in 1998; ASEAN's worst afflicted economy, Indonesia, suffered a 14 percent drop in exports performance in the first quarter 1998. *The Asian Wall Street Journal*, 31 July–1 August 1998, pp. 4–5.

7. Krugman (1994). Jim Walker, Chief Economist of Credit Lyonnais Securities, indicated in January 1995 the potential of Thailand to follow Mexico into a currency crisis. See *The Straits Times*, 23 March 1998, pp. 34–35, and UNCTAD, *Trade and Development Report 1996* (Geneva: UNCTAD, 1998), pp. 104 and 123.

8. See UNCTAD, *World Investment Report 1997: Transnational Corporations, Market Structure and Competition Policy* (New York: UNCTAD, 1998), pp. 5–8; and Barry Wain, Chile's Curbs on Hot Money May Hold Lessons for Asia, *The Asian Wall Street Journal*, 31 July–1 August 1998, p. 1 for an indication of the U.S.$400 billion that flooded Asia (excluding Japan) between 1990 and 1996.

9. See AFP, Reuters, BIS Annual Report, *The Business Times*, 9 July 1998, p. 6, for an institutional view of ''Asian woes'' in which ''between 1996 and the second half of 1997, capital movements to Asia swung from an annual flow of almost U.S.$100 billion

. . . to outflows of the same size''; and Darren Mcdermott, Asia's Chances of Attracting Capital Fade, *The Asian Wall Street Journal*, 14 October 1998, p. 1.

10. See Vikram Khanna, New Risks Threaten Asia's Recovery, *The Business Times*, 29 October 1998, p. 5.

11. See Asad Latif, Is New Asia an Invention of Western Wealth?, *The Sunday Times*, 29 November 1998, p. 53.

12. See Augustine H. H. Tan, IMF Is Not Adequately Geared to Help, *The Straits Times*, 23 January 1998, p. 58 for another (quadrilateral) view of what has caused the Asian crisis, namely, the 1985 Plaza Accord–driven investment flows to Asia to counter the competitive effects of U.S. dollar depreciation against the yen; the revitalization of the U.S. economy throughout the 1990s; the 1994 devaluation of the yuan; and the overinvestment in nonproductive property assets.

13. The cumulative capitalizations of five stock markets in Asia (Singapore, Kuala Lumpur, Manila, Bangkok, and Jakarta) is only about 75 percent of the capitalization of Microsoft.

14. See Jeff Rubin, Worries about Recession Dominate American Corridors of Power, *The Asian Wall Street Journal*, 13 October 1998, p. 15.

15. See *Business Week*, Asian edition, 22 June 1998, p. 103; and *Asiaweek*, 28 May 1999, p. 103 for a comparison of capital market valuations.

16. See Peter Drucker, Rapid Change Has Led to Social Tensions in Asia, *The Straits Times*, 28 March 1998, p. 66, for a critical analysis of the situation in Asia.

17. See Amitav Acharya, Is Democracy Best?, *Asiaweek*, 23 October 1998, p. 80.

18. See David P. Hamilton, Mr. Doom Shakes Up Atmosphere of Optimism at Japanese Agency, *The Asian Wall Street Journal*, 31 July–1 August 1998, p. 1, for a Japanese view of Japan's rigidities; David Asher, Japan Can't Save Asia, *The Asian Wall Street Journal*, 29 October 1998, p. 7, for an analysis of debt, deflation, default, demographic, and deregulation factors in Japan's depressed condition; and Japan May Not Meet Growth Target, *The Straits Times*, 5 December 1998, p. 92, for the likely economic performance of Japan in 1999.

19. See Darren McDermott, Asia's Chances of Attracting Capital Fade, *The Asian Wall Street Journal*, 14 October 1998, p. 1, and Costly Mistakes, *The Asian Wall Street Journal*, 22 October 1998, p. 1.

20. See Eduardo Lahica, Major Lenders Shun 5 Asian Economies, *The Asian Wall Street Journal*, 30 September 1998, p. 2.

21. See Correction, *The Business Times*, 29 October 1998, p. 1.

22. See John Plender, Japan: Stop-Go-Stop, Financial Times, cited in *The Business Times*, 9 June 1998, p. 11; and U.S. Officials, Experts Put Japanese Bad Debt at US$1t, *The Business Times*, 31 July 1998, p. 4, for the trillion dollar black hole that might hasten Asia's downward descent.

23. See Greg Ip, Credit Crunches Just Aren't What They Used to Be, *The Asian Wall Street Journal*, 8 October 198, p. 8.

24. See The Asian Miracle: Is It Over?, *The Economist*, 1 March 1997, pp. 23–25 for figures on collapsing exports from Asia.

25. See Catherine Ong, A Pattern in Asia's Crisis, *The Business Times*, 29 October 1998, p. 14, for an informed view on the Asian values debate.

26. See Special Report, The Family Firm Suharto Inc, *Time Asia Edition*, 24 May 1999, Vol. 153, No. 20.

27. Terry McCarthy, interview with Lee Kuan Yew, Asian Values and the Crisis, *Time*, 16 March 1998, p. 20.

28. See speech by S.M. Lee Kuan Yew in *The Straits Times*, 21 February 1998, p. 48.

29. See Reuters, Asian Banks Still a Long Way from NPL Peak, *The Business Times*, 12 November 1998, p. 8.

30. The world's two tallest skyscrapers, more fitting to Manhattan, are in Kuala Lumpur!

31. See Wong Wei Kong, Property Curbs Were Not Soon Enough: BG Lee, *The Business Times*, 31 July 1998, p. 1.

32. See Harry Harding, Wanted: Asian-US Cooperation, *The Straits Times*, 22 October 1998, p. 32.

33. See Institute of International Finance, Capital Flows to Emerging Market Economies, 29 January 1998, p. 12A.

34. *Financial Times*, 12 January 1998, Internet Version, http://www.ft.com, accessed 23 January 1998.

35. See Bernard Baumohl, The Banks' Nuclear Secrets, *Time*, 25 May 1998, pp. 36–38, for a measure of the serious markets and credit risk in the derivative contracts held by U.S. banks.

36. See Goldman Sachs, Banking Research, Asian Banks at Risk, 4 September 1997.

37. See Sangwon Suh and Santha OorJitham, Alliance-building, *Asiaweek*, 30 October 1998, pp. 22–28.

38. See Goldman Sachs, Thailand Research, 12 September 1997.

39. See Agencies, Asian Markets Continue to Soar, *The Straits Times*, 19 June 1998, p. 1.

40. See Eduardo Lahica, Major Lenders Shun 5 Asian Economies, *The Asian Wall Street Journal*, 30 September 1998, p. 30; and AFP, Capital Flows to Emerging Markets Drying Up, *The Asian Wall Street Journal*, 30 September 1998, p. 2

41. See Chua Mui Hoong, Why Japan Matters So Much to Asia, *The Straits Times*, 27 October 1998, p. 30, for an indication of Japan's capacity to absorb Asian exports and its FDI in Asia.

42. See Direct Investment in Asia Shrinks 7%, *The Straits Times*, 30 April 1999, p. 85.

43. See Harold James, The 1930s Domino Effect, *The Straits Times*, 27 October 1998, p. 32.

44. See AFP, US Companies Put Out Worst Results in 7 Years, *The Straits Times*, 27 October 1998, p. 38.

45. See Jeffrey D. Sachs, The Wrong Medicine for Asia, *New York Times*, Internet Version, 3 November 1997, accessed 30 March 1998 for this viewpoint.

46. See Linda Lim, "Asian Values" Idea: Is It Out?, *The Sunday Times*, 29 March 1998, pp. 36–37.

47. See US Expert Slams "Snake-oil" Cures, *The Sunday Times*, 29 March 1998, p. 4, for the arguments.

48. See Suh Kyung Yoon, Up for Sale: Korea Inc., *The Straits Times*, 12 June 1998, p. 56, for an appreciation of the "opening up" of South Korea.

49. See Brendan Pereira, Nationalism a Key Factor: Mahathir, *The Straits Times*, 11 June 1998, p. 28, for a peculiar view from Asia.

50. See Blue-chip Blues, *The Economist*, 26 September 1998, pp. 69–70, for an analysis of the turmoil in corporate boardrooms.

51. See Protected Wildlife Killed for Food, *The Straits Times*, 30 October 1998, p. 31; Bernama, Criticisms Should Be Made Privately, Says Mahathir, *The Straits Times*, 30 October 1998, p. 35; and Derwin Pereira, Java's Ninja Terror: Politics at Play?, *The Straits Times*, 30 October 1998, pp. 38–39.

52. See Frank L. Bartels and Barry H. Pavier, ENRON in India: Developing Political Capability—An Imperative for Multinational Enterprise in an Era of Globalization, *Economic and Political Weekly*, 32, No. 8, 22 February 1997, pp. M-11 to M-20.

53. See Jeremy Wagstaff, Indonesia's Poverty: How Bad Is It?, Asian Economic Survey 1989–99, *The Asian Wall Street Journal*, 26 October 1998, p. S13.

54. See Diane Brady, Tackling Corruption, Asian Economic Survey 1989–99, *The Asian Wall Street Journal*, 26 October 1998, p. S12.

55. See Lim Chon-Phung, MNCs Need to Learn the Art of Doing Business in Asia, *The Business Times*, 22 February 1999, p. 9.

56. See Toshiba Suffers First Group Loss in 23 Years, *The Straits Times*, 26 May 199, p. 56.

57. See Reuters, Soros Says He Won't Invest in Malaysia, *The Business Times*, 24 May 1999, p. 1; the value of the capital markets in crisis-ridden Asia is paltry compared to the capitalizations of individual MNEs on the capital markets of the world's main financial centers. (See Nick Freeman, Impediments to Foreign Investment: The Complexities of a Changing International Business Environment, Paper presented to the ABAC-PECC Workshop: Impediments to Trade & Investment, 20–21/May/1999, Tokyo.) Consequently, the effort/incentive dynamics for investment portfolios favor activity in Triad capital markets, not in emerging markets.

58. See Ravi Velloor, "Soft Landing Likely" for US, *The Straits Times*, 26 May 1999, p. 57.

59. See Jennifer Lien, Seagate Denies Plans to Pull Out, *The Business Times*, 31 July 1998, p. 3.

60. See Neil Behrmann, Foreign Acquisitions in 6 Key Asian Nations Soar, *The Business Times*, 27 July 1998, p. 1.

61. See Walter Fernandez, Asian Crisis "to Bottom out Soon." *The Straits Times*, 22 February 1999, p. 50; and Andrew Tan, January Trade Jolt Revives Fears of MNCs Moving Out, *The Business Times*, 22 February 1999, p. 1.

62. See GE to Pump $64b into Asia, *The Straits Times*, 30 March 1998, p. 52.

63. See S'pore Government Leads Investment Drive, *The Straits Times*, 14 January 1997, p. 24; Quak Hiang Whai, S'pore Invests in HK Through International Consortiums, *The Straits Times*, 14 January 1997, p. 24; GIC Takes 40% Stake in Prime Manila Property Deal, *The Straits Times*, 7 February 1997, p. 30; and Viet-S'pore Industrial Park Attracts S226 in Investments, *The Straits Times*, 1 April 1997, p. 61.

64. See Christopher Wood, Asia's Still Fragile Recovery, *The Asian Wall Street Journal*, 6 January 1999, p. 8.

65. See David Asher, Japan Can't Save Asia, *The Asian Wall Street Journal*, 29 October 1998, p. 7.

66. See Reuters, US Layoffs May Reach 10-Year High of 625,000, *The Straits Times*, 5 December 1998, p. 1, for the global employment fallout; Elizabeth Douglas, Woes Due to Bad Management, *The Business Times*, 7 December 1998, p. 2; and Worse to Come for US Firms in Asia, *The Straits Times*, 13 June 1998, p. 80, for a striking example of

this instability. Boeing Co., a firm that in 1997 could not find enough production engineers and technicians, in 1998 planned to eliminate 20,000 jobs due to falling demand.

67. See Gary S. Becker, As Nations Splinter, Global Markets Are Merging, *Business Week*, 22 April 1991, p. 8.

68. See The Global Economy: Deja Vu?, *Business Week*, 21 December 1998, pp. 34–36, for an indication of impediments to crisis solution and the fact that according to the World Bank 36 countries are in recession.

69. See Douglas Appell, Funds Aren't Expected to Return to Asia, *The Asian Wall Street Journal*, 30 July 1998, p. 8.

70. See *Business Week*, Age of the Deal, 2 March 1998, pp. 16–20.

71. See G. Bruce Knecht, Recovery Looks Hard to Sustain for Thailand, *The Asian Wall Street Journal*, 26 October 1998, p. 1; and James Clad and David Steinberg, Little Chance of Quick Recovery for Asia, *The Straits Times*, 28 November 1998, p. 78.

72. See Jay Solomon, Habibie's Plans for Asset Sales Worries IMF, *The Asian Wall Street Journal*, 27 October 1998, p. 1.

73. See Peter Waldman, Desperate Indonesians Attack Nation's Endangered Species, *The Asian Wall Street Journal*, 2 October 1998, p. 1.

74. See *Asiaweek*, Special Report, End of the Free Market?, 18 September 1998, pp. 28–38.

75. See Shoeb Kagda, New Indon Rules for Investment, *The Business Times*, 28 October 1998, p. 7.

76. See Christopher Wood, The Sell-Off Behind Asia's Bull Market, *The Asian Wall Street Journal*, 21–22 May 1999, p. 10.

77. See Row Owen and Phil Strause, Asia's Credit-Risk Learning Curve, *The Asian Wall Street Journal*, 25 May 1999, p. 10.

78. See *The Economist*, China Could Prove a Bigger Shocker, cited in *The Straits Times*, 13 June 1998, p. 65.

79. See Lee Siew Hua, ASEAN Is No Longer as United, the US Believes, *The Straits Times*, 7 December 1998, p. 19.

80. See Jon Linden, ASEAN to Change Within Year, *The Asian Wall Street Journal*, 18 August 1998, p. 11.

81. See AFP, Apec Should Ease Trade and Investment Curbs, *The Straits Times*, 24 May 1999, p. 45.

82. See Andrew Marks, US Key Indicators Take Back Seat to Asian Concerns, *The Business Times*, 31 July 1998, p. 10.

83. See Cover Story, The Atlantic Century?, *Business Week*, 8 February 1999, pp. 18–27; and Cover Story, Asia: How Real Is Its Recovery, *Business Week*, 3 May 1999, pp. 24–27.

84. See AFP, Indian Rightwing Group Plans Anti-MNC Drive, *The Business Times*, 30 July 1998, p. 9; and Paul Kennedy, *The Rise and Fall of the Great Powers* (London: Fontana Press, 1989).

REFERENCES

Barrell, R., and Pain, N. (1998). *Developments in East Asia and Their Implications for the UK and Europe*. London: NIESR.

Bartels, F. L., and Freeman, N. J. (1995). European Multinational Enterprises in Two

Francophone Emerging Markets: Evidence from International Joint Ventures in Cote D'Ivoire and Vietnam. Proceedings of the 21st Annual Conference of the European International Business Academy, Urbino, Italy, December, pp. 87–107.

Bartels, F. L., Mirza, H., and Wee, K. H. (1997). International Business in South Pacific Asia: The Regional Foreign Direct Investment and Localization Strategies of TRIAD Multinational Enterprises. Proceedings of the 14th Pan Pacific Conference, Kuala Lumpur, 3–5 June 1997.

Boddewyn, J. J., and Brewer, T. L. (1994). International Business-Political Behaviour: New Theoretical Directions. *Academy of Management Review*, 19(1), pp. 119–143.

Buchman, M., and Wolf, C. (1998). How to Save Japan from Its Own Rescue Plans. *The Asian Wall Street* Journal, 28 October, p. 8.

Chote, R. (1998). Crunchtime. *The Financial Times*, 19 October, Internet Version, http://www.ft.com, accessed 23 October.

Delhaise, P. F. (1999). *Asia in Crisis: The Implosion of the Banking and Financial Systems*. London: John Wiley.

Drucker, P. (1989). *The New Realities*. Oxford: Heinemann.

Drucker, P. (1998). Rapid Change Has Led to Social Tensions for Asia. *The Straits Times*, 28 March, p. 66.

Fallows, J. (1993). How the World Works. *The Atlantic Monthly*, December, Internet Version, http://www.theatlantic.com, accessed 16 June 1998.

Fallows, J. (1994). What Is an Economy For?, *The Atlantic Monthly*, January, Internet Version, http://www.theatlantic.com, accessed 16 June 1998.

Galbraith, J. K., and Kim, J. (1998). The Legacy of the HCI: An Empirical Analysis of Korean Industrial Policy. *Journal of Economic Development*, 23(1), June, pp. 1–20.

Harman, C. (1996). Globalisation: A Critique of a New Orthodoxy. *International Socialism*, No. 73, Winter, pp. 3–34.

Huntington, S. (1996). *The Clash of Civilizations and the Remaking of World Order*. New York: Simon and Schuster.

Jackson, S., and Markowski, S. (1995). The Attractiveness of Countries to Foreign Direct Investment. *Journal of World Trade*, 29(5), October, pp. 159–179.

Krugman, P. (1994). The Myth of Asia's Miracle, *Foreign Affairs*, November/December, pp. 62–78.

List, F. (1837/1983). *The Natural System of Political Economy*, trans. and ed. W. O. Henderson. London: Frank Cass.

McKibbin, W. J. (1998). *The Crisis in Asia: An Empirical Assessment*. Wahington, DC: The Brookings Institution.

McLelland, D. (1979). *Marxism after Marx*. London: Macmillan.

Mirza, H., Giroud, A., Wee, K. H., and Bartels, F. L. (1998). The Investment Strategies of Asian and Non-Asian Firms in ASEAN. Proceedings of the LVMH Conference, INSEAD Euro-Asia Center, Paris, 6–7 February.

Mirza, H., Wee, K. H., and Bartels, F. L. (1998). Towards a Strategy for Enhancing ASEAN's Locational Advantages for Attracting Greater Foreign Direct Investment. In Kurt W. Radtke et al. (eds.), *Dynamics in Pacific Asia*. London: Kegan Paul International, pp. 195–208.

Ozawa, T. (1992). Foreign Direct Investment and Economic Development. *Transnational Corporations*, 1(1), February, pp. 27–54.

Reich, R. B. (1991). *The Work of Nations*. London: Simon and Schuster.

Rodrik, D. (1997). TFPG Controversies, Institutions, and Economic Performance in East Asia. NBER Working Paper No. 5914, 1 February.

Rugman, A. M., and Verbeke, A. (1992). A Note on the Transnational Solution and the Transaction Cost Theory of Multinational Strategic Management. *Journal of International Business Studies*, 23(4), 4th Quarter, pp. 761–772.

Sayle, M. (1998). The Social Contradictions of Japanese Capitalism. *The Atlantic Monthly*, June. Internet Version, http://www.theatlantic.com, accessed 13 June.

Soros, G. (1998). *The Crisis of Global Capitalism*. New York: Public Affairs.

Stopford, J., Strange, S., and Henley, J. S. (1991). *Rival States Rival Firms: Competition for World Market Shares*. Cambridge: Cambridge University Press.

UNCTAD. (1996a). *Sharing Asia's Dynamism: Asian Direct Investment in the European Union*. New York and Geneva: United Nations.

UNCTAD. (1996b). *World Investment Report*. New York and Geneva: United Nations.

UNCTAD-ICC. (1998). The Financial Crisis in Asia and Foreign Direct Investment, Internet Version, http://www.unctad.org/en/pressref/bg9802en.htm.

World Bank. (1993). *The East Asian Miracle*. Washington, DC.

Zakaria, F. (1998). Time for US to Lead the Region Out of Crisis. *New York Times*, cited in *The Straits Times*, 25 July, p. 54.

Zhang, P. G. (1998). *IMF and the Asian Financial Crisis*. Singapore: World Scientific.

Part II

Organizational Restructuring and the Management of the Firm

Chapter 5

Type, Magnitude, and Timing of Organizational Responses to an Economic Crisis: The Case of Thai Construction Companies

Bettina Büchel

INTRODUCTION

Organizational effectiveness and survival have frequently been attributed to the ability of an organization to respond to changes in the external environment (Argyris and Schön, 1978). This ability to respond to the environment is a result of strategic choices made by management (Child, 1972). Management is confronted with a stream of events in the environment and has to make choices about those issues which will affect the organization (Kiesler and Sproull, 1982). ''Identifying issues helps decision makers impose order on the environment'' (Dutton and Jackson, 1987: 77). The issues are identified by selectively attending to emerging trends and categorizing these trends into different categories.

The strategic management literature suggests two strategic issue categories as salient for the description of the external environment: ''threat'' and ''opportunity.'' These labels have been confirmed in empirical studies by Mintzberg et al. (1976) and Nutt (1984), who found that threat and opportunity are relevant and consequential categories for decision makers. Over time, the use of the terms *threat* and *opportunity* has become part of the routines within organizations. While opportunity implies a positive situation in which gain is likely and over which management has a fair amount of control, threat implies a negative situation in which loss is likely and over which there is relatively little control.

The meaning of a strategic issue is not inherent in the environmental events or developments. Instead, the organization's internal environment (i.e., ideology or organizational culture) has a major effect on the meanings that are associated with issues (Lawrence and Dyer, 1983; Meyer, 1982). Decision makers respond to environmental events based on the meanings derived from the internal context. Because organizational actions taken vis-à-vis strategic issues follow from the meanings attached to these issues, organizations may respond differently to similar environmental events (Dutton et al., 1983).

According to Dutton and Jackson (1987: 83), cognitions should, however, predispose decision makers to respond in systematic ways. Since decision makers from a similar industry are more likely to have similar cognitive patterns, they are in fact expected to respond in similar ways.

Some of the dimensions along which organizational responses can vary are type, magnitude, and timing of the response (Levine, 1978; Zammuto and Cameron, 1985). The type of organizational response to a strategic issue can be either internal or external (Miles, 1980). Response magnitude captures the extent to which actions were radical and involve major reorientations (Dutton and Jackson, 1987). Responses of large magnitude are costly to the company and difficult to affect. The timing of an organizational response refers to the speed with which managers decide on a course of action.

With regard to type of response pattern, organizational design initiatives have been classified into three different approaches (see Table 5.1): restructuring, reengineering, and rethinking (Keidel, 1994). The first approach focuses on organizational units, the second on organizational processes, and the third on organizational mindsets. The first and most basic approach centers on the following equation—design equals structure equals organizational chart equals changing the number of people in the departments (Keidel, 1994: 13). The second approach is less concerned with the elimination of organizational units or people within these units than with the way the work is being carried out. It focuses on operational processes that are revised to match the organization's internal and external interdependencies. The third and most complex approach starts with cognitive change leading to behavioral change and eventually producing performance improvements. The three approaches are essentially nested; the third approach encompasses reengineering, while the second includes restructuring. Moving from the first to third approach, we find that the organizational design initiatives increase in complexity and time needed to produce a performance impact.

While previous studies have investigated responses to issues with different labels, there are no empirical studies that indicate how managers with similar cognitive patterns respond to situations with issues labeled similarly, particularly threatening situations. The Thai economic situation in 1997 was the ideal research setting for investigating organization responses to situations of threat. In order to minimize perceptional differences about the environment, companies from one industry, the construction industry, were chosen.

THAI ECONOMIC SITUATION

After a period of continued high growth exceeding 11 percent annually during 1987–1990, the Thai economy grew at a moderate rate of 8 percent between 1991 and 1994. In 1995 and 1996, economic growth continued to slow down

Table 5.1
Approaches to Organizational Design

	Restructuring	**Reengineering**	**Rethinking**
Metaphors	Downsizing Rightsizing Delayering	Process management Process innovation Process redesign	Framing Patterning Learning
Target	Organizational units and hierarchical levels	Business functions and work systems	Individual, group, and organizational culture
Nature	Numerical	Technical	Conceptual
Rationale	Survival or repositioning	Tactical competitiveness	Strategic advantage
Performance Criteria	Efficiency	Efficiency & customer satisfaction	Efficiency, customer satisfaction, and employee development
Organizational Variables Addressed	Control	Control & autonomy	Control, autonomy, and cooperation
Advantage	Reduced costs	Simpler, faster work processes	Richer planning, decision-making, and innovation capabilities
Disadvantage	Organizational trauma	Organizational anxiety	Organizational frustration

Source: Adapted from Keidel (1994).

with a 7 percent growth rate. It was in 1997, however, that the big fall in the economy's growth was felt. The crisis that emerged in 1997 was a sharp departure from the previous years. It was marked by the devaluation of the baht in July 1997 and the need for a rescue package from the IMF. Table 5.2 summarizes the economic development of Thailand between 1987 and 1997.

Growth in the construction industry is closely tied to domestic economic growth. In Thailand, the construction sector was among the first to take off during the period of economic prosperity. As its proportion of GDP rose from 4 percent in the 1980s to 6 percent in the 1990s, the construction business became an integral part of the country's economy. The construction boom started in 1987 and peaked at a 28 percent growth rate in 1989. During 1987–1993, the private sector expansion was the main thrust, boosting construction investment and consuming approximately 70 to 75 percent of total construction expenditure. However, an economic slowdown as well as oversupply brought a slowdown in private construction after 1994, which has in turn made overall construction expenditure grow at a slower rate.

Because of deficiencies in infrastructure, the government increased its budget allocation for this type of expenditure. As a result, growth within the construction industry between 1994 and 1997 was due mainly to the public sector, consisting mostly of infrastructure projects. The proportion of these projects rose from 30 to 40 percent of total construction expenditure. In 1997, public sector investment was expected to be the driving force for the construction sector for the next several years, constituting between 45 and 50 percent of total expenditure.

CASE RESEARCH OF CONSTRUCTION COMPANIES

This exploratory research investigated the response of four construction companies to Thailand's economic crisis in 1997: Italian-Thai Development Public Co., Ltd. (ITD), CH. Karnchang Public Co., Ltd. (CK), Sino-Thai Engineering & Construction Public Co., Ltd. (STECON), and Christiani & Nielsen (Thai) Public Co., Ltd. (CNT). The companies were selected from the top construction players listed in the stock exchange market of Thailand. The revenues the companies were able to generate for the years 1992–1997 are presented in Figure 5.1. All of the investigated construction companies were based in Bangkok and had been serving the Thai construction market for many decades. Table 5.3 summarizes the key characteristics of the four construction companies.

Primary data were collected from respondents of these four construction companies in order to identify the issues that affected their company and their responses to the Thai economic situation in 1997. The respondents were top managers, vice presidents, senior managers, or human resource managers. Top managers seem to be the most sensitive to strategic issues encountered by the organization, as they frequently interact with the environment and represent the key decision makers of the organization. From every organization, three to five

Table 5.2
Summary of Thai Economic Development between 1987 and 1997

High-Growth Years (1987–1990)	Slower Growth (1991–1994)	Slowdown Years (1995–1996)	Crisis (1997)
• Economy grew at an average rate of 11%, the highest in history, called the "boom years" • Big investments in construction, both in public and private sector • Investments from foreign countries poured in, making Thailand a favorite manufacturing base in Asia	• Economy grew at an average rate of 8% • Plagued by world recession and oil crisis due to Gulf War • Investors limited spending	• Economy grew at an average rate of 7% • Liquidity problems in property sector due to high interest rate policy • Big slump in export growth • Current account deficit high • High inflation • Tumbling bourse in the stock market • Decline of private investment index • Increased number of bouncing checks • Thai competitiveness downgraded by World Economic Forum • Political instability	• High interest rates • Current account deficit even higher • Increasing inflation • Decline of private investment index • Lack of investor's confidence • Devaluation of baht • 7% VAT up to 10% • Closure of 58 finance firms • Fiscal austerity plan • Consumer spending down • Heavy foreign debt burden • Diminishing foreign reserves • Rising unemployment • Political instability • IMF rescue plan

Figure 5.1
Revenues of Selected Construction Companies between 1992 and 1997

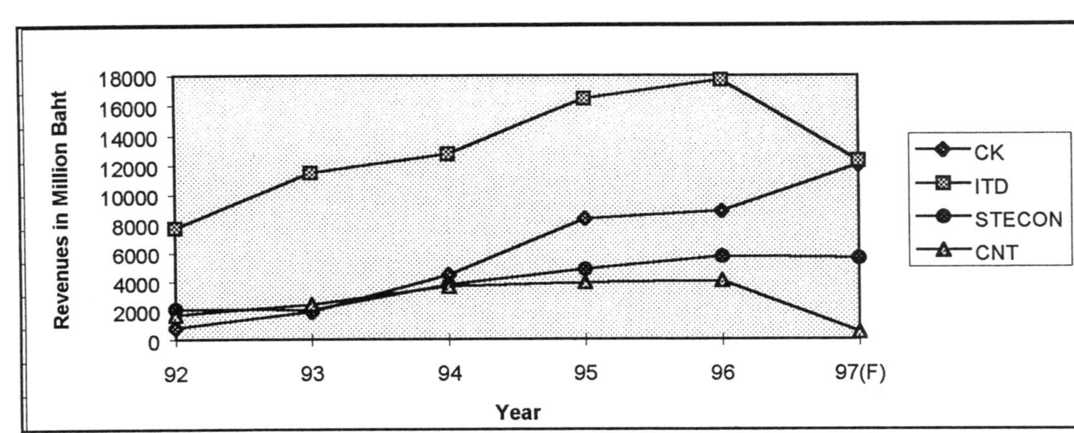

Source: Annual Reports and Research Reports of TISCO, Merrill Lynch, Securities One.

Table 5.3
Features of Construction Companies

	Company Features	ITD	CK	STECON	CNT
1	Size	Largest construction company	Second-largest construction company	One of the top 10	One of the top 10
2	Complexity	Holds 8 licenses	Holds 5 licenses	Holds 2 licenses	Holds 2 licenses
3	Focus of Activity	Public sector	Public sector	Private, some public sector	Private sector
4	Structure	Divisional	Functional	Functional	Matrix
5	Management Competence	High	High	Medium–High	Medium–Low
6	Work Force Competence	High	High	High	Medium–High
7	Product Diversification	High	Medium–High	Medium–High	Medium–High
8	Market Diversification	Medium–High	Low–Medium	Low–Medium	High–Low
9	Technology Diversification	High	Medium–High	Medium–High	High–Medium

respondents participated in a one- to two-hour interview using an open-ended interview guideline. The respondents were interviewed in the last quarter of 1997. The interview guide enabled the researcher to obtain comprehensive views about the respondents' understanding of the current economic situation and the response they had undertaken to overcome the situation.

Perception of the External Environment in 1997

A general consensus was found among the respondents of the four construction companies that the Thai economic situation in 1997 was a threat. Although variations existed about the degree to which certain issues had an effect on the company, all construction companies repeatedly mentioned twelve issues as having a large influence on their response.

1. Devaluation of baht
2. Interest rate increase
3. Stricter banking credit system
4. Liquidity of property sector
5. Cut in government spending
6. Increase in VAT from 7 percent to 10 percent
7. Closure of 58 financial companies
8. Energy price increase
9. Construction material price increase
10. Labor wage increase
11. High inflation
12. Political instability

STECON and CNT perceived a number of issues as being a larger threat than ITD or CK, particularly in reference to the stricter banking credit system, the liquidity of the property sector, and the closure of 58 financial companies. The financially less stable position of STECON and CNT made funding harder to obtain due to the banks' requirement for rigorous documentation. The property sector's liquidity had a greater effect on STECON and CNT as they were concentrating more on the private sector. The closure of 58 financial companies mainly affected STECON and CNT, for they had greater exposure who were dependent on loans from the finance companies.

The cut in government spending had a larger effect on ITD and CK since they concentrated on the public sector. Cuts in government spending caused delays, postponement, and cancellation of contracts owing to the government's inability to pursue all infrastructure projects. At the same time, the cut in government spending meant that STECON and CNT might find it harder to bid and obtain public contracts in the future.

The devaluation of the baht, interest rate increases, the increase in VAT from 7 to 10 percent, energy price increases, labor wage increases, inflation, and political instability were all mentioned as having a severe effect on the construction companies. These issues were perceived to affect all construction companies similarly.

Organizational Responses

Although a number of issues affected the companies differently, there was a high degree of overlap in terms of salient issues that affected all construction companies. When investigating responses to this situation of threat, both similarities and differences in the response pattern of the construction companies were found. Similarities existed regarding the type and area of organizational response. Major differences existed with regard to the magnitude and timing of the response. The magnitude was classified into low, medium, and high. The timing of the response was defined into the four quarters of 1997, with the investigation period ending at the close of 1997.

The largest number of responses was in the area of human resources (see Table 5.4). All of the construction companies stopped further hiring. The magnitude of response was higher for STECON and CNT than for ITD and CK. ITD and CK focused mainly on enlarging jobs for existing employees, monitoring fringe benefits, subcontracting manpower, and freezing salary increases for the year. In addition, ITD started to cut the benefits of top management to symbolize the necessity of cost-cutting measures. CK started replacing foreign employees with Thai nationals. Other than subcontracting manpower and significantly cutting benefits, STECON and CNT laid off workers and planned to decrease the salary of existing employees.

The timing of response was earliest by CK followed by ITD, CNT, and STECON. CK affected most of their responses prior to the devaluation of the baht as they saw the crisis coming. ITD and CNT mainly responded in the spring of 1997. STECON only responded in the latter part of 1997.

In the area of finance, all construction companies were more selective in choosing reputable firms as future customers, cut back on investments, and strictly enforced cost reduction programs. CNT showed the highest magnitude of response, followed by STECON, CK, and ITD (see Table 5.5). Both STECON and CNT were highly affected by the liquidity problems of the property sector and therefore closely monitored their customers' financial position to ensure payment. In some cases, existing projects had to be canceled. In the future, the two companies intended to apply for credits only for attractive projects involving clients who could demonstrate their liquidity. In order to overcome the current crisis, STECON started to sell off land, and CNT started to sell off poor-performing subsidiaries. CK responded to the upcoming crisis by swapping foreign loans prior to the baht devaluation. ITD tried to follow a strategy of risk minimization.

Table 5.4
Human Resource Reponses of the Construction Companies

Company	Human Resource Responses	Response Magnitude	Timing of Response
ITD	Job enlargement or job sharing at all levels	medium	II. Quarter
	Monitoring of fringe benefits	low	II. Quarter
	Cuts of benefits started with top management (no bonus, allowances monitored, reduction in overtime payment)	medium	III. Quarter
	Subcontracting of a large part of labor force	medium	II. Quarter
	No salary increase this year	low	II. Quarter
CK	Job enlargement at management level	medium	I. Quarter
	Contract manpower	medium	I. Quarter
	Replacement of foreigners with Thais	medium	II. Quarter
	Cuts of benefits (no bonus, allowances monitored, reduction of uniforms)	medium	II. Quarter
	Monitoring of fringe benefits	low	II. Quarter
	No salary increase	low	II. Quarter
STECON	Contract manpower	medium	III. Quarter
	Plans to cut salary	medium	II. Quarter
	Cut fringe benefits (no bonus, medical welfare handled internally, no uniforms, holding fund for employees retained, life insurance policy limited to high-risk projects, transportation allowance cut)	high	III. Quarter
	Lay off "poor" performers (quota for layoffs per department)	high	III. Quarter
CNT	Contract manpower	medium	II. Quarter
	Plans to cut salary	medium	II. Quarter
	Cut fringe benefits (medical benefits only to direct employees, cut in allowances and overtime)	high	II. Quarter
	Lay off "poor" performers	high	II. Quarter

Table 5.5
Financial Response of the Construction Companies

Company	Financial Responses	Response Magnitude	Timing of Response
ITD	Avoid risky exposure by joint venturing with locals in foreign countries	low	IV. Quarter
	Cut back on cash outflows	low	III. Quarter
	Enter into long-term contract with suppliers to guarantee price stability	medium	II. Quarter
CK	Swapped foreign loans prior to baht devaluation	high	I. Quarter
	Enter into long-term contract with suppliers to guarantee price stability	medium	III. Quarter
STECON	Apply for credits only for attractive projects	low	IV. Quarter
	Closely monitor customers' financial position to ensure payment	medium	III. Quarter
	Sell off land	high	IV. Quarter
CNT	Apply for credits only for attractive projects	low	IV. Quarter
	Closely monitor customers' financial position to ensure payment	medium	III. Quarter
	Cancellation of projects	high	III. Quarter
	Sell off poor-performing subsidiaries in China and Vietnam	high	III. Quarter

In terms of timing of response, CK was the earliest to respond, followed by ITD, CNT, and STECON. CK anticipated the devaluation of the baht and swapped its-foreign loans. ITD responded fairly late by cutting back on cash outflows and entering into long-term contracts with suppliers to guarantee the price stability of construction material, a strategy that CK adopted as well. After the difficulties of the financial situation became apparent in the second half of 1997, both STECON and CNT had to sell off existing assets. In addition, CNT canceled some of its ongoing projects in the latter part of 1997.

DISCUSSION

The literature suggests that decision makers who perceive an issue in the same manner will respond similarly (Dutton and Jackson, 1987). Here, it was found that similar interpretations of issues from decision makers with similar cognitive patterns can lead to different responses. Although the respondents in the construction companies viewed the Thai economic situation as a threat and showed a high degree of overlap in terms of salient strategic issues, the responses varied in terms of magnitude of response and timing of the response.

Similarties in response were found only regarding the type of response affected by the construction companies. The majority of initiatives focused on cost-cutting measures of mainly human resources. By numerically reducing the number of employees, their benefits and salaries, the organizations were headed for higher efficiency to survive the crisis. According to Keidel (1994: 21), ''restructuring makes the most sense when a firm has little choice but to reduce costs quickly; that is, to 'cut its losses.' '' Specifically, STECON and CNT were faced with the need to survive. If employees had not been laid off, the company may have ceased to exist. As more slack both in terms of time and resources is available, companies can afford to think about reengineering or rethinking. Since the immediate effect of changes is not directly visible, corporations require enough financial cushion so that the short term is sacrificed for the long term. This was not the situation for CNT and STECON. The response by ITD and CK showed that they were thinking about organizational processes, for example, job enlargement before falling back at the last option, downsizing. Yet the underlying idea was to cut costs in order to improve the efficiency. Given the Thai economic crisis and the relatively late identification of issues demanding a response, restructuring may have been the only alternative for all of the construction companies. Yet, early identification of an upcoming crisis may have enabled the companies to reengineer their processes or rethink their cognitive patterns, thereby making them better prepared for the upcoming crisis.

Differences in response were found regarding the timing and magnitude of organizational responses. Two possible reasons may explain these differences. First, the speed of issue identification may have had an effect on the response of the construction companies. Although all companies identified similar issues as being a threat to the company, the timing of issue identification was not similar. CK identified the potential devaluation of the baht earlier than the other companies and took precautionary measures when it swapped all its debts in January 1997. In the first quarter of 1997, ITD was preoccupied with its operational activities, and thus only felt the issues resulting from the economic crisis around April 1997. STECON and CNT were generally late in their response but responded with a higher magnitude. This is consistent with Ansoff (1980) who mentioned that response patterns vary depending on the identification of "weak signals." Early identification of issues leads to correspondingly "weak responses," which progressively strengthen as information becomes more abundant. Early detection of strategic issues increases the time available for a response. Timeliness of response depends on anticipating of changes and on making expeditious use of the time provided by the advanced warning. When organizations do not detect an issue early or do not see the need to react, they may easily come into a situation that leads to responses of high magnitude. In these situations, the time for well-considered responses is limited owing to the inability to collect information of a quality high enough to permit specific and well-considered responses.

STECON, for example, felt the crisis at the beginning of 1997 but did not make any response until the "issues" became pressing. The resulting organizational responses came slowly in the later part of August to September 1997, but led to responses of higher magnitude. In the case of STECON, the issues may have been identified early, but the response was not undertaken until the urgency of the issue required an immediate response. In these situations, the response seems to be of higher magnitude.

Another possible explanation for the findings that similar interpretations of issues can lead to different responses are internal differences. Differences in response may have been influenced by each company's strengths and weaknesses (i.e., the company's position in the construction market, financial situation, and degree of diversification).

Since ITD and CK were primarily involved in the public sector while STECON and CNT focused on the private sector, the economic crisis had a larger effect on STECON and CNT. Although the government reduced its spending, ITD and CK could still expect payment for existing projects. This was not necessarily the case for those construction companies that mainly had private clients. Since the financial situation of STECON and especially CNT was unstable at the beginning of 1997, any additional decrease in revenue had a more important impact on these two companies. Therefore, issues became more urgent to them faster and therefore led to responses of higher magnitude. CNT had already suffered from the slower economic growth of 1996 and its exposure to the property sector's lack of liquidity. Therefore, they were in a financially more difficult situation at the beginning of 1997. CNT, having already been plagued with numerous management problems, had few options but to finish its restructuring and continue with further downsizing. For this company, the strategic issues that emerged from the threatening impact of the Thai economic crisis increased the urgency of the situation and led to immediate responses of high magnitude. Since ITD and CK had a larger number of construction licenses than STECON and CNT, they had more opportunities of diversification into new fields and therefore had more options of response. Because of ITD's and CK's stronger position in the construction market, their financial situation, and their degree of diversification, the response pattern was generally of lower magnitude than STECON's or CNT's.

CONCLUSION AND IMPLICATIONS

This study found that managers from the same industry with similar perceptions of issues can vary in terms of magnitude and timing of response. Magnitude and timing of organizational response in situations of threat depend on the aspects: the timing of issue identification and internal company strengths and weaknesses. The earlier the identification of issues, the more time is available for companies to respond. This ''extra'' time allows companies to collect additional information before an appropriate response is undertaken. Given enough time, the type of response may not necessarily only lead to downsizing, but may allow organizations to analyze their operational processes or cognitive patterns. In addition, a company's strengths and weaknesses determine the degree to which a crisis may pose a threat. Companies in a weak position may have no alternative but to downsize and feel a greater urgency to respond with actions of higher magnitude.

In order to ensure early identification of issues, management could implement a strategic issue management system which tracks important trends and events both inside and outside an organization. Early identification can be assured in the following ways:

- Periodic (e.g., monthly) review and updating of a key strategic issue list.
- Continuous surveillance, both inside and outside the organization for ''urgent'' issues that may arise in between reviews. When such issues arise, a ''red light signal'' alerts management to the need for immediate attention.
- Assignment of responsibility for surveillance to groups that are best equipped to monitor the environment.

The success of a strategic issue management system depends on its ability to identify issues early and to complete the response in time to head off threats and to ''cash in'' on opportunities. As Ansoff (1980) stated, three simple rules can be used to guide the choice for a particular enterprise. First, the approach must be responsive to the complexity of the challenge; second, the approach must be as simple as the complexity permits; and third the approach must be feasible within the company's resources.

ACKNOWLEDGMENTS

The data for this chapter were collected for a research study undertaken at the School of Management at the Asian Institute of Technology by Angela Labriam Prathunam.

REFERENCES

Ansoff, H. I. (1980). Strategic Issue Management. *Strategic Management Journal*, 1(2), pp. 131–148.

Argyris, C., and Schön, D. A. (1978). *Organizational Learning: A Theory of Action Perspective*. Reading, MA: Addison-Wesley.

Child, J. (1972). Organizational Structure, Environment and Performance: The Role of Strategic Choice. *Sociology*, 6, pp. 1–22.

Dutton, J. E., Fahey, L., and Narayanan, V. K. (1983). Toward Understanding Strategic Issue Diagnosis. *Strategic Management Journal*, 4, pp. 307–323.

Dutton, J. E., and Jackson, S. E. (1987). Categorizing Strategic Issues: Links to Organizational Action. *Academy of Management Review*, 12, pp. 76–90.

Dutton, J. E., Walton, E. J., and Abrahamson, E. (1989). Important Dimensions of Strategic Issues: Separating the Wheat from the Chaff. *Journal of Management Studies*, 26, pp. 379–396.

Keidel, R. (1994). Rethinking Organizational Design. *Academy of Management Executive*, 8, pp. 12–30.

Kiesler, S., and Sproull, L. (1982). Managerial Response to Changing Environments: Perspectives on Problem Sensing from Social Cognition. *Administrative Science Quarterly*, 27, December, pp. 548–570.

Lawrence, P. R., and Dyer, D. (1983). *Renewing American Industry*. New York: Free Press.

Levine, C. H. (1978). Organizational Decline and Cutback Management. *Public Administration Review*, 38, pp. 318–357.

Meyer, A. D. (1982). Adapting to Environmental Jolts. *Administrative Science Quarterly*, 27, pp. 515–537.

Miles, R. H. (1980). *Macro Organizational Behavior*. Santa Monica CA: Goodyear.

Mintzberg, H., Raisinghani, D., and Théorêt, A. (1976). The Structure of "Unstructured" Decision Processes. *Administrative Science Quarterly*, 21, pp. 246–275.

Nutt, P. C. (1984). Types of Organizational Decision Processes. *Administrative Science Quarterly*, 29, pp. 414–450.

Zammuto, R. F., and Cameron, K. (1985). Environmental Decline and Organizational Response. In L. L. Cummings and B. M. Staw (eds.), *Research in Organizational Behavior* 7. Greenwich, CT: JAI Press, pp. 223–263.

Chapter 6

Technology and Restructuring of Organization and Assets in an Indian Bank Faced with the Demands from Financial Restructuring and Globalization

Parthasarathi Banerjee

INTRODUCTION

The Asian economic crisis has several direct causes: convertibility, exposure of domestic money markets to international money markets, in-flow of hot money, and several related macroeconomic policies and events. The catastrophic turn of events perhaps began with the contagion effects. Understandably, the crisis could abate because governance of the micro-foundation of the economies had gotten beyond the control of the domestic governance system. Before the onset of the crisis domestic manufacturing and services had a fairly high degree of exposure to both the international money markets and international decisions regarding manufacturing and services. The management of both the macro and micro variables, in particular the nonfinancial domestic management, did not learn from the earlier Latin-American crisis and had not put in place systems and structures that could act as buffers and that could offer immediate contingent managerial decisions. Management of the microeconomic activities also had collapsed. This integration of domestic investment, manufacturing, and services with the international money-market volatility, which had not yet provided for managerial system structures and buffers, resulted in disaster. A certain degree of managerial foresight at both the macro and micro level could have perhaps prevented the enormity of the crisis. Regulation and governance functions in the economy along with the routine management had vanished. Arguably, money-market volatility was the initiating cause, but it was neither the only nor perhaps the most important one. A systemic and institutionalized managerial response coupled with the governance function was missing.

A possible world reasoning, that is, arguing that such a crisis would not have occurred had there been certain managerial systemic responses and a system of governance, or perhaps deconstructing the domestic managerial readings on the unfolding of this crisis, would surely provide us with possible systemic and managerial answers. This crisis is now history. Moreover, it did not happen in India, though it could have. Resorting again to world reasoning, we may wonder if India had provided for certain managerial systems and structures that could act as real buffers. A feature-by-feature or a systemic comparative study on the differences in the management systems between the countries in Asia where it did and where it did not break in may therefore be meaningful. The tacit hypothesis is that a managerial-governance system ought to have been in place and that comparing certain key management systems, especially regarding financial management, is a viable inquiry.

A key feature in banking management, especially in an integrated world, is the management of assets and liabilities (Allais, 1987). This is the virtual core of bank management integrating at the level of a bank's operations of finance—its liability, with the asset captured in the tangibles and intangibles of the real sectors—the organization of manufacturing and services. The systems in place for asset and liability management in the banking sector as such appear to be the crucial governance system. Therefore, reconnaissance of and management of any impending systemic crisis are easily and manageably done within this structure of the banking system. We find it meaningful to identify the structural and systemic asset-liability management parameters of Indian banking, reflected in a large public sector bank. We argue *inter alia* that certain key features of this system offer potential alternatives to those systems that were in place in the management of the crisis-affected banking of the Asian countries. This chapter examines the management of the asset side, in particular the nonperforming asset (NPA), of a large public sector Indian bank. The backdrop is provided by the generalities of Indian banking practices, the liberalization drives, and the signals from the Asian economic crisis.

Institution of Bank Managerial Practice: Close-Governance or Rule-Based

Management of the asset is indeed the governance of the market. The Asian crisis was, first, a failure of the domestic governance system; it was also a failure, though only secondarily, of the international governance system. A crucial difference exists, however, between these two modes of governance. Some domestic systems, as in Germany and Japan, are based on relationship-based transactions, whereas the international system, being similar to the Anglo-American system, is closer to a spot market, arms-length transactions system sometimes also called a securitized system. The Indian banking institution has adopted elements from both systems. There is a merit in this strategy. We may visualize a two-tier system, having as its foundation the relation-based system that interfaces with the international system through securitized systems. This is a prudential domestic financial management system, normatively accepted as the Basle system; it exists in several modes in many countries.

The Indian system of asset management has elements of both the relations-based and the securitized mode. The first tier is the governance system of the domestic creditors achieved through the bank management system; this tier follows the principles of relations-based banking. The second tier interfaces with the global money market and is populated with arms-length auctioneers in a securitized environment. A global shock or its ripple interferes with the second tier, and since this tier follows the same market principles as in currency in the shock-originating system, this tier would be in a situation to generate an immunity system. However, the first tier, comprising domestic economic activities, is being governed through a bank management system, and it follows principles different from the second tier. The manager-governor in this tier receives prior information on the likelihood of the appearance of shock ripples, and the credit system being under its control, the tier two is likely to remain an effective governor-manager.

Governance of the financial setup is thus possible through two types of market governance systems: relations-based and securitized spot-market transactions. Both constitute market transactions, though the two are mediated differently. The relations-based transactions take into consideration the future and repeatability of transactions and provide for a monitoring system that is closed and gives unique, private information to the market governance (Aoki, 1990; Aoki and Patrick, 1994; Baums, 1993; Morck et al., 1989; Frankel and Montgomery 1991; Williamson, 1985, 1988). This monitoring and governance function is undertaken in Japan by the main banking system, in Germany by the universal bank system, and in India, in a limited capacity by its existing system of banking (Berglof, 1990; Baums, 1994; Bhole, 1982; Gupta et al., 1991; RBI, 1985). The governance and monitoring functions are somewhat separate; monitoring on a case-by-case basis by-he case-lender and governance by a variegated network of activities, such as mergers and acquisitions (M&A), and organizations such as the credit rating agencies, and finally by institutions such as securitizations in the American system. Transactions in the latter are spot-market, not necessarily repeating; hence they are not closed and do not generate any privately accessible unique information (Aoki and Patrick, 1994; Jensen, 1988; Morck et al., 1989; RBI, 1987, 1999b; Stiglitz and Weiss, 1981). Management of a bank's internal operations as well as management of market transactions are critically different in these two systems.

In summary, (1) money-market volatility can engender an economywide crisis if there is a mismatch between the type of domestic market-governance institution and the type of financial-governance institution—for example, if the market is governed by a relations-based system and the finance follows a securitized system; (2) the institution of market governance (and monitoring) can be undertaken by the banking system, hence this governance relates bank and industry together in a system—as in the relations-based system—or this governance can relate an interindustry system with the set of financial markets through a number of institutions and organizations—as in the securitized system; (3) a separation between the market-governance function and other money-market functions is conceivable, or in other words, especially during a liberalization phase, these two functions can have different modes of institutionalization; (4) the market-governance function is also simultaneously a monitoring function and a function that integrates the internal management of the bank with the monitoring and governance of the creditor industry—hence, it integrates the internal with the external managerial functions of the bank, at least in a few segments; (5) such an integrated management is conceivable in the areas of asset and liability, especially in the areas of asset management (leaving aside for the purposes of this chapter the treasury operations); and finally, (6) institutional aspects of the asset management of the banking system appear to be essential information toward determining the resilience of the economywide system to an external and perhaps volatile shock.

ISSUES IN ASSET MANAGEMENT IN AN INDIAN BANK

Consequent to the initiation of the liberalization of the financial system in India around 1991 (Reddy, 1999; Jalan, 1999), issues in the internal managerial aspects of a bank as an organization were raised rather systematically. A high-powered committee, the Narasimham Committee (RBI, 1991), examined this domain of internal management rather closely. Earlier, the Chakravarty Committee had gone into these aspects as well (RBI, 1985). The ''Supervisory'' (as the current Reserve Bank governor, Bimal Jalan, puts it), or the governance aspects, were raised in several fora/reports, although the direct linkages between the internal management and the market governance was not established beyond doubt. These supervisory reforms and the managerial reforms, however, came in tandem, establishing perhaps the close causal connections somewhat obscurely. The reform process that was set in motion was systemic in character and did not spare any banking function (Reddy, 1999; RBI, 1999e). Moreover, this process predates the crisis in the Asian economies. Perhaps that was how the financial system in India readied itself to an as yet unforeseen shock arising out of a volatility. Asian crises somewhat strengthened, as we would argue, the indirect causality between the internal managerial reform and the reform of the market governance, including the supervisory function of the Reserve Bank of India.

Asset and liability positions (OECD, 1987; RBI, 1991; Jalan, 1999) of the Indian commercial banks had deteriorated, and in particular, all the banks were burdened with a large NPA. The balance sheets of the banks did not, however, reflect this NPA, and the degree of exposures was not known. Banks in general had a very small capital base (Tier-1 capital), and transparency was virtually absent. Management of the NPA appeared crucial since the industry itself was undergoing liberalization reforms, consequent to which restructuring and turning sick had become commonplace. Reforms of the bank's internal management and the NPA management were thus understood as pertaining to the same issue (RBI, 1991). NPA management, however, was part of the overall policies on and management of the credit—the instrumentality through which the bank can govern the market. A study of NPA management, along with a study of managerial and supervisory reform, should thus provide us with enough clues as how to provide the banking governance function—the management of credit or banking asset, with an institutional buffer against volatility and external shocks.

Toward this, a major public sector bank, (henceforth referred to as B) has been studied. In the next section, we study bank B with reference to the context that has been provided by the general policy drifts in the Indian banking milieu. The following section brings out the general problem of the NPA, and in particular the dimensions of NPA that B faces, followed by a discussion on the specific managerial problems faced by both B and the CB in general on managing the NPA. Next, we observe the extent of relations-based banking, as well as the emerging trends of securitization in the context of the assets market. This is followed by the managerial styles in the relations-based banking and the reengineering initiatives that bank B had taken to improve its management system. We discuss the reengineering drive at B that had a special emphasis on NPA management. The evolution of the managerial system during this period is examined thereafter, in terms of the systemic response and erection of new management information system. Integration of the management of NPA with the internal managerial restructuring creates a systemic and institutional response structure, which is discussed in this section. That is followed by a concluding summary, pointing out the dual strategy adopted by the Indian banking system. As it appears, this dual strategy of combining management and governance functions within the bank management system strategy with the strategy of developing market-led institutionalization for interfacing the management-governance system with the global money market in an environment of liberalization is unique. Such a strategy mix appears to be promising for transition economies in the developing world.

General Banking Policies, Structure, and Bank B

Prior to the initiation of the reform of the banking system in 1991–1992, it was characterized by several features of interest. The first group of policies relate to the structure of this system (RBI, 1985, 1988). The Indian banking system includes the commercial banks (CB), developmental financial institutions (DFI), cooperative banks and rural banks, nonbanking financial institutions (NBFC), and so on. The CBs are mostly public, although private sector banks existed even before the reform; currently, both private and foreign banks operate in India. CBs operate through the branches, and this commercial banking is so greatly dependent on the branches that the banking system is described as branch banking. Branch expansion was seen as reaching the villages and the impoverished—an act of justice "reflecting the concern to achieve a more balanced spatial distribution of credit" (RBI, 1991: 6). It was also seen as the corporate strength of a bank and as the overall strength of the Indian banking. In 1969, the year of bank nationalization, a branch served 69,000 people, and by 1990, this figure had dropped to 12,000; out of a total of 51,000 branches in 1990, as many as 33,600 were in rural areas. Similarly, deposit accounts with the banks rose sharply, and by 1990, it was over 300 million. The deposits accounted for 38 percent, and advances for 25 percent of the gross domestic product in 1990.

The other structural features include a near-absent competition policy, and a near-absence of local/regional specialization and of domain specialization. Competition encouraged through regulation over the branch expansion was not exercised, and neither interbank competition based on branch banking nor interbranch competition based on branch business was practiced. Nearly all the CBs are banks of national stature that have expanded all over India. In addition, all the banks have a poor capital base that does not always satisfy the Basle norms of capital adequacy. Historically, even up to the year of nationalization, most CBs had both a regional bias and a bias or a domain knowledge on specific industry/business houses. This practice of catering to a group of managing agencies (a now defunct system that was close to a holding company) was readily given up following nationalization. However, most banks continued with the traditional customer base. Bank B, for example, has continuously retained a large number of customers over more than 50 years.

The CBs in India are thus small compared to the average international operator and are inadequately capitalized, overstaffed, and overbranched, extremely dispersed spatially, and have lost a large degree of domain specialization. Moreover, as in the case of bank B, which had adopted banking practices relevant to western India, firms have had to compromise with and substantially gives up routines. Each commercial bank, however, is very hierarchic in terms of reporting structure, which has led to a contradiction in structure: branch banking implying a business unit is at the bottom of the hierarchy. With the expansion of banks through an increasing number of branches and spatial expansion, the corporate governance internal to the bank has been seriously debilitated. Most branches are deposit branches acting as post offices and therefore do not experience serious difficulties in reporting. Problems arise in the case of industrial/corporate branches. Bank B, for example, had to reduce reporting levels among the corporate branches. The wide dispersion has led to extremely weak reporting and management control, rendering inert the overall CB structure. This current structure is largely unresponsive to competition. It is difficult to effect any managerial transformation rapidly and with confidence.

Another area of interest is the practice of disbursing directed credit. Through the mechanism of the Statutory Liquidity Ratio (SLR), which ran very high ratios prior to reform, a stipulated minimum percentage of credit is distributed to the public sector. The priority sector lending to agriculture, small-scale industry, and small enterprises, accounted for 40 percent of bank credit by 1990. This also resulted in a phenomenal increase in the number of credit accounts. For example, credit accounts to the priority sector alone rose to over 35 million, resulting in a smallness of each operating credit account and a consequent rise in the unit cost of operation. The high cost of Indian banking is reflected in the average operating cost of banks as a percentage of assets; it was about 2.3 in India during 1990–1991 to 1995–1996, as compared to 1.1 percent in China, 1.6 percent in Malaysia, and 1.0 percent in Japan. Such a high intermediation cost would not allow the system to work on a fine and thin spread, and lower interest. Recently, the Reserve Bank of India (RBI) governor observed: "Operating costs depend on labor productivity, technology, innovation and organizational effectiveness. . . . These factors differentiate the weak from the strong banking system. Without gaining sufficient advantage in this respect, it is difficult to think of a significant improvement in the banking system in future" (Jalan, 1999: 16).

Bank B compares favorably with the others in the CB system. This bank has about 2,500 branches, with four tiers; the branches at the bottom are layered above by 64 regional offices, which in turn are supervised by 15 zonal offices. The head office is at Mumbai, where this bank was formed about a hundred years ago by a group of businessmen. Bank B has foreign operations as well, primarily among the expatriate Indian community, in about 10 countries through 19 branches. Currently, it has about 25,000 employees. It encompasses several spheres of financial activities, including merchant banking, housing finance, leasing, venture capital, credit card, mutual fund, and stock brokering. It has several specialized branches; by 1997–1998, the branches included 29 small-scale industry (SSI) branches, 8 corporate banking branches, 5 agriculture hi-tech branches, 1 lease finance branch, 10 commercial and personal banking branches. By 1997–1998, the bank had 252 fully computerized branches, and 243 were at least partially computerized.

Some of the bank's operating parameters are relevant to our analysis. Bank B had an operating profit growth of 20.2 percent during 1997–1998 and a similar figure during 1996–1997. However, this figure declined sharply during 1998–1999. Two other large banks in India, however, a grew in operating profit in the range of 10 percent only during 1997–1998. Deposits also experienced good growth during 1997–1998: 23.04 percent, which compared favorably with three other major banks—21.63 percent, 14.18 percent, and 18.94 percent. Similarly, the advances had a growth of 20.09 percent during this period, compared to advances of 19.79 percent, 14.05 percent, and 15.59 percent, respectively, for these other three banks. The growth rate in credit during this same period was 20.1 percent for B. Some of the key financial ratios for B are as follows: the return on average assets was 1.01 percent during 1996–1997 and 0.86 percent during 1997–1998; the yield on advances was 13.17 percent in 1996–1997 and 12.20 percent in 1997–1998; the average cost of deposits was 7.50 and 6.90, respectively; the noninterest income to net income was 30.06 and 31.10, respectively; and staff cost to average working funds was 2.01 and 1.83, respectively.

Nonperforming Assets (NPA) and Bank B

Banking assets also have been undergoing reform, both prior to and during the 1990s. Broadly speaking, this asset can be subdivided into investments, credits, and debts (RBI, 1975, 1984, 1999d). The investments involve mostly government securities. Investments in government securities accounted for 64.2 percent of the total in 1991, 69.2 percent in 1994, and 70.1 percent in 1997; investment in other domestic securities was 34.6 percent of the total in 1991, 30.0 percent in 1994, and 27.1 percent in 1997. Other investments, such as in shares and debentures, have been rising steadily: from a meager 2.9 percent of the total in 1991 to 7.9 percent in 1994 to 11.5 percent in 1997; investments in certificates of deposits and commercial papers were nonexistent in 1991 and 1994; beginning in 1995, it rose to 1.1 percent in 1997, and so on. Thus, while overall investments in government securities has been rising steadily, with an increasing dependence on longer-term maturities, and consequently the investments in other domestic securities steadily declining, investments in the debt-market have been singularly rising. Investments by foreign offices have risen only marginally—from a meager 1.1 percent of the total in 1991 to 2.4 percent in 1997.

As a result, the investment-deposit ratio moved from 38.5 in 1991 to 35.7 in 1997, and the credit-deposit ratio declined from 62.9 in 1991 to 54.9 in 1997. Credit from the commercial banks has several components, including loans, cash credits and overdrafts, and bills purchased and discounted. From 1991 to 1997, more than 90 percent of total bank credits was in the loans category and nearly 9 percent in bills purchased. There has been a similar rise in the term loan from the CB; consequently, the proportion of working capital loans has been declining (RBI, 1998, 1999a, 1999c, 1999b, 1999e). Overall, the banking system has been shifting its base toward the practices of universal banking. The increasing proportion of both term loans and debt instruments has made the passage to universal banking smoother and resulted in a declining share of NPA in total credit. Bank B's share in these two segments has also increased. Bank B's domestic credit grew 19.7 percent in 1997–1998, and out of the total nonfood credit that it disbursed during this period, the corporate sector had about a 63 percent share, and the primary sector nearly a 4 percent share. In a regional office of B, the corporate sector had a share of about 57 percent of total credit/advances in both 1993–1994, and 1995–1996, though in absolute terms and at current prices it experienced growth a little above 50 percent.

The NPA problem is not confined to the corporate sector. The corporate sector's share in a bank's total NPA, as well as B's share, is very large though. Next we observe the sources of funds of the corporate before embarking on a discussion of the NPA. With regard to the liability side of some nongovernment nonfinancial companies, borrowings alone constituted 37.8 percent and 37 percent, respectively, in 1993–1994 and 1994–1995 of the total liability. An examination of the financing (for a different set of companies) showed that borrowings constituted 30 percent and 27.5 percent, and total external sources (including borrowings) 67.3 percent and 64.3 percent of these companies' total financing during 1994–1995 and 1995–1996, respectively. Reserves and surplus had meager shares of 12.8 percent and 20 percent of total financing, and 19.5 percent and 21.6 percent of this latter group's total liabilities in 1994–1995 and 1995–1996, respectively. Most large international companies are less dependent on borrowings and ordinarily secure as much as about 80 percent of the fund requirement from internal accruals. The corporate's dependency on the borrowings keeps their bargaining positions vis-à-vis the banks weak, and the debentures and securities floated by the corporate remain unattractive, making the debt market weak. In such a bargaining situation, the operation of the securitized market must necessarily remain weak, and the relations-based banking will be perpetuated. This dependency relation (between bank and corporate) of the corporate on the borrowings, primarily from the banks, is the basic edifice on which the managerial systemic-response has been constructed.

A dependency relation enables a bank to govern its credit customer. Such a relation may be shown through several modes, including the bank presence on the customer's board or the binding conditionalities on the customer regarding the use of funds. Moreover, through information on the company performance, the bank may adjust its credit line, or its own portfolio; it may managerially assist the troubled company; or it may even sensitize its regulator. The RBI, based on sufficiency of evidence, may alert other banks as to a company's or an industry's vulnerability. Much therefore depends on this dependency, which we have described as relations-based banking. The existence of this relation as well as its intensity and nature is a matter needing further probe. The genesis of NPA and its management shows the fault line. How bank management acts on the fault is critical not only to the management of assets but also to governance of the market. A reactive managerial policy would address this matter primarily through bookkeeping, and a proactive managerial policy would address it through change management of its own as well as its customer's system.

Bank B and the Management of NPA

A large number of banks have net NPAs ranging between 10 and 20 percent of their net advances. Bank B recorded figures 6.5 percent and 7.3 percent in 1997 and 1998, respectively (considering only domestic lending); the figures for the same period were 11.8 percent and 11.6 percent, respectively, for the NPA as a percentage of total advances. The desirable figure is only 3 percent for domestic banks and zero for banks with international operations. These figures can be arrived at by adhering to accounts adjustments, such as through adopting the income recognition norms and identifying the quality of assets, using a risk weightage. These bad assets can then be retired through book adjustments and/or through securitizations. However, this recognition and these adjustments can be accompanied by systemic changes in bank-internal management as well as bank governance management. If just an accounting approach is taken, bank management may, among other things, resort to minor changes in the internal reporting format and in its Management Information Systems (MIS), and in its new loan issuance. The RBI may examine the bank's adherence to the specified norm, abandoning the crucial reconnoitered information needed to provide a managerial buffer to any upcoming volatile shock. This strategy, called strategy-1, would therefore require setting up a host of market institutions/organizations, in the form of Merger and Acquisition (M&A) funds and M&A market, securitizations, rating agencies, and so on. Strategy-1 does not, however, provide for a transition management, which also is critical since the transition alone can take several years. Also possible is an alternate strategy, the so-called strategy-2, which, while retiring bad assets, also acts on changing the internal management of the bank itself as well as seeking to change the creditor company's governability by changing bank-company relations. Indian banks have been vacillating between these two strategies; bank B is also following both strategies. Strategy-1, preferred by the market ideologues, is attempting to build up its set of institutions and organizations. However, strategy-2 is being employed by banks seeking to continue Indian banking's tradition of management.

Bank B had initiated the process of recognizing "doubtful advances" in 1976, when it was decided in a board meeting that the bank should cease charging interest on doubtful advances. This decision became operative in 1980. Criteria to ascertain the quality of the assets, primarily through the income recognition route, such as nonpayment of interest, was put in place for all accounts above a minimum level. The RBI subsequently introduced the health code system of classification of borrowers' accounts in 1985. Later, in 1989 and 1990, the RBI required that banks cease charging interest on assets falling under certain health codes (viz., recalled, suit-filed, decreed, and bad/doubtful). Banks thereby started classifying their accounts, as was reflected on their books. This attempt was based on the identification of accounts/assets making use of income norms. This process did not ask for a managerial change or a recognition of the particular creditor company that was in default. Identifying an ailing company or simply a defaulting company could have implied several managerial alternatives to the lender bank, such as following what a typical main bank would have done, salvaging the defaulting company managerially even by changing its board, informing and guiding the lending activities of other banks regarding the limitations of that company, or, for example, tightening that company's financial transactions by exercising control over its principal current accounts with the bank. Apparently, the bank's response remained limited to assets-classificatory and book adjustment activities.

In 1992–1993, as per the RBI directives, bank B initiated classification of assets into four categories: standard, substandard, doubtful, and loss making, and in addition followed the income recognition rules. This was not made applicable to accounts below Rs.25,000. Total NPA for domestic activities as a percentage of total advances was 29.9 in 1993, 28.7 in 1994, and 22.2 in 1995. The foreign branches also had NPA, but B could reduce it substantially. Recognizing the high level of NPA, bank B initiated managerial exercise in 1995–1996 in order to formulate an action plan and a management strategy. At that time, B's NPA percentage (of total advances) was higher than that of the total banking system. A detailed breakdown of NPA distribution shows that accounts above Rs.25,000 had a share of 79.8 percent of total NPA in 1993, 78.5 percent in 1994, and 77.8 percent in 1995. However, in terms of NPA to total advances, accounts above Rs.25,000 constituted only 27.4 percent in 1993, 25.5 percent in 1994, and about 19 percent in 1995. Asset quality distribution shows that the standard category constituted about 75 percent of NPA, substandard only about 3 percent, doubtful about 20 percent, and loss about 1 percent. The account size classification shows a different picture, however. Accounts above Rs.5 million had about 52 percent of the total in the loss category, whereas accounts below Rs.25,000 had about 7 percent of the total in this category. The smallest accounts had higher shares under the substandard and doubtful categories. The health code breakdown of NPA shows that in 1995, B had about 46 percent under the "sick viable" and "sick sticky/nonviable" categories and about 50 percent under the "advances recalled" and "suit filed" categories, and about 4 percent under the "decreed" category.

The first category of assets was in a position to be retrieved, given perhaps managerial assistance. The second category could perhaps be retrieved through control exercises over the transaction-oriented current accounts, although legal difficulties were present. The last two categories are difficult and rather costly to be retrieved; these categories constitute the "doubtful" assets. Quite a few of the "sick viable," numbering about 100 with average credit size of Rs. 38 million, come under the Board of Industrial and Financial Restructuring (BIFR), an institution that looks after and helps to effect the turnaround of sick companies). Assets of B with the small-scale sector (SSI)—a priority sector—were mostly under the "standard" category, a redeeming feature. In fact, the ratio of "doubtful" assets to "standard" assets with the SSI (and from B) was 1 to 3. The corresponding ratio for the corporate sector—a non-priority sector—was about 1 to 9, indicating the relative asset vulnerability in the case of the SSI sector.

THE ASSETS MARKET AND RELATIONS-BASED BANKING

The assets market can be understood in terms of its two components: assets creation and assets disposal. A bank's involvement remains through both stages. In the first stage, assets are created through credit provisioning; credit for working capital, term loans, bonds, and so on are the ordinary routes that the CB in India follows. The assets disposal market, however, is rather limited in India, and in the post-reform phase, securitization, or mergers and acquisitions, have been emerging as the disposal market. Weakness or the near absence of this market for assets disposal demands that once formed, assets must be carefully monitored and managed. The institution to achieve this management is relations-based banking. In the Japanese version of such banking, a few tasks are performed regularly: ex-ante, interim, and ex-post monitoring; managerial support; interlender (the banks') activities; and finally, control over the creditor's main current account. Indian banking does not perform all these activities, although Indian banking performs some of them obliquely, and over the years a corresponding institution has been built up by relations-based banking.

The working capital credit provisioning has thus far been done through a system called cash credit, although in recent years this has been replaced by a system called demand credit. The cash credit system is rather old, and it was originally based on trust. The banker, having knowledge of and trust in the managing agency (a sort of holding company and now legally disallowed), who was looking after the lending company, would start a credit line for the creditor for as much as the lender would require. Such a system was not advantageous for the bank because of the increased cost involved in letting funds remain idle. Monitoring was limited to the credit offtake, and checks on fund diversions also were insured. This credit, especially that devoted to the working capital, had to follow a norm, which was devised by the regulator according to the inventory and other requirements of that particular industry. Since then, the monitoring function has remained based on credit and not lender-based. The credit case, particularly if it is a case of a term loan, is often based on a project, and monitoring is thus limited to the project undertaken. Important data on the creditor's other transactional activities, other projects, or other defaults in payments are not routinely collected. Moreover, the banks' managerial staffs have poor domain knowledge, having never been exposed to real-life industrial activities.

The assets creation in the cash credit system has remained linked to the disposal market, however, because, in the absence of a de facto disposal market, the assets once created have to remain tied up with, if not the original company, then with the group. Assets that turn sick or idle could thus still have a route (though not mediated by the market transaction or dictated by the bank) for transferral to preferred users. In this system, the creation as well as the virtual disposal of assets makes use of transactions and prices. However, these transactions or prices are not decided through auctions or so-called open market transactions. This system can be defined as a market institution, which may he called market-1, and is dependent on relations and trust. The other market, which is dependent on arms-length spot auctions and which would not demand any privileged information, may be called market-2. The most important characteristics of market-1 is the degree to which it can eliminate moral hazards. Bank-customer relations are protracted. Bank B, for example, has retained the same customers over more than 50 years. Knowledge of the customer is therefore deeper than what bank B could otherwise have had from an auctioned market of information. It has not been necessary for B to have control exercised through its own presence on the creditor's board of directors. Neither has it been necessary for B to retain the creditor's principal current account.

Supplying working capital does not, however, mandate a board membership; even term loan or equity financing, while entitling a board membership, is being questioned by influential industrial lobbies. It is also not well established whether and to what extent control can be exercised and privileged information can be accessed through banks having board membership. Moreover, retaining the principal current account of the creditor within itself can be feasible only under an institutional setup of the main bank system. In the absence of such an institution, the banks in India have never been able to continuously monitor, a case of interim monitoring, the tied-up long-term creditor. The latter, through the long-term credit relationship with the bank, provides the institutional platform for relation-based banking. Moreover, the bank's managerial assistance to its creditor in distress or the deputation of bank staff to the creditors, has never been practiced. A bank, such as B, trains its staff on project appraisal and therefore necessarily imparts a degree of domain knowledge, for example, an expertise on textile projects. Such expertise is extremely limited, however. Recruitment by all the major banks is done centrally, and individual banks such as B cannot recruit their own staff alone, nor can they induct senior managers horizontally. As a result, B could never acquire, either through deputation or through horizontal induction, the required domain expertise. Such an expertise can assist the distressed creditor through consultative advice or can evaluate the value of available information.

Bank B therefore could not have access to board-level information. Neither could it possess or monitor the information on an interim basis through the principal current account of its creditor. B also could not, through available domain knowledge or through deputation to a distressed creditor, salvage managerially the assets turning sick. Apparently, B's only privileged information on the creditor is the historical knowledge of the creditor's performance along both the credit lines and the general management. Such information, though not exclusively private, is privileged. B apparently can bargain with the credit-seeker for both ex-ante and ex-post information (on earlier credit lines). As a practice Indian banks take into consideration the level of inventory in the year preceding, while releasing the credit in the current year. This historical information is not routinely shared with the other banks in the region. In fact, the Indian banking structure is not spatially configured; as a result, banks do not compete on the basis of regionality. Neither do they cooperate regionally. The lead bank system is operationally not very effective.

A mismatch between assets creation and assets disposal, in either the market-1 or market-2 system, leads to the NPA. NPA is not a dead asset; rather, it is an asset that is immobile and therefore failing in the value-adding capability. What we need to distinguish is the difference between the types of mobility. Market-1 provides for a circuit that is not created through auctions, whereas market-2 creates its circuits through auctioning. Both markets often fail to clear, and the NPA gets created. Institutions in the market-1 system that are necessary to clear the market relate to governance of the creditor, and hence the market through both the management system internal to the bank and an operational interbank system. Such a governance institution, being embedded in the managerial system, is not just static or is not limited only to the interim governance. It also serves the purpose of reconnaissance by way of accessing information that will be needed in the future governance. This aspect of future orientation provides the basis of a competition policy in the market-1 system. In contrast, market-2 seeks to govern through multiple organizations, M&A through auctioning, and partitioning of and marketing of information relating to market functioning. Banks are not the only governing agency in this market-2 system. The basis of information that can be of use in the future is rather weak, and the market-2 system tends to operate in a static mode or through a mode that is close to equilibrium. In contrast, market-1, which employs relations-based banking, is close to direct governance, offers a parsimonious market organization owing to the absence of multiple organizations, and situates its bank management institution close to market governance as well as to a reconnaissance. The Indian banking system, and in particular bank B, is close to the classic examples of relations-based banking.

Managerial Styles and Reengineering at Bank B

The system of management functioning appears to be crucial. This system, as argued earlier, has two aspects of relevance: (1) the internal and (2) that which relates to its creditors. The former system depends on the latter, and the latter is largely a component of a nationwide institution of governance. Restructuring the internal system by a board is feasible for a particular bank, though it would remain limited by the rules and regulations of the RBI and the Ministry of Finance (MoF). However, restructuring the latter is beyond the jurisdiction of a particular board. The governance restructuring follows the overall discourse regarding governance and market. We define "managerial styles" as the mode and manner in which a management functions and acts, and engages in games, acts strategically, and is poised for the future. A managerial style is therefore not exclusively dependent only on the rules-set, power, and injunctions that are peculiar to internal management. This style is equally dependent on prevailing discourses—that is on the discourses regarding the governance institution. Management values, elements of trust, and attitudes toward both competitors and creditors sustain this style.

Restructuring, or more specifically, reengineering of bank B's internal management, was initiated by its chairman and endorsed by its board around 1995. The initiating chairman retired soon after, and an international consultancy firm was engaged. During the preparation of the consultancy report, the next chairman also retired, and so the consultants presented the report to the third chairman. The implementation of the report appears to have been initiated during the tenure of the fourth chairman. The terms of engagement of the consultants were rather wide, including items relating to restructuring into strategic business units (SBUs) and reengineering. The consultants did not undertake the specific tasks of setting the specific process goals of the to-be-reengineered processes, or even identifying the details of the processes to be changed or the specific modalities of transformational processes leading to SBUs. The board, apparently uninformed about the reengineering concepts or the SBU, could not appear to have evaluated the shortcomings of the consultants' reports and activities. The senior managers, those who were not on the board, also had frequently changed their functional positions in the organization. As a result, the change initiative could not or did not have its root in a specific set of managers, but had to collapse to the functional roles—which ironically, the entire exercise was supposed to change.

Apparently, bank B went to an international consultant primarily because of the contingent demand on bank B to expand its tier-1 capital, through expansion of equity from the public. Bank B was undercapitalized, and in order to satisfy the Basle norm, it was to expand its equity. In fact, the Basle norm could not still be fulfilled, even following the equity expansion since tier-2 capital was still larger than tier-1 capital. The consultant was therefore hired primarily for a certification. With this understanding, the consultancy firm proposed a general structure of functions and operations that was closely in tune with the discourses and rhetoric of market-2 and that was more in tune with the Anglo-American market-2 type of banking organizations. For example, it had proposed opening a very large number of corporate banking branches. Given the banking scenario for the corporate, it was indeed astronomically high. B's board was apparently not happy with the consultants' report. A few rather cosmetic changes were made, such as in the reporting structure. Bank B, as all other CBs, has a mechanism of transfer pricing through which branches that receive deposits much in excess of what the branch can advance are provided with an accounts adjusted. Such transfer pricing does not endow a branch, for example, with the desired degree of freedom required for transforming that into an SBU. As per RBI regulations, a CB is supposed to have a transfer pricing cell.

Similarly, the senior managers of the bank understood reengineering of processes as being a continuation of the hitherto existing practice of organization and method (O&M). In fact, the O&M department was converted into the Reorganization Cell. Functional areas of banking such as credit advance, credit monitoring, large project approvals, human resource development, customer servicing, and MIS were all identified by the consultant as processes to be reengineered. Therefore, senior managers of B unquestioningly accepted this and thought that by reducing the layers through which a report used to travel or by reorganizing the work of the front desk bank clerks, reengineering could be achieved. They naturally did not have any process diagrams; neither did they have any process goals. The bank's current MIS cannot indicate individual, activity, process, or even branch-level productivity. The reengineering therefore could not set any quantitative goal. The consultant apparently borrowed the concept of relation-based management and proposed a new designation called the relations manager. The board, having accepted the concept of relations management, created such managers at the branch level and primarily for the SSIs, as well as for the corporate banking branches. The relation-based concept, which thrives on domain knowledge, intimate and exclusive knowledge of the creditor, and deputation of bank staffs to creditors, was not used. Instead, bank B started practicing a public relations exercise.

The functional areas that have been so far attended to, if not for reengineering, and where certain changes have been effected, are strategy planning, organization structure, credit management, treasury management, counter services and check clearing, human resources, information technology, and MIS. Bank B's policy has been to open at least one corporate banking branch in each zone and at least 75 personal banking branches in the next few years. Apparently, B has not recognized and formulated any particular competition policy or any strategic plans for cooperation. Indian banking is based on branches, although the competition is not defined on branch-based competition. In contrast, a corporate banking branch stimulates branch-based competition, which is only partially a spatial competition. For the ordinary branches, competition, if any, is based only on spatial considerations. Bank B is therefore in the midst of a policy mix, and its personnel do not appear to be happy with the outcome. Most of the branches act as a post office, collecting deposits, and get their share of profits through book adjustment based on transfer pricing. Most investments are made through the treasury department and those, too, in government securities. Competition in the investment market is not yet acute. There appears to be some competitive element with investments in bonds, and so on, of the best managed private companies. In addition, competition in the ordinary deposit market is barely present, and the personal banking branches are meant primarily for new value-added service products. Neither the corporate banking branches nor the personal banking branches appear to be infusing a new culture of competition into B's system of management as such. The managerial style does not appear to have changed much. The senior managers of B often speak of "time-tested practices," and they discuss reengineering and management system restructuring with reference to these time-tested practices.

Systemic Response, Information System, and the NPA

Organizational strategy for the reduction of NPA and the initiative on restructuring and reengineering were taken simultaneously at B, although these two goals do not appear to have been mentioned together. Assets position had been considered much earlier, and definite activities were initiated to reduce NPA prior to engaging the consultants. The reduction strategy for NPA came out of, first, pure rational considerations on assets management. Soon, however, the regulator central bank, the RBI, and the MoF as well as the Indian Banks Association (IBA) got together and created an environment of new norms and regulations, such that banks had to begin activities toward NPA reduction as per the new set of norms and regulations. This was the second factor that began transforming the management systems of Indian banks. The first factor, a pure rational consideration, was derived from within bank B, and the second cause, also derived from rationality, acted on all the banking organizations from without. Yet another factor appeared, from outside the banking institution, and it was the general concern about the rising spectre of the Asian crisis and the general economic slowdown. This third cause, especially because it was dominated by the media, appeared as more rhetoric than substance and hence soon began dominating the discourse through setting standards of values and oughts. Central regulatory policies could not disregard such a discourse, and the rationality exhibited through the second factor soon had to pick up the rhetoric of the third. The first cause could remain relatively free of this rhetoric, though much of the policies resulting from the consultants can be attributed to the third. The systemic responses of B and the banking institution in India in the aftermath of the Asian crisis are thus explainable through these three causes.

The reduction strategy for NPA was initially driven by the first cause, followed by the second and only later did bank B's public utterances lead to the rhetoric of the third. Insofar as it was only the first cause, the strategy adopted did not have to materially change the organizational structure of B and instead depended more on new lines of activities and reporting, information structure, and so on. This strategy soon had to dovetail with the ordinances arising out of the second cause. Bank B now had to commit itself to a set of values on organizational performance. It was somewhat mandatory that B effect changes. Organizational restructuring, though not mandated, was imperative, and with the discourse setting in from the third cause, bank B now thought it wise to at least appear to be restructuring itself. The hiring of an international consultant was thus a necessity arising out of the rhetoric. New jargon, such as SBU and BPR, now appeared in the organizational dialogue. The earlier information system, dependent more on verbal and therefore on hermeneutic connotations, soon became mixed with the apparent rationality of computerized numerical reporting.

The rapidity and effectiveness with which an organization, and hence an institution, can respond to a systemic shock such as was given by the Asian crisis depend not only on the information being exchanged within the organization and institution, but also on the semantic load or the hermeneutically interpreted structure of discourse making use of that information. Thus, studying just the physical structure or the MIS or even the legal and normative parameters of bank B or the Indian banking institution would not enrich us as much as would appreciating the space of events, full of verbal rhetoric. If we look solely at the data on number of new branches opened, new technologies and services initiated, new MIS installed, and even the percentage reduction in NPA, then bank B attained reengineered processes and SBUs. However, if we look at other discourse-related parameters, bank B remained weak. Managing the discourse-related parameters cannot be achieved only within the boundaries of an organization; such a management would demand related changes in both the banking institution and the overall economic institutions. The systemic response of bank B is therefore that building block which crystallizes the contours of institutional response well within the structure of the organization. Hence, it is those blocks within B building up the institutional response that we may refer to as the systemic change within B. Such a change is unlikely to be captured through a few statistics.

The governance function of banking is crystallized through functional blocks within B. The relations-based banking offers a set of such blocks. Monitoring a company ex-ante interim and ex-post, as against monitoring either a project or a credit account; monitoring the company by retaining within itself the principal current account of the company as against monitoring a credit account through its income recognition; or monitoring a company by being on the board as against remaining an outsider dependent on priced information from the market provide us with the key features of alternative building blocks within the organization that can support two different types of governance. The first set of features relate to relations-based banking and are not exactly available with B, whereas B appears to be having the second set. The second set is closer to the securitized institution. B, having more of the second set, however, also depends on the element of trust and privileged information as defined earlier. Therefore, B is an intermediate organization supporting the institution of relations-based banking only partially, while at the same time offering scope to the securitized institution. The systemic response of B and perhaps of other banks in India, when viewed through the statistics of securitized organizations, appears to be driven by the Anglo-American model of market-2 and its related institutions of governance. However, this systemic response, if studied closely and hermeneutically, affords us an alternative picture. B appears to have emboldened the relations-based institutions through what its managers call time-tested practices.

MIS in B, for example, has changed outwardly. Earlier, each department had its own MIS; currently, MIS itself is a department. The reporting structure on transactions is now from the branch to the zonal office, and about two hundred branches report to each zonal office. The regional office, to which the branches earlier reported, gets its required information from the zonal office, which finally sends the information across to the MIS department at the head office. Computerization has helped increase the fields of information being covered, which now collects information on about 40 items regarding credit accounts above a certain size. In order to monitor the assets accounts, this MIS collects information on 40 heads of about 75,000 accounts. However, the privileged information relating to the company is not obtained through the MIS. The bargaining between B and its creditor and the information leaking through long association, and so on, enriches the MIS. This second part ensues from discourses within and outside B. The borrower now has to fill in a longer form providing more information. Thus, bank B argues, the risk rating of credit takes into account all that the consultant had suggested—that is what a securitized banking institution should possess formally. The rhetoric is thus satisfied, and the interpretive domain remains overseeing, guiding the actual credit allocations and assets classification. Bank B therefore receives the meaning of assets information through a relations-based institution while depending partially on the securitized building blocks. The buffer to a volatile shock, as given by the Asian crisis, is thus provided by a mixed institution, which, however, is founded on organization-internal managerial systemic response.

CONCLUSION: MANAGERIAL SYSTEMIC RESPONSE

The response system thus built is managerial and organization-systemic. One may wonder if, indeed, the banking institution-to-respond were to be securitized and built on market-2, there would have been no need to found this institution on the management system. In market-2, the responding institution is built around multiple organizations, partitioned and priced information, rating and M&A, and so forth. Such a system allows checks and balances, as well as assets disposal through auctioning. The presence of multiple auctioning agents and a partitioned multiple market tend to stabilize the system when given a volatile shock, at either the same equilibrium or at another equilibrium. Thus, market-2 institution-to-respond would not demand a managerial system. The very edifice of a managerial system taking care of shock management and assets management cannot be maintained in market-2, and it can only be maintained in market-1. This reasoning establishes beyond doubt that what the Indian banking institution attempted to forge was in fact based on relations-based banking.

Indian banking does not have surfacially a main bank system. The banks, as particularly in bank B, often possess organizational features relevant to market-2. However, these features are not the building blocks of an institution of market-2. Management styles, the systemic response of both B, and, as it appears, other commercial banks, do indeed constitute through a complex intra- and inter-organizational discourse the systemic buffer much needed to absorb volatile shock. Bank B, as we have seen, initiated the strategic management of assets in particular of nonperforming assets much before the Asian crisis. This bank again appointed a consultant to advise it on restructuring and reengineering simultaneously with the Asian crisis. Bank B finally appears to have emboldened its management styles and systems that had been in vogue. The difference was that now the new styles and systems had taken into account the turning-sick assets, disposal of assets, degree of exposure of the assets market to international money market, and the portents of a systemwide volatile shock. Bank B and Indian banks in general did not go for management of nonperforming assets through market-2 mediated organizations. The assets management problem was considered managerially; corresponding management systemic solutions were institutionalized, internal to the organization by the bank itself as in the case of bank B, and internal to the institution of banking by the central bank.

Assets management provides us with an example of an institutionalized managerial solutions. The Indian banking strategy toward not just managing assets liabilities but also toward interfacing with the global money markets appears to be getting shaped around two tiers. The first tier is internal to the bank-creditor system, and the second tier is for interfacing the first tier with the global money markets. A reading of the Asian crisis offers two different strategies as required by these two tiers. Apparently, the first tier is being provided with a managerial system, as a buffer that can see it through crises including shocks. Such a management system and style is based primarily on privileged information, trust, and relations. The banking system is not distinctly relations based. However, the dominant discourse and dependence on the managerial system make it de facto relations based. The first tier, as one of its constituents bank B, has taken in earnest the task of management of nonperforming assets. Such a task permits building up the management system as an institution. Moreover, this system, since it interfaces the bank with its creditor, institutionalizes the system of governance of the assets, and hence the governance of creditor companies. The response to the Asian shock is thus made into a system of management of banking and banks.

The most important element of this system appears to be the function of governance. It is a system of governance and management. In contrast, the second tier that interfaces the first tier with the global money market has proliferated into multiple markets and organizations, partitioned information, and auctioning. This tier of Indian banking is building securitized institutions belonging to market-2 which was described earlier. Indian banking appears to have chosen a dual strategy: strategy-1 for the first tier of banking that relates the bank to the companies through assets; and strategy-2 for the second tier that relates this first tier to the global market. Strategy-1 is driven by considerations of management (of assets and bank organization) and governance of assets (with the companies). Strategy-2 is driven by considerations of auctioning and securitizations. The interfacing of these two different strategies would surely be a challenge to the regulator in the near future. Strategy-1 is founded upon credit market governance through bank management system and management styles. This strategy works essentially on the values and norms of relations-based banking, though not always on its structure. Such a strategy offers privileged information, organizational preparedness, and early reconnaissance of failures in assets markets and therefore offers both a buffer to and an information system on any likely emergent volatile shock. Bank B, being an important bank, has geared itself managerially to provide the systemic response. The strategies of Indian banking in the aftermath of the Asian crisis appear to be unique and hold promise to banking institutions in the developing world.

REFERENCES

Allais, Maurice. (1987). The Credit Mechanism and Its Implications. In G. R. Feiwel (ed.), *Arrow and the Foundations of the Theory of Economic Policy*. London: Macmillan, pp. 137–152.

Aoki, Masahiko. (1990). Toward an Economic Model of the Japanese Firm. *Journal of Economic Literature*, 28, pp. 1–27.

Aoki, Masahiko, and Patrick, Hugh (eds.). (1994). *The Japanese Main Bank System*. Oxford: Oxford University Press.

Baums, Theodor. (1993). Takeover vs. Institutions in Corporate Governance in Germany. In D. D. Prentice and P.R.J. Holland (eds.), *Contemporary Issues in Corporate Governance*. Oxford: Clarendon Press, pp. 46–62.

Baums, Theodor. (1994). The German Banking System and Its Impact on Corporate Finance and Governance. In Masahiko Aoki and Hugh Patrick (eds.), *The Japanese Main Bank System*. Oxford: Oxford University Press, pp. 152–169.

Berglof, Erik. (1990). Capital Structure as a Mechanism of Control: A Comparison of Financial Systems. In Masahiko Aoki et al. (eds.), *The Firm as a Nexus of Treaties*. London: Sage Publications, pp. 23–37.

Bhole, L. M. (1982). *Financial Markets and Institutions: Growth, Structure and Innovations*. New Delhi: Tata McGraw-Hill Publishing Co. Ltd.

Frankel, Allien B., and Montgomery, John D. (1991). Financial Structure: An International Perspective. *Brookings Papers on Economic Activity*, 1, pp. 257–297.

Gupta, N. C., M. N. Kaura, & G. L. Sharma. (1991). *Corporate Finance Emerging Options*. New Delhi: Anmol Publications.

Jalan, Bimal. (1999). Towards a More Vibrant Banking System. *Reserve Bank of India Bulletin*, January, pp. 11–20.

Jensen, Michael C. (1988). Takeovers: Their Causes and Consequences. *Journal of Economic Perspectives*, 2, pp. 21–48.

Morck, Randall, Shleifer, Andrei, and Vishny, Robert W. (1989). Alternative Mechanism for Corporate Control. *American Economic Review* 79, pp. 842–852.

OECD. (1987). Asset and Liability Management by Banks by R. Harrington. Paris: OECD.

Reddy, Y. V. (January 1999). Financial Sector Reform: Review and Prospects. *Reserve Bank of India Bulletin*, pp. 33–94.

Reserve Bank of India (RBI). (1975). Report of the Study Group to Frame Guidelines for Follow-Up of Bank Credit. Mumbai: RBI.

Reserve Bank of India. (1984). Report of the Committee to Examine the Legal and Other Difficulties faced by Banks and Financial Institutions in Rehabilitation of Sick Industrial Undertakings and Suggest Remedial Measures Including Changes in the Law. Mumbai: RBI.

Reserve Bank of India. (1985). Report of the Committee to Review the Working of the Monetary System (Chakravarty Committee). Mumbai: RBI.

Reserve Bank of India. (1987). Report of the Working Group on the Money Market. Mumbai: RBI.

Reserve Bank of India. (1988). Report of the Study Group for Examining Introduction of Factoring Services in India. Mumbai: RBI.

Reserve Bank of India. (November 1991). Report of the Committee on the Financial System (Narasimham Committee). Mumbai: RBI.

Reserve Bank of India. (January 1999b). Harmonising the Role and Operations of Development Financial Institutions and Banks. Mumbai: RBI.

Reserve Bank of India Bulletin. (August 1998). Finances of Private Limited Companies—1994–95. Mumbai: RBI.

Reserve Bank of India Bulletin. (January 1999a). Performance of Private Corporate Business Sector. Mumbai: RBI.

Reserve Bank of India Bulletin. (May 1999c). Finances of Private Limited Companies 1995–96. Mumbai: RBI.

Reserve Bank of India Bulletin. (May 1999d). Investments of Scheduled Commercial Banks (end March 1997). Mumbai: RBI.

Reserve Bank of India Bulletin. (May 1999e). Monetary and Credit Policy for the Year 1999–2000. Mumbai: RBI.

Stiglitz, Joseph E., and Weiss, Andrew. 1981. Credit Rationing in Markets with Imperfect Information. *American Economic Review*, 71(3), pp. 393–410.

Williamson, Oliver E. (1985). *The Economic Institutions of Capitalism: Firms, Markets, Relational Contracting*. New York: Free Press.

Williamson, Oliver E. (1988). Corporate Finance and Corporate Governance. *Journal of Finance*, 43, pp. 567–591.

Chapter 7

Reforms of China's State-Run Enterprises: Chances and Risks for China and for Western Business

Wolfgang Klenner

A FEW REMARKS ON CHINA'S FRAGILE ECONOMIC STABILITY

Asia is sometimes surprising. Its successful market economies, from which the world used to take lessons in economic optimism and pragmatism, have lost their dynamics and fallen into a crisis. China, however, which until recently was considered by many observers to be most prone to political and economic turmoil in the region, presents itself in rather stable conditions (Honkawa, 1998; Richter, 1999). The political transition of leadership, which was thought most critical only a few years ago, went very smoothly. Moreover, contrary to the expectations of all those economists, who give credits only to ''pure'' economic systems, China's mixed economy has proven quite workable. But most surprising is the fact that during a time when most East and Southeast Asian nations are suffering economic troubles, China is displaying considerable stability—at first glance at least. This is most extraordinary, since China, too, experienced an enormous ''bubble,'' with speculative investment taking place within a huge area stretching from China's bordertowns to Vietnam, all along the coast up to Shandong, and further to the North. Investment was often financed by banks on the basis of private connections or, without financial intermediation, through triangular debts. There is the astonishing observation that in China, similar or even worse developments than those in the rest of Asia did not lead to a crash. Contrarily, at present, China's currency is stable, the growth rate of its GDP is high, there is no inflation, and foreign reserves are, according to common criteria, more than sufficient.

The reasons for China's persisting economic dynamics and financial stability are not easy to grasp. But they are obviously the result of something like the specific "China-mix." This refers to economic mechanisms such as credit chains, which often are economically unreasonable, however cemented by personal ties between "entrepreneurs" and their "friends" within the banking system, the administration, and the party organization—features that might be called elements of economic planning. Moreover, strict provisions for financial flows between the outside world and China seem to be decisive. Financial transactions are almost entirely restricted to investment in material assets in China. Foreigners have rather limited access to China's financial assets. They are usually expected to invest in specific projects that cannot easily be liquidated, should there be any rumors and reports about the country's financial problems. As is well known, corresponding reactions of foreign investors in financial capital were among the causes for the financial dry-out of Thailand, Korea, and other Asian countries and the drastic decline of their currencies. China's mixed economic system—which from a theoretical point of view is a less than second-best solution, resulting in misallocations and a waste of manpower and material ressources—in view of all the economic and social problems and economic misery in China's neighboring economies is certainly not too "bad" (Millstein et al., 1998).

REACTIONS OF WESTERN BUSINESS

It might be not surprising that U.S. Treasury Secretary Robert Rubin called China during Asia's crisis an "island of stability" (*Financial Times*, December 1, 1998). Business, however, seems to have a somewhat different perception, and even China's economic leaders are not overly optimistic. It is recognized that the high growth rate of 7 or 8 percent of GDP in 1998 was not merely the result of self-sustained growth, but to a high degree it was the outcome of heavy government spending on infrastructure in order to stimulate the economy. This gives rise to the assumption that, in the near future, business might be less buoyant than expected.

Moreover, it is not just this slowdown that is worrying foreign investors. An ordinary recession wouldn't be considered a serious obstacle. In view of a few extremely attractive business centers such as Shanghai, it might be remembered that Manhattan, too, was built during a recession—but nevertheless became a center of prosperity. The real worries are triggered by other developments and observations. Among those is the handling of the liquidation process of one of China's most prominent financial institutions, the Guangdong International Trust and Investment Corporation. Foreign creditors were told not to expect full or even priority repayment in outstanding loans to the bankrupt company. This decision not to bail out foreign lenders, even though this financial institution had been backed by provincial government, should be welcomed as a matter of principle. It makes a clear distinction between sovereign and nonsovereign debt, a line that had been blurred too often by the "quasi-sovereign-label" attached to loans to many Chinese state-owned companies in the past.

Creditors don't like principles, however, whenever they go against their interests. At the same time, and this is probably a more severe problem, they are shocked by the incompetence and corruption that became evident when they learned more about the downfall of Guangdong's financial institution. They fear that many more companies, including the some 200 regional International Trust and Investment Corporations, are also beleaguered by professional misconduct.

Against this background, different attitudes of Western investors toward China can be observed. There is the wait and see approach of companies, who already dispose of well-established production sites in China and want things to become better before they get more concrete about further extending their business into China. Other companies that started major projects just before the crisis have no other choice but to go ahead. Examples seem to be the steel project of Krupp, together with Pudong Iron and Steel in Shanghai and the BASF project in Nanjing. Another group of companies, especially those that faced problems in the past, are considering exit options, either for a few selected projects or in total. Last though not least, some investors are attempting to benefit from decreasing prices for assets and property and grasp the chances of acquiring shares of Chinese companies. But altogether optimism is on the wane.

Recent statistics show that foreign direct investment through the third quarter of 1998 was down 0.6 percent to U.S.$31.4 billion, as compared to the same period last year—although China was still the world's largest recipient of FDI. The lion's share during both periods went into equity joint ventures and wholly foreign-owned enterprises. Mergers and acquisitions faced a drastic decline. They amounted to only U.S.$2.5 billion in the first six months of 1998, compared to U.S.$6.6 billion in the same period in 1997 (*Handelsblatt* 1998).

This situation could change as a result of the reforms of China's state sector. In the future, mergers and acquisitions could become an important vehicle of foreign investors attempting to participate in China's growth (Capener, 1998). Since mergers and acquisitions of Western companies are a rather new form of capital transfer to China, it shouldn't be surprising that their permitted forms have been only gradually increased and are still limited. In the past, foreign investors were allowed to acquire shares in selected listed companies. Meanwhile, they may purchase shares through private placement in unlisted companies and take over a Chinese business by a newly established joint venture or a wholly foreign-owned enterprise. But substantially more opportunities will be offered as a consequence of the envisaged conversion of selected state-owned enterprises into joint-stock limited companies. It can be expected that reforming China's state sector, which contributes more than 30 percent to China's industrial production, will provide foreign investors with a wide array of chances to buy directly the shares of a going concern.

The Western response remains cautious, but interest will certainly increase should China juridically and economically pave the way for this kind of investment and demonstrate its ability to stabilize the economy.

BASIC STRUCTURES OF CHINA'S STATE ENTERPRISES

In China's socialist past, industrial growth was promoted by allocating most savings to China's state industry. As a result, all big enterprises, some of them with several hundred thousand employees, as well as most medium-scale enterprises, belong to the state sector. This sector still constitutes roughly half of China's accumulated capital in spite of rather high growth rates of private and cooperative enterprises within the last decade.

A substantial portion of the state-run enterprises belong to the heavy and chemical industry. They are usually highly diversified companies producing a wide array of commodities and providing a multitude of social services for their employees. State-run enterprises can be found all over China. However, state-owned capital as a percentage of total industrial capital is highest in the "old" industrial centers such as Northeast China, Beijing, Wuhan, and Lanzhou. In fact, a few regions are dominated by giant, comprehensive companies. Their growth and diversification had been spurred by regional industrial bureaus and enterprise directors aiming at overcoming bottlenecks that resulted from poor overall economic planning. But they were also the result of a deliberate policy during China's Cultural Revolution promoting all kinds of investment initiatives of local cadres and creating self-sufficient enterprises that would be able to continue production, even if external supplies were disrupted by military conflicts.

As is well known, state-run firms, though not always as backward as is often pointed out (Ishikawa, 1997), constitute a serious bottleneck for China's future economic growth and swallow a large portion of China's budget. In order to render them more effective, their transformation into corporations with private Chinese and foreign participation and, simultanously, mergers, splittings, and close-downs will be necessary. This will help to create those enterprise structures that are essential for a functioning market economy.

Questions such as who should be in charge of restructuring, what concepts should be applied, and which speed will be appropriate are still under discussion. China's policymakers are aware that it makes sense to give modern enterpreneurs rather than the administration the say in restructuring enterprises. However, it would be difficult to attract managers and private capital for state-run enterprises in their present shape. Apart from this, enterpreneurs might favor decisions that are socially unacceptable. There seems to be the conviction that, at least preliminarily, an involvement of bureaucrats will be necessary. Various privatization concepts already applied in Eastern Europe, such as handing out vouchers and other schemes, are being analyzed. At present, however, most policymakers seem to prefer selling shares at market prices. They are aiming at widening the capital basis of former state-run enterprises rather than initiating a mass give-away of shares. Speed is obviously not very important. Minimizing social, political, and economic risks, which follow from the transformation of state-run enterprises, has a high priority (Klenner, 1994).

CHANCES AND RISKS OF ENGAGING IN STATE-RUN ENTERPRISES

Enormous amounts of private funds will be required to restructure China's undercapitalized large enterprises, which had been shaped according to the requirements of central control. Heavy resentment of the sellout of China's "property of the whole people" to wealthy Chinese capital owners, who are more clever and less scrupulous than the ordinary citizen, and to foreign companies will certainly come to the fore. However, especially foreign capital has demonstrated its ability to modernize China's production. In 1997, for instance, foreign-funded firms were involved in 47 percent of the country's foreign trade (*China Daily*, Business Weekly, Beijing, November 29–December 5, 1998). In view of the beneficial effects of foreign participation, it can be expected that the state sector's technological backwardness and increasing financial burden will induce the government to open the state sector to foreign companies and offer a broad range of possibilities for participating within this process.

These possibilities will accompany the attractive chances. Investors could decide whether they aim at a majority stake in order to gain executive power or just a small percentage in order to build up relations and become part of information networks. They would be able to tap the potential of China's old core industries, providing basic inputs for the whole economy and thereby obtaining pivotal positions in China's economy. Getting access to China's vast industrial labor force is another opportunity. Investors will certainly be confronted with all the burdens of pre-market labor relations and organizational structures, but the staff of former state-run companies might turn out to be more experienced and more loyal than many job-seekers and job-hunters of joint ventures. Finally, even if state-run firms represent a comparatively low technological level and turn out commodities that are hardly competitive on world markets, their products might still be in demand in China and less developed countries. Former state-run enterprises could be attractive for those Western firms that aim at transferring less modern technologies in line with the so-called flying-geese pattern, in which economic changes in the more advanced countries come to be repeated in the less developed countries, with time lags.

But engaging in China's state sector poses considerable risks. At first, shares of former state-run enterprises might be comparatively low priced. However, even low-priced shares could turn out to have been too expensive. This can be best illustrated by German experiences with Treuhand: At the beginning of Treuhand's work of restructuring and sell-out of East German enterprises, estimates put the value of those assets at approximately 600 billion DM. Treuhand, however, closed its business, with debts amounting to roughly 180 billion DM. It thus became obvious that huge amounts of capital built up during decades of socialist planning had turned into negative assets, when evaluated on the basis of market criteria. But Germany's experiences might not be valid for China. China's productive assets will generally not be devaluated as dramatically as in

East Germany, since Chinese wages will not rise as they did in East Germany. Moreover, China, being a developing country, provides a vast market for ''second-grade'' and ''third-grade'' commodities.

By participating in the management of former state-run enterprises, foreign firms will have to deal with outdated equipment which produces high pollution—for which they might be made responsible. Moreover, China's administration could make enterprises responsible for previous damages to the environment and raise pollution norms. In all these cases, costs might increase dramatically and turn former assets into a heavy burden.

China's transition toward a market economy poses yet other risks. Western investors should be prepared for dramatic changes in the business climate of China's former state industry, demanding an extremely high degree of flexibility. During the initial stage, foreign investors will have to deal with the old-fashioned type of Chinese cadres, who might be inefficient but whose decisions are easily predictable. They will have to cope with former contracts and agreements, business relations, and personal connections they have concluded and built up. This will become different, when a new type of Chinese manager comes into existence together with a dynamic, aggressive, and rather unscrupulous emerging middle class—probably much like the Japanese managers who came up after the abolition of the more samurai-like *zaibatsu* after World War II.

Further changes will come to the fore, if formerly state-run enterprises are totally or partly taken over and managed by Chinese businessmen from Taiwan, Singapore, Hong Kong, Southeast Asia, and Korean and Japanese companies. East and Southeast Asian capital and management know-how would flood into China's state sector aiming at getting into personal networks, taking command of important enterprises, and establishing springboards for further penetration of China's market. With these newly arising entities that might determine the rules of the game, Western firms will probably find it more difficult to develop partnership relations and to compete than with previous state-run enterprises.

In spite of all these changes, it cannot be excluded that even the new corporations will still be connected to state officials in different ways. They might therefore, on the one hand, act like ''normal'' competitors, and on the other hand, exploit state subsidies for their purposes. In the latter case, Western investors could turn out to be less able than their Asian competitors to obtain support of influential Chinese bureaucrats, since they do not dispose of established networks based on personal or family relations.

It goes without saying that ''atmospherics'' and other economic features, which had been shaped during China's previous socialist system, would be tilted more decisively toward the market economy. State officials would feel more committed to rational economic behavior, transparency, and clear regulation. Managers, being confronted with comparatively ''hard'' budget constraints, would feel obliged to obey market rules and would no longer expect a bailout by the state bureaucracy and banks. Moreover, with the ceremony being subject to market pressure, the necessary microeconomic conditions would be created, under which modern instruments of monetary and fiscal policy could be effectively applied. At present, costs do not matter much to state enterprises since they can rely on subsidies from the administration. Therefore, a rise is the interest rate or changes in taxes hardly influence firms' demand for capital. This would change as a result of harder budget constraints, enabling China's authorities to better regulate the economy by means of modern economic policy.

Only a few years ago, these results would have been indiscriminately welcomed. But on the basis of the recent financial turmoil in Asia, it has become evident that this transformation goes together with considerable risks for China's economic and social stability. As has been outlined before, economic deficiencies caused by the state sector are limiting China's growth. At the same time, they are helping to prevent China's fragile economy from collapsing. Moreover, restrictions imposed on the dealings of foreign investors in financial assets are limiting China's access to foreign capital and, hence, economic growth. On the other hand, foreign investors cannot withdraw their capital from China at the push of a bottom, should there be any troubles with China's finances.

The envisaged reform of China's state sector and the acceptance of foreign investment have to be seen in a differentiated way. Further reforms will certainly be required for paving the way toward the necessary productivity gains in China's former state sector. However, the introduction of market mechanisms will put an end to those traditional mechanisms that helped to prevent a fragile economy from crashing. A comprehensive set of supportive measures will be required in order to prevent China's economy and society from tumbling into new problems. Chances and risks will not only depend on the economic and legal provisions for restructuring state enterprises. Also important will be China's ability to create the necessary economic and social conditions under which instruments of modern economic and social policy could be effectively applied.

There are already a few examples of Western mergers and acquisitions of former state-run enterprises. Most of them are still struggling to find solutions for integrating their business. During this initial stage they are quite understandably willing to talk neither about problems nor about achievements. However, it will be most exciting to learn about how partners from completely different economic systems, with dissimilar cultural backgrounds and business practices, are attempting to integrate operations and work for common goals.

REFERENCES

Capener, C. R. (1998). M&A in China Comes of Age. *The China Business Review*, July–August, p. 14

China Daily, Business Weekly, Beijing, November 29–December 5, 1998.

Financial Times. (1998), December 1.

Handelsblatt. (1998). Düsseldorf, November 3.

Honkawa, H. (1998). China Unavoidable Influence from the Asian Currency Crisis. *JETRO China Newsletter*, Tokyo, 2(133), p. 18.

Ishikawa, S. (1997). China's ''Open Door'' and Internal Development in Perspective of the Twenty-First Century. In Fumio Itoh (ed.), *China in the Twenty-First Century: Politics, Economy, and Society*. Tokyo, New York, and Paris: United Nations University Press, p. 48.

Klenner, W. (1994). Privatization of Large Enterprises in Europe, a Comparative Approach—Lessons for China? *Proceedings of the International Symposium on Reform of China's State Owned Enterprises*, Institute for Reform and Development, Haikou.

Millstein, I. M. et al. (1998). *Corporate Governance. Improving Competitiveness and Access to Capital in Global Markets*. Paris: OECD.

Richter, F. J. (1999). Industrial Restructuring in Post-Deng China: Toward a Network Economy. In F. J. Richter (ed.), *Business Networks in Asia: Promises, Doubts, and Perspectives*. Westport, CT: Quorum, pp. 237–249.

Part III

Allying and Venturing: The Unfolding of a New Interfirm Rationality

Chapter 8

Venturing Jointly: Oriental and Occidental Perceptions

John Kidd

INTRODUCTION

This chapter explores the potential for misperceptions which can arise in the day-to-day interaction of managers while they are working in joint ventures. These managers will carry different personal paradigms relating uniquely to their individual circumstances, though some will be close to the learning of others if they are from the same country, or firms, or have followed similar training through their educational background. Such joint ventures, if they are located in Asia, are often set up with the help of "trading houses" such as the so-called Japanese *sogo shosha*, the Korean *chaebol*, the Taiwanese *jain duang*, and the Chinese *Foreign Trading Houses*. If they are located in Europe or the United States, then local Chambers of Commerce or Regional Development Agencies are often the intermediaries between the local firm, the relevant government departments, and the foreign investor. In both cases, management behaviors in the joint venture will be strongly directed by the majority partner and by the associated persons in the region of the location.

After some time, often quickly—particularly in times such as the current Asian economic crisis—the parent firms may reorganize their joint venture. We would hope from the outset that the staff, and thus the organization, might operate in an open and transparent mode—more acceptable to Western firms, institutions, and governments, yet still understandable to the traditional managers of firms in Asia. Yet this may not be possible, for repositioning of both Western and Oriental personnel in such ventures will be problematic since many shibboleths will be affected. In this chapter we of necessity ground our discussion on Western models and philosophies (it is our natural background), though from time to time we will reflect on pertinent Asian influences and thoughts, and illustrate these by comparing, say, Chinese to American scenarios—but simply by way of example because we do not wish to comment precisely on one distinct national aspect against another. The bulk of the chapter concentrates on West-East differences, often contrasting the role of culture and how this may affect the managers in the MNEs: whether for problem solving, process modeling, or the effective exchange of knowledge, whether for work or leisure.

In this time of great uncertainty in Asia, as economic turmoil takes its toll many Asian practices are tumbling when placed in the vise of global economic measures. The traditional methods of business management in Asia may not be appropriate within the new global order but whether such scenarios may be viewed in such a black and white manner is questionable. Often we may discern two well-held models derived from an Oriental or an Occidental viewpoint, but unless communicated will not be perceived by the other side. This chapter attempts to portray several twinned models that may operate in developing a joint venture.

As background, some data relating to the role of foreign direct investment (FDI) are presented in helping to develop the global enterprise culture: and within this framework the recent rise in cross-border merger and acquisition (M&A) activity can be noted. Generally, the enterprise is supported by the exchange or brokering of knowledge–be it between peers, within the hierarchy, or with individuals in other firms. Brokering has been widely studied in monocultural firms, and it is not our intention to report on brokering here. Rather, it is to consider the potential for conflict as one's well-held beliefs in paradigms are revealed to others in the organization. If this results in conflict, one might fail to exchange knowledge in an effective manner. Thus, an embryonic firm may have to consider, as well as trustworthy brokering between its members, many other impacts due to theories in good standing relating to individuals, processes, and organizations. Thus, many drivers can be considered in this overview.

Investment Churn

In recent years, the forces of globalization have determined and been determined by great flows of investment, not only between the developed nations but also from developed to undeveloped nations. Indeed, some might argue that this was ever so in historical times. See Frank (1998) who argues that bullion flows from the Americas and Africa helped the Europeans to purchase arms to subdue Asia, which had China as the center of the global economy up to the 1800s. The modern reasons for globalization are many but often are related to technology transfers wherein some economic advantage can be discerned by the firms or nations concerned. There is also a strong flow within some of the Southeast Asian nations: the surprising nation is perhaps China, which has absorbed a vast inflow (much was in fact from Japan). One might also note that Singapore, Malaysia, and Indonesia have received considerable inward investment over the recent past. The recent surge in FDI is due generally to the upsurge in cross-border merger and acquisition (M&A) activity, following the global restructuring of power, telecommunications, pharmaceuticals, general chemicals, and financial institutions, and following the general easing of regulations pertaining to foreign ownership of local enterprises.

The further analysis suggests a freeing up of markets which the United Nations Conference on Trade and Development (UNCTAD) says is strongest in the developing countries where emphasis is placed on cross-border merger and acquisition. This is indicated by the reduction of restrictive FDI regulations. According to UNCTAD, cross-border M&A activity now represents about one-quarter of all recorded M&A. In turn, this represents an increase from 49 to 58 percent of total FDI in-flows. The growth in FDI, with its undoubted ''churn'' between countries in the short term, strongly implies the need for very precise knowledge management to help enterprise partners looking to build synergistic relationships. The fact that such partnerships are difficult to forge is clearly expressed by Doz and Hamel (1998), yet there are distinct advantages to be achieved through new alliances, be they local, national, or global. However, once one accepts partners ''in the next village and beyond'' as it were, there will be difficulties in absorbing the others' cultural norms and expectations.

Relationships between BPR, OL, and KM

Figure 8.1 sets out views of the relationships between knowledge management (KM) and other fields. Many regard KM as merely an exercise in using information technology (IT)—for example, undertaking Data Mining or installing Lotus Notes. But it is more than this, and it has a strong cultural element. Looking at three elements that have pushed KM into the limelight, namely—Business Process Re-engineering (BPR), Knowledge Based Systems (KBS), and Organizational Learning (OL)—we see the importance of KM. In OL, culture was taken for granted, but its importance is now realized; BPR succeeds best when it encompasses the need for cultural change in the organization. Many of the failures of KBS development resulted from ignoring culture, especially of those persons who were supposed to use the system when developed (see Talwar, 1994).

As Figure 8.1 shows, KM implicitly covers a wide set of paradigms described well in a recent book by Davenport and Prusak (1998) wherein they elaborated many Western ideas pertaining to KM. Their ideas are too extensive to report in this chapter. Herein we concentrate throughout on the development of a ''brown-field'' joint venture (JV)—in other words, a JV created from parts of organizations already in existence. This is the most useful focus for a discussion on globalization. It should be noted that we are not describing this JV in a legalistic sense. Rather, this is a firm with senior staff members of the two or more ''joint'' partners and with the majority of the staff recruited from the local host country. Although the theoretical concept of a ''green field'' development

Figure 8.1
Determinants of Change

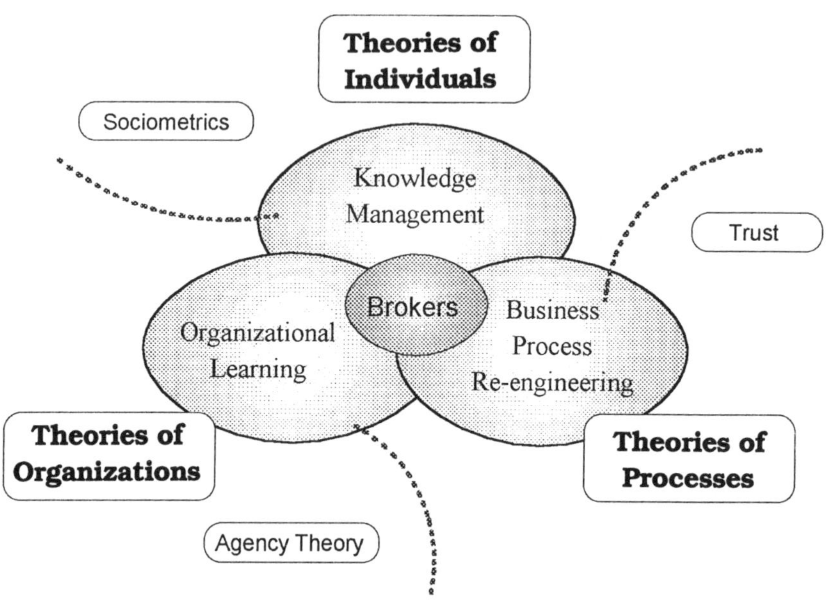

is a useful one, in practice no JV is ever staffed by persons who have no preconceptions brought with them from their homes, schools, or parent company firms. This means that members of the JV will probably not have benign expectations of the actions to be received from their senior managers, and so junior managers will inevitably carry some sense of vulnerability. In a new venture, the seniors have to instill a sense of trust so that all may pull together knowing that frequent change will be an inevitable outcome of the brown-field venture. These ''states of trust'' are well documented by Baier (1986), Sako (1994), Blois (1998), and Butler and Gill (1997). They are fundamental to the well-being of the organization, which ultimately will be one wherein the brokering of knowledge should become an accepted norm. In a similar vein, there are ''push technologies'' such as Agency Theory or Sociometrics which underpin studies in OL and KM, respectively. Agency Theory has been well documented by Baiman (1982, 1996) and will not be further addressed: Sociometrics based on the works of Hofstede and others is discussed later in the chapter. Following the structure of Figure 8.1, we go on to consider specific areas in which cultural differences may manifest themselves, one from each of the three sets of background theories.

THEORIES OF PROCESS

Today there is great pressure to review processes that enterprises use to ascertain whether improvements may be made; this follows the marketing of Business Process Re-engineering as the "saviour of business." It is unfortunate, yet natural, that often only one attribute at a time is changed through a manager's understandable conservatism. This diminishes the overall gains that might be achieved, since, if there is a strong complementarity of attributes, it is necessary to institute massive change along a number of dimensions. To be able to successfully implement change, the firm must research its processes and model them for the greater comprehension of its actors and players.

Inevitably, these changes include vast investment in information technology, presuming it to be useful in helping management decision making through having better access to data and to information, and in allowing easier knowledge sharing. This emphasizes the need for more education and training, but the United Kingdom and continental Europe are somewhat reluctant to spend on this aspect of the firm's operations, placing budget constraints on this factor. Yet it has long been recognized in Japan and Korea that such training is simply absorbed as part of the production cost and does not have a clear budget.

Systems Modeling: Western and Eastern

In the United Kingdom the Soft Systems Modeling (SSM) approach is widely accepted (Checkland, 1981; Checkland and Scholes, 1990; Checkland and Holwell, 1998). In this approach, a strong attempt is made to initiate and maintain discussions between the client and the consultant to be sure of jointly understanding the issues and to ensure that the correct problems are being addressed. Later the same conversational cycle can be used to assess the quality of the proposed solution prior to implementation. In some ways this process is quintessentially British; it is pragmatic, it draws on such quantitative and qualitative techniques as needed during the evolution of the study, and it is multidisciplinary. It is based in the tradition of the scientific method, but its interpretative, phenomenological stance makes it softer than the "hard" science, positivist, functional view embodied in (for example) the mathematical optimization paradigms of Operational Research. However, for multinational clients, the SSM approach may seem sloppy and not rigorous enough. (This is especially so for the U.S. academic community, which seems to prefer a data-rich scenario leading to a hard-science analysis of the problem.) In contrast, some Asians view even SSM as too hard a science; they may prefer to "commune" and to use a Zen-like approach.

Consider the work of Li and Li (1998). They state that in ancient China the social situation was believed to consist of two parts: *Wu* (objective existence) and *Shi* (human activities and their mechanisms). Both *Wu* and *Sh*i have governing laws, *li*, hence *Wuli* and *Shili*. Following *Shili* systems theory becomes a knowledge system about the laws of people's actions wherein *Shili* emphasizes information collecting, understanding, and decision making and implementing to develop the linkage of the perceived target system to the proposed target system derived through these *shili* processes. The whole becomes a learning system during which the *wuli* process transfers the target system from its initial

Figure 8.2
The *Shili* Process Logic

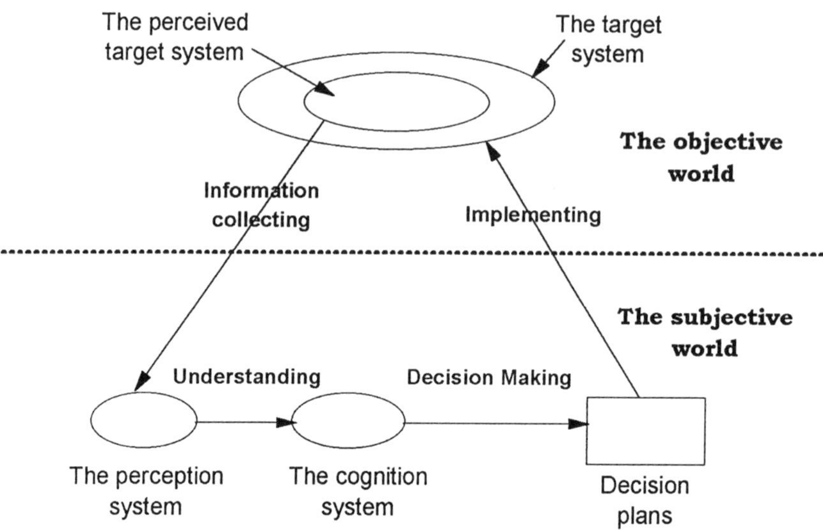

Source: Li and Li (1998). Reprinted with permission.

state to its goal state; and a *shili* process whereby the subject organizes the process. Their ideas are presented in Figure 8.2. Furthermore, *renli* concerns the sociopolitical patterns of interaction; thus, it deals with the effects of the overlaps of different cultural and belief systems. When one is oriented toward *renli*, one ensures that the designed systems support human needs as well as objective needs. Thus, the effectiveness of *wuli* and *shili* can work only when *renli* is recognized and undertaken. It is said that problem solving for the Asians deals with a myriad of component parts that can be finely categorized, and managed best by consciously knowing *wuli*, sensing *shili*, and caring for *renli* so that one can bring all the *WSR* into holistic consideration—though some will contend that certain *li* are more crucial than others in individual cases (see Zhu, 1998).

Wu and *shi* to some extent parallel Checkland's distinction between designed systems and human activity systems, but there is an important difference. Checkland, as a phenomenologist, does not attempt to address the objective world (if one indeed exists); his view is that only the perceived target system can be known, although a change in the perception system may mean that a somewhat different target system may be perceived. With that important difference, the steps of Li and Li are very similar to those of the usual model of SSM. Also, the *wuli* and *shili* process resembles the double-loop of cybernetic interventions in organizations, as described in Beer (1972) or Espejo and Harnden (1989) in which an inner loop is concerned with solving the problem and the outer loop with creating the conditions in which the problem may be solved effectively. Further, they bear a resemblance to the three categories of human interests described by Habermas (1989)—namely, the technical, the practical, and the emancipatory.

In many ways, however, the acceptance of many *lis* being able to address the mega-issues of a mega-country like China is the key to successful cross-cultural learning for the Westerner entering China (cf. population studies embracing 1.3 billion persons). Even so, when management gurus such as Prahalad "tell" the Chinese managers they should forget history and do as Americans do—venture as though there were no historical encumbrance—these gurus forget the innate sense of history sensed as a living force, which is totally realistic for most Chinese, and it is that which makes them hesitate (see Prahalad, 1998).

We must admit that Prahalad has made an interesting point: that most Western managers come from a data-rich environment, and if they have passed through a formal business education program, they will have been instructed in data modeling. In contrast, the Orient is data-poor, as often respective governments either did not collect national or sector statistics or did so in such a loose way as to collect a mass of meaningless data (cf. the tonnage of good quality iron produced in China during the Cultural Revolution). Even today official data throughout the region has to be carefully scrutinized. If there is a lack of quality data, formal analytic methods will not generate statistically valid models; indeed, many models will not be computable due to a lack of data (Haley and Tan, 1996). They emphasize that Asian managers will tend to look to their networks for personal, subjective data and that the senior managers will busy themselves much more and more deeply in the minutiae of their organizations than will an Occidental manager who may rely more on data analyses. Li and Zheng (1993) also state that many Chinese managers, even if well educated, will put aside their foreign books on management and rely on intuition and experience based on their personal wishes and values. This apparently yields characteristic random decision making. They suggest there is a huge problem in helping such managers select the best theoretical approach to their problems since there are few applicable models to help Chinese managers generate practical approaches to management in China. Implicitly, perhaps overdrawing the argument of Li and Zheng, we may infer that there is no room in China for the Western manager who does not network well, who does not work with *guanxi*, and who wishes to work with analytical models.

Summary 1

The two process models illustrated earlier show different approaches to the assessment of business scenarios. While we recognize that myriad methods are available to assess uncertainty, to address the place of the individual in a process that may not be working well, and so on, the Chinese method (widespread throughout the Orient) is based on a Confucian system that emphasizes the primacy of societal harmony demanding an observation of laws, which in turn emphasize the rule by the top of the organization, even the state, and thus a subjugation of the needs of an individual (as understood by a Westerner). In contrast, the Western view emphasizes civil and political rights and thus the role of the individual, following, for instance, Jean-Jacques Rousseau's *The Social Contract* written in 1762, and the development of Bills of Rights in the constitutions of France and the United States.

Ostensibly the two systemic models do the same thing–and they have the same aims: namely, to improve a situation but through different processes. Thus, if there are two strong managers working side by side, one from the Occident and the other from the Orient, they will end up with a different modus operandi for their solutions. The models that offer solutions, and the failure to progress toward these solutions by each manager, may not be disguised as stemming from errors in language translation; so these well-held beliefs in their models may develop into unreconcilable conflict.

THEORIES OF INDIVIDUALS

Sociometrics

One set of descriptors that has stood the test of time is due to Hofstede (1980, 1991). He ''measured'' culture on five indices derived from data on 100,000 individuals spanning 50 countries. His studies have been replicated more or less by others: see, for instance, Trompenaars (1993). Smith (1996) notes that the Hofstede indices have been confirmed by other large-scale surveys, for instance, Smith and Peterson (1994), Yang (1988), and Smith and Bond (1993). Partial replications have been undertaken by Hoppe (1993) and McGrath et al. (1992) on businesspersons and by Merritt (1998) on airline pilots. Generally in this chapter, we are contrasting the Occidental to the Oriental. As an illustration, we offer subjective thumbnail sketches based on the works of Hofstede (1980, 1991), Hall (1976), and Hoppe (1993); see Table 8.1. Furthermore, as these studies were derived from the perceptions of individuals as to their relationships to their organizational life, we may consider that the indices of Hofstede and others indicate how individuals make an organization what it is and operate how it does. In some ways, the indices describe organizational behavior and how these behaviors differ across nations and cultures.

Thus to recapitulate within these contrasts—

- Organizations in the ''family'' cluster (Hoppe), as in China, Japan, or Korea, tend toward top-down management (high Power Distance Index–Hofstede), and so juniors do not take responsibility for their decisions. There is much involvement in ''face giving and saving'' (low(ish) Masculinity Index–Hofstede), inclining one to be considerate of others: yet they will accept 'rule by law', allowing the head of the firm, or the state, to define behavior. They are High Context (HC) persons, always networking

Table 8.1
Comments on Country Index Values

<table>
<tr><th rowspan="2">Description by Hoppe</th><th rowspan="2">Indicative Country</th><th colspan="5">Indices of Hofstede</th><th colspan="2">and Hall</th></tr>
<tr><th>PDI</th><th>UAI</th><th>IDV</th><th>MAS</th><th>CD</th><th>H / L</th><th>M /P</th></tr>
<tr><td>Family</td><td>China</td><td>80</td><td>60</td><td>20</td><td>50</td><td>100</td><td>HC</td><td>P</td></tr>
<tr><td colspan="2">Business implications</td><td colspan="7">Organizations in this cluster tend toward top-down management (high PDI). Juniors do not take responsibility for their decisions (high CD). There is much involvement in "face giving and saving" (low(ish) MAS), inclining one to be considerate of others. They are HC in a guanxi sense, and polychronic.</td></tr>
<tr><td>Pyramidal</td><td>Japan</td><td>54</td><td>92</td><td>46</td><td>95</td><td>80</td><td>HC</td><td>P</td></tr>
<tr><td colspan="2">Business implications</td><td colspan="7">The moderate PDI allows seniors to be the leaders but the high UAI and moderate level of individuality indicates group cohesion. The high MAS inclines toward institutions as a "home" rather not the natural family. They are HC (much verbalization within their peer group) and polychronic.</td></tr>
<tr><td>Pyramidal</td><td>Korea</td><td>60</td><td>85</td><td>18</td><td>39</td><td>75</td><td>HC</td><td>P/M</td></tr>
<tr><td colspan="2">Business implications</td><td colspan="7">CEO is recognized as the "authority" (strong PDI). With high UAI and low IDV the population accepts all rules. In contrast, the low MAS supports a conflicted-fawning attitude to manage their long-term HC view of life; they are mixed mono/polychronic.</td></tr>
<tr><td rowspan="2">Village</td><td>UK</td><td>35</td><td>35</td><td>89</td><td>66</td><td>25</td><td>LC</td><td>M</td></tr>
<tr><td>US</td><td>40</td><td>46</td><td>91</td><td>62</td><td>29</td><td>LC</td><td>M</td></tr>
<tr><td colspan="2">Business implications</td><td colspan="7">Both the U.K. and U.S. data have been presented as they are so similar. They do not care for hierarchy and are also very accepting of structural uncertainty while being highly individualistic, moderately materialistic, and short-term. They are LC and monochronic. All in all we find their organization may be loosely structured and personal learning fragmentary, focused on "now" and "me."</td></tr>
</table>

Note: Summary descriptions of the Hofstede Indices, and the work of Hall and Hoppe are in the Notes.
Source: Based on Hofstede, Hall, and Hoppe.

(Hall), using *guanxi* [see later], and polychronic (Hall) in the sense that they treat time as having parallel streams and so may seem illogical in decision making.

- The members of the organizations in the ''village market'' cluster (Hoppe), as in the United States or the United Kingdom, do not care for hierarchy (low Power Distance Index). They are also very accepting of structural uncertainty while being highly individualistic, moderately materialistic, and short-term. They are Low Context (LC) and monochronic (Hall) following time paths and models faithfully. Their organization may be loosely structured and personal learning fragmentary, focused on ''now'' and ''me''; individuals do not network extensively and stick to their schedules; and they rely on the ''rule of the law'' to solve disputes.

These summaries are brief, but they indicate underlying differences due to the cultural predisposition of persons from the indicated countries. They show that attitudes, sociometrics, and behaviors are quite different and thus that JV firms may suffer greatly if their cultural fit is widely divergent, with staff who are disinclined to change or do not accept the differences. This will inhibit development of stronger relationships.

Chinese Interpersonal Relationships

In Chinese society, the exchanges of favor involving *guanxi* are not strictly commercial; they are also social involving *renqing* (social or humanized obligation) and the giving of *mianzi* (the notion of face) in society (see Lou, 1997). But more recently, as China opens up, *guanxi* has become known as social capital, which taking a Western view is used to "tidy" commercial contracts between corporations, so leading the Westerner toward an overreliance on gift giving and banqueting in China as a means of conducting business. The latter activities are both normal facets of Chinese *guanxi*, but many Western firms operations go too far and operate too close to bribery. Western individuals can become known as "meat and wine friends" defeating the object of true *guanxi*–which is the offering of favors during the development of a personal relationship, naturally promoting business in China, between the Chinese.

Guanxi is given to strengthen personal relationships and so may be called back in later times. Thus, the development of long-term relationships is the normal expectation of the Chinese and in general in the Orient: it is what interlinks managers personally in their business networks (not via legal contracts as in the West). Individuals give *guanxi*, increasing *renqing* and in difficult times allowing a defaulter to survive while maintaining *mianzi*. Thus, the Chinese, even if they are quick to take advantage of a business opportunity, will allow space for the vanquished to maintain his or her face—for "to become faceless" affects all the relationships in a family, making their *guanxi* continuance problematical. In brief, there are five main aspects to *guanxi* (see Table 8.2).

The outsider observer can easily become confused insofar as the Chinese appear to passively follow rules in a family situation and denigrate their individuality, while in relationships outside the family they may be very active in initiating *guanxi* exchanges. Even for the Chinese such interweaving can become complex to maintain and nurture. It is clear, however, that the Western notion of networking, or dealing with people, is far removed from the Chinese *guanxi*, and when Westerners copy *guanxi* they do so badly.

Interactions between Sociometrics and Business Attitudes

Culture and Accounting

It is pertinent to note the global pressure to have organizations conform to GAAP (Generally Accepted Accounting Principles). This was driven first by U.S. accountants looking for easier-to-apply rules yielding greater transparency,

Table 8.2
The Meanings of *Guanxi*

Transferable	If A has *guanxi* and knows B who knows C, then B can introduce A to C. Without such an introduction A cannot deal with C.
Reciprocal	A person who does not return a favor loses *mianzi*. In unequal exchanges the weaker person may later request a far greater favor than his or her rank would normally command.
Intangible	The persons sharing *guanxi* exchanges do so in silent ways using unwritten codes. Disregarding long-term commitment will lead to grave loss of face.
Utilitarian	. . . rather then emotional. Exchanges are expected to be of favors and essentially are bonds, but they need not be between friends. When no longer profitable for both parties, mutual exchanges can easily be broken by accord.
Personal	Organizations do not have a group identity—it is the *guanxi* between individuals that bind firms. However, in modern firms there is much more pressure to reward people for their *guanxi* operations—so the personal element is transforming to an organizational form, which promotes "value added," even in *guanxi*.

Source: Lou (1997).

which in turn, would promote clearer comparability across firms in different states in the United States or even between firms located in different countries. Accounting regulators in many countries have agreed that their national methods would incorporate GAAP. During the summer of 1997, China publicly agreed to adhere to GAAP, as the Japanese do already, but the Chinese authorities said they would do it their way.

It is prudent to think about the meaning of "generally acceptable" as it may apply in Asian countries since it has been shown that accounting disclosure, at least historically, is strongly correlated with cultural measures (cf. with those measures of Hofstede) and that Oriental cultures are biased toward secrecy (non-transparency). See Gray (1988), Gray and Radebaugh (1993), Gray (1996), Gray and Vint (1995), Salter and Niswander (1995), and Zarzeski (1996). Thus, one may now ask whether different regularity practices and the more open financial markets in these regions will force firms to be more transparent (in a GAAP sense). In fairness, we should note that opaqueness is not a unique East/West issue since the Channel Islands, Belgium, Spain, and Switzerland all practice low levels of financial disclosure (see Gray, 1996).

Research on the Oriental concept of probability and risk has shown that Asian persons may be "fate-oriented" and less willing to take a probabilistic view of the world (see Phillips and Wright, 1977). This might suggest that sophisticated accounting is not needed in Asia since "what will be—will be," and ultimately no subtle provisioning will hide poor performance. On the other hand, the Asian collective spirit will carry an ailing firm without loss of face. This is often noted when discussing the profit of a firm. Most Japanese CFOs have stated at some time that the profit of a subsidiary can be calculated based on the bottom line; thus we understand the need to protect it. In contrast, in the West, the rules and clarity of accounting might well report a technical failure, and the firm will be forced to liquidate, notwithstanding any mitigating circumstances. The lack of disclosure in Asian accounting and the degree to which management accounting is not undertaken in Asia are seen as quite deep research issues by Western academic accountants–even to the extent that some question whether accounting practice might indeed change Asian culture (see Baydoun et al., 1997: 422).

Bribery

As noted earlier, the Asians deploy opaque accounting practices, and they also practice gift giving on a scale that to an American seems nothing short of bribery. We have noted briefly the universal practice of *guanxi* in China. (*Note*: the same word and social process are endemic in Japan.) We should also note the darker, and also widespread, practice of bribery which has come under considerable public scrutiny in recent years in China and elsewhere. Even leaders of Third World countries seem to have diverted, for their own purposes, international aid funds originating in the developed nations (such as those from the International Monetary Fund [IMF]). This was almost with the explicit consent of the donors as formerly they have ''looked the other way'' and not insisted on clear accounting for the cash flows. Now, with the pressure brought to bear by the OECD, by several national leaders, and by the CEOs of major multinationals, there is a conspicuous movement against the use of bribery.

The World Bank and the IMF are now ready to ''be whistle blowers'' when they detect funding diversions, and other organizations now more publicly claim that they resist bribery. Since 1977, the the United States has had laws that criminalize commercial payoffs to public servants abroad by their national personnel. The Royal Dutch/Shell Group in its April 1998 annual report said that it fired 23 of its workers on ethical grounds and terminated contracts with 95 firms, also on ethical grounds (see Walsh, 1998). Japan has been paralyzed for years in being unable to disentangle its opaque systems resting on bribery and extortion. Similarly, China has a strong history of *guandao*, or official corruption, which, according to Walsh, is more pervasive than it is in Japan. President Jaing Zemin declared war on this ''evil'' when it became obvious that a $2.2 billion scandal had involved Chen Xitong who was a former party chief and Politburo member, and his deputy Wang Baosen (who committed suicide). Altogether some 500,000 persons in China in recent years have been reprimanded or punished for taking kickbacks, but the use of extortion is still rife in China (see Walsh, 1998).

Thus we have to suppose that the following ruling of the OECD will prevail:

In 1994, the OECD Council adopted the ''Recommendation on Bribery of Foreign Public Officials in International Business Transactions'' which calls on Member countries to act to combat illicit payments in international trade and investment. As part of that Recommendation, reference was made to the need "to take concrete and meaningful steps including examining tax legislation, regulations, and practices insofar as they may indirectly favour bribery": C(94)75. Following this, the OECD's Committee on Fiscal Affairs undertook an in-depth review of tax measures which may influence the willingness to make or accept bribes. The Committee concluded that bribes paid to foreign public officials should no longer be deductible for tax purposes, which will require many Member countries to change their current practices. [The Recommendation was adopted by the Council of the OECD on 11 April 1996.]

In a very public fashion, Transparency International (see http://www.tranparency.de) supports the OECD ruling through the publication of a Corruption Perception Index on the World Wide Web. Eighty-five countries are on their 1998 list, with the ideal least-corruptible having a score of 10. Only nine countries score above 9.0—namely, Denmark (1st with 10.0), Finland (9.6), Sweden (9.5), New Zealand (9.4), Iceland (9.3), Canada (9.2), Singapore (9.1), and with a score of 9.0, there are The Netherlands and Norway. The United Kingdom is 13th with 8.7, the United States 18th with 7.5, Japan 25th with 5.8, Taiwan 31st with 5.3, South Korea 43rd with 4.2, and China 52nd with 3.5—the bottom is Cameroon 85th with 1.4. They emphasize that estimating is a subjective art and that their rankings depend on many factors (openly discussed in their Web pages). Thus China may not be the 52nd next year. They also say that in *all* countries bribery is officially not acceptable and often is a criminal offense—yet it takes place: hence the ranks and absolute scores.

Summary 2

The sociometric indices due to Hall, Hoppe, and Hofstede (plus their replications over time) show how well they discriminate between cultures and, by extension, between individuals of different cultures. The indices predict quite different behaviormodes, with different ways of handling personal interactions that may offend the other. Naturally there is "clannish behavior," but that is usual in all societies. No, it is more gross, with the Oriental operating an impenetrable insider/outsider regime. This extends to holding very different views on ethical behavior, to honesty, and to openness in business and private life. The author has frequently heard expressions such as "I am honest in my way" (being offered, not as an excuse, just as a fact); or "We are never quite sure how we interact except on money matters—here the Chinese keep all cash flow data to themselves so our parent company knows little about the current worth of the 'joint' venture."

Similar differences are seen in the exchange of favors with the Occidental generally discharging a debt through one episode, whereas the Oriental will maintain a debt-list for life so as to give and receive honor in the correct way (once more governed by *li*, observing the laws pertaining to behavior). Their way of life is more than etiquette; it is inbuilt and different.

THEORIES OF ORGANIZATIONAL LEARNING

Earlier we noted several factors that differentiate the Eastern from the Western person: these differences will also affect their management style—individualistic in the Occident and more socially cohesive in the Orient. We wish to present some theories of Organizational Learning (OL) that also appear to be culturally biased, but first let us note that some have described Organizational Learning as an oxymoron, saying that *only* people can learn and an organization cannot: (see Weike and Westley, 1996). Easterby-Smith (1997) notes the recent growth in the volume of the literature on OL. Importantly, he argues that the learning organization is but one area of study in OL which may be studied within a wide spectrum of disciplines—psychology and organizational design, management science, strategy, production management, sociology, and cultural anthropology. He proposes that there is, as yet, no comprehensive theory of OL.

Huber (1991), whom Easterby-Smith classifies as analytic within the management science discipline, has identified several aspects of OL. When some unit of an organization acquires new knowledge, it is a sign of the existence of learning, but as long as the knowledge rests inside the unit, there is no chance of organizational learning. Furthermore, when other units interpret this information from their own perspectives, the data are elaborated and amended into more thorough know-how. This is akin to the organization learning by its development of cases and exceptions, even moving close to a Case-based Reasoning approach. Huber suggests the key points in designing interaction patterns for OL:

- To encourage individual units to acquire new knowledge
- To make each unit distribute its own knowledge to others
- To interpret it for each other
- To make a database for organizational usage

Similar evidence has been found in studying cultural differences in ''learning to learn'' about the implementation process (see Kidd and Kanda, 1997). Here the research questions were simple: given the CEOs in either the United Kingdom or Japanese firms have expressed an idea, how do their junior managers enact this idea? Do the United Kingdom and the Japanese undermanagers undertake implementation differently? The research was conducted in firms in the United Kingdom and in Japan; they were not joint ventures. The answer was emphatically ''yes, they do undertake implementation differently,'' but curiously with a pattern of social interaction that is almost complementary—a form of United Kingdom–Japanese management (*Lego*). But it is a form of management style, which if not subject to carefully decoding one culture to another, will result in each side saying of the other, ''I would not have done it that way,'' even though the individuals were assumed to be encouraged to collect information in order to learn. Thus, if they were working in a joint venture, their incomprehension might result in a breakup of the firm.

Huber presents a simple approach to learning, whereas others present a more complex model embedded in a form of action research (see Senge, 1990, or earlier, Eden et al., 1983); or in "theories-in-use" (see Agryris and Schon 1978). Later Argyris (1993) presented the "double loop" learning approach whereby individuals are said to learn first from the observation of others and then to talk over their models with colleagues and thus come to some greater "learning and understanding" and so set themselves up for another cycle of development. Indeed, this is also posed by Nonaka (1994), Nonaka and Takeuchi (1995), and Nonaka and Konno (1998). Checkland treats this process differently, but in many ways the approaches are similar: one has to "get into the mind of the other" in order to communicate meaning adroitly.

In Nonaka's thesis, organizational data will be dynamic, and its interpretation will change with the individual's learning. Further, the data collected may alter over time to reflect new needs. However, it is necessary to access certain initial data in order to commence the broader development process. Yet it must be remembered that stored data representing knowledge does not describe perfection—only a currently well-held belief in a theory-in-use. If the bureaucratic strength of the managers is over-heavy, the data set may not be allowed to change. Consequently, free-thinkers in the organization will be inhibited from developing the data or be fearful of making mistakes and so learning will be inhibited (see Schein, 1993).

Nonaka and his co-researchers describe tacit knowledge as having two dimensions. First is the technical—the know-how. The second dimension is the cognitive, comprising the beliefs and mental models we all develop and carry over the years whose schema are hard to change as we often take them for granted. Their SECI model is presented diagrammatically as Figure 8.3. It has four quadrants:

1. Socialization: This is the sharing of knowledge between two persons—here put as a philosophical concept of pure experience, which is related to Zen learning. It is developed by being together and by sharing experience over time, not through written or verbal exchanges. We have to allow ourselves to empathize with others and not just sympathize. So we become larger through self-transcendence.
2. Externalization: This requires the expression of tacit knowledge through metaphor, analogies, or narratives. By so doing, the individual can become integrated with the group's mental world. But this process may also call for deductive, inductive reasoning or creative inferences in order to make the sharing of knowledge clear and transparent.
3. Combination: Here the key processes are communication and diffusion involving (a) collecting externalized new explicit knowledge, (b) the dissemination of this knowledge by meetings for instance, and (c) the editing of new material to make it more usable.

Figure 8.3
The Dynamic Learning Model (the SECI model)

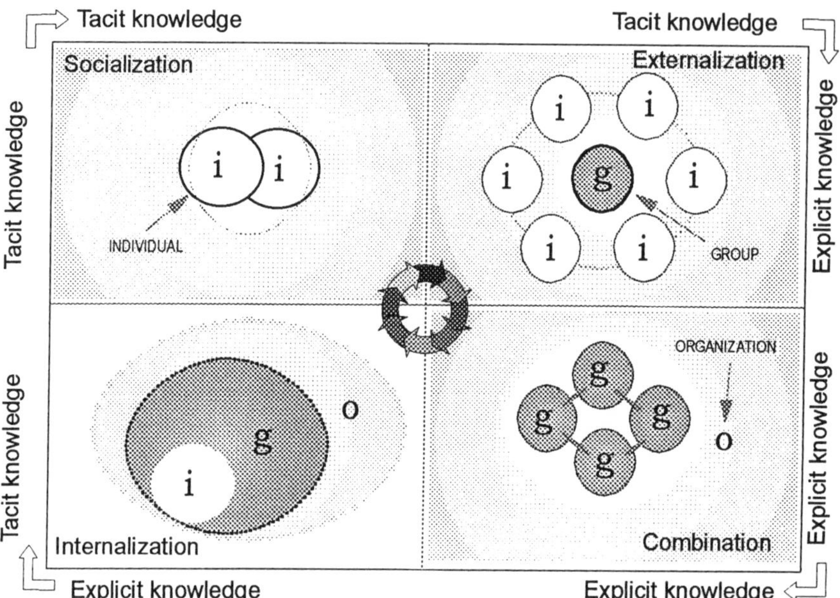

Source: Nonaka and Konno (1998). Reprinted with permission.

4. Internalization: This is the conversion of explicit knowledge to the organization's tacit knowledge by identifying the knowledge needed by one's self for working in the organization, by (a) being involved in training programs, and (b) engaging in simulations of learning-by-doing to trigger the learning process.

Summary 3

Again we see obvious differences between the Occidental and the Oriental: building upon the earlier differences, we consider that the knowledge management process constructed by following Huber's model suits the short-term, low-context nonnetworking Occidental. A much slower, deeply committed workforce, as in traditional Japan, fits Nonaka's model well. Here there is time to learn in an apprenticeship (there is also a feeling that such a slow process of learning is also "good for the soul"), and later the successive processes also take a long time to enact. Each model clashes with the other, and one wonders how a modern, virtual organization might learn to work together even if from very different cultural backgrounds.

We see an outcome with respect to knowledge management in the Orient which is predicated on acceptance of the rule by the law, acknowledgment of patronage (through the *guanxi* processes), and a sense of family in which they are insiders. The strong belief in Western individuality clashes with all these themes, thereby creating very different stances—us against them; one group inscrutable; the other too talkative and open.

DISCUSSION

Inevitably that during the development and early years of an organization there will be changes, and these will be frequent. There will be many disturbing aspects in enjoining the attitudes and working-day inclinations of people from different cultures. Some of these will affect the daily lives of people at all levels of the organization, especially with respect to control, financial planning, and probity. Nevertheless, if the firm is to prosper, the members must learn how to exchange knowledge. Earlier we saw how individuals differ greatly in their networking, ethics, and propensity to pull together. Huber suggests it is sufficient to collect and collate data, and once this data is made accessible to all in the organization "it" can be said to be learning. However, this seems to us to be a fairly simplistic approach, though one suited to a group of persons, as described by various sociometric indices, to be short term and individualistic.

Nonaka and Konno (1998) advocate the study of the Japanese concept of *ba*, which they say translates to the English word "place." It can be thought of as a "shared space for emerging relationships." This space can be physical such an office, it can be virtual as with e-mail or teleconferencing, mental as with sharing ideas or expressions, or any combination of these. They stress that the differentiation between *ba* and ordinary interventions is the concept of knowledge creation—it is *ba* that provides the platform. They are saying that *ba* offers a transcendental perspective that integrates all needed information, and there is a recognition of self in all this. So, following existential theory, *ba* is a context that harbors meaning. It follows, they say, that *ba* is a shared space that serves as a foundation for knowledge creation.

If knowledge is separated from *ba*, it turns into information that can be transmitted independently from *ba*. Information resides in media and networks, and it is tangible; but knowledge resides in *ba*, which is intangible. *Ba* is the world where the individual realizes himself as part of the environment on which life depends. More realistically, *ba* is grounded in sharing, so individuals in knowledge-creating firms can have *ba*. Furthermore, this *ba* will unite teams, informal groups, and even organizations. The self is embraced by the collective when an individual enters the *ba* of teams; later on, the organization is the *ba* for these teams, and the market environment is the *ba* for the organization.

It may be seen that the concepts of *ba* are quite close to those of WSR (*wuli, shili*, and *renli*); they emphasize the wholeness of the perspectives perceived in the study of the issues in a firm. In contrast, much of Western management literature emphasizes reductionism and particularization—a search for the *one* truth. Vertinsky et al. (1975) has provided a checklist for organization, to break this singular approach and allow individuals in the firm to be better placed to develop a learning framework. Vertinsky says individuals have to

- have a longer-term perspective;
- abandon personal experience as a primary basis for decision making;
- abandon interpersonal competition in the firm; and
- accept the scientific paradigm.

Here there are two Oriental aspects (longer-termism, lack of interpersonal competition) and two Occidental aspects (scientific decision making and the scientific paradigm). What is possibly unusual in this approach is the strong sense of *ba* in the checklist: the long-term perspective and the consensual approach which indicate that maybe, just maybe, there can be a move away from acceptance of the positivist view of the world to one where alternative methods are debated, and that simple cognitive models may be replaced by holistic thinking. Indeed, this plea is expressed by Hampden-Turner and Trompenaars (1997).

CONCLUSION

We have described several themes indicating how individuals in global organizations might find some difficulty in understanding what their Oriental and Occidental partners are saying, or meaning, or how they are trying to progress toward a goal and naturally several aspects interact as one attempts to merge norms or values to better manage knowledge. At least the MNE must be viewed as a differentiated company loosely pulling toward some form of comprehensive goal using a myriad of methods and techniques appropriate to the host site of each of its branches. Yet these have to be understood by the head office. Such an idea is expressed strongly by Nohria and Ghoshal (1997). Yet, with the same strong insistence on networking, Min Chen (1995) expresses the way of the Asian business somewhat differently. As a baseline, the managers in the head office must be willing to accept data, facts, and suggestions evolving from paradigms diverging widely from their own in order that the MNE will progress along a viable trend.

If we follow the direction of Nonaka et al., and if the managers of the firm give appropriate support to knowledge acquisition, retention, and exchange, its individual members may be persuaded to accept long-term employment in the firm and so grow with the firm. On the other hand, in the currently fashionable virtual organization model, we see a need to have flexible employment arrangements. Here the slow learning pace of individuals will be difficult to accommodate since learning implies an exchange of knowledge; that in turn implies either open management or being on the inside. Even so, in the virtual organization, there is the need to provide space and mechanisms for growth, learning, and knowledge sharing. Yet the research thrusts remain—we have to ascertain how the various major theories, perhaps fads, link to generate a viable business, or indeed how the "little" and more personal drivers such as the relationships between trust, agency theory, and sociometrics lead to new business paradigms helping to create a new BPR, OL, or KM theory. In practice, we have to guard against a too hasty judgment of "the other" when we do not in fact understand the other's background and ethical drivers.

Perhaps the real key to success in the MNEs will be through development of a deeper awareness of each member of the other, so that the individual persons in the firm will learn how to be supportive of the other even when the other seems to be clumsy and to be missing the point.

NOTES

Hofstede

There are very few measures of culture; indeed, the definition is also elusive: "culture is the collective programming of the mind which distinguishes the members of one human group from another" (see Hofstede, 1980). From his extensive data he derived a set of indices that may be summarized as follows.

- *Power Distance (PDI)*: Some societies like hierarchies, and others wish all to be as equal as possible. There is also an aspect of interpersonal independence in this measure, in which a tall hierarchy will be said to maintain a high PD index.
- *Uncertainty Avoidance (UAI)*: Some societies prefer few rules, less stable careers, less fixed patterns of life (i.e., more uncertainty and risk than others would like).
- *Individualism (IND)*: Some societies like to see individuals express themselves, while others wish for collectivism, having close relationships that even extend to permitting the firm to look after one and in return expect one's loyalty.
- *Masculinity (MAS)*: The more "masculine" a society, the more it values assertiveness and materialism. It cares less for the quality of life or concern about other people (i.e., the more caring or "feminine" aspects).
- *Confucianism (CD)*: This dimension relates to the long- or short-termism of the society. A long-term person can be thought of as being persistent and thrifty, ordering relationships by status and looking to maintain this order.

Hall

Time Frames

If we note the argument that "it is not cultures which collide—but people," we find that Hall (1976: 17) maintains that the most natural time frame of all humans is that which is in accord with nature: according to the rise and fall of the sun, and according to weather patterns. He suggests that the industrial revolution, initially in England, is to blame for the development of monochronic persons. Thus, the linear time person, the monochronic (M-time) person, is in fact trained to be so, while the polychronic, P-time person has a more natural lifestyle.

Hall suggests that the majority of managers and workforce in the European/North American regions, working in M-time, are grounded in this heredity and tradition, which creates psychological tensions since their working mode is not in accord with their body clocks, or of those clocks with whom they may work—if they are from a different culture, working in P-time. We should note that the monochronic person emphasizes schedules, segmentation of activities, and promptness: M-time is almost "real." It is said that "time may be wasted/lost/saved" as though it were a real commodity. The M-person will compartmentalize his/her life, accepting that schedules are "sacred and unalterable" so that they yield to an ordered lifestyle with clear priorities.

Polychronic persons are rather different. They are characterized by being at the center of many simultaneous events and by a great involvement with people. They focus strongly on the completion of human transactions regardless of any ongoing schedules (such as they are). P-time is *experienced* as being much less tangible than M-time: in this sense it can't be lost. The P-person can jump from one point to another in a seemingly random way, rather than accepting the notion that time is understood to be a road along which the person travels without deviation.

Contexts

Hall (1976: 83) discusses the nature of *context*. He suggests that one function of culture is to provide a selective screen between people and the outside world. This screen protects the nervous system from information overload, which when transgressed can lead to many disorders ranging from cognitive dissonance to full mental breakdowns. People handle some of these overloads by delegation, whereas organizations employ other methods, increasing the mass and complexity of the system and hopefully the reactivity of the organization. Ashby (1958) in his Law of Requisite Variety ruled that "only variety can overcome complexity—so more complex systems need more complex solutions to remain viable." This is carried forward into modern systems thinking; see Beer (1972), and Espejo and Harnden (1989). These concepts lead to an acceptance of the idea that individuals obtain their formative learning from their home, from their school(s), and from their work. They have constructed their own model of the world, which, in Soft Systems Modeling is called their W: that is, their Weltanschauung or World View.

LC persons will often need a full briefing from their support team, demanding contextual information from them. Therefore, much time passes before making a decision, but HC persons can make decisions personally and rapidly since they are networked and well briefed. Difficult interactions arise: HC persons are impatient if given lots of information by LC persons. In turn, LC persons are at a loss when not told anything by the HC person. Thus, the hesitation of the LC person when out of context can be seen as obstructionist by an HC person.

We can also see subtle shifts carried by the coded messages between two persons: if one person gives too much information, more than is required by the recipient, it may be seen as a form of status maintenance or as a reprimand.

The HC/LC mix creates further issues; consider the advisors to a CEO. They are "gatekeepers" since they not only filter information but do so according to their personal model, though this may conform neither to the CEO's model the vision of the organization, nor the model of the supplicant attempting to make a case to the CEO. Furthermore, a low-context CEO sees only the LC persons relevant to his or her day's work, all of whom must be on the appointment schedule.

In order to cope with complexity, or working in a different world, Hall suggests one resolution is to pre-program individuals through "contexting," to cope with events that are usually more complex than the language used to describe them. In other words, rather like an actor, a person should learn to recognize a complex, yet novel, situation and thus have internalized methods to cope with this complexity. Discussing with a mentor would be an example of how one might learn to deal with context overload. Indeed, this was done explicitly in Japanese firms that supported lifetime employment principles. This is the *sempai-kohai* approach whereby a superior holds the responsibility for a junior staff member and so can develop that junior over a period of years as each progresses upward in the firm.

Hoppe

The Hoppe data derive from studies of executives rather than the general worker class that Hofstede used and so may more readily link to the discussions in this chapter. The McGrath study relates to entrepreneurs and found that the "usual" indicators of the entrepreneur were magnified when cultural differences were taken into account. Thus, we understand that the international entrepreneur has to be somewhat larger than life. However, in firms that are entering a period of stability, it is natural that they should look to less flamboyant characters. But this is to deny the forces of change which demand that the firm, if globalizing, should be searching for excellence, novel ideas, and so forth, and thus be in continuous flux. In other words, there is a natural barrier between the staid worker class which looks for stability and the outward-looking entrepreneur.

The descriptions derived from Hoppe's approach typify how organizations in different nations work: in one they work as a *family* unit where the head is old and revered, and in another as a *well-oiled machine* where many rules account for most situations and thus the more senior persons are not bothered by general queries. People from other nations prefer a logic of hierarchy, so we find that they prefer to work with a *pyramid of people* in their organization. Through the work of Hofstede, Hoppe, and others we see that attempts to merge firms with differing modes of operation may causes angst, if not actual revolt, especially if the merger is seen as a direct order from some distant owner based in a different culture.

REFERENCES

Argyris, C. (1993). *Knowledge for Action: A Guide for Overcoming Defensive Behaviors.* San Francisco: Jossey-Bass.

Argyris, C. and Schon, D. (1978) *Organizational Learning: A Theory of Action Perspective.* Reading, MA: Addison-Wesley.

Ashby, W. R. (1958). Requisite Variety and Its Implications for the Control of Complex Systems. *Cybernetica*, 1, pp. 83–96.

Baier, A. (1986). Trust and Antitrust. *Ethics*, 96(2), pp. 231–260.

Baiman, S. (1982). Agency Theory in Management Accounting: A Survey. *Journal of Accounting Literature*, pp. 154–213.

Baiman, S. (1996). Agency Theory in Managerial Accounting: A Second Look. *Accounting, Organisations and Society*, 15(4), pp. 341–371.

Baydoun, N., Nisimura, A., and Willett, R. (1997). Reflections on the Relationship between Culture and Accounting in the Asia-Pacific region. In N. Baydoun et al. (eds.), *Accounting in the Asia-Pacific Region.* New York: John Wiley, pp. 400–426.

Beer, S. (1972). *The Brain of the Firm.* London: Allen Lane.

Blois, K. (1998). The Costs and Benefits of Trust in Business to Business Relationships: A Case Based Discussion. *Working Paper Series*, no. 9809, Templeton College, Oxford University. See also Keith.Blois@templeton.oxford.ac.uk.

Brynjolfsson, E. (1994). An Incomplete Contracts Theory of Information, Technology and Organisation. *Management Science* 40(12), pp. 53–67.

Butler R., and Gill, J. (1997). *Knowledge and Trust in Partnership Formation.* Presentation to the Fourth International Conference on Multi-Organisational Partnerships and Co-operative Strategies, Oxford, July, pp. 8–10.

Checkland, P. (1981). *Systems Thinking, Systems Practice.* Chichester: John Wiley.

Checkland, P., and Holwell, S. (1998). *Information, Systems and Information Systems.* Chichester: John Wiley.

Checkland, P., and Scholes, J. (1990). *Soft Systems Methodology in Action.* Chichester: John Wiley.

Davenport, T. H., and Prusak, L.(1998). *Working Knowledge: How Organisations Manage What They Know.* Boston: Harvard Business School Press.

Doz, Y. L., and Hamel, G. (1998). *Alliance Advantage: The Art of Creating Value Through Partnering.* Boston: Harvard Business School Press.

Easterby-Smith, M. (1997). Disciplines of Organisational Learning: Contributions and Critiques. *Human Relations*, 50(9), pp. 1085–1113.

Eden, C., Jones, S., and Sims, S. (1983). *Messing about in Problems.* Oxford: Pergamon.

Espejo, R., and Harnden, R. (1989). *The Viable Systems Model.* Chichester: John Wiley.

Frank, A. G. (1998). *ReOrient: Global Economy in the Asian Age.* Berkeley: University of California Press.

Gray, S. (1988). Towards a Theory of Cultural Influence on the Development of Accounting Systems Internationally. *Abacus*, 24(11), pp. 1–15.

Gray, S., and Radebaugh, L. H. (1993). *International Accounting and Multinational Enterprises.* New York: John Wiley.

Gray, S. J. (1996). International Comparisons of Business Performance: Measurement and Disclosure Issues. *International Review of Business*, 1(1), pp. 1–15.

Gray, S. J., and Vint, H. M. (1995). The Impact of Culture on Accounting Disclosures: Some International Evidence. *Asia-Pacific Journal of Accounting*, 2, pp 33–43.

Habermas, J. (1989). *Knowledge and Human Interests*. Cambridge: Polity Press.

Haley, G. T. and Tan, C. T. (1996). The Black Hole of South East Asia: Strategic Decision Making in an Informational World. *Management Decision* 34(9), pp 37–48.

Hall, E. T. (1976). *Beyond Culture*. New York: Doubleday.

Hampden-Turner, C., and Trompenaars, F. (1997). *Mastering the Infinite Game: How East-Asian Values Are Transforming Business Practices*. Oxford: Capstone.

Hofstede, G. (1980). *Culture's Consequences: International Differences in Work-Related Values*. London: Sage Publications.

Hofstede, G. (1991). *Cultures and Organisations: Software of the Mind*. London: McGraw-Hill.

Hoppe, H. M. (1993). The Effects of National Culture on the Theory and Practice of Managing R&D Professionals Abroad. *R&D Management*, 23(4), pp. 313–325.

Huber, G. P. (1991). Organisational Learning: The Contributing Processes and the Literature. *Organizational Science*, 2(1), pp. 88–115.

Kidd, J. B. and Kanda, M. (1997). Organisational Learning in Practice: The Behaviour of Senior Production Managers in Britain and Japan. Presentation to the 14th EAMSA Conference, Asian Firms Looking Towards the Global Market, Metz, France, October 23–25, pp. 239–256.

Li Xibin, and Zheng Huaizhou. (1993). GUIFAN Management Aproach—A New Branch of Management Science. *Modernisation of Management*, pp. 1–5.

Li Ya, and Li Xibin. (1998). *The Shili Process Theory and the Evolution of Systems Methodology*. In Proceedings of the 3rd International Conference [ICSSE '98], Gu Jifa (ed.), Systems Science and Systems Engineering, Beijing, China, August. Beijing: Kedya Press, pp. 318–322.

Lou, Y. (1997). Guanxi: Principles, Philosophies and Implications. *Human Systems Management*, 9, pp. 1–9.

McGrath, R. G, MacMillan, I. C., and Scheinberg, S. (1992). Elitists, Risk-Takers, and Rugged Individualists? An Exploratory Analysis of cultural Differences between Entrepreneurs and Non-entrepreneurs. *Journal of Business Venturing*, 17, pp. 117–135.

Merritt, A. C. (1998). *Replicating Hofstede: A Study of Pilots in Eighteen Countries*. http://www.psy.utexas.edu/helmreich/hofrep.htm.

Min Chen. (1995). *Asian Management Systems: Chinese, Japanese and Korean Styles of Business*. London: Routledge.

Nohria, N., and Ghoshal, S. (1997). *The Differentiated Network*. San Francisco: Jossey-Bass.

Nonaka, I. (1994). A Dynamic Theory of Organizational Knowledge Creation. *Organizational Science*, 5(1), pp. 16–35.

Nonaka, I., and Konno, N. (1998). The Concept of ''Ba'': Building a Foundation for Knowledge Creation. *California Management Review*, 40(3), pp. 40–50.

Nonaka, I., and Takeuchi, H. (1995). *The Knowledge-Creating Company*. Oxford: Oxford University Press.

Phillips, L. D., and Wright, C. N. (1977). Cultural Differences in Viewing Uncertainty and Assessing Probabilities. In H. Jungermann and G. de Zeeuw (eds.), *Decision Making and Change in Human Affairs*. Dordrecht: D. Reidel Publishing.

Prahalad, C. K. (1998). Internationalisation, Globalisation and Chinese Firms. A presentation to the China Europe International Business School [CEIBS] Annual Conference '98, Competing in Chinese Markets. Shanghai, July 27.

Sako, M. (1994). The Informal Requirement of Trust in Supplier Relations: Evidence from Japan, the UK and the USA. Paper presented at the Workshop on Trust and Learning, Paris.

Salter, S. B., and Niswander, F. (1995). Cultural Influences on the Development of Accounting Systems Internationally. *Journal of International Business Studies*, 26(2), pp. 379–398.

Schein, E. H. (1993). *Organisational Culture and Leadership*. San Francisco: Jossey-Bass.

Senge, P. (1990). *The Fifth Discipline: The Art and Practice of the Learning Organization*. New York: Doubleday.

Smith, P. (1996). National Cultures and the Values of Organisational Employees. In P. Joynt and M. Warner (eds.), *Managing Across Cultures: Issues and Perspectives*. London: International Thompson, pp. 92–104.

Smith, P. B., and Bond, M. H. (1993). *Social Psychology across Cultures: Analyses and Perspectives*. Hemel Hempstead: Harvester-Wheatsheaf,

Smith, P. B., and Peterson, M. F. (1994). Leadership as Event Management: A Cross-Country Survey Based upon Middle Managers from 25 Countries. Presentation to a symposium at the International Congress of Applied Psychology, Madrid.

Talwar, R. K. (1994). Re-engineering—A Wonder Drug for the 90s? In C. Coulson-Thomas (ed.), *Business Process Re-engineering: Myth and Reality*. London: Kogan Page, pp. 40–59.

Trompenaars, F. (1993). *Riding the Waves of Culture: Understanding Cultural Diversity in Business*. London: The Economist Books.

Vertinsky, I., Barth, R. T., and Mitchell, V. F. (1975). *A Study of OR/MS Implementation as a Social Change Process*. In R. L. Schultz and D. P. Slevin (eds.), *Implementing Operations Research/Management Science*. New York: American Elsevier, pp. 253–270.

Walsh, J. (1998). A World War on Bribery. *Time*, June 22.

Weike, K. E., and Westley, K. (1996). Organizational Learning: Affirming an Oxymoron. In S. R., Clegg, C. Hardy, and W. R. Nord (eds.), *Handbook of Organisational Studies*. London: Sage Publications, pp. 440–458.

Yang, K. S. (1988). Will Societal Modernisation Eventually Eliminate Cross-Cultural Psychological Differences? In M. H. Bond (ed.), *The Cross-Cultural Challenge to Social Psychology*. Newbury Park, CA: Sage Publications.

Zarzeski, M. T. (1996). Spontaneous Harmonisation Effects of Culture and Market Forces on Accounting Disclosure Practices. *Accounting Horizons*, 10, March, pp. 18–37.

Zhu Zhichang. (1998). Cultural Imprints in Systems Methodologies: the WSR Case. In Proceedings of the 3rd International Conference [ICSSE '98]—Gu Jifa (ed.), Systems Science and Systems Engineering, Beijing, China, August. Beijing: Kedya Press, pp. 402–407.

Chapter 9

Reorganizing Japanese Business Groups in Times of Crisis: Sony's Bold Experiments

Yoshiya Teramoto and Caroline Benton

INTRODUCTION

Japan is in the midst of an economic crisis and has been undergoing fundamental change over the last seven to eight years as a result of a lingering recession, deregulation, intense foreign and domestic competition, and new investor attitudes. These factors are reshaping the Japanese business environment by opening up the market to new players and products/services, and by pressuring corporations to disclose and improve their financial position. To survive in this new environment, corporations are reviewing their business and corporate group management models.

Japanese corporate groups have been especially hard hit by the economic crisis, since many of their subsidiaries accumulated massive debts on speculative investments during the bubble period of the late 1980s. The authors suggest that in the new market environment, which calls for greater financial strength and greater management accountability, Japanese corporate groups must review their business and corporate group management models, and place more emphasis on intragroup networking and group synergy to create greater knowledge and value (Teramoto, 1996).

This chapter therefore attempts, first, to give a synopsis of the socioeconomic changes that are occurring; second, to present emerging types of business models for corporate groups; and third, to discuss future trends in corporate group management. An analysis of recent moves by Sony, Toyota, and Toshiba to redesign their corporate group management models is presented to elucidate these points. Although the changing environment has affected both horizontal and vertical corporate groups, this chapter focuses on trends in management of the latter type, which is represented by the industrial groups held together by complex business relationships and is epitomized by the supplier-assembler networks of major manufacturers such as Toyota (Teramoto, 1990). In contrast, horizontal corporate groups refer to the six groups built around the four largest prewar industrial groups, or *zaibatsu* (Mitsui, Mitsubishi, Sumitomo, and Fuyo), and two major banks (Dai-ichi Kangyo Bank and Sanwa Bank).

THE CHANGING BATTLEFIELD OF JAPANESE BUSINESS

Although there are other influential socioeconomic factors, four in particular are reshaping the Japanese business environment, or corporate ''battlefield.'' These are (1) the deepening recession, (2) accelerating deregulation, (3) intensifying competition in today's global economy with fading borders, and 4) changing investor attitudes. These factors, which are described individually in this chapter, are interacting in varying degrees.

Deepening Recession

During the heyday of the economic boom of the mid- to late 1980s, there was little need for Japanese corporations to make strategic change or to redesign their business or corporate group management models. Economists and business gurus lauded the Japanese business system and portrayed it as well adapted to thrive in a growth environment. Western corporations were told to emulate the Japanese way of doing business, including long-term employment, stable relationships with shareholders, and the *kanban* system of manufacturing (Seike, 1995).

With the burst of the bubble in the early 1990s, the value of corporate and individual investments in stocks and real estate fell drastically. The consequence was severe for the economy, causing a long-lasting recession (Figure 9.1). Companies are now struggling to compete in an era of shrinking demand and to improve their weakened financial position by redeeming unconverted corporate bonds issued during the late 1980s and by selling off unnecessary investments.

All this has had a tremendous effect on corporate groups, many of which have accumulated huge losses on their subsidiaries' speculative investments in stock and real estate (Dirks and Teramoto, 1996). No longer able to rely on the old certainty that stock and real estate prices would rise, Japanese corporations and banks have become far less willing to maintain a relationship of mutual holding of stocks among group companies. The volatile state of the stock market has also driven off most substantial domestic purchasers. This situation is painful for Japanese companies and is opening up corporate groups to foreign and Japanese companies outside the traditional group network. Recently, it was announced that during the first quarter of 1999, foreign investors accounted for over 40 percent of trading on the Tokyo Stock Exchange.

Figure 9.1
Trends in Japanese GDP

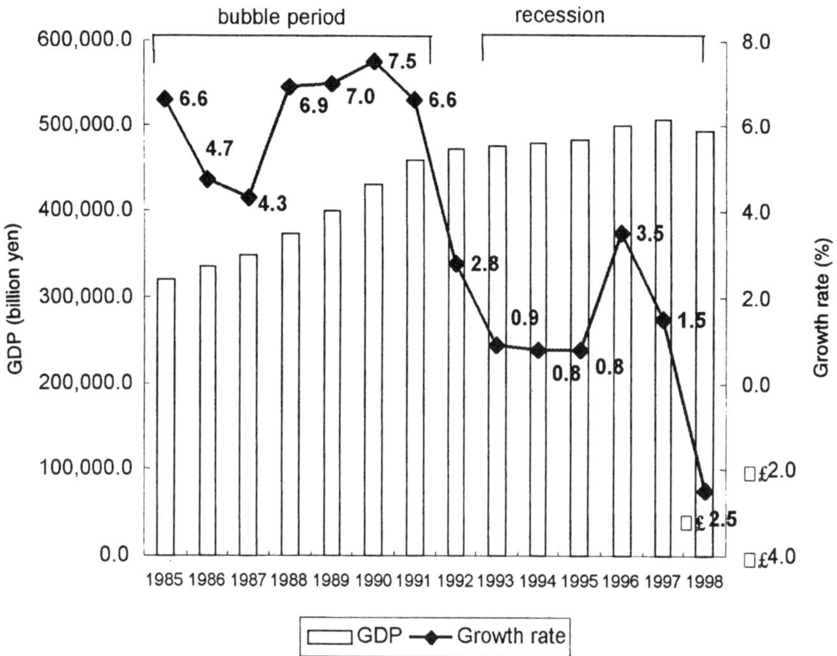

Source: Economic Planning Agency.

Accelerating Deregulation

In order to jump start the economy out of its present downward spiral of recession and deflation and to revitalize the stock market (and also as a result of intense international pressure), the Japanese government has been proposing and implementing relaxation of restrictions over the last several years. The government hopes that the ensuing competition of the ''freer'' market will force Japanese companies to review their old and no longer viable business models, leading to an increase in their productivity and competitiveness.

Deregulation of Pure Holding Companies

Among the proposed deregulatory measures, the relaxation of the antitrust law is one that will have great impact for Japanese corporate groups. After the end of World War II, ''pure holding companies'' that did not have an operational base and existed only to hold stock in other companies were prohibited under the antitrust law so that wealth/power would not be concentrated among the pre-war industrial groups (*zaibatsu*) and other large conglomerates. Recently, however, the antitrust law was revised, deregulating pure holding companies as of December 17, 1997.

This relaxation of the antitrust law will allow corporations to concentrate control and monitoring functions at corporate headquarters, while leaving the responsibility of day-to-day operations to its subsidiaries. With stronger control over group entities, a corporation can also ensure better coordination and consolidation of resources for greater group synergy. In summary, the merits of a holding company are as follows:

- Group headquarters can control, monitor, and coordinate the strategies, direction, and resources (including human resources) of group companies.
- The concentration of these functions at corporate group headquarters allows for faster and more efficient decision making and response.
- New businesses and companies can be formed more easily.
- Existing businesses and companies can be sold off more quickly

New Accounting Practices

Another measure that will affect corporate groups significantly is the change in accounting practices. In the past, corporations had to consolidate only subsidiaries in which they had over 50 percent ownership. It could choose whether or not to consolidate a subsidiary in which it had only between 20 and to 50 percent ownership.

Over the past year, changes in standards for accounting practices have been implemented to promote consolidation. Under the new standards, a corporation must consolidate any subsidiary over which it has substantial controlling power, regardless of ownership ratio (such as in the case where board members are sent to manage the affiliate) as of March 2000. Other changes in accounting practices that have been decided or are being discussed by the government are (1) valuation of stocks held for investment purposes using market price (expected to be implemented in March 2002); (2) disclosure of consolidated cash flow from March 2000; (3) disclosure of insufficient accumulation of funds to cover pension obligations, if any; and (4) consolidated taxation for corporate groups.

The most significant consequence of these proposed changes in accounting standards is greater disclosure and transparency for shareholders, which means that corporations will have to take greater responsibility for the performance of their group as a whole. Thus, there will be greater incentive for corporations to ensure that their subsidiaries are performing satisfactorily through stronger control and monitoring; those that do not will have to answer to investors and will face declining stock value.

Stock Exchange Scheme

A bill has been sent to the National Diet to introduce a corporate stock exchange scheme that will permit corporations to exchange their stocks for those of other companies in order to promote merger and acquisitions. Through this scheme, corporations will be able to privatize publicly listed subsidiaries by exchanging their own corporate stock for stock held in their subsidiaries based on an appropriate exchange ratio.

In summary, the Japanese government has been implementing regulatory changes to force domestic corporate groups to strengthen their corporate group management capabilities so that they can compete successfully in the global economy. The set of "games rules" by which corporate groups can operate in Japan has been changed, significantly affecting the way they do business.

Intensifying Competition

Deregulation and the deepening recession have fueled competition among both foreign and domestic corporations. In particular, competition in the finance, medical, telecommunications, temporary staffing, and retail industries has become fierce, with entry by new market players promoted by deregulatory measures (Table 9.1). To compete for the over 1,200 trillion yen in personal savings, domestic investment trust companies are rushing to enter the market, while domestic banks are consolidating the knowledge and expertise of their financial subsidiaries. WorldCom and British Telecommunications are also taking advantage of the newly deregulated telecommunications market to expand their business in Japan and recently became the first two foreign companies to be granted a Type 1 Telecommunication Business permit, which allows them to install their own telecommunication circuit facilities and cables.

Competition from domestic corporations from other industries is also intensifying: insurance companies has been able to enter the banking business since October 1999 (the date for allowing banks to enter the insurance business is under discussion); and since March 31, 1999, convenience stores can compete with drug stores and sell certain medical products, such as disinfectants and nutrient-filled drinks, that require less medical knowledge.

Such deregulatory measures are blurring the borders between markets and industries and leave no corporation exempt from heated competition. Corporations can no longer survive by merely following their old ways of doing business, but must self-organize and review their business and corporate group management models to consolidate resources and compete as a group. By doing so, they will be able to fully utilize their group resources and capabilities to create new knowledge and value.

Changing Investor Attitudes

Japanese corporations have been traditionally noted for seeking market share and sales growth as opposed to corporate profits and net worth. However, the slowdown in the economy has caused a significant change in investor attitudes. With stock and real estate values plummeting, investors have become more

Table 9.1
Major Deregulatory Measures Affecting Corporate Group Management

	Targeted regulations		Deregulatory measures (implemented and proposed)	Implications of deregulatory measures
1	Antitrust law	1	Revised to allow for holding companies as of Dec. 17, 1997.	Corporate groups can consolidate control and monitoring power, while delegating responsibility for operations to subsidiaries. This can lead to greater group synergy.
2	Accounting practices	1	Revised to promote consolidation of subsidiaries as of March 2000.	New practices should lead to greater disclosure and transparency for shareholders. Corporations will have to take greater responsibility over their group as a whole.
		2	Revised to consolidate subsidiaries over which a corporation has controlling power, regardless of ownership ratio as of March 2000.	
		3	Valuation of stocks for investment purposes based on market value (proposed for March 2002).	
		4	Revised for disclosure of consolidated cash flow as of March 2000.	
		5	Disclosure of insufficient accumulation of funds to cover pension obligations (under discussion).	
		6	Consolidated taxation (under discussion)	
3	Stock exchange scheme	1	Permit exchange of own stock for stock held in other companies (bill sent to Diet).	Stock exchange scheme can be used to privatize subsidiaries and will promote M&A.

sensitive to the value of their stock and are seeking greater return on investment. In particular, there has been an increase in institutional investors who are "active investors," a term made popular by Sony president Nobuyuki Idei that denotes investors who take an assertive interest in maximizing returns.

This has resulted in a shift from a business philosophy in Japan that places emphasis on employees, as was once demonstrated by the promise of long-term employment, to a more complex view that places importance on investors and other stakeholders as well as employees (*Shukan Toyo Keizai*, April 3, 1999). Japanese corporate groups must now try to maximize shareholder value by improving ROE, ROI, EVA (economic value added), and other performance measures. Even corporate investors who were once stable, long-term shareholders have begun to seek greater return on their investments and are now more reluctant to engage in mutual holding of stock among group members.

EMERGING BUSINESS MODELS

In the new environment, Japanese corporations will self-organize and move toward business models that place more importance on group networking to generate synergy and create new knowledge and value. At the same time, corporate groups will also pursue greater financial strength and shareholder value. A business model for a corporate group comprises the following two elements.

- Business strategy for the corporate group
- Corporate and group business process

The first element, business strategy, provides the direction for a corporation and its subsidiaries, including what its business will be, and when and where it will be carried out. The second element, corporate and group business process, refers to how, or the method in which, the business is to be carried out to create value, and incorporates such factors as alliances and marketing and sales activities.

Over the last decade with advances in information technology, companies have pursued business models that provide customers with both hardware and software to create greater value and profits. The most obvious examples are manufacturers of personal computers that bundle OS and application software with their hardware. There are also less obvious examples, such as automobiles sold with navigation systems (which are increasingly prominent in Japan), and cellular phones sold with e-mail and bank transaction functions.

The mere bundling of hardware and software, however, has become insufficient; product quality is no longer an adequate differentiating characteristic, and discriminating consumers are demanding sophisticated service. Japanese banks, which did not provide sophisticated financial advice, are now rushing to enter into the newly deregulated investment trust business by providing investment advice. Recent newspaper advertisements placed by major banks all stress to varying degrees that they are now financial partners and advisors for their retail customers.

SECOM, which provides security for homes and buildings, is an example of a corporation that has succeeded by offering a combination of hardware, software, and service. The hardware of course consists of the alarm, sensors, and cables that connect the corporation's customers to its control centers, while the software is the computer system that operates and runs the security system. SECOM's services include the monitoring of its alarm systems and the dispatch of emergency response personnel from local depots when an alarm or emergency is registered. Its growth has been exceptional in the recessionary economy, with a compound growth rate in sales of over 8 percent, and an even larger increase in profits, over the last several years.

SECOM's current business model focuses on utilizing its information infrastructure to the fullest extent and on strengthening its networking among its business units so that it can offer a wider range of services and create a "social system industry." For example, it now provides home medical care for the elderly, such as the dispatch of nurses and delivery of intravenous solutions, and on-line educational services for children through its security system. These services are made possible by strong networking among its different business units (SECOM Home Medical System Co. and SECOM Lines Co.) and its control centers to maximize usage of its hardware and software system.

SECOM's example shows the emergence of a business model based on networking of group companies and customers. To utilize their group resources to the fullest extent and to provide a greater range of products and services to customers, forward-thinking corporate groups are strengthening their networks and alliances. This leads to greater sales and profits and an improvement in cash flow, as sales per customer can be maximized, which results in greater operational efficiency and minimization of variable costs.

This type of business model, which is abstractly and loosely represented in the following equation, is a shift from a pursuit of increasing market share to a pursuit of increasing sales per customer through networking. The "Service (Hardware + Software)" portion of the equation connotes the use of service to bundled hardware, and software for differentiation and for continuous generation of revenues. The "Network" refers to the integration of the various services, hardware, and software to make multiple offerings to customers (Teramoto, 1996).

$$\text{Network} \iint \text{Service (Hardware + Software)}$$

In order to implement a network business successfully, a corporation must control and monitor the activities of its group companies so that coordinated synergy can be achieved. The need for such control and monitoring has catalyzed the emergence of corporate group management models that are new to Japan, such as (1) the establishment of holding companies, (2) the adoption of a system of in-house companies, and (3) the appointment of corporate officers.

Holding companies and in-house companies both allow corporations to concentrate control and monitoring activities at group headquarters, while leaving the responsibility and accountability of day-to-day operations to the management of business units. With a system of corporate officers, corporations can transfer board members to strategic business units. This will improve the management capability of these units, while reducing the number of board members to expedite top-level decision making.

PIONEERING CORPORATE GROUP MANAGEMENT: SONY'S EXPERIMENTS

Throughout its history Sony has been an innovator in a market that has been traditionally noted for companies that copy the products and services of American and European companies. Sony has been a pioneer of corporate management by being the first to introduce in-house companies in Japan and to restructure its corporate board through a system of corporate officers. In addition, Sony has gone against the traditional practice of listing subsidiaries on the stock market, with recently announced plans to privatize three publicly traded subsidiaries.

In-House Companies

In 1994, Sony reorganized its business divisions into ten in-house companies based on their different businesses. A system of in-house companies is similar to having a set of legally autonomous companies within a corporate group. It is, however, different from a system of business divisions in that in-house companies have much greater responsibility; each in-house company is allocated capital and is responsible for investments and all performance measures such as return on investments and cash flow.

From the viewpoint of the business units, the benefits of a system of in-house companies are (1) speedier operational decision making, (2) increased vitality of business units as a result of increased motivation, and (3) clear definition of responsibility and accountability. From the perspective of corporate headquarters, the system simplifies the duties of top management, leaving more time for development of overall strategy and for control/monitoring of business units; helps train the next generation of top management; and increases the efficiency of resource allocation. Accordingly, the system allows top management to focus on networking and coordination among its companies to create group synergy, leading to the creation of new value and knowledge.

In the context of organization theory, setting up a system of in-house companies is one step away from establishing a "pure" (nonoperational) holding company. With the recent relaxation of restrictions that prohibited pure holding companies and limited the total value of stock that a corporation could hold in other companies, Sony announced plans in March 1999 to further reorganize its in-house companies and subsidiaries to achieve even greater group synergy.

Restructuring of the Corporate Board

In June 1997, Sony overhauled and restructured its corporate board by reducing the number of board directors from 38 to 10, while simultaneously introducing a system of corporate officers to manage and oversee day-to-day business operations. The persons taken off the board filled most of the new corporate officer positions.

Sony established these new positions (1) to reduce the number of board members and speed up decision making and (2) to separate the responsibility of mid- to long-term strategy and policy (board members) from day-to-day management of operations (corporate officers). With the increasingly complex business environment and the growing need for networking and alliances, Sony wished to simplify its board of directors so that it could focus discussions on important policy and strategic issues that affect the group as a whole. In this manner, it hopes to better control, monitor, and coordinate its business units.

Realigning Corporate Group Architecture

On March 9, 1999, Sony announced a forward-thinking plan to ''realign and strengthen its group architecture'' to enhance shareholder value through a concept that it calls value creation management. This is defined as the creation of completely new values (i.e., new products and services) by combining elements of various businesses (Richter and Teramoto, 1995). For example, Sony's satellite business was developed through the combined expertise of its professional-use broadcasting equipment, AV equipment, and contents businesses.

The basic three pillars of the new group architecture are (1) privatizing three group companies that are listed on the Tokyo Stock Exchange; (2) strengthening its core electronic business; and (3) strengthening its group management capabilities. Its goal is to implement a ''unified dispersed'' management model that allows for consolidation of overall control and monitoring functions at group headquarters, while dispersing responsibility of day-to-day operations to each business unit. In this manner, Sony hopes to consolidate corporate group strength and produce greater synergy among business units in this ''network-centric era.''

The first pillar of the new architecture calls for turning three publicly traded companies–Sony Music Entertainment, Sony Precision Technology, and Sony Chemicals–into wholly owned subsidiaries by January 1, 2000 through a stock exchange scheme. Though this realignment, Sony's highly profitable computer game subsidiary, Sony Computer Entertainment (SCE), will also become in actuality a wholly owned subsidiary. Currently, Sony Music Entertainment and Sony both own a 49.8 percent share of SCE.

The privatization of subsidiaries goes against traditional Japanese business practice where the listing of subsidiaries on the stock market has been viewed as a sign of success. Idei, however, stated that it has been his philosophy to bring subsidiaries fully into Sony and that the board had been discussing why these companies were being publicly traded over the last several years. He also said that the privatization of these subsidiaries declares to the public that these companies are the resources of Sony and that if the corporate architecture is appropriately structured, corporate value (i.e., stock value) can be increased without privatizing peripheral businesses (*Nikkei Business*, March 22, 1999). In other words, Sony hopes that the privatization of these subsidiaries will allow it to strengthen the ties within its network of companies, while increasing shareholder value.

The second pillar of Sony's new group architecture is to strengthen its core electronic business by revising its system of in-house companies. As of April 1, 1999, its set of ten in-house companies were regrouped into three—Home Network Company, Personal IT Network Company and the Core Technology & Network Company. Combined with Sony Computer Electronics, these three, companies now make up the core of Sony's electronic business. Sony hopes this will strengthen the networking among its business units by combining those in similar fields, and will help train and develop the next generation of top management.

The ten companies were regrouped based not only on their business field, but also on their business models. Companies that exhibit decreased profits after a certain level of sales as a result of greater investment needs (decreasing returns to scale) were separated from companies that exhibit increased profits with increased sales (increasing returns to scale), since these two types of companies require different business models. Examples of the first type of companies are those involved in television and audio video equipment; information technology and electronic game companies are examples of the latter type.

Sony also hopes to link these two types of businesses by investing in networking technology that link these businesses (*Shukan Diamond*, March 27, 1999). For example, it hopes to create a network platform for providing customers with digital content such as movies, music, and financial services. Sony's current network businesses, such as its Internet and satellite broadcasting businesses, were left under the direct control of the head office (see Figure 9.2). These businesses are still at a very young stage and require considerable investment, although they are expected to exhibit exponential growth in profits if successful.

The third pillar of Sony's new group management policy is to strengthen its group management capabilities and decision-making speed through the following changes.

- Further separation of board and management duties by reviewing its current list of board members, by reducing the number of members of its Management Committee and by increasing the number of external directors.
- Strengthening the group headquarters' function as an active investor that will control and monitor operations and allocate resources. Support functions will be transferred to companies, enabling them to operate autonomously.
- Implementing a new value-based performance measurement system to pursue "value creation management." The new performance system hopes to accurately allocate and reflect cost of capital to the companies, and is to be based on the concept of economic profit, which is calculated by subtracting the cost of debt and equity from after tax operating profit.

Figure 9.2
Sony's New Organizational Structure

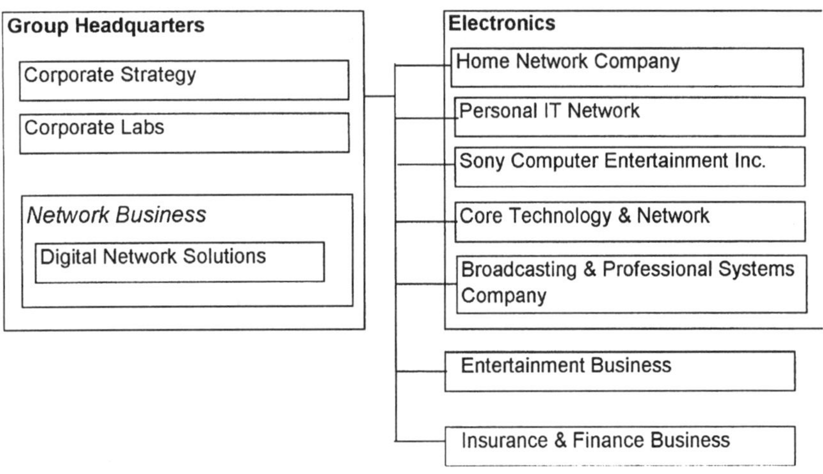

Source: Sony Corporation.

In accordance with these changes, the redefined functions of Sony's headquarters are to establish and evaluate overall goals and strategies for the group, to allocate resources, and to develop and grow the next generation of management.

FUTURE TRENDS IN CORPORATE GROUP MANAGEMENT

Corporate Group Management Models of Other Corporate Groups

The changing environment has affected not only Sony, but also other major corporate groups, such as Toyota, Hitachi, and Toshiba. This section briefly discusses the recent actions taken by these corporations to consolidate the capabilities of their group by strengthening their corporate group management models.

Toyota, one of the brightest stars of the economic miracle of post-war Japan, has been facing difficulties recently due to the recession, heightened competition, deregulation, and international pressure to decrease exports. Although Toyota is still financially sound, its credit rating was lowered by Moody's in August 1998 as a result of decreased productivity (sales per head office employee decreased from 59 in 1989 to 49 in 1998). To increase its productivity and create group synergy, Toyota is moving toward a holding company style of group management. Over the last two years it has increased its share in publicly traded subsidiaries; Toyota increased its share in Hino Jidousha Kogyo, Toyota Sha Tai, and Denso during its 1997–1998 fiscal year, and in Daihatsu Kogyo the following year to strengthen their joint product development, manufacturing, sales, procurement, and distribution capabilities (*Shukan Toyo Keizai*, January 23, 1999). In addition, Toyota dispatched corporate executives to management positions at various subsidiaries to fortify ties and coordination among group companies.

Toshiba is also facing difficulties and is expected to barely break even on a consolidated basis in its 1998–2999 fiscal year. As a result, it is reviewing its corporate group management model and has realigned its business lines to strengthen group control while delegating responsibility of day-to-day operations to its business units. It introduced a system of in-house companies in April 1999 by merging units and spinning off unprofitable noncore businesses. Fifteen business units were regrouped into nine companies that are fully responsible and accountable for their own performance and growth. Corporate officers and support staff at headquarters were also dispatched to the companies to manage and operate them, respectively. At the same time, a department for auditing the companies was established at headquarters.

To strengthen the networking among its business units, Toshiba also began redesigning its internal information system in 1995. The project is well under way, and as of April 1999, all units including the in-house companies and factories will be linked with Oracle's ERP program.

Hitachi, which will record a loss of over 37.5 billion yen on a consolidated basis in its 1998–1999 fiscal year, has also reviewed its corporate group management model. As of April 1999, its "group system," which it first established in February 1995, was reorganized into ten "groups," each responsible for its own businesses, much like an individual company

To ensure that each group can act independently, Hitachi simultaneously established a system of corporate officers who are to manage the day-to-day operations of the individual businesses, and reorganized its head office. The functions of its Executive Committee and its Vice President Committee were merged into a new Senior Executive Committee, which will focus on corporate strategies related to restructuring, intercompany alliances, and other top management decisions. Hitachi also plans to propose a reduction of board members at its next shareholders' meeting in June 1999 and to create a post of vice chairman of the board who will be specifically responsible for consolidated management. It hopes that these changes will clarify responsibility and accountability, and speed up top-level decision making

Hitachi's home page states that there is an "urgent need to extend the concept of consolidation beyond a mere method of accounting to encompass stronger management aimed at boosting the efficiency of the more than 1,000 companies of the Hitachi Group." In order to meet this need, it established a Hitachi Group Committee composed of the group chairman, group president, and representatives from group companies in October 1998.

Further Trends in Corporate Group Management

As discussed in the previous sections, socioeconomic changes are transforming the way corporate groups manage their businesses. Increasingly, corporations are concentrating overall control and monitoring power at group headquarters, while delegating responsibility for all aspects of day-to-day operations to their companies. This allows for stronger mid- to long-term directional control, by the head office, while giving subsidiaries the flexibility to adapt to environmental changes in the short term

These trends in corporate group management, however, are still unfolding as deregulatory measures are implemented and as the recession deepens. There are two possible future scenarios for corporate group management—one is a move toward the Western (Anglo-American) style of corporate group management, and the other is the development of a new style that is particular to Japanese corporations.

The Western style of corporate group management is one in which head offices are mainly holding companies focused on controlling wholly owned subsidiaries. ABB, General Electric, and many U.S. financial institutions are representative of corporations with this style of group management. Sony's recent group realignment is a step toward this style. In an interview with a respected business magazine, Idei (president and co-CEO of Sony) stated that he studied the group management of ABB for reference (*Nikkei Business*, March 22, 1999).

Whether a new style of corporate group management that is particular to Japan will be formed is uncertain. Corporate groups may move toward increased share in, but not privatization, of their subsidiaries, such as Toyota has done. Or corporate groups may choose to have a mix of wholly owned subsidiaries and privatized subsidiaries.

In either scenario, corporate groups will have to reconcile their business model, or way of doing business, with their corporate group management model in order to maximize the utilization of group resources and shareholder value. In other words, the method in which corporations manage their groups must be appropriate for the way in which they run their business to create profit and value.

CONCLUSION

The recent trends in corporate group management show that successful corporations like SECOM and innovative corporations like Sony will respond to crises by undertaking successive efforts to redesign their business and corporate group management models. A crisis, by definition, is a period of chaos in which it is impossible to foretell how events will play out or what strategies will be successful. Thus, corporations must first implement strategies and policies that they believe will be most successful, and then fine tune or redo them as events unfold. In other words, successful corporations are those that undertake continuous self-organization to respond to the changing environment.

Corporations and group companies that adapt successfully to environmental change are also those that accumulate and increase their power to learn and create knowledge/value. A learning organization is one that monitors, interprets, and internalizes environmental change (Teramoto et al., 1994). SECOM and Sony are both learning organizations that are attempting to increase their ability to create knowledge and value, as shown by their pioneering products and services, with the united resources of their group.

REFERENCES

Dirks, D., and Teramoto, Y. (1996) Lessons from the Recession: Indication for a New Type of Japanese Management. Best Paper Proceedings, AJBS annual conference, pp. 389–402.

Nikkei Business. (1999) Idei Nobuyuki Shacho Ga Kataru Sony No Daitan Kiko Kaikaku (Interview with President Idei on Sony's Bold Realignment). *Nikkei Business*, March 22.

Richter, F. J., and Teramoto, Y. (1995). Interpreneurship: A New Management Concept from Japan. *Management International Review*, 35(2), pp. 91–104.

Seike, A. (1995) *Nihon Gata Soshiki Kan Kankei No Management* (Japanese Style Management of Interorganizational Relationships). Tokyo: Hakuto Shobo.

Shukan Diamond. (1999). Kigyo Kachi No Sozo Wo Mezasu Sony Soshiki Kaikaku No Yomikata (How to Read Sony's Organizational Realignment Aimed at Creating Corporate Value). *Shukan Diamond*, March 27.

Shukan Toyo Keizai. (1999). Group Kigyo No Kiriuri Ga Kasoku (Acceleration of Selling off Group Companies). *Shukan Toyo Keizai*, January 23.

Shukan Toyo Keizai. (1999). Kyoso Rule Ga Kawaru (The Rules of Competition Are Changing). *Shukan Toyo Keizai*, April 3.

Teramoto, Y. (1990). *Network Power*. Tokyo: NTT Shuppan.

Teramoto, Y. (1996). Japanese Corporate Group Re-management. *Economic Journal of Hokkaido University*, .125, pp. 1–26.

Teramoto, Y. et al. (1994). *Gakushu Suru Soshiki* (Learning Organization). Tokyo: Dobunkan.

Chapter 10

The Increasing Competitiveness of Indo-German Joint Ventures: The Role of Joint Venture Autonomy for Success

Brij N. Kumar and Markus Khanna

INTRODUCTION AND OBJECTIVE OF THE STUDY

The necessity of making a deeper inquiry into the difficulties of managing Indo-German equity joint ventures derives from two separate developments:

1. After several years of reform-led economic expansion, some spine-chilling signs indicate that India hasn't been left unscathed by the turmoil plaguing East Asia (Sidhva, 1999: 83). Finance Minister Yashwant Sinha's assertion in November 1998 that "India is not in trouble" now sounds like sheer bravado in the face of some worrying macroeconomic figures. According to estimates by the independent Centre for Monitoring the Indian Economy in Bombay, the cumulative trade deficit reached $5.8 billion in the first seven months of fiscal 1998–1999, compared with $2.7 billion in the corresponding period in 1997–1998, which has helped to reduce foreign-exchange reserves slightly. They stood at $27.5 billion in August 1998, compared with a peak of $30 billion a year earlier, according to the Reserve Bank. Overall growth in industrial production in April–September 1998 was 3.6 percent, compared with 6 percent a year earlier. Another fact indicating that India could be headed for big trouble is the recent decline of foreign investment. Several reasons can be mentioned for explaining that total foreign direct investment (FDI) in the April–September 1998 period amounted to $1.2 billion, compared with $1.8 billion during the same period in 1997. One compelling explanation is that although India has liberalized FDI into the country substantially since 1991, its policies essentially remain restrictive, especially considering the amount of FDI in other similar newly industrializing countries (NICs).

As compared with China and Brazil, for instance, FDI flows into India are merely a trickle. The reasons for these reservations are many, but nationalism as indicated by the latest nuclear tests in May 1998 seems to be the underlying force. For example, immediately after the tests, foreign institutional investors withdrew more than $400 million from the stock markets, and Moody's Investors Service downgraded India's sovereign rating to speculative.

Being faced with these economic and political difficulties, foreign companies in India, especially international joint ventures, have to focus on possibilities to increase their efficiency. In this context, defining the right degree of joint venture autonomy plays a sensible role.

2. Germany is among the leading foreign investors in India, with a total stock of 1,045 billion DM (1996). According to several experts, the recent tightening up of policies on the Indian side has had adverse effects on Indo-German companies. For instance, in one case expansion into adjacent markets was curtailed, and in another production of new products was hampered by restricting import licences. The main consequence of such problems is that it becomes difficult for the German parent company to plan and include Indian operations as part of their global strategy. Coordination and control of the Indian activities cannot be put on a reliable base. Subsequently, as a result of such uncertainties in the host-country environment, autonomy of the Indian subsidiaries becomes an important problem—that is to say, as to how far business is left to the discretion of the local management to plan and operate within the contingencies of the host country without having to bear global coordination risks. From this perspective, the question of the autonomy of Indian operations becomes an issue of being able to compensate restrictions imposed by the host country unhampered by parent-company control. On the other hand, some amount of coordination of joint venture (JV) operations may also be inevitable, depending on certain economic imperatives.

The objective of this study is to investigate the autonomy of Indo-German joint ventures (JVs) and its impact on joint venture success. Joint venture autonomy is defined as the degree of decision-making discretion of joint venture management. The right amount of subsidiary autonomy has been proven to be crucial for performance (e.g., Geringer and Hebert, 1989: 235–237; Yan and Gray, 1994: 1478) and is in itself dependent on an intricate interplay of many diverse influencing factors. The focus of the study is specifically on the relationship between the German parent and the Indo-German joint venture in India because the aforementioned problems basically arise in this context. The chapter will attempt to provide answers to the following questions:

- What degree of autonomy do the German parent companies provide their JVs in India with respect to major functional areas?
- How does the degree of autonomy relate to the success of the joint ventures?
- What are the major influencing factors of autonomy and success, and what role do they play in the Indo-German sample joint ventures?

CONCEPTUAL FRAMEWORK

Basic Variables: Joint Venture Rationale and Autonomy

The concept of foreign subsidiary autonomy is used to a great extent in studies of international management (see, for example, Kumar, 1987: 113; Kieser and Kubicek, 1992: 281–282; Welge, 1992: 579–584; Frese, 1995: 74–88). Traditionally, a hierarchical perspective is taken where headquarters control the subsidiaries and make the strategic decisions (e.g., Stopford and Wells, 1972; Doz and Prahalad, 1981; Baliga and Jaeger, 1984; Porter, 1985; Egelhoff, 1988).

This chapter demonstrates the concept of autonomy in the sense that physical separation between parent and joint venture and the difficulties associated with managing joint ventures in NICs call for coordinated action and control by the foreign parent company—in our case by the German parent. In this sense, in this study we regard autonomy as the degree of control excercised by the German parent company in various functional areas in their Indian joint venture.

Although foreign subsidiary autonomy has received considerable attention in the literature (e.g., Doz and Prahalad, 1981; Cray, 1984; Bartlett and Ghoshal, 1989; Hedlund and Rolander, 1990), there is a paucity of research on control of joint ventures (e.g., Geringer and Hebert, 1989: 250). It is obvious that whatever the shared modus of control and joint venture autonomy, both partners will see this as being instrumental for achieving their initial individual and shared strategic objectives and eventually maximizing joint venture performance. Previous studies on the relationship between joint venture control and performance are, however, largely inconclusive (Geringer and Hebert, 1989: 25–26).

In this chapter we propose that the rationale underlying the decision of the partners to establish a joint venture with each other (rather than wholly owned subsidiaries) for pursuing their strategic goals offers help in explaining the extent and structure of the autonomy granted and subsequently accounting for the relationship between exercised partner control and performance.

According to Culpan and Kumar (1994: 268–270), compelling theoretical explanations for joint venture existence are offered by three concepts: (1) transaction cost economics; (2) resource dependency approach; and (3) competitive advantage theory.

Perspective of Transaction Cost Economics

Our guiding hypothesis is that joint venture autonomy is instrumental for minimizing transaction costs. The relationship is explanable by three factors immanent in transaction cost theory: (1) trust between the partners, (2) commitment of the partners to the common venture, and (3) cross-cultural competence of the partners needed to interact with each other.

Role of Trust

Trust as an informal control mechanism has been identified as a substitute for ownership-based control (formal control) and as a viable alternative to other potential control mechanisms. If a trustworthy relationship is developed between economic agents (the parents), opportunism and thus agency costs will be reduced. Therefore, it is predicted that the impact of management control will become weaker when informal control mechanisms are present (Schaan, 1988: 13). Thus, in a trustful relationship the foreign parent company, being geographically separated from the JV, need not necessarily install expensive control mechanisms to ensure that decisions in the JV are made in accordance with his wishes (Inkpen and Birkenshaw, 1994: 204). Conversely, a lack of trust probably leads directly to the foreign partner's demand for a broader control focus and for tighter controls. An atmosphere of trust is typically reflected in a *consensus on mission, strategy, and operating procedures* as well as in the type of reporting and *communication and openness* between the JV partners. These indicators of trust reflect the willingness and ability of the JV partners to share information, and in particular, information or knowledge embodied in organizational skills and routines.

In trying to link trust and JV success, one may postulate that a lack of trust in the other JV partner adversely affects JV performance. Typical statements such as "if you ask parent company personnel about the success of their JVs, in nine of ten answers the idea of trust will figure prominently" point in the same direction (Killing, 1983: 82). The assumption that building trust in interorganizational partnerships has significant positive market performance and efficiency implications has empirically been substantiated in a variety of intra- and interorganizational contexts (Baird et al., 1990; Bleeke and Ernst, 1991) and also suggested in cross-border partnerships (Beamish, 1985; Parkhe, 1993; Madhok, 1995). A summary of the arguments presented above yields the following proposition:

Proposition 1: In a trustful relationship the foreign (German) partner has a more relaxed attitude toward control, and JV management enjoys a higher degree of autonomy than in partnerships characterized by a low degree of interpartner trust (ceteris paribus).

As reliable measures of trust and trust-building in joint ventures, the following items seem appropriate:

1. Frequency with which the joint venture must report to the German parent company
2. Duration and kind of partner relationship and communication between the German and Indian partner
3. Congruence of partner strategic interests and mission between the German and Indian partner

Role of Commitment

Commitment is probably the most important attribute in the ongoing management of a joint venture (Beamish, 1988: 64). Commitment is required to overcome initial uncertainties associated with a new country or partner. Sense of duty to the venture and partner is the basis on which problems are addressed and solved, changes are made, and help is provided (Beamish, 1988: 64). Where joint ventures are established in a spirit of commitment to long-term success, opportunism is believed unlikely to emerge (Beamish and Banks, 1987: 11). This indicates that in the absence of opportunism less control is necessary and the JV will enjoy a higher degree of autonomy. Especially applied to JVs in developing countries, there is empirical evidence that the foreign partner's commitment to the JV is positively correlated with JV autonomy (Beamish and Banks, 1987: 11). The degree of commitment to a venture is likely to be conditional upon certain characteristics of the venture. It is likely to be higher, for example, the more *strategically important* the output is deemed to be for a given parent. Commitment will also tend to be higher if the distribution of rewards from the venture, when it is successfully completed, is deemed equitable by all parties. Envy of the share of gains appropriated by the other partner cannot only diminish motivation, but can encourage cheating, which may be ''justified'' as a means of generating a more equitable outcome. Commitment in the relationship allows for long-term scenario planning by both partners. Thus, several researchers (e.g., Schaan, 1983; Buckley and Casson, 1988: 99–101; Kogut, 1989: 185; Cullen, Johnson, and Sakano 1995) have emphasized that commitment in the relationship leads to higher market performance of the partnership. Also, Beamish (1988: 43) found a strong correlation between commitment and performance in JVs, noting that most of the commitment characteristics in the high-performing LDC JVs were related to the foreign partner's willingness to do something (e.g. supply special skills like technology). The reasoning of the previous arguments leads to the following proposition:

Proposition 2: The greater the parental German commitment toward the joint venture, the higher the degree of JV autonomy (ceteris paribus).

As a reliable indicator of (German) partners' commitment is the importance of the joint venture for their total business activities (sales, profit).

Role of Cross-Cultural Competence

The cross-cultural competence of the partners facilitates understanding between them by helping to overcome cultural barriers posed by language, nonverbal communication, and value differences. The more managers have attained cross-cultural competence, the better they become at exploiting the benefits of shared ownership and shared risk (Harrigan, 1986: 45). In accordance with

Buckley and Casson (1988: 32), to be able to appropriately configure a JV, intercultural competence gathered in connection with the experience with other JVs in which the participants are involved turns out to be crucial. The parents' venturing experiences show, in general, a positive relationship with the delegation of decisions to the subsidiaries (Pahlberg, 1996). Some researchers postulate that the greater the cross-cultural competence and the more experience the foreign parent company gains in developing countries via the JV form of organization, the greater are its understanding and empathy toward the local partner and the less inclined it will be to try to force home office policies and practices on the JV in the host country (Fayerweather, 1978: 353; Kumar and Esslinger, 1998: 144). But the developing country partner's foreign experience gained in other business cooperations with Western companies can also have a considerable influence on the Western partner's attitude toward control. Contacts with foreign companies and businesspeople can enhance the local partner's understanding of and familiarity with Western business attitudes. They can also prove to be a valuable attribute in developing knowledge, skills, and values concerning modern management methods. Furthermore, cross-cultural business dealings are likely to sharpen the sensitivity toward competitiveness in the international market and increase the reciptivity toward demands regarding quality standards, commitment in pre- and after-sales service considerations, and the values of industrial society in general (Kumar, 1995: 69). Being familiar with these considerations can generally increase the local company's ability to communicate with the foreign partner and better understand his requirements with respect to management control (Kumar and Esslinger, 1998: 145).

These findings can be related to the *experience curve*, which is associated with cooperative strategies (Harrigan, 1985: 58). For instance, firms use their multiple JV experience as a credential when forming new JVs. The more experience firms gain from previous cooperations, the greater the probability that they will be able to organize the new ventures more effectively and avoid earlier mistakes (Zielke, 1992: 241; Eisele, 1995: 180). Most researchers addressing the venturing experience of partners found a positive impact on JV performance. In particular, the acquaintance of the local partner with Western values can support the openness of the mind for further enculturation of individual attitudes advantageous for successful market performance of the JV (Kedia and Bhagat, 1988). A summary of the arguments presented above yields the following proposition:

Proposition 3: The greater the cross-cultural competence of both partners, the higher the degree of joint venture autonomy (ceteris paribus).

The measure used for the German and Indian partners' cross-cultural competence is their past experience with international joint ventures.

Resource Dependency Approach

From the point of view of the resource dependency approach, joint ventures are formed by partner firms for pursuing a variety of strategic objectives and mutually defined goals not attainable by acting autonomously (Buckley, 1992: 91; Inkpen and Birkenshaw 1994: 202). These objectives can be (1) reducing costs (e.g., by attaining economies of scale), (2) obtaining market access, (3) obtaining access to know-how, and (4) reducing risks (e.g., sharing investment) (Porter and Fuller, 1986; Harrigan, 1986: 16; Beamish, 1988: 23–41).

The objectives that are important to a given partner should lead to different patterns of management control exerted over the JV. However, no existing research evidence links between partners' objectives and JV control system choices and JV success. Thus, it becomes difficult to pinpoint the possible relationships that really matter for understanding the impact of parents' objectives on the autonomy and success of JVs.

Nevertheless, plausible theoretical arguments can be made. A promising avenue is to connect control over JV activities with the specific competencies a parent brings in. The contributions made and contemplated by partners to their JV pertain mainly to the partners' expectations and strategies reflected in their objectives for the JV. According to Yan and Gray (1994: 1481), the possession of crucial resources such as technology or market know-how that could be contributed to the JV gives a parent bargaining power vis-à-vis its partner. They relate this bargaining power to management control that a party can exercise over the JV. In their opinion, the relative possession of crucial JV resources determines the distribution of management control that between the parents (Yan and Gray, 1994: 1480). The underlying question is: how do the contributions of the parents influence the manner in which they exercise control over the JV?

Empirical results of prior research on JVs show that, for example, technology and control affect each other (Kumar and Esslinger, 1998: 140–142). Technology is one of the most important bargaining chips that firms possess when negotiating the terms of their cooperative strategies (Harrigan, 1986: 41). Thus, it is scarcely surprising that firms seek as much control and close coordination with their ventures if they contribute and seek to protect technological knowledge and other shared information that comprise their strategic core. And, for example, if the JV is dependent on the foreign parent for continuous updating of important technology, the foreign parent may exercise considerable control, even though the local partner possesses the majority of the paid-up capital (Kumar and Steinmann, 1987: 93).

With most firms from developed countries expanding into developing countries, goals or objectives include not only lucrative sale and use of their sophisticated technology, but also access to domestic markets and utilization of cheap labor cost production. For these reasons, one can expect that managers of German firms will tend to actively participate in the technology-related decisions but remain passive shareholders in decisions where the local partner has the relevant expertise (e.g., in marketing/sales, personnel/staffing, and procurement).

Market access may be the most attractive resource to control because it provides a competitive advantage that is more durable than most technological resources, especially where product and process technology changes rapidly (Harrigan, 1986: 39).

Local firms possess specialized information on the country's economy, political situation, culture, and so on, information that is costly and time consuming for the foreign partner to gather. But the local partner lacks the production technology necessary to produce high-quality goods (Becker and Tiehl, 1983: 60). In sum, the complementary skills and resources of the parents determine what functional areas each parent aims to control and how competitive the venture will be as compared to local firms.

Differences in objectives among participants in developing country JVs are common, and, unless the venture is designed and managed so that each of the partners perceives that its objectives will be attained, the JV is likely to encounter conflicts, bureaucratic delays, and other performance problems. Thus, it is imperative that the parents be aware of and take into consideration the objectives of each partner when attempting to design and implement an effective JV control system. Complementarity of parents' objectives subsequently moderates the joint venture performance, and attention must be devoted to the creation of a ''win-win'' situation in which each partner attains its goals. This reasoning leads to the following proposition:

Proposition 4: The greater the need of one parent (German parent) for the contributions of the counterpart (Indian partner), the more inclined the former is to exercise relaxed control over the joint venture and thus the higher the degree of JV autonomy (ceteris paribus).

The measures used for investigating resource dependence are the German and Indian partners' strategic objectives with reference to each partners' expected contribution toward fulfilling these.

Competitive Advantage Perspective

The competitive advantage perspective focuses on achieving gains through coordinating the joint venture activity within the global framework of the German parent. Coordination, on the other hand, is restricted by the necessity of local responsiveness (adaptation of management and functional issues) created by specific host-country influences. The amount of coordination and local responsiveness together reflect the degree of interdependence between the joint venture and the German parent, and therefore the German parent's role in the joint venture decision-making process. Subsequently, coordination (local responsiveness) and interdependence can be regarded as important contingencies for joint venture autonomy (Welge, 1982: 820; Kobrin, 1991: 207). This reasoning yields the following proposition:

Proposition 5: The greater the interdependence between the total corporate system and the joint venture, the greater the coordination needs, the lower the degree of joint venture autonomy (ceteris paribus).

In accordance with the most common measures used for coordination/local responsiveness (interdependence), the amount of goods exchanged between the joint venture and the German parent and the degree of adaptation/variance practiced in the joint venture management will be used as proxy.

METHOD

The propositions are investigated in connection with a sample of Indo-German joint ventures located in the New Delhi region. A questionnaire was mailed in March–May 1998 to 70 companies in the area, out of which 28 qualified for inclusion in the research (40% response). Seven branches of industry were represented in the sample (chemicals, mechanical engineering, automobile parts, software, electrical, leather/textile, and food/beverage), most of them belonging to the consumer goods sector, and were small and medium-sized enterprises (less than 800 employees and less than 2,000 Mill. Rs. ≈ 100 Mill DM sales). In administering the questionnaire to the joint ventures, the view of the joint venture management was appraised. The respondents were 82 percent top-level Indian managers (partners) and 18 percent German expatriates.

FINDINGS

Joint Venture Autonomy and Success

As indicated earlier, joint venture autonomy was appraised as the degree of decision-making discretion of joint venture management in the functional areas and joint venture success as the degree of goal attainment. Figure 10.1 presents the findings.

Our results show that by and large performance is considered to be medium, and the joint venture autonomy is greatest in the personnel/staffing function, and the least in production. Apart from marketing and product policy, in all other functional areas, the degree of German parent control exercised and joint venture success show a significant positive relationship.

The relationship between autonomy and success as investigated by the empirical study may be analyzed. It was expected that the joint venture's flexibility and adaptivity would be viewed as contributing positively to the performance of the JV. But the results provide strong evidence to the contrary. In all management functions except marketing and production policy, there is obviously a

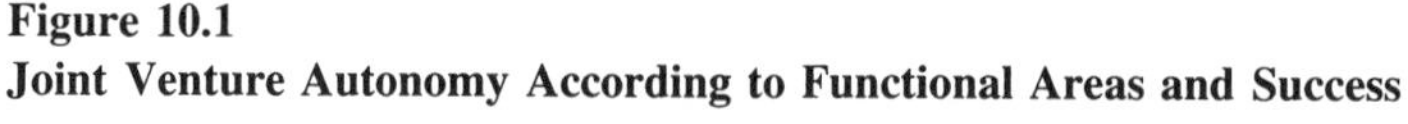

Figure 10.1
Joint Venture Autonomy According to Functional Areas and Success

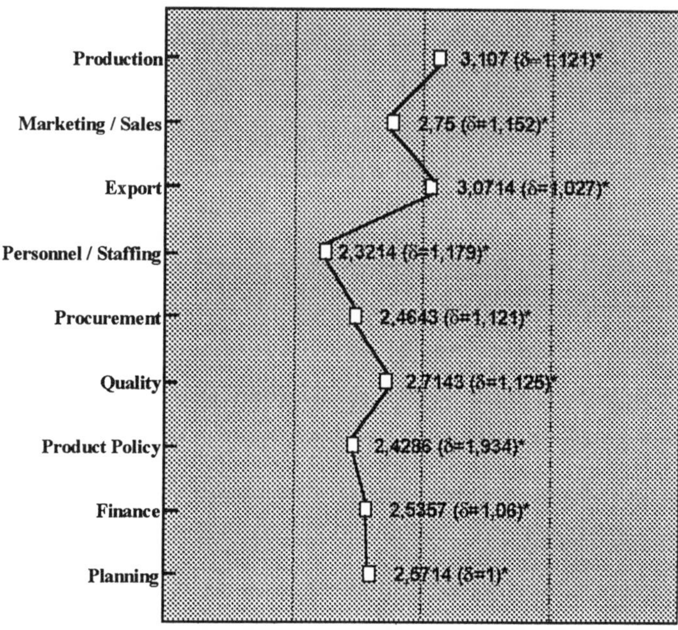

*Mean value of a 5-point scale: The higher the score, the higher the perceived influence of the German parent, the lower the joint venture autonomy.
(∂) Standard deviation.

need for assistance from the German parent. Generally speaking, the results indicate that JVs in a lesser developed market like India require a high degree of assistance or control by the German parent company, especially in areas like production, export, procurement, and quality control to adequately attain German partner's goals.

Thus, the underlying proposition that in India joint venture autonomy would be positively related with JV success has to be refuted. The analysis in the following sections sheds light on the most important influencing factors and thus on relating autonomy and success to the particular settings in which the JVs are embedded.

Influencing Factors of Autonomy

The Impact of Trust

Duration of acquaintance indicates previous partner interactions that preceded the joint venture formation. It can be assumed that trust has been built up in the meantime. The German firms knew their Indian partners prior to joint venture establishment on the average for a long period of time. But as indicated by the findings that does not necessarily indicate a positive influence on the degree of joint venture autonomy. The distribution of firms along the two dimensions, "duration of acquaintance" and "autonomy," shows contraindicative results. One would expect that the longer the partners knew each other prior to the JV formation, the greater the German partner's willingness to grant a higher degree of autonomy to the respective JV.

However, the positive correlation gives support for the contrary: the longer the partners knew each other prior to the JV formation, the greater the control of the German partner in the majority of the functional areas, especially in quality control ($r_s = 0.635$; $p \leq 0.05$), planning ($r_s = 0.524$; $p \leq 0.05$), export ($r_s = 0.425$; $p \leq 0.05$), personnel ($r_s = 0.434$; $p \leq 0.2$), product policy ($r_s = 0.348$; $p \leq 0.2$), and production ($r_s = 0.308$; $p \leq 0.2$).

The positive correlation ($r_s = 0.526$; $p \leq 0.05$) between frequency of reporting in the area of quality control and decision-making control of the German parent suggests lack of trust, which would be in line with proposition 1. The more personal relations exist between the partners, the lesser the JV autonomy in planning ($r_s = 0.366$; $p \leq 0.2$). In spite of a weak correlation, the latter finding is quite contraindicative regarding the emphasis of personal relations in the question of joint venture autonomy (Figure 10.2).

The findings show no significant influence of communication on joint venture autonomy. This indicator concerning trust follows the definition developed by Gupta (1987) around the notion of the German partner's willingness to share information about, for example new developments in technology and so forth. The weak negative correlation ($r_s = -0.303$; $p \leq 0.2$) shows a tendency in the presumed influence on joint venture autonomy. The positive correlations between congruence of mission and parent company control ($r_s = 0.581$; $p \leq 0.05$) actually indicate lack of trust, or that congruence of mission doesn't necessarily lead to trust. The presumed relationship to the German partners' control could not be verified; as with the congruence of mission, the practiced control by the German parent rose.

The Impact of Commitment

The factor of commitment was measured on a 5-point scale indicating the importance of the joint venture in India for the German parent company. Their commitment is generally in the medium range, and the impact on degree of exercised control is generally positive, that is, the control of the German partner increases with his commitment, which refutes proposition 2.

The Impact of Cross-Cultural Competence

The cross-cultural competence of the German and Indian partners was measured in the basis of their previous joint venture experience. Our findings show that in both cases the experience and presumed cross-cultural competence is not great, the German partner being a little more experienced than the Indian.

Figure 10.2
Impact of Trust Criteria on Autonomy

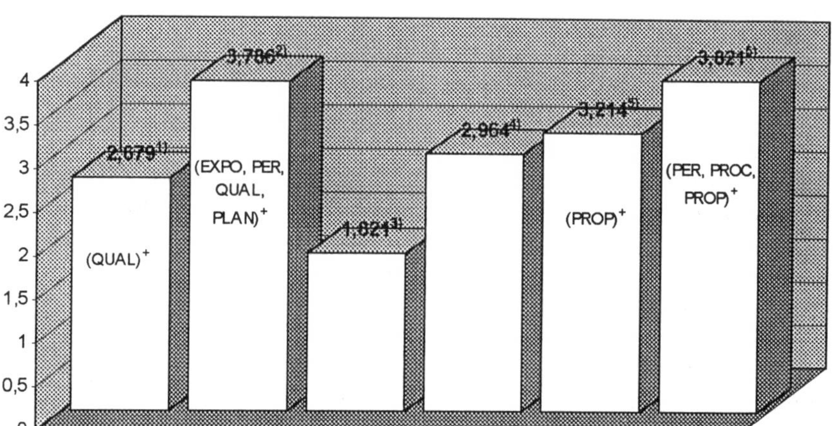

+p ≤ 0,001 − 0,1 (Spearman rank correlation to autonomy in various functional areas: MA: Marketing; EXPO: Exporting; PER: Personnel; QUAL: Quality; PLAN: Planning; PROP: Product Policy; PROD: Production)

(1) Mean value of 5-point scale: The lower the score, the less frequent the required reporting, the greater the trust.

(2) Mean value of 5-point scale: The higher the score, the longer the partner acquaintance, the higher the trust.

(3) Mean value of 3-point scale: The higher the score, the friendlier the relations, the greater the trust.

(4) Mean value of 5-point scale: The lower the score, the more open the communication, the greater the trust.

(5) Mean value of 5-point scale: The higher the score, the greater the congruence, the greater the trust.

The German partner's experience has no influence on the degree of control in the joint ventures. It is striking that the Indian partner's venturing experience is positively related to the German partner's control exerted in quality concerns ($r_s = 0.46$; $p \leq 0.05$), planning ($r_s = 0.449$; $p \leq 0.1$), finance ($r_s = 0.443$; $p \leq 0.1$), production ($r_s = 0.391$; $p \leq 0.1$), and export ($r_s = 0.36$; $p \leq 0.1$). It seems on the whole that the German firm considers the previous experience of the Indian partner to be as a basis of a strength that could threaten its decision-making autonomy. Hence, there is a perceived need for higher control in the mentioned, cases, and consequently proposition 3 must be refuted.

Impact of Partners' Strategic Objectives and Partner Contributions (Resource Dependencies)

German Partner

Figure 10.3 shows that in a descending order of emphasis the German partner's objectives to form the JV with the Indian partner were low-cost production

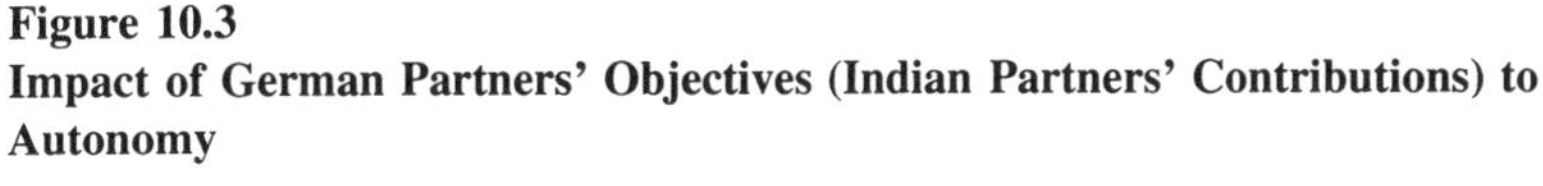

Figure 10.3
Impact of German Partners' Objectives (Indian Partners' Contributions) to Autonomy

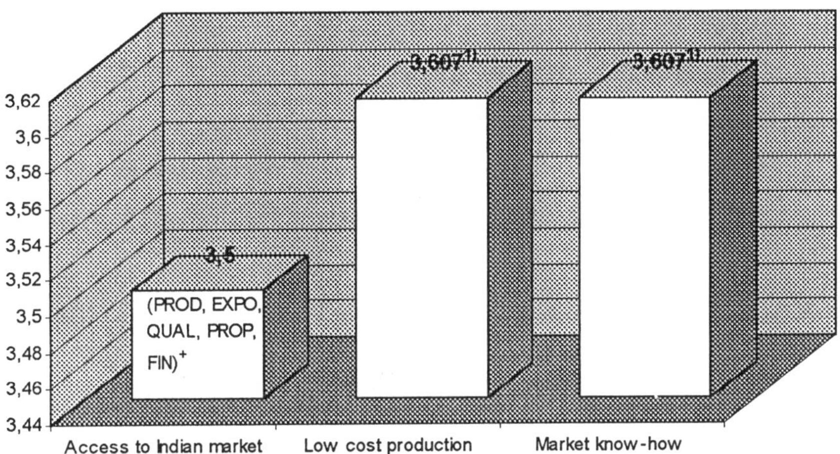

+p ≤ 0,05 (Spearman rank correlation to autonomy in various functional areas: MA: Marketing; EXPO: Exporting; PER: Personnel; QUAL: Quality; PLAN: Planning; PROP: Product Policy; PROD: Production).

(1) Mean value of a 5-point scale: The higher the score, the greater the importance of the objective and expected contribution of Indian partner.

for export to Germany or global markets (3.607), use of market know-how (3.607), and access to the Indian market (3.5). As discussed in the theoretical part, the objectives of a given partner should lead to different patterns of management control.

The positive correlations indicate that, contrary to our initial assumption, the more the German partner seeks the special knowledge of the Indian partner in order to get access to the Indian market (e.g., knowledge concerning negotiations with government agencies or in dealing with the bureaucracy), the more German partner is also inclined to control the following areas: finance (r_s = 0.571; $p \leq$ 0.05), export (r_s = 0.511; $p \leq$ 0.05), and production (r_s = 0.446; $p \leq$ 0.01). Only a weak negative correlation between the need for access to the Indian market and control in product policy points in the presumed direction (r_s = – 0.426; $p \leq$ 0.2). The other two objectives show no significant relationship to the control phenomenon.

Indian Partner

As Figure 10.4 shows, the Indian partners value their German counterparts as collaboration partners mainly because of the high standards of their technology (3.84) or because of their reputed products and brands (4.0). The findings show positive correlations to German parent control throughout in the areas indicated. The more the Indian partner seeks access to modern technology of

Figure 10.4
Impact of Indian Partners' Objectives (German Partners' Contributions) to Autonomy

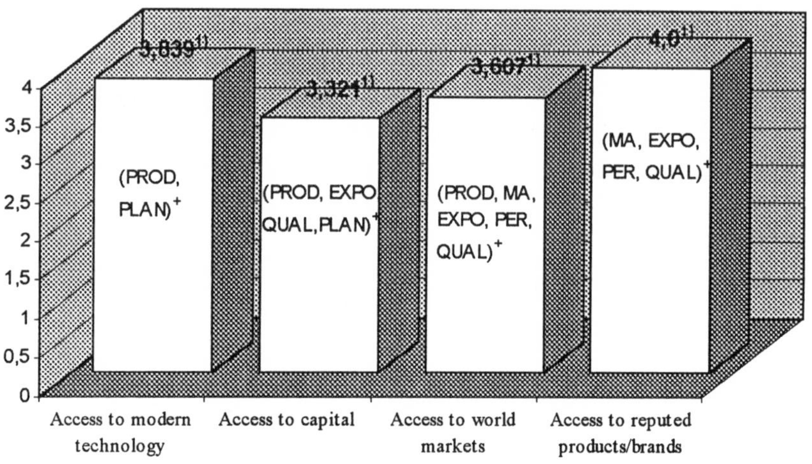

+p ≤ 0,005 – 0,05 (Spearman rank correlation to autonomy in various functional areas: MA: Marketing; EXPO: Exporting; PER: Personnel; QUAL: Quality; PLAN: Planning; PROP: Product Policy; PROD: Production).

(1) Mean value of a 5-point scale: The higher the score, the greater the importance of the objective and expected contribution of German partner.

the German counterpart, the more is the German counterpart inclined to exercise tighter controls in production ($r_s = 0.495$; $p \leq 0.05$) and the planning function, ($r_s = 0.504$; $p \leq 0.05$). Similarly, if the German partner contributes his products and brands, he focuses his control activities on marketing ($r_s = 0.546$; $p \leq 0.05$), export ($r_s = 0.485$; $p \leq 0.05$), personnel ($r_s = 0.776$; $p \leq 0.005$), and quality control ($r_s = 0.585$; $p \leq 0.005$). By condensing the data another step further, one immediately sees that the Indian partners' desire for access to German partners' capital and world markets leads directly to tighter controls in the depicted functions (Figure 10.4).

Access to modern technology and reputed brands constitutes the most important reason for the Indian partner to collaborate with a German firm. In order to interpret the tight controls exerted in this connection by the German partners in the majority of management functions that go along with an increase in the Indian partners' need for sophisticated technology and especially reputed products and brands, Geissbauer and Siemsen (1996: 56) provide the following explanation: "When the corresponding technology is brought into the joint venture, the temptation for the local partner can be overwhelming to want to use the products and processes without any participation of the inconvenient German partner. In the past there have been several cases, in which German partners have been rudely pushed out of the collaborations, or in which former employees of the ventures have turned themselves into independent businessmen with the stolen technology.'' Thus, German partners have to protect their contributions and prevent the local partner from absconding with their competencies.

The protection of sophisticated technology, products, and so on, is even more justified when considering that in India Western ideas of protection of intellectual property rights often meet with only unappreciative disapproval. Effective legislation regarding the protection of patents and trademarks and of copyrights as well is being developed slowly. India has specified a number of statutory regulations for protection of patents, trademarks, technology, and other proprietary know-how. Existing legislation is being revised along the lines of the Paris Convention. By condensing the data another step further, one realizes that an increase in the Indian partners' need for capital and access to the world markets in which the German counterpart operates leads directly to tighter German controls. This indicates in turn that if the German partner contributes capital and access to the world markets, he is aware of the danger that the Indian partner may use the capital for unintended purposes or that his business activities in his target markets may collide with the increasing export activities of the Indian parent or even the JV.

In summarizing the latter findings, the following conclusions can be drawn. Obviously, both partners seek their complementary skills and resources which go along with protection of related contributions. The German partner protects his sophisticated technology, products and brands, capital, and know-how concerning world markets by exercising control, whereas the Indian partner does not necessarily connect his contributions with similar demands. Proposition 4 is only partly validated.

Impact of Coordination Strategy (Competitive Advantage)

The coordination strategy as a global competitive advantage was measured by two indicators: the degree of variance of management from the German parent and the amount of exchange of goods within the global system of the German partner. Investigating the variance in management, relevant factors, and resources in the joint venture from the German parent company and considering that in most areas there is more similarity with the German parent than variance, we can expect some coordination potential, though not high. Furthermore, all items have a positive correlation with the degree of German company control as suggested in the proposition. The most significant correlations have been observed for the following items: finances, qualification of personnel, and knowledge of the Indian market.

The impact of the second important proxy of global competitive strategy on autonomy is as follows. We see that the role of the individual criterion varies. There seems to be no impact of global procurement on autonomy, a positive influence of intracompany sales, and a negative correlation between domestic sales and German control. The results are by and large consistent with our proposition: intracompany and international sales have to rely on standardized products and quality, hence stronger coordination and German control, domestic sales rely more on local responsiveness, which is left to joint venture management, which requires more autonomy.

DISCUSSION AND CONSEQUENCES

Our findings show that Indo-German joint ventures in our sample have a considerable amount of autonomy in decision making, even though variant according to functional areas. Interesting, however, are the results that Indo-German joint ventures with relative lower autonomy, that is, higher German parent control were, by and large more successful than that those had less control. Initially, we had assumed that, especially owing to the uncertainties in the Indian environment, more joint venture autonomy than German parent control would be the better strategy for goal attainment. However, certain economic and social imperatives seem to have an interesting influence, so that more control and coordination seem to be the more favorable strategy. What are these main factors which indicate more German parent control?

Trust between the partners does not appear to be overwhelmingly high, which apparently results in higher control by the German partner. Factors that could have been considered as trust-building criteria often showed negative influences, for instance, the "duration of acquaintance." Apparently, the longer the relationship, the more knowledge the German partner gets about the resources and capabilities of the Indian counterpart and the more convinced he is about the necessity of control. Similarly, the "congruence of mission" does not seem to be a warrant for building trust, but rather a feature fortifying the German parent's determination to attain set joint objectives in the cooperation by exercising more control and coordination. The same is the case with *commitment* which appears to enhance the felt necessity for stronger control of the joint venture in order to fulfill the defined role of the Indian operations. Even so, the achieved *cross-cultural competence* of the Indian partner through venturing experience also does not suffice to build up trust. On the contrary, it may be seen as a basis of strength of the Indian partner threatening goal attainment, hence the tendency for stronger control.

The major factor that puts the German partner in a more favorable position enabling him to enforce more coordination, even in the face of trust-building measures, is apparently his power base vis-à-vis the Indian counterpart. The contributions of the German partner sought after by the Indian partner are apparently valued so highly by the latter that the inputs are seen as a legitimate base for the German partner's decision-making authority. Finally, we have indication that the Indian joint ventures to a certain extent are considered to be part of the global integration strategy by the German partner. Many functions are standardized according to German specifications, which make direct control and coordination necessary. Standardization also seems plausible in the light of the fact that the Indian partner seeks contributions through which his competitive edge can be improved.

The most important functional areas where coordination and control proved to be crucial for success were: quality control, exportation, production, and personnel/staffing. Quality control is one of the most difficult issues in Indo-German joint ventures. German parent companies are known to be uncompromising on this question to the extent that cooperation has been dissolved in the past when the Indian partners did not abide by these standards. Coordination and control in exportation are considered necessary while protecting foreign markets already being served directly by the German parent or other subsidiaries. Conflict with own joint ventures in India over this issue also occurs quite often, because the joint ventures are generally very keen about exporting in order to generate foreign exchange. Coordination in the production area is necessary for technology transfer from Germany and is also readily accepted by Indian partners. German parent-company influence in the personnel function, of course, pertains to staffing key positions in the joint ventures.

While evaluating the influencing factors, one must keep in mind the many interdependencies and their multivariate impact. These could not be examined in this study, especially because of the small sample. Apart from this shortcoming, the study could perhaps help practitioners organize their relationships with their foreign partners more effectively.

REFERENCES

Baird, I. S., Lyles, M. A., and Wharton, R. (1990). Attitudinal Differences Between American and Chinese Managers Regarding Joint Venture Management. *Management International Review*, 30(3), pp. 53–68.

Baliga, B. R., and Jaeger, A. (1984). Multinational Corporations: Control Systems and Delegation Issues. *Journal of International Business Studies*, 12(1), pp. 25–40.

Bartlett, C. et al. (eds.). (1990). *Managing the Global Firm*. London and New York: Macmillan.

Bartlett, C. A., and Ghoshal, S. (1989). *Managing across Borders: The Transnational Solution*. Boston: Harvard Business School Press.

Beamish, P. W. (1985). The Characteristics of Joint Ventures in Developed and Developing Countries. *Columbia Journal of World Business*, 3 (Winter), pp. 13–19.

Beamish, P. W. (1988). *Multinational Joint Ventures in Developing Countries*. London: Routledge.

Beamish, P. W., and Banks, J. C. (1987): Equity Joint Ventures and the Theory of the Multinational Enterprise. *Journal of International Business Studies*, 18(2), pp. 1–16.

Becker, F., and Tiehl, K. (1983). Strukturen und Bewertungen Deutsch-Indischer Joint Ventures in Indien. Ein Beitrag zur Entwicklungsforschung. In K. Hottes and C. Uhlig (eds.), *Joint Ventures in Asien*. Munich: Beck, pp. 32–78.

Bleeke, J., and Ernst, D. (1991). The Way to Win in Cross-Border Alliances. *Harvard Business Review*, 2, November/December, pp. 127–135.

Buckley, P. J. (1992). Alliances, Technology and Markets: A Cautionary Tale. In P. J. Buckley (ed.), *Studies in International Business*. London: Macmillan.

Buckley, P. J., and Casson, M. (1988). A Theory of Co-operation in International Business. *Management International Review*, Special issue on Co-operative Strategies in International Business, pp. 19–38.

Buckley, P. J., and Ghauri, P. N. (eds.) (1994). *The Economics of Change in East and Central Europe*. London: Haworth Press.

Cray, D. (1984). Control and Coordination in Multinational Corporations. *Journal of International Business Studies*, 15(1), pp. 85–98.

Cullen, J., Johnson, J., and Sakano, T. (1995). Japanese and Local Partner Commitment to IJVs. *Journal of International Business Studies*, 26(1), pp. 91–115.

Culpan, R., and Kumar, B. N. (1994). Cooperative Ventures of Western Firms in Eastern Europe: The Case of German Companies. In P. J. Buckley, and P. N. Ghauri (eds.), *The Economics of Change in East and Central Europe*. London: Haworth Press, pp. 267–277.

Doz, Y., and Prahalad, C. (1981). Headquarters Influence on Strategic Control of MNCs. *Strategic Management Review*, 23(1), pp. 15–29.

Egelhoff, W. G. (1988). *Organizing the Multinational Enterprise: An Information-Processing Perspective*. Cambridge, MA: Ballinger.

Eisele, J. (1995). *Erfolgsfaktoren des Joint Venture-Management*. Wiesbaden: Gabler.

Fayerweather, J. (1978). *International Business Strategy and Administration*. Cambridge, MA: Ballinger.

Frese, E. (1995). *Grundlagen der Organisation. Konzept-Prinzipien-Strukturen*. 6th ed. Wiesbaden: Gabler.

Geissbauer, R., and Siemsen, H. (1996). *German Direct Investments in China, India and Indonesia: A Comparison of Investment Locations*. Bonn: DIHT.

Geringer, J. M., and Hebert, L. (1989). Control and Performance of International Joint Ventures. *Journal of International Business Studies*, 20(2), pp. 235–254.

Ghauri, P. N., and van Rossum, W. (1996). Interdependence in International Joint Venture Relationships: The Role of the Technology. Working Paper, University of Groningen, pp. 1–16.

Gupta, C. B. (1987). *Contemporary Management*. Singapore: South Asia Books.

Harrigan, K. R. (1985). *Strategies for Joint Ventures*. Lexington, MA: Lexington Books.

Harrigan, K. R. (1986). *Managing for Joint Venture Success*. Lexington, MA: Lexington Books.

Hedlund, G., and Rolander, D. (1990). Action in Heterachies—New Approaches to Managing the MNC. In C. Bartlett et al. (eds.), *Managing the Global Firm*. London and New York: Macmillan, pp. 15–46.

Hottes, K., and Uhlig, C. (eds.) (1983). *Joint Ventures in Asien*. Munich: Beck.

Inkpen, A. C., and Birkenshaw, J. (1994). International Joint Ventures and Performance: An Interorganizational Perspective. *International Business Review*, 3(3), pp. 201–215.

Kamminga, P. E. (1997). Management Control Aspects of Joint Ventures. Working Paper, University of Groningen, pp. 1–15.

Kedia, B. L., and Bhagat, R. S. (1988). Cultural Constraints on Transfers of Technology across Nations: Implications for Research in International Comparative Management. *Academy of Management Review*, 13(2), pp. 559–571.

Kieser, A., and Kubicek, H. (1992). *Organisation*. Vol. 3. Berlin and New York: De Gruyter.

Killing, J. P. (1983). *Strategies for Joint Venture Success*. New York: Praeger.

Kobrin, B. (1991). An Empirical Analysis of the Determinants of Global Integration. *Strategic Management Journal*, 12(4), pp. 17–31.

Kogut, B. (1989). The Stability of Joint Ventures: Reciprocity and Competitive Rivalry. *Journal of Industrial Economics*, 38(2), pp. 183–198.

König, W. et al. (eds.) (1987). *Betriebliche Kooperationen mit den Entwicklungsländern*. Munich: Beck.

Kumar, B. N. (1987). *Deutsche Unternehmen in den USA: Das Management in amerikanischen Niederlassungen deutscher Mittelbetriebe*. Wiesbaden: Gabler.

Kumar, B. N. (1995). Partner-Selection Criteria and Success of Technology Transfer: A Model Based on Learning Theory Applied to the Case of Indo-German Technical Collaborations. *Management International Review*, 1(4), pp. 65–78.

Kumar, B. N., and Esslinger, A. S. (1998). Corporate Management in German Companies in East Asia: Similarities and Differences in Parent-Company Control in Japanese and Chinese Subsidiaries. In Y. Takahashi, M. Murata, and K. M. Rahman (eds.), *Management Strategies of Multinational Corporation in Asian Markets*. Tokyo: Chuo University Press, pp. 133–148.

Kumar, B. N., and Haussmann, H. (eds.) (1992). *Handbuch der Internationalen Unternehmenstätigkeit*. Munich: Beck.

Kumar, B. N., and Steinmann, H. (1987). Führungskonflikte in internationalen Joint Ventures des Mittelstandes. In W. König et al. (eds.), *Betriebliche Kooperationen mit den Entwicklungsländern*. Munich: Beck, pp. 81–97.

Madhok, A. (1995). Opportunism and Trust in Joint Venture Relationships: An Exploratory Study and a Model. *Scandinavian Journal of Management*, 11(1), pp. 57–74.

Pahlberg, Cecilia. (1996). *Subsidiary-Headquarters Relationships in International Business Networks*. Uppsala, Sweden: HSC.

Parkhe, A. (1993). Strategic Alliance Structuring: A Game Theoretic and Transaction Cost Examination of Interfirm Cooperation. *Academy of Management Journal*, 36 (4), pp. 794–829.

Porter, M. E. (1985). *Competitive Advantage: Creating and Sustaining Superior Performance*. New York: Free Press.

Porter, M. E. (ed.) (1986). *Competition in Global Industries*. Boston: Harvard Business School Press.

Porter, M. E., and Fuller, M. B. (1986). Coalitions and Global Strategy. In M. E. Porter (ed.), *Competition in Global Industries*. Boston: Harvard Business School Press, pp. 363–400.

Schaan, J.-L. (1983). Parent Control and Joint Venture Success: The Case of Mexico. Unpublished doctoral dissertation, University of Western Ontario.

Schaan, J.-L. (1988). How to Control a Joint Venture Even as a Minority Partner. *Journal of General Management*, 14(1), pp. 4–16.

Sidhva, S. (1999). No Escape. *Far Eastern Economic Review*, 1(2), p. 83.

Stopford, J. M., and Wells, L. T., Jr. (1972). *Managing the Multinational Enterprise: Organization of the Firm and Ownership of the Subsidiaries*. New York: Basic Books.

Takahashi, Y., Murata, M., and Rahman, K. M. (eds.) (1998). *Management Strategies of Multinational Corporations in Asian Markets*. Tokyo: Chuo University Press.

Welge, M. K. (1982). Entscheidungsprozesse in komplexen, international tätigen Unternehmungen. *Zeitschrift für Betriebswirtschaft*, 52(9), pp. 810–832.

Welge, M. K. (1992). Strategien für den internationalen Wettbewerb zwischen Globalisierung und lokaler Anpassung. In B. N. Kumar and H. Haussmann (eds.), *Handbuch der internationalen Unternehmenstätigkeit*. Munich: Beck, pp. 569–590.

Yan, A., and Gray, B. (1994). Bargaining Power, Management Control, and Performance in United States-China Joint Ventures: A Comparative Case Study. *Academy of Management Journal*, 37(6), pp. 1478–1517.

Zielke, A. E. (1992). *Erfolgsfaktoren internationaler Joint Ventures. Eine empirische Untersuchung der Erfahrungen deutscher und amerikanischer Industrieunternehmen*. Frankfurt am Main: Gabler.

Chapter 11

New Economic Development and Strategic Alliances in the Japanese Finance Sector

Caroline Benton and Yoshiya Teramoto

INTRODUCTION

There are two widely different types of industries in the Japanese market—one modern and technically advanced and the other backward and behind the times. The manufacturing sectors of the automobile and electronics industries with their high-quality products and cost-efficient production methods are representative of the first type, whereas the finance and retail sectors exemplify the second.

In the aftermath of World War II, Japanese manufacturers such as Toyota and Matsushita concentrated their efforts on meeting the standards of their American and European counterparts. They rigorously studied, improved on, and created state-of-the-art products and production technologies through incremental improvements, and today they are global leaders in their fields. As a result, their exports are major trade friction concerns.

In contrast, in areas such as the finance and retail sectors Japan is acutely lagging behind global standards. These sectors are still playing catch-up to their Anglo-American competitors because they had been protected from competition and thus had not been strongly motivated to acquire sophisticated expertise. With the Japanese Big Bang and the relaxation of the large-scale retail stores law, these sectors are coming of age, however.

This chapter describes the macro- and microeconomic factors affecting the finance sector and then discusses efforts by domestic institutions to survive the Japanese Big Bang in the context of alliance theory. An analysis of the recent alliances of major domestic institutions is presented to elucidate these points.

SHAKING THE CRADLE

The environment of the Japanese finance sector can be said to have been a safe cradle watched over and protected by the government. This section discusses the major macro- and microeconomic trends that have been shaking the once safe cradle of the finance sector.

Macroeconomic Trends

Economic Crisis

The burst of the Japanese economic bubble in the early 1990s has brought about the country's longest recession of the post-war period. As the bubble (1985–1991) was fueled by unfounded speculative investments, with its bursting Japanese corporations accrued huge losses on their investments. Financial institutions, in particular, have been critically hit for the following reasons.

- Japanese financial institutions backed a significant percentage of the speculative investments of the bubble period with loans, many of which have since gone bad. In January 1998 the government estimated that the total value of the bad debts held by Japanese financial institutions was over 76.7 trillion yen, which amounted to roughly 12 percent of their outstanding loans.
- Japanese financial institutions were not immune to the attractiveness of the speculative investments of the bubble period and were active participants of *zaitech* (a term made popular in the mid- to late 1980s, which refers to the technology of aggressive investments). With the collapse of the stock and real estate markets, many financial institutions also accumulated huge losses on their own investments.
- The value of financial institutions' own publicly traded stock also declined in the early 1990s with the fall in the stock market. A comparison of the stock values of the six largest city banks is shown in Table 11.1.

Major domestic banks and other financial institutions topped global asset rankings during the bull market of the late 1980s and were once praised as the energy behind the Japanese post-war economic miracle. However, as a result of the current economic crisis, the value of Japanese financial institutions' assets has declined significantly, threatening their financial viability. Even the once excellent credit ratings of the largest banks have been downgraded by international credit rating agencies. Japanese financial institutions must now pay a premium—an embarrassing situation for these once proud firms—for financing in international markets due to their increased risk.

From the perspective of the market in general, the burst of the bubble has caused a shift from indirect to direct financing by industrial corporations, a change in investor attitudes, and a weakening of the once stable mutual shareholding among group companies. These microeconomic trends have affected the finance sector as well and are discussed separately. In terms of the finance sector, Japanese institutions are now trying to catch up with global standards with regard to their financial health and expertise by writing off bad debts, limiting the number of new loans, and forming strategic alliances.

Table 11.1
Bad Debts of the Six Major Banks (Unit: trillion yen)

	Total Assets	Bad Debt Ratio
Tokyo Mitsubishi Bank	81.95	2.5%
Sumitomo Bank	58.08	2.5%
Sanwa Bank	52.71	2.3%
Dai-ichi Kangyo Bank	53.80	3.2%
Sakura Bank	51.65	3.2%
Fuji Bank	51.09	3.7%

As of March 1998.
Source: Compiled by Kiyoshi Shimano.

Deregulation: The Japanese Big Bang

Faced with a severely weakened finance sector and intense intentional pressure, in the shape of the Bank for International Settlement's (BIS) minimum capital ratio requirements, then Prime Minister Ryutaro Hashimoto announced plans in 1996 for a Japanese Big Bang, or fundamental deregulation of the finance sector. The government hoped to revive the economy by modernizing the finance sector through deregulation leading to competition and stronger enforcement of global standards for financial health. The BIS capital adequacy standard is an 8 percent capital ratio for internationally active institutions. For those active only in the domestic market, the Japanese Ministry of Finance has a 4 percent standard.

The government's three major principles for the Japanese Big Bang are free competition, fair competition through disclosure, and globalization of existing laws. The major deregulatory measures of the Big Bang needed to achieve these principles are outlined in Table 11.2.

Traditionally, Japanese banks and other institutions tended to follow each other's business practices and lead; they offered the same services and products at similar, if not identical, fees and interest rates. In this manner, they were able to gain huge profits on their favorable interest schemes for those given on deposits and received on loans, and they did not have to differentiate themselves through unique services. For example, they never nurtured sophisticated risk management capabilities, and they more or less offered the same interest rates regardless of different risk levels. Japanese banks also focused mainly on corporate customers and never developed their retail banking business beyond basic financing services such as saving accounts, home loans, and credit cards.

Currently, Japanese financial institutions are being tested in a free market as government barriers to market entry and new products/services are eliminated.

Table 11.2
Summary of Major Measures of the Big Bang

Deregulation of Holding Companies

1 Deregulation of pure holding companies as of December 1997

Deregulation of Services

1 Deregulation of investment trusts by December 1998

2 Deregulation of investment management by banks by December 1998

3 Deregulation of stock derivatives by December 1998

Competition among Different Areas of the Financial Sector

1 Deregulation of fees for non-life insurance by July 1998

2 Deregulation of transaction fees for stocks by December 1999

3 Elimination of operation restrictions on the security subsidiaries of banks

4 Complete deregulation of entry by insurance companies and banks into each other's markets by March 2001

Improved Customer Services

1 Change to disclosure based on consolidated accounts from March 2000

2 Establishment of funds to insure insurance payments by December 1998

3 Establishment of funds to protect investors by December 1998

Source: Compiled by Kiyoshi Shimano.

They can no longer maintain their game of conformity, and they must start to differentiate themselves by creating unique value for their customers. For example, with the deregulation of the investment trust and insurance business, domestic banks are being forced to respond to the aggressive market entry of foreign institutions (e.g., Citibank and Merrill Lynch) by offering new retail financing services, such as mutual funds, to target the over 1,200 trillion yen in personal savings.

Microeconomic Trends

The macroeconomic factors mentioned in the preceding section have brought about microeconomic trends that are also affecting the finance sector. These are (1) a change in investor attitudes, (2) a decline in mutual shareholding relationships, (3) a shift to financing of investments by industrial corporations, and (4) a rush to form alliances to survive in the new competitive environment.

Changing Investor Attitudes

Japanese corporations had been known for seeking market share and sales growth as opposed to corporate profits. Similarly, institutional and corporate investors had placed more importance on long-term capital growth than on short-term dividends and had been mainly stable shareholders. With stock and real estate values plummeting, investors have become more sensitive to the short- to mid-term value of their investments and are demanding greater returns.

This has caused a shift in Japanese business philosophy from one that places emphasis on employees, as was once demonstrated by the promise of life-long employment, to a more complex one that places importance on investors and other stakeholders as well (*Shukan Toyo Keizai*, April 3, 1999). Japanese financial institutions must now try to maximize shareholder value by improving ROE, ROI, EVA (economic value added), and other performance measures, as well as by providing greater added value to their customers.

A Decline in Mutual Shareholding Relationships

The economic crisis and the change in investor attitudes are impacting large conglomerates, including the *zaibatsu* groups centered on the largest banks (Mitsui, Mitsubishi, Sumitomo, and Fuji). In order to survive in the global environment, Japanese financial institutions have to prioritize improving their financial position and capital ratio to meet global standards.

Since capital ratio is calculated as total equity divided by total assets, Japanese financial institutions are trying to decrease the denominator of this equation by selling off nonessential stock and real estate and by limiting credit and loans. In other words, they are more reluctant to engage in mutual holdings of nonessential stock (i.e., not related to core business), and they are beginning to seek greater returns on their investments.

A Shift to Direct Financing by Industrial Corporations

In the past, Japanese corporations relied on bank funding to finance investments. This made having a sound and stable relationship with a main bank extremely important for Japanese industrial corporations. Recently, however, Japanese banks are causing a credit crunch to bring their capital ratio to global standards. This has led to (1) a decreased reliance by industrial corporations on financial institutions, (2) the adoption of new direct methods of raising capital by industrial corporations, and (3) a weakening of ties between industrial corporations and their main banks.

For Japanese banks, this has caused a dilemma: while they can improve their capital ratio by limiting their funding and credit, they lose interest revenues as their corporate customers begin to rely on direct financing. This means that Japanese banks must look to other sectors—such as the retail banking sector—to fill the gap in their business left by this shift to direct financing.

In particular, this has had a dire effect on the three specialized financial institutions (long-term credit banks) that serviced the corporate and industrial sectors—the Nippon Credit Bank (NCB), The Long-Term Credit Bank of Japan (LTCB), and the Industrial Bank of Japan (IBJ). These institutions had held a special position in the Japanese economy and were established to offer long-term financing for corporations. But NCB and LTCB failed during the last year as a result of massive bad debts and the decline in the market for long-term corporate financing through these banks.

Formation of Alliances

As the waves of globalization and deregulation increase in intensity, companies are finding it increasingly difficult to operate and expand their business by themselves using their own capital, staff, and expertise. This is also true for the Japanese finance sector; over the past year, domestic institutions have been rushing to improve their weakened financial position and to organize alliances in response to the mega-competition that has been catalyzed by the Big Bang. Examples of these alliances are presented in the following section.

ALLIANCES IN THE JAPANESE FINANCE SECTOR

Alliance of Sumitomo Bank and Daiwa Securities

In July 1998, Sumitomo Bank and Daiwa Securities announced plans to create joint ventures for the wholesale securities, derivatives, and asset management businesses. Under the arrangements of the alliance, two joint ventures—one for the first two businesses and another for the last—were established into which Daiwa Securities transferred its operations, becoming somewhat like a holding company (Figure 11.1). Sumitomo's securities subsidiary, Sumitomo Capital Securities, was also consolidated into the whole securities joint venture, while Sumitomo group companies, SB Investment Management and SBIM Investment Trust Management, were merged with the asset management joint venture. The new subsidiaries, which began operating in April 1999, are Daiwa Securities SB Capital Markets (for the wholesale securities and derivatives business) and Daicam SB Asset Management (for retail asset management business).

Faced with decreased financial strength after the burst of the bubble, Daiwa Securities was looking to find a strong business partner for capital influx and business synergy. It had basically three objectives for entering into an alliance: (1) to increase its financial strength through capital influx, (2) to increase its product/service development ability, and (3) to obtain access to a global sales channel (*Nihon Keizai Shimbun*, July 28, 1998).

In contrast, Sumitomo Bank, which was relatively quick to deal with bad debts by making provisions to cover over 120 percent of their value, wanted to gain know-how regarding securities and investment management, and to restructure its noncompetitive securities and wholesale investment business (*Nihon Keizai Shimbun*, July 28, 1998). Sumitomo did not have the human resources or capital to grow its securities company to be a major player that could survive the Japanese Big Bang. With the new alliance, it transferred its wholesale securities and investment businesses to Daiwa Securities SB Capital Market, one

Figure 11.1
Sumitomo Bank and Daiwa Securities Alliance

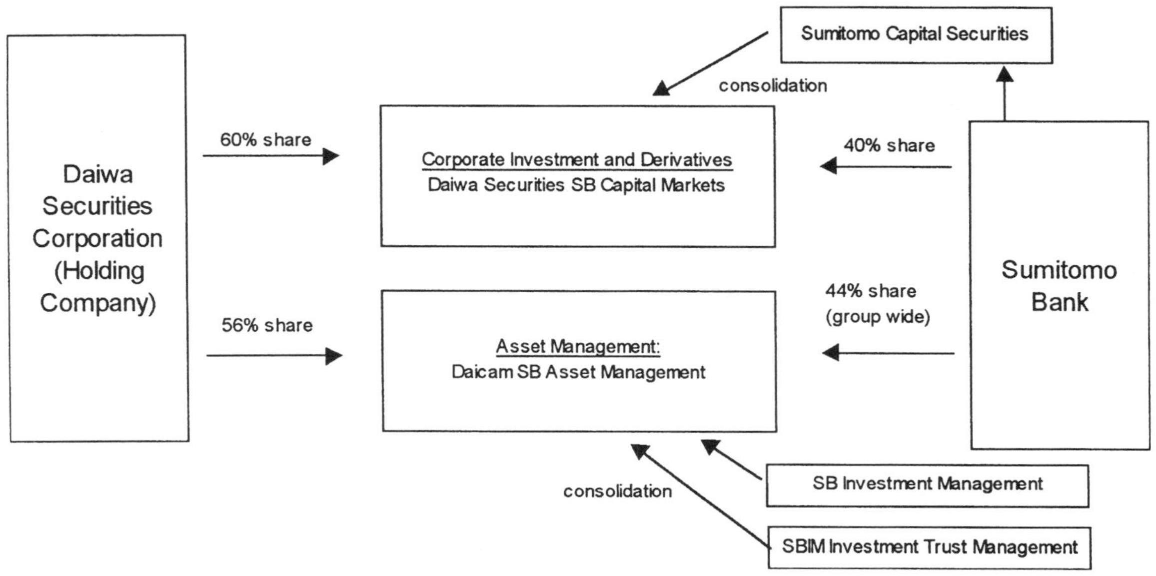

of the new joint ventures. By doing so, it desired to focus its own in-house human resources and capital on growing its retail banking business.

The partners also announced simultaneously that they intend to recruit foreign institutions and other domestic institutions from the Sumitomo *zaibatsu*, including Sumitomo Trust and Banking, Sumitomo Marine and Fire Insurance, and Sumitomo Life Insurance. Bringing in group companies will allow Sumitomo Bank to reduce investment redundancy and consolidate group strength, while foreign firms will help the partners to enhance their capabilities and acquire global business channels. Yoshifumi Nishikawa, president of Sumitomo Bank, stated that he hoped to include an alliance with a foreign-affiliated company and offer uncommon (in Japan) services (*Nihon Keizai Shimbun*, July 29, 1998).

In January 1999, Daiwa and Sumitomo finalized their plans for an alliance with a foreign institution and signed a letter of intent with T. Rowe Price Associates. The agreement outlines plans for the foreign institution to invest in Daicam SB Asset Management and for this joint venture to ally with Robert Flemming and T. Rowe Price in an overseas joint venture for non-Japanese securities portfolios for Japanese customers.

Alliance between the Industrial Bank of Japan and Nomura Securities

An example of an emerging alliance between Japanese financial institutions that do not belong to a *zaibatsu* is the recent partnership between the Industrial Bank of Japan (the last surviving long-term industrial credit bank) and Nomura Securities (the leading securities company) that was announced in May 1998 (see Figure 11.2). Under the terms of the alliance, the companies created two joint ventures—IBJ Nomura Financial Products Holding, which is based in the United Kingdom and is involved in the development of sophisticated products such as derivatives-based investment tools; and Nomura-IBJ Investment Services, which offers asset management and pension funds services. IBJ Nomura is a holding company that has established a wholly owned U.K. subsidiary, IBJ Nomura Financial Products plc, with a branch office in Tokyo.

The partners' motive for the alliance was to pool resources to compete against the aggressive market entry of foreign institutions with the full implementation of the Japanese Big Bang. Masao Nishimura, president of the Industrial Bank of Japan, stated that it is most important not to have the Japanese market taken over by foreign institutions (*Nihon Keizai Shimbun*, May 14, 1998).

As a long-term credit bank, IBJ is strong in corporate investment banking and weak in retail banking. This situation is potentially fatal to the long-term survival of IBJ: Japanese industrial companies are depending less on bank financing and are following Western practices of raising funds directly on the market. Through its alliance with Nomura, IBJ intends to nurture new businesses for long-term survival by gaining retail financing skills, sharing the necessary investment, and making use of Nomura's large base of consumer and corporate clients. The

Figure 11.2
Nomura Securities and the Industrial Bank of Japan

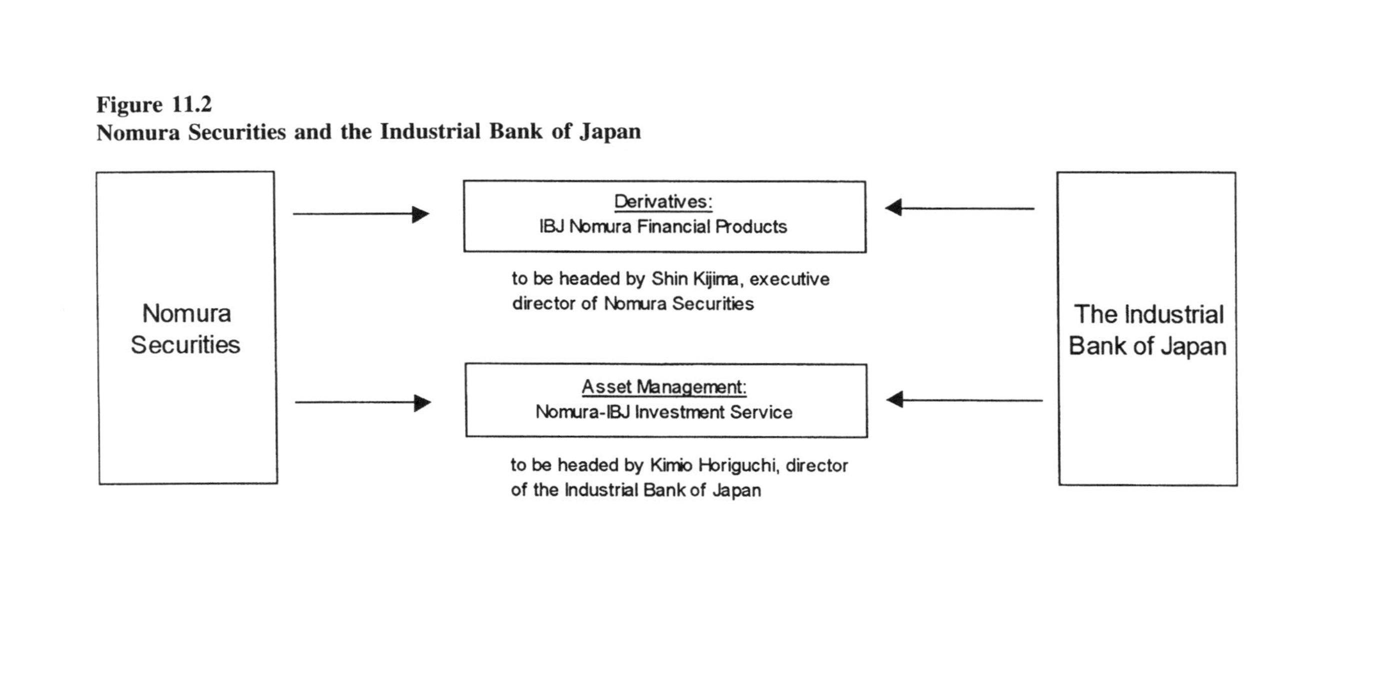

partners also have complementary intelligence with regard to derivatives: Nomura has experience in equity derivatives, whereas IBJ is strong in credit derivatives.

Nomura Securities, on the other hand, hoped to be able to contact/approach IBJ's rich wholesale corporate client base for pension schemes (for example, 401K products) that are new to Japan and to share the investment for growing its assessment management and derivatives businesses. In addition, with the separate joint ventures, Nomura Securities can institute different salary levels for its different businesses that have different profitability ratios and can halt the outflow of professional employees departing to take higher paying positions at foreign institutions.

In spite of the partners' exceptions, many industry experts have expressed doubts regarding whether the alliance alone will be enough to raise each partners' market value over the long term. An executive director of Morgan Stanley stated that, although the cooperation between two relatively strong domestic companies is interesting, the alliance has little impact compared to the drastic merger measures for survival of foreign financial institutions (*Nihon Keizai Shimbun*, May 14, 1998). Furthermore, the alliance does not directly help the companies to compete in the global market or bring in the leading-edge technology of foreign financial institutions.

In addition to the alliance with Nomura Securities, in October 1998 IBJ announced plans for a separate and comprehensive alliance with the Dai-ichi Mutual Life Company (DML). The agreement calls for cooperation "within every possible business area" (announcement on IBJ home page dated October 2, 1998), and includes (1) providing complementary products to each partner's individual and corporate customers, (2) cooperating in asset management (possibly consolidating the companies' asset management businesses), (3) establishing a joint venture for the development of advanced products in the fields of banking, insurance, pension, securities, and asset management, and (4) for DML to invest in IBJ. The third action was implemented in April 1999 with the formation of IBJ-DL Financial Technology.

The benefits of the alliance for IBJ are that it will receive capital to improve its financial position and regain trust, and it will be able to build a retail customer base. (DML has a network of sales branches in every prefecture.) DML, on the other hand, will be able to secure a foothold in the banking business that is to be deregulated for insurance companies by March 2001.

Alliance between Dai-ichi Kangyo Bank and JP Morgan

The alliance between Dai-ichi Kangyo Bank (DKB) and JP Morgan—which was announced in October 1998—is an example of a partnership between a Japanese bank and a foreign institution (Figure 11.3). Under the terms of the alliance, the companies jointly established DKB Morgan, an investment trust and asset management company in May 1999. The 50–50 joint venture is to

Figure 11.3
Dai-ichi Kangyo Bank and JP Morgan Alliance

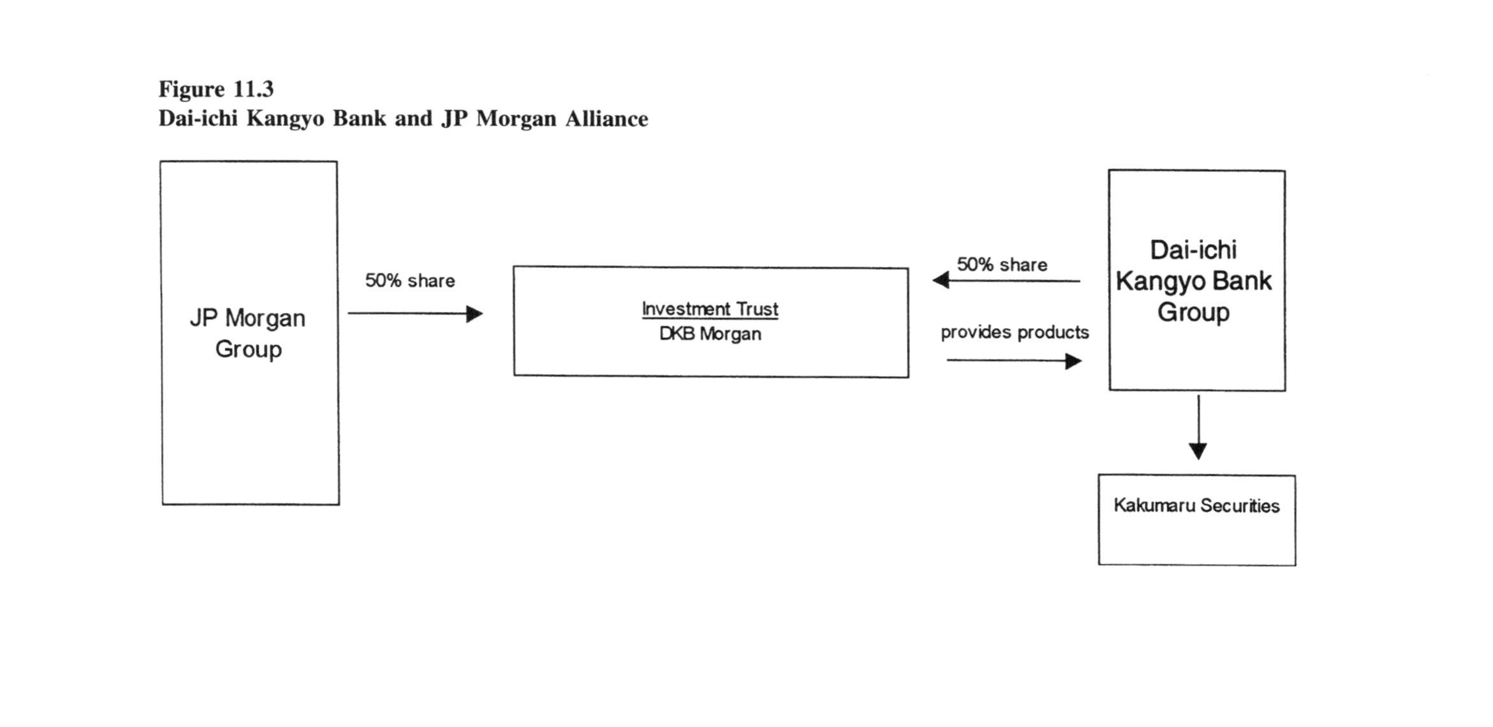

develop foreign currency investment products—an area that DKB has not been strong in—for the Japanese bank to offer to the retail and wholesale sectors. This alliance follows DKB's earlier acquisition of Kakumaru Securities, a second-tier securities company.

DKB's motive for entering into the alliance was to bring in JP Morgan's global asset management, investment trust, and product development skills. DKB, which is not part of a *zaibatsu*, is not strongly affiliated with any leading Japanese life insurance or securities company. Thus, it turned to a foreign institution with global experience for building its investment trust business. The partners also announced that they are considering allying in the field of private banking.

After experiencing losses in the Russian and Asian markets in 1997 and 1998, JP Morgan entered into the alliance with DKB to catch up with Citibank and Goldman Sachs in the Japanese market. Through the alliance, JP Morgan wanted to take advantage of DKB's domestic sales network and retail/wholesale customer base. Historically, JP Morgan has been stronger in corporate investment and weaker in retail banking (*Nihon Keizai Shimbun*, October 2, 1998).

Dai-ichi Kangyo Bank also announced in November 1998 that it has agreed to an alliance with Fuji Bank in the area of trust banking. The partners proposed to create a new trust bank—which will focus on pension-fund management and custodial business—by merging their trust banking subsidiaries (Dai-ichi Kangyo Trust & Banking and Fuji Trust and Banking) on an equal basis. The joint venture, which was initiated by Fuji Bank, will allow the two banks to restructure/consolidate their trust banking subsidiaries, leading to greater efficiency, and to combine their large client base.

The joint venture also took over the pension trust, custodial, and stock transfer agency services of Fuji Bank's other trust banking affiliate, Yasuda Trust & Banking (YTB). Fuji Bank had wanted to use its trust bank business as a vehicle for competition and survival after the Big Bang. However, YTB was heavily burdened with bad debts and needed the proceeds obtained by the transfer of these three businesses to improve its financial position.

NEW DEVELOPMENT MODEL THROUGH KNOWLEDGE-BASED ALLIANCES

Typically, companies choose to ally in order to enhance their strengths or to compensate for their weaknesses by seeking partners with the resources they need. These resources differ by industry but can be broadly categorized into two types—knowledge-based and operation-based resources. The first category includes nontangible elements such as proprietary technology, professional employees with state-of-the-art skills, and market intelligence. In contrast, operation-based resources refer to the tangible items necessary for a business, such as operational staff (e.g., clerks, plant workers), facilities, and capital. For the finance sector, important knowledge-based resources are leading-edge financial tools, such as derivatives and investment/asset management services, and risk management proficiencies. Essential operation-based resources include capital, branch offices, and operational staff.

In the past, regulatory protection and interest schemes that were highly favorable to financial institutions (large differential between interest given on deposits and received on credit) made it possible for domestic companies to accumulate a huge operational base (branch offices, staff, etc.) with less emphasis on developing sophisticated financial products and services. *The Economist* reports that "Japan's financial firms are a decade or more behind their foreign rivals. The risk-management revolution and cost-cutting mergers seen elsewhere have largely passed Japan." The magazine also writes that "big domestic investors are also starting to deal with foreign intermediaries. The reason is that few Japanese stockbrokers offer much but execution" (*The Economist*, May 16, 1998). This emphasis on execution is illustrated in the importance Japanese stockbrokers had placed on promoting the frequent buying and selling of stocks to earn transaction fees over growing clients' assets over the long term. In contrast, major Anglo-American financial institutions have survived in their relatively freer markets by accumulating financial savvy and product development capabilities. However, these foreign firms have not been able to build a significant operational base in Japan due to restrictions and regulations.

As discussed in the case studies, Japanese financial institutions are trying to catch up with their Anglo-American counterparts by attempting to reduce this gap in knowledge-based resources through alliances. This is in contrast to the business models that Anglo-American financial institutions have had for competing in their home countries (see Table 11.3). These models have tended to be based not on alliances and coexistence, but on merger and acquisitions and the natural selection of the fittest and the weeding out of the weakest. This section analyzes the alliances discussed in the previous section in terms of the partners' resources and objectives.

March (1991) proposed a model of exploration and exploitation in organization learning for adaptation. This model has been expanded to alliances (Koza and Lewin, 1998), which can be broadly divided into these two categories based on their motivations. Exploitation alliances are those formed for making greater use of existing capabilities by pooling complementary resources to streamline businesses or enter into new markets. In contrast, exploration alliances are those for discovering or learning new business opportunities.

In terms of the first alliance discussed in the preceding section, Sumitomo Bank aimed to secure securities and investment/asset management know-how, whereas Daiwa Securities hoped for capital influx and access to its partner's global sales channel. Accordingly, Sumitomo Bank wanted an exploratory alliance to develop new investment services for the retail and wholesale sectors. In contrast, Daiwa Securities aspired to make greater use of its securities business through an exploitation alliance while receiving capital influx as well. With the inclusion of T. Rowe Price, a major foreign financial institution, Sumitomo

Table 11.3
Business Models Used by Japanese and Anglo-American Financial Institutions

	Japanese Model for Survival	Anglo-American Model for Survival
Objective of Business Model	To gain new knowledge and expertise through alliances to survive in the new hyper-competitive environment.	To expand and grow business by nurturing their own knowledge, and by developing and/or acquiring operational resources.
Business Model	Formation of alliances, such as joint ventures, with one or more of the following types of institutions: —other types of domestic institutions —foreign banks	In their home markets, Anglo-American firms have tended to rely on the following to grow their businesses: —merger and acquisitions —competition through natural selection

Bank and Daiwa Securities intend to increase both their knowledge-based and operation-based resources with the inclusion of the new partner's expertise and global channels.

By definition, the two different types of alliances are closely related to the partner's resources. In an exploration alliance, a corporation partners with another firm for new businesses in which it has little experience. It seeks the knowledge-based resources of a partner and in exchange shares its operation-based resources. An example of one of these alliances is a joint venture between a domestic company and a foreign company with new technology. The domestic company offers its operation-based resources, such as offices, sales force, and capital, and in return receives the foreign partner's new technology. Conversely, a corporation with excess capacity builds an exploitation alliance in a new business area/market to maximize the usage of its existing resources.

From the perspective of Dai-ichi Kangyo Bank, its alliance with JP Morgan is an example of an exploratory alliance between a Japanese company and a foreign partner. Dai-ichi Kangyo Bank sought to take advantage of JP Morgan's long history in the areas of investment trust, asset management, and private banking. In other words, Dai-ichi Kangyo Bank expects to be able to transfer back the knowledge of the joint venture. JP Morgan, on the other hand, had both exploratory and exploitative objectives for the alliance: by allying with Dai-ichi Kangyo, it intended to exploit its global product development capabilities, while gaining experience in the retail banking sector—an area in which it has been weak globally—in Japan.

Similarly, in its partnership with Fuji Bank, Dai-ichi Kangyo Bank desired an exploratory alliance for wholesale trust banking focused on pension-fund management and custodial business. Dai-ichi Kangyo Bank, which had not been strong in trust banking, wished to pool its resources with those of the two trust banks affiliated with Fuji Bank in order to generate greater efficiency in developing new products and services targeted at the soon-to-be-deregulated corporate pension market. Fuji Bank, on the other hand, had a more dire reason for the alliance: it and its affiliate, Yasuda Trust & Banking, were severely weakened financially and needed the proceeds of the transfer of YTB's operations.

In comparison, the objectives of exploratory alliances are more difficult to achieve than those of exploitative alliances because knowledge-based resources are harder to transfer and require more effort and time to accumulate than tangible operation-based resources. Furthermore, it is harder for a corporation to evaluate accurately and objectively a potential partner's expertise and skills.

In the alliance between the Industrial Bank of Japan (IBJ) and Nomura Securities, the partners had both exploitative and exploratory objectives. They desired to streamline their current derivatives and asset management businesses by sharing resources and to utilize each other's customer base (exploitative objectives). They also wanted to achieve the exploratory objective of gaining from each other complementary expertise in derivatives, as the Nomura Securities is strong in equities and the IBJ in credit. IBJ needed to transform itself from a long-term credit bank for continued survival by obtaining retail banking and securities experience (exploratory).

It has been reported that there are different opinions within IBJ and Nomura with regard to the effectiveness of the partnership, which may cause problems in the future. After the alliance announcement, Nomura board executives met with President Yasuhiko Ujiie, and one director stated that, while he understood that derivatives and asset management were important, he wondered about the choice of IBJ as a partner (*Nihon Keizai Shimbun*, May 16, 1998). This statement reflects the opinion of many Nomura directors that IBJ may not be the leader in credit and credit rating, and may not be the ideal partner.

In its alliance with Dai-ichi Mutual Life, IBJ has both exploratory and exploitative objectives. The credit bank aspired to increase its operation-based resources by receiving capital and making use of the insurance company's nationwide customer base, and to obtain knowledge-based resources regarding retail banking and the soon-to-be deregulated insurance business.

CONCLUSION

Major Japanese financial institutions have chosen alliances and coexistence as their business model for survival, as opposed to the Anglo-American models of M&A and competition that leads to weeding out the weak. Nevertheless, the reshaping of the Japanese finance sector is still in the early stages, and this current trend of alliances may be only transient. Different models for business survival may appear in the future as deregulatory measures and ensuing competition play out.

Nonetheless, it will not be easy for Japanese banks to achieve the exploratory objectives of these alliances, because knowledge-based resources are harder to accumulate and require greater effort and time to transfer. Consequently, their partners with these types of resources can exert uneven power. To avoid this unequal advantage, it is important that the banks seeking the knowledge-based resources are active in the joint ventures by involving key staff and management on a day-to-day basis and do not merely invest capital. Knowledge of the dispatched staff must also be consciously transferred back to and internalized in the head office.

Since the alliance partners have different objectives, they must also work to ensure that the arrangements are mutually beneficial, or the partnership will not last. Speed is of utmost importance as well, since the window of opportunity will narrow quickly as companies from different industries and foreign markets enter the newly deregulated finance sector. Because of the effort and time required for obtaining knowledge-based resources, Japanese financial institutions should focus their business strategies on specific areas of retail and/or wholesale banking and finance. If they try to attack all areas and spread resources too thin, they will not be able to accumulate real expertise in any area within a reasonable time span.

All that said, the continued survival of any Japanese financial institution is also heavily contingent on how quickly it can improve its financial position. There are still many rumors and stories in the media of undisclosed bad debts. If the amount of hidden unrecoverable loans of an institution is too great, it may not be able to survive regardless of its alliances.

REFERENCES

The Economist. (1998). Japanese Finance: Rich Pickings for the Gaijin. *The Economist*, May, 16, pp. 11–13.

Koza, M., and Lewin, A. (1988). The Co-evolution of Strategic Alliances. *Organization Science*, 9(3), pp. 255–264.

March, J. G. (1991). Exploration and Exploitation in Organizational Learning. *Organization Science*, 2(1), pp. 71–87.

Nihon Keizai Shimbun. (1998). Kogin, Nomura Teikei Happyo, Nennai Ni Kyogo De Nisha Setsuritsu (IBJ and Nomura Announce Alliance, Will Establish Two Companies within the Year). *Nihon Keizai Shimbun*, May 14.

Nihon Keizai Shimbun. (1998). Kogin To Nomura Shoken Teikei, Anarisuto Ni Kiku (IBJ–Nomura Securities Alliance—Asking Analysts). *Nihon Keizai Shimbun*, May 14.

Nihon Keizai Shimbun. (1998). Kogin, Nomura Teikei No Shogeki (The Shock of the IBJ–Nomura Securities Alliance). *Nihon Keizai Shimbun*, May 16.

Nihon Keizai Shimbun. (1998). Big Bang Kachi Kumi He Rengo (Alliance for Winning After the Big Bang). *Nihon Keizai Shimbun*, July 28.

Nihon Keizai Shimbun. (1998). Aseru Togin, Gaishi Teikei Wo Mosaku (Japanese City

Banks Apprehensive, Considering Alliance with Foreign Firms). *Nihon Keizai Shimbun*, July 29.

Nihon Keizai Shimbun. (1998). Sumitomo Bank, Daiwa Securities Ga Teikei Happyo, Sarani Gaishikei Teikei He (Sumitomo Bank and Daiwa Securities Announce an Alliance, and Are Considering Bringing in a Foreign Institution). *Nihon Keizai Shimbun*, July 29.

Nihon Keizai Shimbun. (1998). Dai-ichi Kangin, JP Morgan Teikei, Gaishi To Renkei, Togin Ni Hakyu (Dai-ichi Kangyo Bank and JP Morgan Ally; Alliance with Foreign Firms Spreads). *Nihon Keizai Shimbun*, October 1.

Nihon Keizai Shimbun. (1998): JP Morgan Ni Nani Wo Manabu Ka (What to Learn from JP Morgan). *Nihon Keizai Shimbun*, October 2.

Nishiura, Y. (1998). *Marketing Innovation of Financial Services*. Tokyo: Toyo Keizai Shinposha.

Shimano, K. (1998). *Kinyu Gyokai Saihen Chizu* (A Map to the Realignment of the Finance Sector). Tokyo: Pal Shuppan.

Shukan Toyo Keizai. (1999). Kyoso Rule Ga Kawaru (The Rules of Competition Are Changing). *Shukan Toyo Keizai*, April 3.

Teramoto, Y. (1990). *Network Power*. Tokyo: NTT Shuppan.

Part IV

In Search of an Asian "Post-Crisis" Management Paradigm

Chapter 12

The Evolution of Management in Thailand after the Asian Crisis

John Kidd, Kriengsak Niratpattanasai, and Frank-Jürgen Richter

INVESTMENT AND THE ASIAN CRISIS

The mass of FDI flows tends to move to and from the developed countries with the exception of (greater) China, which has absorbed a huge flow of inward investment for many years. That said, it is clear that Thailand has also managed to benefit from a significant inward flow of investment over the recent past, with no indication of a slowdown in the last recorded year, 1998.

The recently prevailing view of Thailand's emergent economy and its ''good'' management practices changed radically at the start of the Asian economic crisis in 1997. The bubble burst, and the economy fell into disarray. The exchange rate collapsed following the decision to float the currency in July 1997, a humiliating IMF bailout had been agreed to, and general confidence in the country's economic institutions was shattered. In almost every industry, output volume dropped dramatically: in the first six months of 1998, automobile sales dropped by around 75 percent compared to the same period of 1997 (Warr, 1998); real estate business posted a negative growth of 80 percent; and clothes sales declined by 30 percent. Only Instant Noodle reported a growth, a substantial 30 percent growth! Instant noodles in Thailand cost about 5 baht, whereas rice with curry (considered a local fast food) costs 20 baht. In short, instant noodles became one of the key indicators for the economic downturn and is perhaps a general indicator across Asia. A research student of one of the authors (Kidd) comes from a poor Japanese farming family wherein he, being the second son, grew up on a noodle diet rather than rice (rice was reserved for the number-one son). We might suggest that variations in potato sales may be a similar indicator in Europe.

This chapter reviews five major economic trends in Thailand and their implications for Thai management. Since publication of Naisbitt's *Megatrends Asia* (1997), times have changed dramatically. Consequently, we will try to present a realistic view, illustrating post-crisis economic trends and moving to the development of an evolutionary model of management for the Thai business environment. It will stimulate discussion on the sectors and indicate how Thai managers would have to modify their business attitudes. We acknowledge that change is a part of human evolution—which is the message in *Business Week*'s Annual Special Issue (European Edition, March 20, 1999) featuring "the 50 best performers." Their Executive Officers state that "above all, companies must be prepared to change fast." The grounds and perspectives of change in Thailand are quite painful. Especially since the years of boom, Thais did not prepare themselves for any significant downturn of the bubble economy that they were generating.

THE FIVE TRENDS IN POST-CRISIS THAILAND

Until the outbreak of the crisis, Thailand was one of the best places to do business in Southeast Asia. Today, it is one of the worst hit by the economic turmoil. Yet at the turn of the millennium we can see more clearly the root causes of the crisis and perceive a way forward for Thailand. Over the next few years, Thailand will need a significant upgrading of a range of business-related institutions and processes. Although the first steps in restructuring debts and restructuring businesses have already been completed, the makeover of Thailand Inc. will take several years, if not generations, to achieve since the underlying enduring attitudes of the Thai people are deeply embedded in their culture and in their learning processes.

The following sections describe five major shifts taking place in Thailand in the short term.

First Trend: From Local Ownership to Foreign Ownership

The devaluation of the baht in 1997 ensured that most Thai firms would lose most of their wealth. Hence, they need immediate cash injections to improve their balance sheets. Quite often, the only available and remaining source is inward foreign investment, given that most of the domestic investors were in severe trouble regarding their own cash-flow situation. Hence, many industries might become dominated by foreign firms or become local joint ventures with foreign firms. The ownership is being transferred from purely Thai to partially or wholly foreign; as a consequence, the management methods will change, and sometimes not subtly.

Foreign firms dominate the manufacturing sector: they mostly arrived during the early phase of import substitution (1960–1975) in order to maintain their shares in the Thai market by taking advantage of local production. Foreign investment surged again after the Plaza Accord (1986 onward) and caused currency appreciation. Foreign investment took place mainly in the acquisition of finance institutions. In the finance sector, for example, foreigners can now hold majority shares in banks for up to ten years. So far, two banks—Thai Danu and the Bank of Asia—have deals allowing foreign banks to take majority positions.

The implications for Thai managers are as follows:

The Way Thais Do Business Will Be More Transparent

In the past, Thais used to do business in grey areas as well. For example, if Thais had to contact government officers on business-related issues, they had to spend some portion of the expense for "Tea Money." This may not be accepted by foreign venture partners. Foreign investors might be aware of this practice and consequently forbid any kind of bribery.

On this aspect [The Recommendation was adopted by the Council of the OECD on April 11, 1996.]

Perceiving Other Cultures

Thais have been getting used to seeing foreigners who come to Thailand adapt to Thailand's culture and management style. But now the game is different. Foreigners are the new shareholders or the new bosses. They come in with high expectations of a quick return in their investments. The Thais' new role is to understand the incoming culture and work with them effectively. Thais have to learn how to work in a multicultural environment. (The cultural aspect is discussed in more detail later in this chapter.)

English Communication Skills

It is imperative that Thai managers use English more fluently as the medium of business communication since, like it or not, English is the global business language. The old belief of Thai managers who were not good at English was that "as long as you work in a Thai firm, you are not required to be efficient in English." This notion is out of date. Since Thailand was never colonized as Singapore or Malaysia were, Thais use English as a second language. Only young executives who graduated overseas are fluent in English, but unfortunately these people are still the minority in their local organizations. In common with many Asians, Thais are too shy to speak English with foreigners because they are afraid they might pronounce the words incorrectly and thus lose face.

Second Trend: From Protected Market to Deregulated Market

Thailand used to have a protected market, especially in banking, insurance, energy, petrochemicals, and telecommunication industries. The government erected trade barriers, worrying that local organizations could not compete with foreign competitors. But GATT (now the WTO), and the IMF are forcing Thailand to deregulate their market to allow free competition. This means that the level of competition will increase dramatically, so new strategies to win customers have to be deployed.

The implications for Thai managers are as follows:

Competitive Advantage

Since the new players in the market are now global or regional brands, Thais can no longer play by their old rules. Actions that worked in the past will not likely work in the future. Thais need to find a particular competitive advantage to differentiate their products or services since the success of "Me-too products" has now ended. Products and services that do not have unique selling points will not be on the market for long since consumers will ignore them.

The Thai economic crisis is due in part to the inability of Thai firms to generate enough added value in their products to overcome the deficit stemming from their importation of raw materials and components. In order to relieve such a situation, the technological capability and competitive advantage of Thai industry have to be strengthened.

Customer Focus

Most of the firms within the protected industries never took good care of their customers. For example, bankers used to think that customers came to the bank solely to ask for loans. So, they thought that providing loans to customers would be a special favor. When Citibank came to Thailand 15 years ago, it launched an aggressive marketing campaign that focused on the retail customers. It gained a substantial market share, although it operated only one branch (to the owing government's general protection in allowing only one branch for foreign banks). The retail bank customers were asked about the service expectations compared to the actual deliveries. The result was a big perceptual gap. One of the local bank chief executives argued that "the reason that our bank is still the market leader is not because we are much better than other local banks, but rather that we are not as bad at what we do." In the near future, customers will demand really good service (not the lip-service that every bank is currently claiming). Consequently, customers will see value being given in return for investing their private money in the banks.

Privatization

The IMF advised the Thai government to privatize state enterprises and government functions. Inevitably with privatization, there will be massive layoffs of nonproductive employees as the work processes in these organizations are redesigned. Office automation and new technologies will replace several manual work processes (for the good of the workers sometimes—using robots to spray paint on cars, for instance). In many ways, this may be seen as a prudent step toward being integrated in the global economy (it is like using the English language). It is through the creation of the commonality of computer-based applications packages to aid management that the Thai managers will become more attuned to the business and communications mechanisms of the inwardly investing firms. But there are drawbacks, as seen in Japan, where the "bubble" has also burst. This has led to layoffs, and as a consequence, a huge loss of face for the company-aligned employee who becomes a nuisance at home where his wife once reigned supreme. In some cases this has led to the suicide of the once-proud worker (Bremner et al., 1999).

Third Trend: From Bubble Economy to Real Demand

Before the crisis, Thailand enjoyed double-digit growth rates, but now many of Thailand's industries are not growing or at least they will take some time to recover. In exports, Thailand enjoyed the benefit of low labor costs, thereby promoting "assembly" products such as garments, shoes, and computer components. To export these products, Thailand now has to compete with China, which is becoming a tough competitor. Growth in these product sectors is quite uncertain. In addition, sales in real estate, housing, and automobiles are falling. In short, economic activity in luxury products is declining.

The implications are as follows:

Cost Cutting

Because future real demand will be less than today, many firms will be unable to operate their business at the same cost. Managers have to lead their organizations to produce more output with fewer resources. Unnecessary expenses have to be cut at a time when wage growth will be rising, and the demographic trends in the country show there will be fewer young (cheap) nimble-fingered workers who in several years time will be a drain on the economy as they 'demand' a state pension. These pensions, as in all developed economies, have to come from their government's current account.

Information Base

Since markets and consumer behavior are difficult to predict, Thais have to generate information systems to be able to react to market changes in a timely way. In fact, to be proactive will be a prerequisite of a modern enterprise (see *Business Week* cited earlier "on change"). We will have to wait to see whether or not the traditional Thai will become so entrepreneurial. This new reliance on information technology cuts across the traditional role of interpersonal networking that is operating throughout Asia.

Planning

Thais are not experienced corporate planners. In the old days, when Thailand was rich with natural resources, Thais used the motto "In the river we have fish, in the field we have rice," which means that food was usually available right in front of the house. Why bother to hold inventories? Furthermore, natural disasters like earthquakes or snow in winter have not occurred in Thailand, so there was no need to fight with nature. Hence, there was no perceived need to plan ahead.

There is a local joke regarding the meaning of "plan-ning" "Ning," when pronounced in the Thai language, means "unmoving." When Thais say "planning," it sounds like "plan!—and do nothing." Unfortunately, Thais do not have sufficient enthalpy (i.e., stored energy) in their economy or in relation to a global economy that came "knocking on their door." Planning is an absolute must in an increasingly integrated global economy.

Fourth Trend: From Diversification to Focus

As major Thai conglomerates prospered they diversified their businesses into unrelated enterprises. To mention a few examples: Siam Cement diversified from being a cement producer to a construction-related business plus telecommunications and automobiles; Charoen Phokaphan Group (CP) diversified from an agricultural base to telecommunications, cable TV, retail business, motorbikes, and energy; United Communication (UCOM) diversified from telecommunications to retail business, regional airlines, and cable TV. Notably it would seem that Thai conglomerates are often led by ethnic Chinese entrepreneurs who are seen to dominate all Southeast Asian economies (Pyatt, 1996). Just as in the neighboring countries of Malaysia and Indonesia, the ethnic Chinese expanded into businesses in which they had no experience. The general word-of-mouth networking between other expatriate Chinese rapidly led to these simple expansions.

A contrast can be seen between the data collection modes of the Oriental and Occidental countries. In the Occidental much of this data is open to analysis, so generations of business students and others have become used to developing statistical models for forecasting futures. In the Orient, data is also collected: but if collected by the state, it may not be made available. If collected by a firm it will be only accessible internally and often on a limited access base. Thus, the fastest way to assess a new situation in Asia is to call one's trusted friends to form a judgment based on their collective subjective model. In this we note the centrality of the concept of "trust" and reciprocity implied by the networking.

Most of the diversified conglomerates are now learning the need for fiscal conservatism and sharper focus on core industries. Today, the Thai conglomerates pay the price of their past profligacy—their appetite for new markets and new industries knew no bounds. Now they are forced to focus on what they do best. Siam Cement, for example, is selling off or reducing its stakes in dozens of noncore operations to focus on just three of its strongest lines: cement, petrochemicals, and paper, which account for about 60 percent of the company's total sales and have a similar share of its assets. The idea is to specialize only in lines where the company has strong profits, returns on investment and long-term competitiveness. But we must mention some general concerns here. Take a general manufacturer of, say, bricks. It gets bigger and so needs a computer system for inventory control and fiscal management, and it acquires a logistics operation to aid its goals. Eventually, this fictional firm finds that its expertise lies in computing and telecommunications, and not in the original core business.

The implications for Thai firms are as follows:

Mix of Management Style

The high-calibre persons who transfer back to the core business will have to adapt rapidly to their new environment. For example, if they transferred from a Telecom industry to the agriculture sector, it would take some time to become attuned to their new industries knowledge base. They may bring some innovative ideas; however, they have to be able "to sell new tricks to the old dogs." Unfortunately, they might find it quite difficult, because the existing executives might have wrong perceptions. Lots of balancing by top management is needed to best utilize their mix of management styles—and in general, until the old cadre retire, there will be many lost battles.

Product Development and Research Budget

Many organizations stopped spending on new product development in order to save as much as possible. Nowadays Thai corporate restructuring does not allow expenditure on projects that cannot indicate a strong return on investment—and typically R&D can offer no guarantees. This is not an unusual problem, but it needs a sensitive approach with a well-educated workforce. They have to hold many workshops and seminars to change the culture.

Corporate Culture

The big conglomerates once threw securities analysts out of shareholder meetings. Now they consider good media and investor relations a matter of best practice. Greater openness will help companies build their share price, making it easier and cheaper to raise funds as needed. In effect, by promoting a trustworthy business base, they hope to be free of nepotism and opaque practices that have dogged most Asian management practices for decades (and that from the boom times the Western managers have to accept blame, too, for they were party to these practices by implication). In the new regimes, the openness of accounting and the acceptance of GAAP (Generally Accepted Accounting Principles) will allow the economic sectors' performance to be measured and thus the comparability of economic performances to be seen. Once this is so, investors will be much happier with local Thai firms.

Fifth Trend: From Market Rate Pay to Pay by Performance

During the bubble economy, finding a good employee was not easy; companies had to buy their senior managers at a high price. The executives' compensation and benefits included a company car with driver, cellular phone, secretary, and unlimited travel and entertainment budget. Because of market shrinkage and unstable demand, it was hard to identify who was a good manager and who was just the lucky guy. In general, in every person's resume were stories of success in sales upon profit increases, as well as business expansions. Apparently, the compensation level was related to the market rate and not to formal qualifications. Today things are different. Most of the Thai companies have had to cut unnecessary expenses, and many also cut salaries by approximately 30 percent.

The implications are as follows:

Ability to Spend Decreased

Thai senior executives were formerly able to send their first child to study overseas. The second child went to Europe or the United States on short-term educational trips. They could afford to buy residences in Bangkok and condominiums in tropical resort areas like Pattaya or Huahin. Most of them did not save their earnings. With the fall in income, they had to reallocate their funding and entrench their way of life, becoming more prudent and conservative, and leading by example.

Long-Term Employment

Thais are skilled in relationship building. In Asia day-to-day living and business practices, including the employment of staff, normally depend on relationships. Thais used to believe that "regardless of how lazy or incapable employees are, as long as they do not steal money or property, they will not be laid off." This belief can no longer be applied. Honesty alone is not enough; providing real contributions to the organization is crucial, and so formal performance-related pay assessments are becoming the norm.

Learn to Stand on Your Own Feet

Most organizations are about to reduce their workforce, and executives have to handle more responsibilities. They may no longer have company car, personal driver, and personal secretary. They have to drive by themselves (with their own car in some cases) and have to share a secretary with colleagues or the boss. This means they have to pour their own coffee, dial telephone calls, type memos and letters, send e-mails and faxes; but now they have to learn basic administration skills. The critical factor is that Thais are very concerned about losing face. Many care so much about showing others how rich and big they are that it may be difficult for them to do "clerical work," and, what's worse, to be seen doing it.

META-LEARNING: A CATALYTIC PROCESS

The acceptance of national differences in political and economic systems, which are driven by their own internal logic, supports the rapid movement of people and communications between business communities. Yet cultural systems, which are fundamentally irrational and value-driven, often block real understanding and transfer. Various studies suggest that management methods vary by culture. Just as there is a Thai-style management, there is also an American style and a Country X style (Hofstede, 1980, 1991; Kidd & Lu, 1999). Cultures cannot carry another's culture as a mantle since the mature character of a culture is unchangeable, or at least highly resistant to transformation, and we each carry our own.

There are many differences that the workers and managers in joint ventures have to accommodate in their daily lives. Others who have studied this area are Hall (1976) and Hoppe (1993).

To illustrate several national cultural differences we refer to Hofstede (1980, 1991). We may observe that the Thais would appear to be caring, collectivist, and medium to long term in their goals, which may conflict with their need to accept the "laws of hierarchy," yet they wish to be clear about issues. One may see considerable differences between the sociometrics of its near-neighbor countries, which may have stronger economies such as Korea and Japan, and certainly with the values expressed by the British and Americans.

This summary, though brief, nevertheless highlights the underlying differences due to the cultural predisposition of persons from the indicated countries. They show that attitudes, sociometrics, and behaviors are quite different, and thus JV firms may suffer greatly if their cultural "fit" is widely divergent, especially if staff are disinclined to change or do not accept these differences.

In a situation such as the current economic crisis in Thailand, certain culturally bound behaviors and attitudes seem to have provoked the inflating of the economic bubble. Random, illogical, and gross speculation at the Bangkok stock exchange, and the use of "Tea Money," have to be overcome. It would not be right, however, to impose an American style of management, as Thai managers historically and culturally carry their own distinctive perceptions of how things have to be done (Tiralp, 1998). In a highly original argument, Unger (1998) considers the unique organization of Thai society and the impact it has had on the country's institutions and their political and economic outcomes.

Hence, we would like to suggest the approach of Argyris and Schön (1978) who suggest "meta-learning" as a mechanism to reflect on one's own culturally bound behaviour and by which one might develop new models of knowledge creation and perception. Meta-learning is proposed here to involve the management style of organizations accepting that this is always rooted in the history of a given organization. The future could be a hybrid of Thai and Western style of management rather than the domination of any one system. Indeed, domination will be fatal (as in an underground guerrilla war) since it can erupt over some small affair that reflects the wider issues of lack of trust and lack of co-evolution between the two management groups.

Meta-learning consists of the identification and development of learning processes. With this learning mode as part of a holistic approach, previous learning processes themselves become an object of contemplation. Symbolic events are reread, concepts are reinterpreted, and the points of reference for learning instances are changed. With meta-learning the ability of organizations to learn is improved. The question not only arises upon whether an organization learns, but whether it is learning fast and penetratingly enough to realize its use. This can only happen by removing learning barriers and stimulating the willingness to learn. Note that some of this process will entail the acceptance of "loss of face" as individuals. Westerners, as well as Thais, make mistakes, and through these mistakes they should be able to learn.

In the rarest cases, meta-learning leads directly to a "cultural revolution." But more likely it will be a stepwise evolution until a balance between wanted and actual behavior has occurred. The amount and the necessary speed of meta-learning depend on the gap that lies between the established culture and its environment. If the gap is large and the organization is willing, that progress may be rapid. The influence that the corporate culture has on the learning processes is relatively undisputed (Keough and Doman, 1992). It influences the interpretation of models, and it is used to compare experiences with its norms and determinants leading to the filtering of information. If, for example, the manufacturing of a certain product or technology is an integral part of the corporate culture, the signals for change are often not perceived for a long time. Generally, only after a failure is experienced is the organization willing to make changes. Basically, we are talking about a human condition, not one restricted to Thai people. We do not perceive the facts until they are overwhelmingly obvious—a point repeatedly stressed by Bayesian statisticians. See, for instance, Kahaneman et al. (1982).

META-LEARNING AND MENTAL THERAPY

Having illustrated the underlying rationale behind meta-learning, it can be concluded that Thais need to relearn. Yet naturally, when the word *learning* is mentioned, the general perception of Thais is to recall the formal education at school or university. In Thailand, most classified advertisements for recruitment put a major emphasis on formal education rather than on the key capabilities to get the work done. Thais need to realize that learning has nothing to do with formal education but is a rather complex process of knowledge creation based on formal education, and strongly influenced by the organizational and national culture that reeducates "in the university of life." What has to be promoted is the capacity to learn how to learn, as noted in Figure 12.1.

Meta-learning is often hindered by depression and an unwillingness to enter new territory. The economic crisis caused a huge general depression among Thai executives, and some managers try to use traditional Thai ways of therapy and to enter Buddhist temples, worshiping as believers. Generally, Buddhist monks are not good at counseling skills focused on business issues. Nevertheless the ongoing changes in the economy, society, and culture will force Thais to change

Figure 12.1
Meta-Learning Applied to the Thai Situation

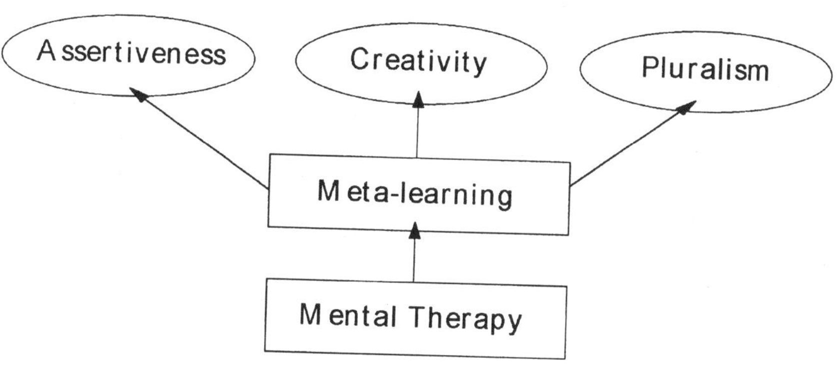

and adapt their values and beliefs. Mental therapy is one of the solutions needed to trigger the necessary processes of meta-learning.

Mental Therapy—To Counteract the Detractors

Mental therapy is very new to Thais: they traditionally perceive visits to a psychiatrist as shameful (generally this is so globally). Nonetheless, just as one visits a medical doctor for treatment of some physical ailment, it should be just as acceptable to visit a mental therapist. This will be the major barrier preventing Thais from visiting a psychiatrist. There might be a solution to this "face" issue. One might change the name of mental therapy to career counsellor, who could then exert influence right from the base of the organization. The staff in this department must have basic skills in dealing with depressed employees and can naturally provide basic healing for them.

The government can help cope with this issue. Because Thailand is a Buddhist country, the temple is a place where people feel comfortable visiting. Therefore, if the government would offer to train monks to be first-hand career counselors, the incidence of depression among Thais, would greatly decline, and might in turn trigger meta-learning. But this is quite a wild proposal!

Three subfields can be considered as hindrances to channel meta-learning before it can change the grounds of Thai-style management: namely, assertiveness, creativity, and pluralism.

Assertiveness

Thai culture encourages humility and politeness. For instance, the Thai language offers no distinction between the two words "aggressive" and "assertive." Generally, Thais don't like confrontation. If they disagree with others (particularly with respect to foreigners), they just keep quiet—and in part, this attitude is due to the fact that English is their second language. They don't make decisions quickly, and they prefer to speak with colleagues outside the meeting room after a formal discussion. The result is that their apparent degree of commitment is usually low.

Many expatriate executives find that Thais often seem to agree in the meeting room, but there is no progress. Many such cases are due to a failure to understand the concept of commitment (see also Tayeb, 1996). When Thais nod their head during a discussion with foreigners, it means they are listening to you; it doesn't mean that they agree or understand. Because they are polite, they just want to accommodate others' feeling. Thais therefore have to be more assertive so that they can express thoughts and ideas without feeling thay might be "disliked" by others. Note the similar aspect of the Japanese uttering "hai"—which literally translated means "yes," but in fact it simply means "we are listening, please continue." This mistranslation caused much confusion for U.S. managers in early negotiations with the Japanese.

Creativity

Thailand's education system did not prepare managers to do their job creatively. Furthermore, since Thais have been ruled by a monarchy for a long time, this encouraged their habit of waiting for commands and suggestions. Thais have to realize their creativity to respond flexibly to the market.

What Thais should emphasize is the fostering of creativity in areas where products and processes incorporate a large measure of (local) knowledge. The question is, how can such business be done more creatively? Undoubtedly, the answer entails a wholesale restructuring of the teaching programes in schools, as well as changes to the practices used by companies to develop their human resources. Naturally the policies employed by the government to promote education must also be changed. The reforms in each area need to be aimed at unleashing the creative potential of the individual and in preparing conditions by which this potential can be exercised to the fullest.

Pluralism

Conflict per se is almost universally perceived as a bad thing. Looking at the synonyms for the word "conflict," we see battle, disharmony, antagonism, and argument. Most of these words reflect a negative force in human interaction. But conflict is one way people make progress. If people do not have conflict, humankind will not enter deep discussion and so potentially do not evolve. But if people just say whatever they think, and others respond generally, saying "Yes, I agree," they might have a lot of problems later if they do not explore other possibilities. Again as an example, one of the authors (Kidd) experienced many difficulties in an e-mail relationship with an Asian research partner who said little in response to repeated, and increasingly hostile, questioning. The two persons were, at that time, locked in their social histories—one incapable of disagreement, and the other wishing to use "conflict" as a creative process. The partnership eventually floundered. On the other hand, Pascale (1990) is confidant that conflict, if handled well, may be one of the best forces for developing U.S. enterprises.

Avoidance or compromise are the preferred approaches frequently used by the Thais in dealing with conflict. While having a goal of harmonizing within their culture, Thais are not familiar with confrontation and pluralism. Thus, while easily said, Thais should practice more open pluralism in order to become better at creating and managing conflicts in their international ventures.

CONCLUSION

Before the crisis in 1997, Thai management was instrumental in propelling Thailand's dramatic growth, but it has ceased to function as smoothly as it once did because the environment has fundamentally altered. What was an industrial and commercial system propelled by passive involvement through absorbing considerable inwards investment has now become a proactive management system searching for new inward investment based on joint management. In some cases, the older mechanisms reliant on fast growth have become counterproductive: they are holding the companies back. We need to induce creative learning show potential inward investors that Thais mean business once more—but jointly.

REFERENCES

Argyris, C., and Schön, D. A. (1978). *Organizational Learning: A Theory of Action Perspective*. Reading, MA: Addison-Wesley.

Bremner, B., Thornton, E., and Kunii, I. M. (1999). The Fall of a Keiretsu. *Business Week*, European Edition, March 15, pp. 34–40.

Hall, D. (1998). *Business Prospects in Thailand*. London: Prentice Hall.

Hall, E. T. (1976). *Beyond Culture*. New York: Doubleday.

Hofstede, G. (1980). *Culture's Consequences: International Differences in Work-Related Values*. London: Sage Publications.

Hofstede, G. (1991). *Cultures and Organizations: Software of the Mind*. London: McGraw-Hill.

Hoppe, H. M. (1993). The Effects of National Culture on the Theory and Practice of Managing R&D Professionals Abroad. *R&D Management*, 23(4), pp. 313–325.

Kahneman, D., Slovic, P., and Tversky, A. (1982). *Judgement under Uncertainty: Heuristics and Biases*. Cambridge: Cambridge University Press.

Keough, M., and Doman, A. (1992). The CEO as Organization Designer: An Interview with Professor Jay W. Forrester. *The McKinsey Quarterly*, 28(2), pp. 3–30.

Kidd, J., and Lu, J. (1999). Networks as Comparative Advantage: The Role of Chinese Sogo Shosha in Managing Paradox. I. In F. J. Richter (ed.), *Business Networks in Asia: Promises, Doubts, and Perspectives*. Westport, CT: Quorum, pp. 211–236.

Krungthep Thurakij (Bangkok). (1998). White Collar Research by Spa Advertising Company. September 9.

Naisbitt, J. (1997). *Megatrends Asia.* London: Nicholas Brealey Publishing.

The Nation (Bangkok). (1998). September 23.

Pascale, R. (1990). *Managing on the Edge: How Successful Companies Use Conflict to Stay Ahead.* London: Penguin.

Pyatt, T. R. (1996). Chinese Business Networks and Entrepreneurial Clans in Thailand. *Asia Pacific Business Review,* 3(2), pp. 1–25.

Tayeb, M. H. (1996). *The Management of a Multicultural Workforce.* Chichester: John Wiley.

Tiralp, A. (1998). Japanese Direct Investment and Technology Transfer in Thailand. In Y. Takahashi, M. Murata, and K. M. Rahman (eds.), *Management Strategies of Multinational Corporations in Asian Market.* Tokyo: Chuo University Press, pp. 91–111.

Unger, D. (1998) *Building Social Capital in Thailand: Fibres, Finance, and Infrastructure.* Cambridge: Cambridge University Press.

Walsh J. (1998). A World War on Bribery. *Time,* June 22.

Walsh, J. P., and Ungson, G. R. (1991). Organizational Memory. *Academy of Management Review,* 1, pp. 157–191.

Warr, P. G. (1998). Thailand. In R. H. McLeod and R. Garnaut (eds.), *East Asia in Crisis: From Being a Miracle to Needing One?* London: Routledge, pp. 49–65.

Chapter 13

The Crisis of Japanese Management and Its Transferability Abroad: The "Hybrid Model"

Lucrezia Songini

INTRODUCTION

This study aims to analyze Japanese management in order to point out how its characteristics are changing as a result of the recent economic crisis in Japan. The analysis of the transferability abroad of Japanese management can help us to hypothesize the future of Japanese management. In fact, in the foreign transplants, Japanese management was transferred by introducing some changes in its original structure, owing to the need to cope with different local environments. The "hybrid management model" was developed in many of the foreign subsidiaries, which is formed by a mix of traditional features and new characteristics. Because it emphasizes a change in those elements which are now criticized in Japan, the "hybrid model" can be used as a benchmark for Japanese parent companies willing to change their management systems. We are in the presence of a new stage in the evolution of Japanese management: the previous phase of its transferability abroad has now been followed by a new phase, characterized by the importation in Japan of the "hybrid model," originally developed by foreign transplants. This model could represent a strategic option to those Japanese companies that are dealing with a crisis in the traditional management systems in Japan.

THE DEBATE ABOUT JAPANESE MANAGEMENT

In the 1980s and until the early 1990s, Japanese management was considered to be the most innovative answer to the crisis of Taylorism and Fordism. The success of Japanese management in the international arena has caused a strong debate between two different schools: the "culture-bounded" and the "culture-free'' theories. The first theory states that Japanese management cannot be transferred successfully abroad because it is highly dependent on the peculiar ethics and culture of Japanese society. This is the opinion of mostly Japanese authors, from different disciplines, who were the first to study Japanese management, such as:

- Nakane (1970), who considered the collectivist tradition of Japanese society to be one of the fundamentals of the Japanese company development. She referred to the institution of the traditional family (*Ie*), which was formed not only by the family's blood members, but also by other kinds of people. The same structure would be transferred into the first entrepreneurial firms in Japan and the organizational structure of Japanese companies.
- Morishima (1982), who pointed out the influence of religions (Shintoism and Confucianism) on Japanese culture and ethics and, consequently, on early Japanese companies. In particular, Shintoism influenced the development of the nationalistic spirit and the sense of respect for the authority of Japanese people, while Confucianism supported the Japanese worker's spirit of abnegation and sense of duty to the company and stimulated search for harmony and cooperation within groups.
- Doi (1971), who gave a psychoanalytic interpretation of the social behavior of Japanese people and particularly of the individual's sense of dependence on the belonging social groups (family or company). This dependence forced people to maintain harmonious relationships within the group and not to act in contrast with the collective will.
- Yamamura (1986), who gave a historical interpretation of the evolution of the Japanese company, coming from the first monopolistic and familiar groups (*zaibatsu*) to the modern industrial groups (*keiretsu*).

The ''culture-free'' school has been formed mostly by Western authors, who started to study Japanese management in the 1980's, when Japanese companies gained leadership in the international markets. They agree to consider Japanese management an innovative and rational answer to the problems, which are peculiar to the age of *lean enterprise*, such as the search for efficiency, production flexibility, timeliness, and quality (Cooper, 1995). Because of its rational superiority, this management model would be applicable in different contexts from that of the original one. The authors belonging to this school are as follows:

- Aoki (1988), who gave a microeconomic interpretation of the Japanese model with regard to the ''incentive theory.'' It stated that the core of Japanese management is represented by the particular employment system, based on a merit hierarchy and a centralized structure of incentives.
- Coriat (1991) and Womack, Jones, and Roos (1990), who considered the achievement of the Toyota Production System (TPS) a ''Copernican revolution'' as far as the labor and production organization is concerned. Actually, the TPS overturns the traditional rules of the Tayloristic and Fordistic system.
- Dore (1987), who compared the allocative efficiency of Western companies with the bureaucratic style of Japanese enterprises, which is based on some social agreements

peculiar to the Japanese employment system, which assure authority acceptance and the cooperative and diligent participation of workers to company activities.

- Cooper (1995), who studied the competitive strategies of Japanese companies: they developed a new strategy, the *confrontation strategy*, which got over the rigid partition between cost leadership and differentiation strategies (Porter, 1985). *Confrontation strategy* can develop and manufacture differentiated products, with high quality and low cost.

Because Japan remained quite isolated from the rest of the world economy until the 1970s, we can state that Japanese management represents the results of a peculiar evolution. As a consequence, it is difficult to directly apply the various existing management theories. However, a comparison with two theories that concern the evolution of the modern enterprise allows us to evaluate the real innovation introduced by Japanese companies.

First, a comparison can be made with the evolutionary theory of the American big corporation, developed by Chandler (1962). He stated that the rational answer of big differentiated corporations to the growing environmental complexity was represented by the adoption of the multidivisional organizational structure. In contrast, the Japanese market structure drove Japanese companies to manage the complexity in a different way, not based on the number of hierarchical levels and internal specialization. In fact, the post-war privations, which forced the emerging Japanese enterprises to produce small quantities of differentiated products, caused a more organic development of Japanese companies, focused on despecialization and internal flexibility. As a consequence, the production flexibility would enter into the ''genetic inheritance'' of Japanese companies, since their first stage of development.

In addition, it is noteworthy to compare the development of Japanese management with the evolutionary theory of Di Bernardo and Rullani (1990), who predict an organization based on ''modules'' as a future stage of modern company evolution. The modules will be connected to each other by information networks, to which responsibilities for decisions are delegated. This characteristic is peculiar to the Japanese companies too. In fact, they give great importance to the decision-making decentralization and information sharing among the organization, by the creation of informal communication networks among workers. According to this theory, Japanese enterprises are ahead of their time and anticipated the future organization of modern big global corporations.

In conclusion, the evolution of Japanese enterprise followed a peculiar path, which allowed it to develop autonomously some organizational solutions that Western companies have been discovering only in the last few years and that are typical of the so-called lean enterprise (Cooper, 1995).

THE ''TRADITIONAL'' JAPANESE ENTERPRISE AND MANAGEMENT

The evolution of Japanese management reflects some features, that are typical of many Japanese enterprises (Guatri and Vicari, 1992; Songini, 1991, 1994):

- The stakeholders' group is open to many actors. The company is considered a center of fulfillment of people in a group and a center of cooperation of different subjects, such as suppliers, financial institutions, customers, and the state. Management and employees are more essential stakeholders than the shareholders (Aoki, 1988).
- The strategy is focused on information and knowledge creation and accumulation, incremental innovations, total quality, and kaizen philosophies. It is pragmatic and does not emphasize formalized strategic planning mechanisms (Quinn, 1990; Johansson and Nonaka, 1996).
- Japanese companies pursue mainly growth, competitiveness, company image, and productivity efficiency goals. In contrast, financial goals such as ROI, ROE, and EVA are considered less important (Kono, 1984; Kagono, Nonaka, Sakakibara, and Okumura, 1985).
- Decision-making processes are both formal (*ringi*) and informal (*nemawashi*), participative and consensual. The main advantage is a wider acceptance of proposals among the organization; the obvious disadvantage can be a waste of time (Hayashi, 1988).
- The company is the center of a broad network of suppliers. The relationships between different actors extend to the information and technology sharing, employees' training, cooperation in product and process development, cost reduction, and quality improvement activities (Aoki, 1988; Coriat, 1991).
- The employment system, characterized by the so-called three pillars (lifetime employment, seniority-based wages, and company-based unions), is based on a moral commitment to mutual loyalty between the company and employees. In a period of sustained economic growth, this mutual commitment allowed Japanese companies to accumulate significant know-how, specific to each firm. As a consequence, generally employees closely identify with their company and develop a strong sense of belonging (Aoki, 1988; Coriat, 1991; Takahashi, 1990).
- The Toyota Production System (TPS), invented by Taiichi Ohno, in the post-war period, in order to adjust the production systems to the shortage of raw materials and energy sources, is based on some typical practices, which are related to both *Human Resource Management—HRM* (teamwork, flexibility, job rotation, training on-the-job) and *Production Organization* (Just-in-Time [JIT], kaizen practices, partnership with suppliers, and target costing).

Figure 13.1 points out the relationships between the three pillars of the employment system and TPS. They interact among themselves in a synergistic way and influence the manufacturing core of the model, which is represented by TPS. More in specifically, the "three pillars" form a support that sustains and assures the functioning of TPS, because they guarantee medium and long-term stability. Similarly, synergistic relationships occur among different elements of TPS; each aspect supports the other and performs a complementary function.

The following analysis of both the changes that involve "traditional" Japanese management (see Figure 13.1) and its transferability abroad refers particularly to the three pillars of the employment system and TPS. In fact, they represent the core of Japanese management and some of the most changing aspects.

Figure 13.1
The "Traditional" Japanese Management Paradigm

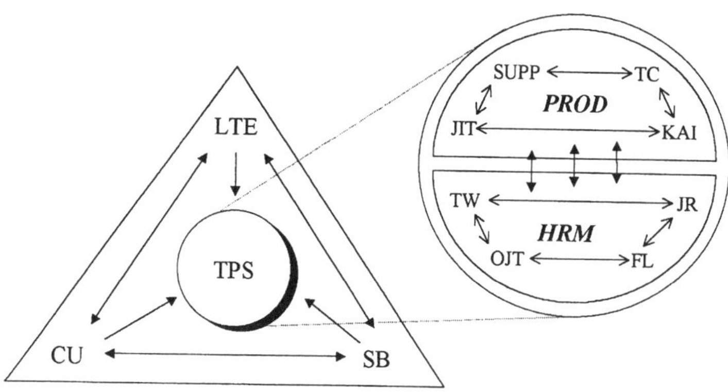

Note: CU = company-based union; SB = seniority-based wage; LTE = lifetime employment; TPS = Toyota Production System; HRM = human resource management; JR = job rotation; OJT = on-the-job training; FL = flexibility; TW = teamwork; PROD = production organization; JIT = just-in-time; KAI = *kaizen*; SUPP = relationships with suppliers; TC =target costing.

THE CRISIS OF JAPANESE MANAGEMENT

The Macroeconomic Context

Until the early 1990, the idea that the success of Japanese companies derived mostly from the "traditional" Japanese management and that it was static and immutable was brought into question by some external factors such as the collapse of the *bubble economy*, the slump in investments and consumption, and the yen revaluation (Molteni, 1996; Woronoff, 1991, 1996). In particular, the *bubble economy*—that is, the period of uninterrupted growth in the Japanese economy from 1986 to 1991—represented, at the same time the last stage of Japanese economic development and its degeneration. The origin of the bubble economy derived from the surge of land and share price, which caused huge speculative shares. Fiscal and monetary policies, which were implemented by the Japanese government in order to sustain the companies, made excessive amounts of money available, which were invested in the stock and real-estate markets, with the consequence of inflating prices. A number of companies added to the manufacturing activities a speculative activity too, while banks began to grant loans against the security for shares or property, with excessive confidence.

In 1991 the bubble burst. Land and share values slumped. As a consequence, the enterprises that were involved in speculative activities posted huge financial losses and caused serious difficulties for Japanese banks. The economic crisis, which has been troubling the Southeast Asian area for the last few years, worsened the Japanese economic situation because that area represents a major export market for Japan.

The Social Context

Compared to other economic crises, which Japanese companies overcame successfully (for instance, the two oil shocks), the current crisis is compounded by significant changes in the mentality and social structure in Japan as well.

Some features of "traditional" Japanese management, which in the past were considered points of strength, are weaker owing to some sociological and demographic trends.

A first trend is represented by the aging population, resulting in part from the low birthrate. In the near future, the lack of young people in Japan could force Japanese enterprises to compete for a smaller and smaller number of young employees, who will be increasingly demanding. They may keep employees who reach the age of retirement, with the consequence of an increase in expenditures, for evaluation and remuneration systems are based on length of service and seniority.

A second trend concerns the gradual westernization of behaviors and values, which is introducing destabilizing elements into Japanese society when compared to the thinking and habits typical of Japanese people in the past. The westernization of society is mostly widespread among young people and is gradually changing the thinking that is the basis for Japanese employment system and the relationships between the employer and employees (Brown, Lubove, and Kwalwasser, 1994; Ohmae, 1995; Woronoff, 1991, 1996). For instance, a wider number of young people seems less willing to sacrifice their private lifes and spare time for their companies.

Other significant determinants of change are as follows:

- New behaviors of Japanese consumers, who are no longer willing to pay higher prices in Japan for products and services similar to those offered in the international markets at low prices (Ohmae, 1995).
- Quality and costs of buildings, which have a negative influence on the life quality, especially that of young couples.
- The gradual disappearance of the so-called one middle-class, owing to the emerging division between "new riches and new poors" (Woronoff, 1996).
- The greater attention to the labor conditions of foreign workers and the female condition.

Effects of the Crisis on "Traditional" Japanese Enterprise and Management

The consistency between Japanese management features and the characteristics of the external context has lost its strength. This phenomenon has forced Japanese companies to gradually change some elements of their management model. However, it is noteworthy that TPS, especially its aspects related to production organization, does not seem to be under discussion in the same way as are the "three pillars" of the employment system.

The lifetime employment system was negatively and heavily influenced by the recession, which slowed down the growth of Japanese companies. During the "economic miracle" of the 1980s, the growing enterprises could offer solid career development paths. On the contrary, in a recession, the commitment to honor the lifetime employment system left the enterprises excessively crowded, especially with white-collar workers. Moreover, in the past, the white-collar workers' low productivity was hidden by the blue collar workers' high productivity (Hori, 1993). In the early 1990s, the transfer of most production activities abroad, due to the revaluation of the yen and increases in labor cost in Japan, reduced the number of blue-collars and, consequently, sharply revealed the different rate of productivity among different kinds of worker.

Another effect of the recession on the lifetime employment system was represented by the so-called "window workers" (*madogiwa zoku*). These are "in-company unemployed" workers, who remain on the company payroll but do not do any work. This is a biased effect of the lifetime employment system. In fact, the informal commitment to make every effort to maintain the employees inside the organization forces companies to guarantee the job to employees, at any expense, until legal retirement.

In the last few years, Japanese enterprises tried to cope with the *impasse*, due to lifetime employment, by introducing some practices aimed at reducing the number of employees, without compromising the reputation and competences accumulated by the organization (Suziki, 1996). The practices are as follows:

- Voluntary resignation programs for middle management members who are retiring. If a manager agrees to retire early, he receives an exceptional golden handshake, in addition to the usual retirement bonus (Aoki, 1988). For instance, in 1992, at TDK, 50 senior managers were asked to resign in exchange for 90 percent salary until the age of retirement (Hori, 1993).
- The veto on hirings: Mazda Motor Corporation did not hire any graduate in 1996; Sakura Bank hired 400 graduates in 1995 but only 100 in 1996; Nissan, which was used to hiring about 1,500 to 2,000 new employees each year, in 1995 hired only 55 (Schmidt, 1996).
- The transfer of employees in excess to those subsidiaries which can better deal with additional costs. This practice (*koyo chosei*) helps the bigger enterprises to reduce internal unemployment, without dismissals. Moreover, the expatriates can act as coordinators between the headquarters and subsidiary and contribute to information diffusion.
- The establishment of subsidiaries which could hire the surplus of employees and undertake on contract activities such as transportation or cleaning. For instance, NTT established autonomous subsidiaries in order to place in it 5,000 employees (Schmidt, 1996).

- The transfer of employees who are nearly retiring or giving voluntary resignation to foreign plants, in order to train local workers.
- Drawing up agreements with outplacement companies, who help the older workers to find employment. Sometimes, the enterprise itself established an outplacement company. For instance, Nippon Steel established Bright Carrer in order to find 17,000 workers new jobs (Hori, 1993).
- The payment in goods produced by the company (*genbutsu shikyu*). NEC, for example, in November 1992, announced that a portion of winter bonuses for management above section-head level would be paid in coupons for NEC-made products, which would range from 100,000 to 300,000 yen.

In some cases, the length and the intensity of the economic crisis required, more dramatic measures, such as shutting down factories or employee reduction. For instance, Nissan shut down the up-to-date plant in Zama and laid 2,000 workers off; Sony in 1999 announced 17,000 redundancies in its workforce.

The crisis affected evaluation and compensation systems, too. In this case, however, the driver of change was more the mentality of young workers than the economic recession. This new class of ambitious managers would like to progress faster than the seniority-based wage system will allow. As a consequence, many enterprises were driven to introduce performance-based salary and promotion systems, which are based on merit. The major risk associated-with the aforementioned trends is that the introduction of Western performance-based compensation and promotion systems further strengthens the individualistic attitude that is widespread among young people and upsets the collectivistic ethics of Japanese society.

Even though TPS does not seem to be changed, compared to the lifetime employment system, Japanese companies are beginning to revise a few production practices in order to moderate some negative aspects and to adapt them to the new competitive environment.

Toyota itself introduced the *21st Century Toyota-Style Manufacturing* into the plant of Miyata (Katayama, 1996). The shortage of young workers and the consequent need of a growing number of women and older employees drove the company to revise the workload and reorganize the production lines according to more human-oriented solutions. The new production allowed the organization both to manage smaller teamworks, which can be more easily governed and to reduce the distance between production lines and component storage areas, improving the supplying timeliness. Moreover, it accepted limited work-in-progress stocks in order to allow workers to cope with production problems, without negative consequences downstream.

The excesses of strong automation have also been reduced owing to the fact that during the recession Japanese companies found serious difficulties saturating production capacity. Greater attention has been paid to working conditions too.

Product and supply strategies are changing in a significant way. The recession made evident the points of weakness of *time-based competition* (Stalk and Webber, 1993). The reduction of product cycles for some items to only a few months, the continuous introduction of new models, and the great differentiation forced Japanese companies to produce innumerable varieties of interchangeable parts, to cope with a number of shrinking production lots, and so on. This strategy had negative consequences, such as losing economy of scale, decreasing efficiency, confusing customers, and reducing all products to commodities. In order to deal with this situation, and the related reduction in demand, Japanese companies have reduced product variety, lengthened product cycles, simplified product features, and reduced and standardized the number of variable parts. Toyota, which in the early 1990s was theoretically able to maintain lead times for new models down to ten months, in 1992 decided to lengthen the life cycle of its new cars to between five and six years rather than four years (with a saving of 100 billion yen for each year added). In the same period, Mazda decided to eliminate 76 variations of its 929 car models, while Nissan programmed to reduce the number of motors by 40 percent in the following five years. In electronics, Sony cut many model sizes, such as 27" and 31" televisions; Mitsubishi Electric Corporation, in 1993, decided to trim its product line from 34 fax modes to 7 in only one year; Matsushita, after having discovered that only 10 percent of its 220 television models and 62 VCRs achieved adequate levels of sales, decided to cut them back dramatically (Stalk and Webber, 1993).

The economic crisis led many companies to overcome traditional strong barriers among rival industrial groups (*keiretsu*). The need to cut costs drove many companies, especially those of the automobile and motorcycle industries, to reach agreements to jointly source standardized parts from one or a few suppliers, usually belonging to one of the *keiretsu* involved in the agreement. In August 1992, Toyota and Nissan reached a broad agreement to cooperate in the procurement of parts. In the same month, Suzuki and Mitsubishi Motor agreed to cooperate in sourcing parts for light cars. In 1992, Suzuki, Yamaha, and Kawasaki announced an agreement to standardize and jointly source about 20 items, in order to cut production costs. Honda later joined this agreement, too. This phenomenon represents quite a revolution in industrial relations in Japan, because rival *keiretsu* did not usually cooperate with each other; they had closed relationships with their suppliers and shared with them firm-specific and confidential technologies, know-how, and R&D activities.

Some other fundamental aspects of Japanese management are also changing significantly. The typical Japanese decision-making systems, such as *nemawashi*, were criticized because they do not allow precise identification of responsibility for decisions. The relationships between small suppliers and big companies, based on commitment and cooperation in the long term, are changing owing to the need of large companies to gain efficiency and cut costs at the suppliers' expense, which had to sustain the cost related to restructuring the Japanese industrial system. Finally, the weakness of Japanese corporate governance systems has become increasingly evident owing to the lack of some corporate control mechanisms which are widespread in the Western context, such as the strong role of external and internal auditors and accounting standards to ensure balance sheet transparency.

In conclusion, Japanese management seems to be in a radically new stage of its evolution: the actual economic crisis is quite different from the previous crisis, which Japanese companies were able to cope with because of its length, origin, and features. Moreover, the current Japanese society is quite different from that of the recent past too. The most significant consequence of change concerns the weakness of the relationships based on trust and common interests between different internal actors and between the company and the external subjects, owing to the gradual abandonment of lifetime employment, the introduction of merit-based compensation and promotion systems, the weakening of identification of workers in their company, and the emergence of new relationships between the companies and their suppliers. The crisis particularly involved the more peculiar aspects of Japanese management, such as the ''three pillars'' of human resource management, especially lifetime employment and the seniority wage system.

THE TRANSFERABILITY OF JAPANESE MANAGEMENT

The question of the transferability of Japanese management abroad emerged for the first time as a result of the internationalization process of big Japanese enterprises, which started in the 1970s.

Since then, many authors have studied the transferability of this model in other sociocultural contexts, characterized by peculiar management systems, habits, employment systems, unions, and so on. To understand in depth the question of transferability of Japanese management, we need to analyze the relationships between its ''production core,'' represented by the Toyota Production System, and lifetime employment. In fact, the Toyota Production System represents the optimal solution to problems that affect all companies in the *lean production age* (Cooper, 1995). Conversely, lifetime employment, summarized by the ''three pillars,'' derives from peculiar aspects of the Japanese context.

A number of authors pointed out that the transferability of Japanese management usually asks for at least a partial change of *humanware* aspects, in order to favor its assimilation in different cultural environments. Its transferability concerns not only the implementation of production techniques, such as JIT or TQM, but also the adoption of peculiar labor organization practices and industrial relations (Oliver and Wilkinson, 1988), and it cannot be considered completed without a consistency with the sociocultural environments where it occurs (Fukuda, 1988). As a consequence, the *soft* aspects of Japanese management are usually adapted in Japanese transplants in order both to avoid the possibility that their weakening could damage the stability of the entire management model and to assure the functioning of its fundamental principles, such as long-term employment. The local adaptation led to the use of some ''para-Japanese'' elements, which are similar to the original ones, but more consistent with the sociocultural context where they are used (Takashi, 1987; Bonazzi, 1993).

An answer to the crisis that involved Japanese management in Japan can be derived from study of the transferability of Japanese management abroad. By comparing the characteristics of Japanese transplants that were realized in various foreign countries (the United States, United Kingdom, Australia, Southeast Asia, Italy), we can point out some common features, which we define "as the hybrid model." Because of significant changes that have involved Japanese society for the last few years, such as, for instance, the westernization of mentality and habits, the adoption of the "hybrid model" could be useful to Japanese parent companies too.

The Employment System in Japanese Transplants

Japanese transplants are located in agricultural areas that have no industrial traditions, in order:

- To look for unemployed labor, without previous experience on the job, who can be trained *ex novo*.
- To look for areas with high unemployment rates in order to represent the only occupational alternative and guarantee a high commitment by local workers.
- To gain funds to industrialize underdeveloped areas and take advantage of laws supporting foreign investments.
- To look for wide areas and where to install suppliers' plants too.

The differences among the behaviors of Japanese and Western workers (and to a smaller extent, the Asian in general) drove Japanese companies to look for environmental contexts that favor the selection of young workers willing to create employment relationships similar to those used in Japan. Actually, because Japanese companies usually represent the only labor opportunity, they can achieve high levels of trust and commitment by their workers and, consequently, invest adequately in employees' training.

In addition, the relationships between local trade unions and Japanese transplants are similar throughout the world. The choice of agricultural areas, where local trade unions are less deeply rooted, allowed Japanese companies to gain a strong position in comparison with trade unions. Japanese enterprises stipulated very favorable agreements with only a trade union, which often emerged through real competition among various unions. In that way, the company-based union was transferred to no-Japanese contexts too, characterized by strong trade unions, such as in the United States and Great Britain. The agreements drawn up by Japanese enterprises and local unions are very similar in all foreign countries and provide for company commitment to assure long-term employment and continuous training. Trade unions are committed to making the introduction of

Japanese management easier; to reducing the number of classified jobs; to pushing labor flexibility; to avoiding energetic protests; to maintaining cooperative relationships between management and workers; and to solving controversies on the job without compromising union relationships based on trust.

Moreover, Japanese transplants are characterized by the informal commitment to guarantee employment to local workers. Even though it is not Japanese lifetime employment, this solution represents an effective ''functional equivalent'' because it allows for the adoption of significant aspects of TPS, such as continuous training, labor flexibility, and teamwork. Nevertheless, Japanese companies assure employment in foreign subsidiaries only when a company's financial solidity is not in danger. They adopt long-term employment, instead of lifetime employment, which on the one hand is less compulsory, and on the other hand allow enterprises to establish long-term labor relations, which, in some ways, are similar to Japanese lifetime employment. The partial and informal adoption of lifetime employment represents one of the most important ''para-Japanese'' elements.

Seniority-based wage is not transferred abroad. In fact, Japanese enterprises always follow local employment conditions and pay salaries consistent with the average, in order to avoid controversies with unions, due to low salaries, and to keep production costs low and avoid competing with local companies for their workforce with the institution of inflated wages. Although in traditional Japanese management, seniority-based wage is the fundamental aspect that guarantees the worker's loyalty, in Japanese transplants seniority does not significantly influence wages.

Figure 13.2 outlines the Japanese ''hybrid model.'' Some linkages that connect different aspects of the Japanese model are not transferred abroad, while a few others are modified so that they can work more effectively in local contexts.

In comparison with the traditional model, we can outline some differences:

- Seniority-based wage was not usually transferred abroad.
- Life-time employment was informally transferred following a less rigid way.
- Company-based union was generally transferred, as a consequence of the agreement with local trade unions.

In conclusion, only two pillars support TPS abroad. Nevertheless, because of the aspects that are generally transferred (company-based union) or adapted to local contexts (lifetime employment), it seems that Japanese foreign transplants implement mainly the synergies between different aspects of the employment system, which are typical of the traditional Japanese model.

The Toyota Production System in Japanese Transplants

With regard to the Human Resource Management (HRM) area of TPS, in most important Japanese direct investments (the United States, Great Britain,

Figure 13.2
The "Hybrid Model"

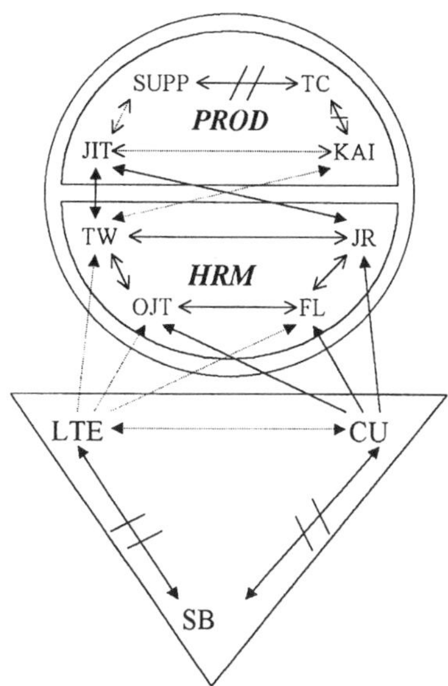

and Australia), job rotation, teamwork, on-the-job training, and labor flexibility are transferred for the most part, especially in case of strategic transplants involved in high value-added production activities. In Southeast Asia, where Japanese investments were established in order to take advantage of low labor costs, labor flexibility and teamwork were introduced. However, low complexity of production activities had not required job rotation practices.

As far as the relationships between HRM and the production organization aspects of TPS are concerned, the traditional model deals with strong linkages between the two areas, while in the "hybrid model" only some linkages take place; a few other aspects are required to be modified or are not transferred at all.

The relationship between teamwork, job rotation, and JIT is usually completely transferred. JIT is introduced in those transplants that have to cope with strategic production activities. In the United States, U.K., and Australia, JIT sourcing is used in the biggest transplants, especially in the automobile industry. However, at the beginning stage, JIT is used only by Japanese transplants themselves. The shortage of local suppliers able to cope with JIT and the requested timeliness and quality standards force Japanese enterprises to implement a "hybrid" version of JIT, characterized by different production planning methodologies (Bonazzi, 1993). In Figure 13.2, the linkage between JIT and suppliers is represented as a partial one, owing to the difficulties realized by Japanese subsidiaries in interacting with local suppliers. In fact, a common trend identifies the relationships between Japanese transplants and local suppliers, which lead Japanese enterprises to establish sourcing agreements similar to those carried out in Japan, by an accurate selection of local suppliers. In order to raise the performance reliability of local suppliers to the levels assured by Japanese suppliers, many Japanese transplants organized specific units devoted to train local suppliers.

The linkage between JIT, teamwork, and *kaizen* is modified abroad, whereas in Japanese enterprises those aspects are strictly related. In fact, teamwork activity requires involvement in continuous improvement programs, which pursue the goals of waste removal and productivity enhancement. On the contrary, Quality Circles and suggestion systems do not always succesfully operate abroad. *Kaizen* has to fight against mostly cultural barriers, because in many companies the worker consider this kind of activity to be uncompensated over time and to be made after working time. This situation occurs in Southeast Asia too, although it has a more similar culture to Japan. *Kaizen* adoption is hindered by local managers too, who do not give workers incentives for involvement in Quality Circles activities, as a consequence of a superficial knowledge of Japanese production philosophy and practices.

Target costing is rarely transferred to local subsidiaries, even though it is considered one of the most significant pillars of Japanese management (Cooper, 1995). This could be due first to the fact that Japanese production transplants were recently established, causing Japanese companies to defer the introduction of TC and opt for more well-known management accounting methodologies, until they reach a more mature stage in their evolution.

Second, a stable relationship between local suppliers and Japanese transplants is not usually fully developed, not permitting the involvement of suppliers in target costing activities. On the contrary, in Japan relationships based on mutual trust allow individual suppliers for specific target costs.

Third, the involvement of Japanese subsidiaries in value-chain activities, such as sales and production, and seldom in research and development, as well as the role played in the multinational networks explain the limited adoption of TC abroad. Actually, because target costing is a cost planning methodology carried out during research and development stages, it is employed most of all by research and development units, which are centralized in Japanese headquarters or in a few American or European centers, and local subsidiaries are involved in target costing only by the development of prototypes and industrialization stages.

CONCLUSION

The transferability of Japanese management abroad has taken place in a number of different ways. In some cases, the same methodologies and tools used by the parent company have been adopted abroad. In other circumstances, Japanese management was partially modified in order to deal with different local contexts.

Eventually, in many situations the Japanese transplants implemented Western management practices (Songini, 1991). In particular, adoption of the "hybrid model" is likely to be related to the difficulties in finding or reproducing in foreign subsidiaries the same consistency both between company features and external context and among various elements of traditional Japanese management.

Because significant changes have taken place in the population structure and mentality of Japan since the early 1990s, the hybrid model could represent a worthwhile strategic option to be carried out by Japanese companies in Japan too. Interestingly, the aspects of Japanese management that were most modified in Japanese transplants were those more closely linked to the specific Japanese context and now criticized in Japan as well.

Japanese companies are dealing with a new stage in their evolution. The phase of exporting Japanese management abroad and adapting it to local contexts is now being followed by a new stage of importing a Westernized version of Japanese management, developed by foreign transplants, which is more consistent with the changing conditions of the Japanese labor market and the collective consciousness of its people.

REFERENCES

Abdullah, S., and Keenoy, T. (1995). Japanese Managerial Practices in the Malaysian Electronic Industry: Two Case Studies. *Journal of Management Studies*, 6, p. 747.

Abegglen, J., and Stalk, G. (1985). *Kaisha: The Japanese Corporation*. New York: Basic Books.

Abo, T. (1994). *Hybrid Factory: The Japanese Production System in the United States*. New York: Oxford University Press.

Aoki, M. (1988). *Information, Incentives and Bargaining in the Japanese Economy*. Cambridge: Cambridge University Press.

Athos, A. G., and Pascale, R. T. (1981). *The Art of Japanese Management*. New York: Warner Books.

Beechler, S., and Bird, A. (1994). The Best of Both Worlds? HRM Practices in US-based Japanese Affiliates. In N. Campbell and F. Burton (eds.), *Japanese Multinationals: Strategies and Management in the Global Kaisha*. London: Routledge.

Bonazzi, G. (1993). *Il tubo di cristallo*. Bologna: Il Mulino.

Bromwich, M., and Shinichi, I. (1994). *Management Practices and Cost Management Problems in Japanese Affiliated Companies in the U.K.* London: CIMA.

Brown, W., Lubove, R., and Kwalwasser, J. (1994). Karoshi: Alternative Perspective of Japanese Management Styles. *Business Horizons*, March–April, pp. 58–60.

Chandler, A. D. (1962). *Strategy and Structure: Chapters in the History of the Industrial Enterprise*. Cambridge, MA: MIT Press.

Cooper, R. (1995). *When Lean Enterprises Collide*. Boston: Harvard Business School Press.

Coriat, R. (1991). *Penser à l'envers*. Paris: Bourgois Editeur.

Dedoussis, V. (1994). The Core Workforce—Peripheral Workforce Dichotomy and the

Transfer of Japanese Management Practices. In N. Campbell and F. Burton (eds.), *Japanese Multinationals: Strategies and Management in the Global Kaisha*. London: Routledge.

Dedoussis, V. (1995). Simply a Question of Cultural Barriers? The Search for New Perspectives in the Transfer of Japanese Management Practices. *Journal of Management Studies*, 6, p. 731.

Delbridge, R., and Turnbull, P. (1994). Diventare giapponesi? L'adozione e l'adattamento dei sistemi di produzione giapponesi in Gran Bretagna. In M. La Rosa, *Modello giapponese e produzione snella: la prospettiva europea*. Milano: Franco Angeli.

Di Bernardo, B., and Rullani, E. (1990). *Il management e le macchine*. Bologna: Il Mulino.

Doi, T. (1971). *Anatomy of Dependence*. Tokyo: Kodansha International.

Dore, R. F. (1987). *Taking Japan Seriously*. London: Athlone Press.

Durand, J. P. (1994). Un nuovo modello produttivo: la via francese. In M. La Rosa, *Modello giapponese e produzione snella: la prospettiva europea*. Milano: Franco Angeli.

Durand, J. P., and Sebag, Y. (1994): MBK: un investimento produttivo della Yamaha in Francia. In M. La Rosa, *Modello giapponese e produzione snella: la prospettiva europea*. Milano: Franco Angeli.

Fukuda, K. J. (1988). *Japanese-Style Management Transferred: The Experience of East Asia*. London: Routledge.

Gnan, L., and Songini, L. (1995). Management Styles of a Sample of Japanese Manufacturing Companies in Italy. In B. N. Kumar (ed.), *MIR—Management International Review, Special Issue*, 35(2), pp. 9–26.

Guatri, L., and Vicari, S. (1992). *Il capitalismo industriale nelle economie avanzate*. Milano: EGEA.

Hashimoto, T. (1997). The Sony Group's New Management Structure. *Japan Update*, 2 (6), p. 12.

Hayashi, S. (1988). *Culture and Management in Japan*. Tokyo: University of Tokyo Press.

Hori, S. (1993). Fixing Japans's White-Collar Economy: A Personal View. *Harvard Business Review*, November–December, pp. 157–172.

Johansson, J., and Nonaka, I. (1996). *Relentless: The Japanese Way of Marketing*. New York: HarperCollins.

Kagono, T., Nonaka, I., Sakakibara, K., and Okumura, A. (1985). *Strategic versus Evolutionary Management: A US-Japan Comparison of Strategy and Organization*. Amsterdam: North Holland.

Katayama, O. (1996). *Japanese Business into the 21st Century*. London: Athlone Press.

Kenney, M., and Florida, R. (1993). *Beyond Mass Production: The Japanese System and Its Transfer to the U.S.* New York: Oxford University Press.

Kim, C. S. (1995). *Japanese Industry in the American South*. London: Routledge.

Kono, T. (1984). *Strategy and Structure of Japanese Enterprises*. New York: Sharpe.

Molteni, C. (1996). *Rapporto Giappone: quale ruolo nei nuovi equilibri dell'area Asia-Pacifico*? Torino: Fondazione Agnelli.

Monden, Y. (1994). *Toyota Production System*. London: IIE.

Morishima, M. (1982). *Why Has Japan Succeeded?* Cambridge: Cambridge University Press.

Morris, J., Munday, M., and Wilkinson, B. (1993). *Working for the Japanese*. London: Athlone Press.

Nakane, C. (1970). *Japanese Society*. London: Weidenfeld & Nicholson.

Ohmae, K. (1995). Letter from Japan. *Harvard Business Review*, May–June, pp. 154–158.

Ohno, T. (1988). *Toyota Production System: Beyond Large-Scale Production*. Portland, ME: Productivity Press.

Oliver, N., and Wilkinson, B. (1988). *The Japanization of British Industry*. Oxford: Basil Blackwell.

Porter, M. E. (1985). *Competitive Advantage: Creating and Sustaining Superior Performance*. New York: Free Press.

Quinn, J. B. (1990). *Strategies for Change Logical Incrementalism*. Homewood, IL: Irwin.

Schmidt, R. J. (1996). Japanese Management, Recession Style. *Business Horizons*, March–April, pp. 70–76.

Schroeder, R. G., Sakakibara, S., and Flynn, J. E. (1992). Japanese Plants in the U.S.: How Good Are They? *Business Horizons*, July–August, pp. 66–72.

Songini, L. (1991). Il trasferimento dei sistemi di gestione giapponesi. *Economia e Management*, 2(5), pp. 12–25.

Songini, L. (1994). Capitalismo e impresa industriale giapponesi tra cultura, efficienza e competizione. In G. Bertoli, A. Farinet, C. Guerini, A. C. Mauri, and L. Songini, *Il capitalismo industriale nelle economie avanzate: Europa, Stati Uniti e Giappone*. Milano: EGEA.

Songini, L., Gnan, L., and Kidd, J. (1999). A Comparison of Management Styles of Japanese Manufacturing Firms in the UK and Italy. In L. Songini (ed.), *Political and Strategic Challenges in Asia and Europe: New Prospects in Economics and Management*. Milano: EGEA.

Stalk, G., and Webber, A. M. (1993). Japan's Dark Side of Time. *Harvard Business Review*, July–August, pp. 93–102.

Suziki, N. (1996). Middle-Aged and Older Japanese Employees in Japanese Corporations: Their Plight During the Process of Major Historic Change in Employment. *Journal of Management Development*, 15(8): 7–15.

Takahashi, K. (1990). *Human Resource Management in Japan*. Berlin: De Gruyter.

Takashi, Y. (1987). The Theoretical Problems of the Transferability of Management Style. In M. Trevor, *The Internationalization of Japanese Business*. Frankfurt: Campus.

Thompson, J., and Rehder, R. (1995). Nissan UK: A Worker's Paradox? *Business Horizons*, January–February, pp. 48–57.

Trevor, M. (1988). *Toshiba's New British Company*. London: Policy Studies Institute.

Vogel, E. F. (1980). *Japan as Number One: Lessons for America*. London: Harvard University Press.

Womack, J., Jones, D. T., and Roos, D. (1990). *The Machine That Changed the World*. New York: Macmillan Press.

Woronoff, J. (1991). *Japan as—Anything But—Number One*. Basingstoke: Macmillan Press.

Woronoff, J. (1996). *The Japanese Economic Crisis*. Basingstoke: Macmillan Press.

Yamamura, K. (1986): L'industrializzazione del Giappone. In *Evoluzione della grande impresa e management*. Torino: Einaudi.

Chapter 14

Are Firms in Southeast Asia Ready for Knowledge Management? Validating a Framework for Knowledge Creation in Thai Telecommunication Firms

Bettina Büchel and Steffen P. Raub

INTRODUCTION

In recent years, knowledge has claimed its place as one of the defining factors of the competitive landscape. This trend can be observed at both the macro and micro levels. At the macro level, the long predicted ''information society'' and ''knowledge economy'' are now emerging as tangible realities. As a result, today's worldwide knowledge environment is structurally much more complex than it was only a few decades ago. Increased complexity is due to several factors:

1. *Exponential growth of the worldwide stock of knowledge.* Following Gutenberg's invention of the printing press, it took more than 300 years for the worldwide volume of information to double for the first time. Since then, it has doubled virtually every five years. Between 1950 and 1975, for example, as many books were produced as in the 500 years following the invention of the printing press (Badaracco, 1991).
2. *Increasing specialization and fragmentation of knowledge.* A century ago, a competent scholar might have possessed an overall grasp of the state of research in almost all areas of science; today, even within one subject, people of different specializations may have trouble understanding each other.
3. *Globalization of knowledge creation.* At the beginning of the 1970s, the United States still produced more than 70 percent of the world's new technologies; now, centers of scientific and technical excellence are spread around the world. The world center of software production around the area of Bangalore, India, is a prime illustration of the fact that the globalization of knowledge is little affected by boundaries between developed and less developed countries (Probst, Raub, and Romhardt, 1999).
4. *Growing importance of knowledge-intensive firms for the economy.* It has been estimated that for industrialized countries approximately 75 percent of the total value added is generated by knowledge-intensive firms (Badaracco, 1991).

At the micro level, it has been pointed out that the value of a company's intellectual capital is often several times that of its material assets (Handy, 1990). The market capitalization of some of the hottest Internet stocks provides support to this perspective. As a result, some companies have published accounts of their intellectual assets, as a supplement to the traditional annual reports (Skandia, 1998).

Leading business firms have reacted to this challenge. New positions have been created: many companies now have a Director of Intellectual Capital, or a Director of Knowledge, or a Knowledge/Intellectual Asset Manager. The common factor in their work is that all of them are responding to the challenge of an increasingly competitive environment in which improved management of intellectual assets can bring critical advantages. Knowledge management is also being supported by the use of new communication technologies and telecommunication infrastructures.

While many companies perceive the increasing complexity of the knowledge-environment as a threat, some have also recognized new opportunities. Innovative companies are finding that they can increase the value of products that have relatively simple basic functions by making them more knowledge-intensive. This may mean enabling a product to adapt itself to changing conditions, or to collect and store information and apply it for the benefit of the user. Simpler examples of intelligent products are textiles that change their characteristics according to the prevailing temperature and humidity, or window glass that reflects or absorbs sunlight according to the weather, thus keeping room temperature constant. More sophisticated applications include Goodyear's project of an "intelligent tire," which registers sinking air pressure via a computer chip and triggers a warning signal, or Citibank's system which recognizes atypical spending patterns in the use of credit cards, thus alerting customers to the possibility of loss or misuse (Davis and Botkin, 1994).

In industrialized countries, increased knowledge intensity and efforts to install knowledge management systems in organizations are pervasive trends. As far as the economies of Southeast Asia are concerned, little systematic research has been conducted. Some recent developments highlight an increased recognition of the importance of information and knowledge. Malaysia's Multimedia Super Corridor, for instance, is designed to elevate the country to developed nation status by the year 2020. The intention of the project is to move Malaysia from being a mere user of multimedia products to being a supplier and developer of information technology. In this chapter, we will attempt to focus on the company level of analysis and analyze whether "Western" models of knowledge management may be applied in a Southeast Asian context.

The first part of this chapter outlines a theoretical framework of knowledge creation. This framework links the strategic implications of knowledge as a resource with the organizational processes for its creation and the catalysts necessary to facilitate the creation of knowledge. The second part then attempts to validate this framework in the context of the telecommunication industry of Thailand.

KNOWLEDGE AS A STRATEGIC RESOURCE

A great number of contributions to the strategic management literature have sought to establish explicit or implicit links between organizational knowledge and competitive advantage. Relevant approaches have used the terms *distinctive competence* (Hitt and Ireland, 1985), *core competence* (Prahalad and Hamel, 1990), *core capabilities* (Leonard-Barton, 1992, 1995), or *strategic assets* (Dierickx and Cool, 1989), to name only a few.

A common line of reasoning underlying these approaches is that over time firms develop knowledge or capabilities that enable them to produce superior products. The development of core competencies or capabilities is a long-term investment. It yields an interrelated mix of organizational knowledge which leads to an increase in the problem-solving capacity of an organization. Competencies and capabilities thus represent the unique set of strategically relevant organizational knowledge, which eventually leads to increased returns for a company (Hamel and Prahalad, 1994).

The resource-based view of the firm offers a useful set of criteria for assessing the competitive value of organizational knowledge. According to Barney (1991: 101), firm resources "include all assets, capabilities, organizational processes, firm attributes, information, knowledge, etc." When regarded from a resource-based perspective, knowledge that leads to a sustainable competitive advantage has to satisfy several criteria. Strategically valuable resources must be (a) *valuable*, (b) *rare*, (c) *imperfectly imitable*, and (d) *cannot have strategically equivalent substitutes* (Barney, 1991: 105–106).

Compared with other organizational resources, knowledge exhibits a number of unique characteristics. One is the lack of permanence. Once acquired, knowledge cannot always be drawn upon in unlimited fashion. It can only be used within certain time limits; it quickly ages and may suddenly become worthless. On the other hand, knowledge may also be rapidly created, as a result of a group discussion or simply in the shape of a novel idea. Moreover, once created, knowledge can be shared almost without limits while still remaining with the original owner.

The rapid transition processes that organizational knowledge may undergo suggest that a traditional, static view of this organizational resource is inappropriate. In order to create a more meaningful framework of knowledge-based competitive advantages, we suggest that the focus instead be placed on learning processes that emphasize the dynamic aspect of creating knowledge. Competitive advantage does not depend on the ability to collect knowledge and hoard it indefinitely. Much rather it stems from the ability to gain access to relevant knowledge and to create new knowledge, or, in a nutshell, on the organization's

Figure 14.1
Processes of Knowledge Creation

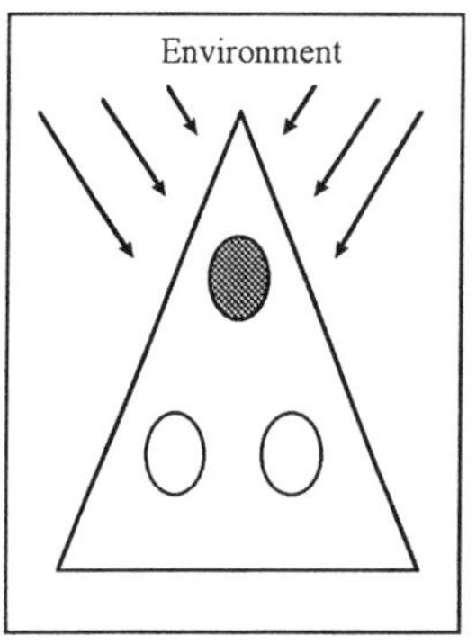

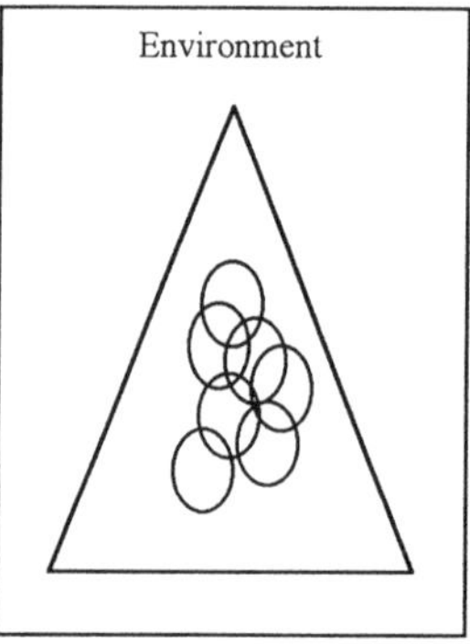

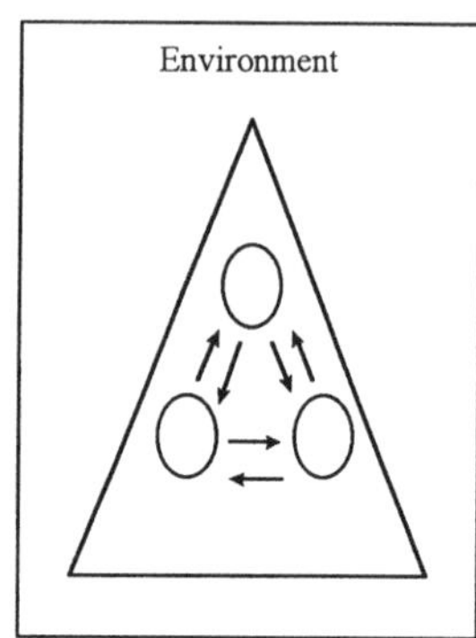

Knowledge Acquisition | Knowledge Synthesis | Knowledge Distribution

ability to learn. In order to incorporate this aspect, we will take a closer look at processes of organizational knowledge creation.

PROCESSES OF KNOWLEDGE CREATION

Information and knowledge are critical resources for managerial decision making and action (Daft and Macintosh, 1981; Daft and Huber, 1987). Interpreting the external environment, coordinating internal activities, handling problems, participating in meetings, sending and receiving reports all require the processing of these resources. Thus, knowledge may justifiably be regarded as the raw material of managerial work. In a similar vein, organizational learning is the process that permits the permanent updating of this resource in order for organizational knowledge to remain competitively relevant.

Organizational learning may be described as a process of knowledge creation (Fiol, 1994; Nonaka, 1994). In his theory of knowledge creation, Nonaka (1994) stresses the particular importance of the knowledge conversion process. Through socialization, externalization, internalization, and combination, knowledge is transferred, distributed, or embedded within the organization. These dynamic processes of knowledge conversion are closely linked to Daft and Huber's (1987) concept of organizational learning which focuses on acquiring, interpreting, distributing, and storing information.

For the purpose of this chapter we will assume that knowledge creation involves three distinct processes: knowledge acquisition, knowledge synthesis, and knowledge distribution (Figure 14.1). Knowledge *acquisition* refers to the search for information about events and trends in an organization's external environment and its integration with the existing knowledge base. Knowledge *synthesis* involves a cognitive process in which knowledge is selected, combined, weighed, and altered (Ungson et al., 1981). Knowledge *distribution* requires the transmission of knowledge among members of the organization.

Knowledge Acquisition

Theories of organizational learning have often emphasized internal aspects and neglected the acquisition of external knowledge (MacDonald, 1995). An organization learns when information is acquired outside the boundaries of the firm and is integrated with existing knowledge (Huber, 1991). It is essential to recognize that a large proportion of all information and knowledge that is potentially relevant for an organization is located outside its boundaries. A critical process of knowledge creation involves the incorporation and integration of some parts of this vast reservoir.

Yet, the integration process poses a challenge. The organizational knowledge base is modified through recombinations of existing and new knowledge (Kogut and Zander, 1993: 392). Organization members "must bring home this new information to be mixed with resident information to shape a novel pattern of knowledge into a package that can be used" (MacDonald, 1995: 562). Sufficient compatibility between old and new is an important condition for external knowledge to be considered valuable. Thus, knowledge acquisition requires organizational members to recognize the connection between existing and new knowledge in order to be able to integrate both. In reality, however, the need for change connected with the acquisition and integration of external information frequently leads to a preference for the use of internal knowledge (also known as the "not invented here syndrome").

Different catalysts may be employed to integrate external information that exploits opportunities and neutralizes threats. Informal networks are a useful strategy for obtaining external information. Informal networks of organizational members across different organizations allow for an exchange of information that may be integrated with existing knowledge. The likelihood that organizational members have received knowledge that is compatible with what is already in use is high in informal networks (MacDonald, 1995). Hence, the importance of boundary spanners, individuals who provide the link between internal and external systems.

Knowledge Synthesis

By acquiring external knowledge, the company increases its strategically valuable knowledge base, thereby fulfilling one criterion for sustainable competitive advantage. However, acquisition is only a first step towards usable organizational knowledge. The organizational learning literature convincingly argues that the whole of the organizational knowledge base is more than the sum of its parts (Probst and Büchel, 1997). However, the connection between the individual and organizational levels of knowledge is perhaps the weakest link in the chain of arguments forwarded by organizational learning theorists. One of the most challenging steps to describe in a framework of knowledge creation, therefore, is the transformation of individual skills into organizational routines (Nelson and Winter, 1982).

We propose that the development of organizational knowledge is mediated through multiple levels. At the individual level, interpretation of the environment leads to the revision of individual knowledge structures (Walsh, 1995). At the group level, individual knowledge structures are synthesized to create shared beliefs. At the organizational level, the routinization of shared beliefs leads to organizational knowledge.

Whereas learning at the individual level focuses on the assimilation of new information into past experiences, learning at the group level entails the transformation of individual experience into group knowledge. Since any single person's knowledge is incomplete, effective organizational action requires communication and combination of individual knowledge (Klayman and Schoemaker, 1993: 163). This process goes beyond the mere aggregation of individual knowledge. Through social interaction between individuals, knowledge is synthesized. As Wiley (1988: 258) states, ''intersubjectivity is emergent upon the interchange and synthesis of two, or more, communicating selves.'' Through the process of interpreting actions and events, the group reaches consensus about action-outcome relationships that provide the negotiated norms base on which the group acts. The interaction creates agreements in a communication process and thereby leads to shared beliefs. Thus, it is not the aggregation or multiplication of individual interpretations but their synthesis which leads to group knowledge.

The organizational level of knowledge synthesis has been labeled ''interaction representation'' (Weick, 1995), referring to the process of consciously documenting the exchange between individuals. Put in different terms, this level results in the routinization of knowledge through representation of interactions manifested in organizational systems. Organizational routines are a set of tasks that individuals and groups conduct in a coherent manner based on shared beliefs between group members (Nelson and Winter, 1982). The key feature of knowledge synthesis is the complex relationship between different levels of emergence it creates. Through exchange, individual knowledge is synthesized to arrive at group knowledge, which eventually becomes routinized at the organizational level. Thus, the transformation of individual knowledge into organizational routines leads to complex and embodied organizational knowledge. The criteria of rareness and imperfect imitability are simultaneously addressed in this process. As a result, knowledge synthesis provides an additional contribution to knowledge-based competitive advantage.

Knowledge Distribution

In order to synthesize and routinize individual interpretations into organizational knowledge, there is a need for a certain amount of consensus between individuals about the content of knowledge. Yet, organizational learning may also be defined as the development of different interpretations which leads to an increase of the organizational knowledge base (Fiol, 1994). This conflict is at the heart of the debate about the role of knowledge distribution in the knowledge creation process.

Although it can be argued that shared interpretations about the content of organizational knowledge are required for coordinated and consensus-based organizational action, different interpretations are said to increase the potential for problem-solving in the future. As Huber (1991: 102) puts it, "it seems reasonable to conclude that more learning has occurred when more and more varied interpretations have been developed, because such development changes the range of the organization's potential behaviors, and this is congruent with the definition of learning." Yet, he also argues that there is a need for a common or shared understanding among the organization's units that various interpretations exist, thus requiring consensus about interpretations.

It must be assumed that both consensus and diversity are necessary for learning to occur (Fiol, 1994). Balancing these two ends is a question of the organization's need for change and the desired stability. When organizational members have developed consensus about that knowledge which produces organized action, they are guided by agreement about the anticipated consequences of their behavior (Gray et al., 1985). These rules which govern organizational behavior are distributed through their repeated application and become embodied in norms and values.

Once organizational knowledge is distributed throughout the organization in the form of rituals and norms and is difficult to localize, it fulfills the criteria of imperfectly imitable knowledge. The lack of imitability lies in the unique historical conditions of development, the ambiguity of shared interpretations, and the complexity of consensus. Thus, the process of knowledge distribution contributes to the competitive value of organizational knowledge.

CATALYSTS OF KNOWLEDGE CREATION

Knowledge acquisition, synthesis, and distribution lead to an enlarged and improved organizational knowledge base which, in turn, may lead to sustainable competitive advantages. However, these processes do not occur automatically. Rather, in order for knowledge to be acquired, distributed, and synthesized, organizations need to be able to create an environment that is conducive to knowledge creation (Nonaka, 1994). Such an environment is characterized by the presence of certain "knowledge catalysts" which facilitate information processing and enable organizational knowledge creation.

Based on their Global Best Practices database, Arthur Andersen has identified four factors that serve as primary catalysts for organizational knowledge creation processes. These "enablers" include leadership, corporate culture, technology, and measurement (Arthur Andersen and APQC, 1995). Each enabler is characterized by a number of items specifying an effective environment for knowledge creation.

"Leadership" refers to the strategic and HR implications of knowledge creation. Using this enabler effectively implies that

- knowledge is recognized as central to the organization's strategy;
- the organization grasps the revenue-generating potential of its knowledge base and consciously tries to manage its knowledge assets;
- the organization uses learning to support existing and create new core competencies;
- individuals are appointed, evaluated, and paid on the basis of their contribution to the organizational knowledge base.

An effective "corporate culture" for knowledge creation acts as a catalyst by

- encouraging and enabling knowledge sharing;
- creating a climate of openness and trust;
- focusing on customer value creation as a basic guiding principle for knowledge management.

"Technology" promotes knowledge creation by

- interconnecting individuals through the use of user-friendly, human-centered, real-time, integrated, and "smart" information technology;
- creating an institutional memory that can be accessed by employees throughout the organization;
- fostering improved collaboration between employees.

"Measurement" of knowledge may facilitate knowledge creation by

- linking knowledge management to financial results;
- developing a balanced set of indicators (both financial and nonfinancial) for guiding knowledge management activities.

Taken together, generic knowledge creation processes and "knowledge enablers" can be regarded as an integrated framework for knowledge creation. The following Figure 14.2 illustrates the framework developed in this chapter.

As Figure 14.2 shows, effective knowledge management may contribute to achieving sustainable competitive advantage. Nonaka and Konno (1998: 14) have recently pointed out that facilitating knowledge creation is key to successful knowledge management. Moreover, as our theoretical framework illustrates, knowledge catalysts will determine the extent to which organizations are able to create knowledge. If one follows this line of argument, it is reasonable to assume that the "readiness" of Thai firms for knowledge management will

Figure 14.2
Knowledge Creation Framework

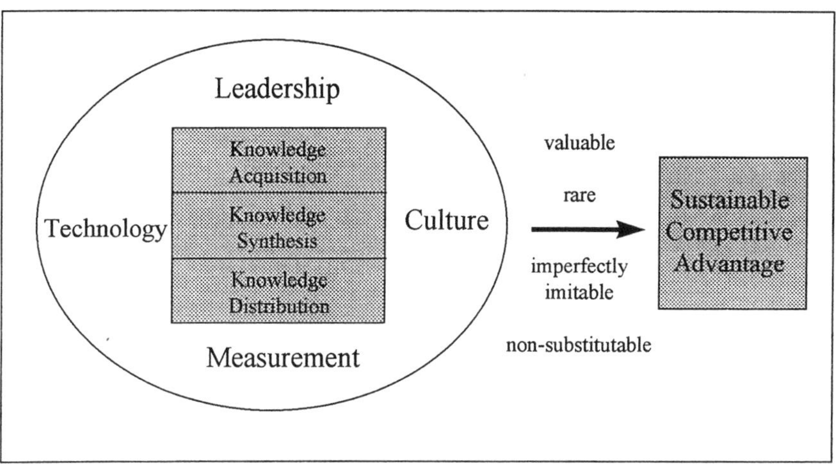

depend to a large degree on their current practices in terms of both the key knowledge creation processes and the enabling factors supporting these processes.

METHODOLOGY

The present focuses on the current state of knowledge creation catalysts within the Thai telecommunication industry. The sample chosen for the purpose of this study consisted of five companies:

- International Engineering Company Limited (IEC)
- Jasmine International Public Company Limited
- Shinawatra Computer and Communications Company Limited (SC&C)
- TelecomAsia Corporation Company Limited (TA)
- Thai Telephone and Telecommunication Company Limited (TT&T)

The five companies are either operators or suppliers of computer and communication technology to the telecommunication industry in Thailand.

Based on the framework, the four knowledge creation catalysts—leadership, corporate culture, technology, and measurement—were operationalized into properties that reflected company practices in these areas. Data were collected by using a questionnaire survey. The questionnaire focused on managers' perceptions of existing company practices within the domain of the four catalysts of knowledge creation. Questionnaires were distributed to managers in a broad range of departments, including finance, marketing, human resources management, information technology, and R&D in order to ensure a relatively complete coverage of each organization's management practices. Survey data were complemented by a series of interviews.

Analysis of data from the chosen firms allows us to present the state-of-the-art of knowledge-related management practices in an industry that is relatively competitive and dynamic and also, by its very nature, is intimately related to the exchange of information and knowledge. Thus, our assumption would be that this sample comes close to representing the most advanced knowledge management practices among private sector firms in Thailand, with the possible exception of consultancy firms.

RESULTS

Data analysis revealed the role of the four knowledge creation catalysts in supporting knowledge acquisition, distribution, and synthesis. In the following section, examples from the practices of the five Thai telecommunication companies are used to illustrate the general findings of the study.

Leadership

Managers in all of the five companies indicated their awareness of a close link between organizational knowledge and the need for leadership initiative. Within the Thai telecommunication companies, a leadership focus on knowledge management found its expression in the conscious acquisition of information from suppliers, customers, and competitors.

Close links with suppliers, customers, and competitors help organizations foster knowledge acquisition. TelecomAsia, for instance, implemented an Executive Information System, which provides daily updates about external indicators for top management decision making. Through the use of this system, top managers are aware of current external developments and can make timely decisions.

Leadership at TA and SC&C showed a particular focus on customer knowledge. Both firms regularly welcomed customer visits to the organization to discuss new ideas or business needs. Through increased information gathering from the environment, the telecommunication companies are able to gain greater awareness of the threats and opportunities in the environment and thereby increase their "absorptive capacity" (Cohen and Levinthal, 1990)—that is, their ability to recognize the value of new external information, assimilate it, and apply it to commercial ends.

From a human resource point of view, collaborating with universities as sources of future employees, rewarding employees for knowledge sharing, and joint setting of learning objectives with employees were viewed as important mechanisms for showing leadership in managing knowledge. SC&C, for instance, started rating employees on job competencies and used this system as a basis for promotion. Rewarding and promoting employees for their willingness to share knowledge facilitates the distribution of knowledge. The joint setting of learning objectives helps in synthesizing knowledge since each individual's goals for knowledge creation can be tied to organizational goals.

Corporate Culture

Managers in most companies described their corporate culture as being dominated by a climate of openness and trust. This facilitates knowledge synthesis by encouraging employees to share information at different levels. An important tool for supporting knowledge sharing is the use of cross-functional teams. Both Jasmine and TT&T regularly identified companywide projects which are managed by cross-functional teams. In the context of these projects, employees volunteered to help one another, even when they may came from different departments or functional areas. SC&C implemented an activity called IT talk whereby individuals share their knowledge about the latest IT developments in the context of a regular weekly meeting.

Another significant practice across all organizations was the encouragement of informal meetings. The existence of informal networks facilitates the organizationwide distribution of knowledge. Through network relationships, organizational members may benefit from "what they know" and "who they know." Burt (1992) argues that the information benefits derived from network ties lie in access to, timing of, and referral to information. Access to information results in the reception of relevant information whereby the sender knowingly distributes the information within the network. The benefits of timing allow the receiver to have quick access before the information loses relevance or before others are able to exploit it. Referral to information is beneficial when opportunities are identified, which may provide the basis for creating new knowledge.

This is a also a dominant feature within Overseas Chinese companies where owners are often also top managers, staff are expected to form strong links with the company, and employees are encouraged to form strong social relationships with one another (Miley et al., 1997). Within this context, the employees tend to display high levels of loyalty to the company and will distribute information and knowledge that may lead to business opportunities in the future.

Technology

The results of the survey indicate that all firms in the sample were aware of the role of technology for knowledge creation. Yet, none of the firms has so far employed information technology to a large extent. The availability of information technology infrastructures within the five different firms is quite different. Despite the partial lack of infrastructure, employees in all five firms were encouraged to learn new technologies and are provided with training for these technologies. TA and TT&T started pilot projects on groupware, and TA, TT&T, and SC&C were in the process of developing corporate Intranets. The firms generally perceived investment in information technology as a tool for improving internal communication. By allowing the firm to respond to customers' complaints or problems in a speedy manner, improved communication was ultimately viewed as leading to higher customer satisfaction.

Measurement

A surprising finding was that all firms established ways of linking knowledge management to financial results. IEC, Jasmine, SC&C, and TA calculated returns on their knowledge investment by tracking the costs of getting information into their processes and products. TT&T introduced cost-benefit analyses to evaluate information technology projects. IEC, SC&C, and TA developed knowledge indicators such as the number of employee development plans, training expenditures per employee, number of associations with learning institutions, and types of customer relationships.

Measurement is generally considered to be one of the most difficult areas of knowledge management. Given the gaps between the best-in-world practices and the state-of-the-art observed in the remaining three catalysts, the high commitment to measurement and the sophistication of the measurement tools used by the firms in our sample are an astounding result.

Measuring knowledge is a catalyst of a somewhat different nature in comparison to leadership, corporate culture, and technology. Rather than facilitating knowledge creation, it tracks knowledge creation indicators by linking investments in knowledge creation and their support systems to short- or long-term financial results. By tracking knowledge creation indicators, organizations are aware of the potential shortcomings in their investment into knowledge creation. This increases the likelihood of future investments. Measurement therefore does not directly support one of the knowledge creation processes but acts as a secondary facilitator by increasing the awareness to take action in favor of knowledge creation.

DISCUSSION

In this chapter we argue that knowledge creation consists of generic processes of knowledge acquisition, distribution, and synthesis, which are facilitated by catalysts in the shape of leadership, corporate culture, technology, and measurement. Based on this framework, the knowledge management practices of five Thai telecommunication firms have been analyzed. The results suggest that the hypothesized links between knowledge catalysts and knowledge creation processes do exist. Although leadership and corporate culture were important catalysts for knowledge creation processes, technology was found to facilitate knowledge creation to a lesser degree within the context of the Thai telecommunication companies.

Although the firms in the sample recognize the importance of focusing on knowledge as a key strategic resource, technology as a facilitator of knowledge creation seems to be in an early stage of development. It is used primarily as a facilitator for knowledge distribution. Except for one company, technology is not employed as a tool for knowledge acquisition. The boundaries between the organization and the environment seem to be firmly entrenched within the culture of most Thai telecommunication companies, hindering people and technology to absorb outside information and integrate them into the existing knowledge base.

Assessment of the state-of-the-art in knowledge practices within Thai telecommunication firms provides an indication of links between knowledge catalysts and knowledge creation processes. There are two possible explanations for the finding that technology seems to play a minor role as a knowledge creation catalyst. One may relate to the context within which the survey was conducted. In Thailand, the employment of information technology is still an emerging trend. Another explanation relates to the knowledge creation framework. Technology may be less important as a catalyst for knowledge creation than the framework assumes.

The functional area that received the greatest attention in terms of knowledge management within the Thai telecommunication companies was human resources. By highlighting the importance of this resource, the companies were making a concerted effort to integrate individual knowledge with the organizational knowledge base. This finding is somewhat less surprising given the challenges of liberalization. In an increasingly competitive environment, the ability to attract qualified human resources will become a key success factor.

More rigorous research is needed to refine the operationalization of knowledge catalysts and to link these to operationalized knowledge creation constructs. By establishing links between these elements, a contribution has been made to the operationalization of knowledge management. In order to rule out the effect of country context, companies from both industrialized and newly industrialized countries need to be studied in order to be able to verify the validity of the knowledge creation framework and the findings of this research.

From a research perspective, the next step should be to develop a more sophisticated survey instrument that develops measures for all constructs of the knowledge creation framework. Links between knowledge catalysts, knowledge creation processes, and the performance of an organization need to be investigated. This will allow verification of the connections between various constructs and point out necessary conditions for effective knowledge management within companies. More precisely, it will show how catalysts enable knowledge creation that leads to a sustainable competitive advantage.

From a managerial perspective, this preliminary survey can help to identify areas of improvement for knowledge management. By providing feedback to the Thai telecommunication companies about their practices and areas for improvement, they can invest further into knowledge management to help develop a competitive advantage.

ACKNOWLEDGMENT

The authors acknowledge the support of Ms. Choojit Chantrasoot for data collection in Thailand.

REFERENCES

Arthur Andersen and APQC. (1995). The Knowledge Management Assessment Tool, released at the Knowledge Imperative Symposium, Houston, Texas.

Auster, E., and Choo, C. W. (1994) How Senior Managers Acquire and Use Information in Environmental Scanning. *Information Processing & Management*, 30, pp. 607–618.

Badaracco, J. L. (1991). *Knowledge Link: How Firms Compete Through Strategic Alliances.* Boston: Harvard Business School Press.

Barney, J. (1991). Firm Resources and Sustained Competitive Advantage. *Journal of Management*, 17, 99–120.

Burt, R. S. (1992). *Structural Holes: The Social Structure of Competition.* Cambridge, MA: Harvard University Press.

Cohen, W., and Levinthal, D. (1990). Absorptive Capacity: A New Perspective on Learning and Innovation. *Administrative Science Quarterly*, 35, pp. 128–152.

Daft, R. L., and Huber, G. P. (1987). How Organizations Learn: A Communication Framework. *Research in the Sociology of Organizations*, 5, pp. 1–36.

Daft, R. L., and Macintosh, N. B. (1981). A Tentative Exploration into the Amount and Equivocality of Information Processing in Organizational Work Units. *Administrative Science Quarterly*, 26, pp. 207–224.

Davis, S., and Botkin, J. (1994). The Coming of Knowledge-Based Business. *Harvard Business Review*, 72(5), pp. 165–170.

Dierickx, I., and Cool, K. (1989). Asset Stock Accumulation and Sustainability of Competitive Advantage. *Management Science*, 35, pp. 1504–1511.

Fiol, C. M. (1994). Consensus, Diversity, and Learning in Organizations. *Organization Science*, 5, pp. 403–420.

Fiol, C. M., and Lyles, M. A. (1985). Organizational Learning. *Academy of Management Journal*, 10, pp. 803–813.

Gray, B., Bougon, M. G., and Donnellon, A. (1985). Organizations as Constructions and Destructions of Meaning. *Journal of Management*, 11, pp. 83–98.

Hamel, G., and Prahalad, C. K. (1994). *Competing for the Future: Breakthrough Strategies for Seizing Control of Your Industry and Creating the Markets of Tomorrow.* Boston: Harvard Business School Press.

Handy, C. (1990). *The Age of Unreason.* Boston: Harvard Business School Press.

Hitt, M. A., and Ireland, R. D. (1985). Corporate Distinctive Competence, Strategy, Industry and Performance. *Strategic Management Journal*, 6, pp. 273–293.

Huber, G. P. (1991). Organizational Learning: The Contributing Processes and the Literatures. *Organization Science*, 2, pp. 88–115.

Huber, G. P., and Daft, R. L. (1987). The Information Environments of Organizations. In F. M. Jablin et al. (eds.), *Handbook of Organizational Communication.* Newbury Park, CA: Sage, pp. 130–164.

Klayman, J., and Schoemaker, P.J.H. (1993). Thinking about the Future: A Cognitive Perspective. *Journal of Forecasting*, 12, pp. 161–186.

Kogut, B., and Zander, U. (1993). Knowledge of the Firm and Evolutionary Theory of the Multinational Corporation. *Journal of International Business Studies*, 24, pp. 625–645.

Leonard-Barton, D. (1992). Core Capabilities and Core Rigidities: A Paradox in Managing New Product Development. *Strategic Management Journal*, 13, pp. 111–125.

Leonard-Barton, D. (1995). *Wellsprings of Knowledge: Building and Sustaining the Sources of Innovation*. Boston: Harvard Business School Press.

Lyles, M. A., and Schwenk, C. R. (1992). Top Management, Strategy and Organizational Knowledge Structures. *Journal of Management Studies*, 29, pp. 155–174.

MacDonald, S. (1995). Learning to Change: An Information Perspective on Learning in the Organization. *Organization Science*, 6, pp. 557–568.

Mahoney, J. T., and Pandian, J. R. (1992). The Resource-Based View Within the Conversation of Strategic Management. *Strategic Management Journal*, 13, pp. 363–380.

Miley, F., Canberra, F., and Read, A. (1997). Internal Controls in Overseas-Chinese Family Companies: A Cross-Cultural Exploration. *Asian Manager*, June, pp. 19–24.

Nelson, R., and Winter, S. G. (1982). *An Evolutionary Theory of Economic Change*. Cambridge, MA: Harvard University Press.

Nonaka, I. (1994). A Dynamic Theory of Organizational Knowledge Creation. *Organization Science*, 5, pp. 14–37.

Nonaka, I., and Konno, N. (1998). The Concept of "Ba": Building a Foundation for Knowledge Creation. *California Management Review*, 40, pp. 1–15.

Prahalad, C. K., and Hamel, G. (1990). The Core Competence of the Corporation. *Harvard Business Review*, 68, pp. 79–91.

Probst, G.J.B., and Büchel, B.S.T. (1997). *Organizational Learning: The Competitive Advantage of the Future*. London: Prentice-Hall.

Probst, G.J.B., Raub, S. P., and Romhardt, K. (1999). *Managing Knowledge—Building Blocks for Success*. Chichester: John Wiley and Sons.

Sandelands, L. E., and Stablein, R. E. (1987). The Concept of Organization Mind. *Research in the Sociology of Organizations*, 5, pp. 135–162.

Skandia. (1998). *Balanced Report on Intellectual Capital*. Stockholm.

Ungson, G. R., Braunstein, D. N., and Hall, P. D. (1981). Managerial Information Processing: A Research Review. *Administrative Science Quarterly*, 26, pp. 116–134.

Walsh, J. P. (1995). Managerial and Organizational Cognition: Notes from a Trip Down Memory Lane. *Organization Science*, 6, pp. 280–321.

Walsh, J. P., and Ungson, G. R. (1991). Organizational Memory. *Academy of Management Review*, 16, pp. 57–91.

Weick, K. E. (1995). *Sensemaking in Organizations*. Thousand Oaks, CA: Sage.

Wiley, N. (1988). The Micro-Macro Problem in Social Theory. *Sociological Theory*, 6, pp. 254–261.

Chapter 15

Chinese Network Management: An Alternative Strategic Management Model

George Haley

INTRODUCTION

In recent years, increasing notice has been taken of the management practices of Chinese business networks (hereafter referred to as the Networks). Analyses have largely fallen into two camps: awed admiration and virulent condemnation. Generally, awed admiration emphasizes the Networks' blazing speed in making and implementing their decisions (Chu and MacMurray, 1993; Wada, 1992). Critics have decried the Networks' tendencies toward conglomerate diversification (Chu and MacMurray, 1993), cronyism (Backman, 1999), and seemingly reactive fashion in which major decisions are made (Ghosh and Chan, 1994). Both positive and negative critiques have an element of truth, yet few add to an understanding of the Networks' management style.

A primary factor that interferes with this understanding is that most of those individuals passing judgment are doing so based on the Western historical and cultural content without considering that the historical and cultural influences of the Chinese will produce different practical and theoretical perceptions of business environments. In additional, whether most authors have been positive or negative has often depended on whether they were writing when the Asian economies were strong or during the recent crisis.

Among those authors whose explanations of managerial decisions are not dependent on the state of the Asian economies, the best known explanations include the following. Hofstede (1992), in his well-known research, proposed culture as a primary determinant of decision-making styles. Haley and Stumpf (1989) found that personality type influenced decision making, and U.C.V. Haley (1997) found evidence that managerial cadres from different nations may be made up of different personality types, thereby implying that personality types capture many national differences in decision styles. With respect to the Networks' decision-making style, the Chinese culture's Confucian belief structures (Hsu, 1984; Pan, 1984; Redding, 1995) have often been cited in explanation of their decision-making style. Haley and Tan (1996) offered competitive advantage as an explanation; it tends to exclude new entrants without the established communities' experience and connections.

The true situation probably includes all the different explanations, and more. Whatever the reason, many major Asian firms exhibit unique strategic-management style. The Asian firms' somewhat holistic, intuitive, decision-making style appears well-suited to information-scarce environments, or environments where market-survey data seem highly suspect, a situation that exists in many emerging and lesser developed economies. Since Asian decision makers have not generally desired more information, the region is an informational void for those who do, and it is an excellent environment for the creation of an alternative, potentially more versatile, strategic management system—one that would benefit executives, entrepreneurs, and policymakers from other emerging and less developed economic regions.

Fei (1992) argued that to understand the differences between Chinese and Western societies, one must recognize that there is not merely a cultural divide between the two societies but a civilizational chasm. In Western societies, the primary social unit is the individual, whereas in Asian societies, the primary social unit is the community. Similarly, as Haley and Haley (1997) maintain, the primary units of Western economies are their individual companies, whereas the primary units of Asian economies are their Networks. While Fei may be correct, this does not mean that Western management theories cannot be used to describe, analyze, and understand the Networks' strategies. To do so, however, one should begin by examining the historical and cultural root structure from which the Networks and their management have sprung.

THE HISTORICAL INFLUENCES ON THE CHINESE NETWORKS

The Chinese merchant classes struggled against periodic campaigns of persecution in China and in the various countries to which they moved. Owing largely to the influence of Confucianism, Chinese culture has long been antagonistic to the commercial classes. To prosper, the commercial classes frequently had to ignore or circumvent rulings from the central authorities. The individuals who would most frequently ignore the center's directives were the merchant classes living in regions remote from the central authorities and who had the greatest incentive to do so (e.g., the southern coastal regions of China from which the bulk of today's Nanyang Chinese originated). These regions are the Hokkien and Teochiu homelands. Both lack good farmlands but possess relatively good ports. Hence, their incentive was purely economic, for the regions simply could not prosper when limited to agricultural pursuits. During the few expansionist periods when international trade was supported, their efforts to build trading relationships brought wealth into their provinces and family coffers. When, periodically, the Chinese emperors tried to block overseas commerce, contacts, and emigration through repressive acts, such as one in 1661, when the Manchu emperor, K'ang-hsi, banned travel and evacuated the coastal regions of China to a point of about ten miles inland (Haley, Tan, and Haley, 1998), it was difficult for the coastal traders to surrender their prosperity. Their reaction was to circumvent the central authorities whenever and however they could. They used their domestic trade and shipping, as well as their contacts in local and central governments, to cover their activities and maintain their foreign trading activities. Secrecy and trust in commerce were necessary, and so the Networks were born.

CONFUCIANISM

Confucius believed in authority and opposed rebellion against a legitimate prince under any circumstance (Legge, 1970; Waley, 1996). One consistent conclusion about the Networks' management is that it is a top-down, authoritarian system. In recent years, many other aspects of Confucian thought have worked their way into the Networks' management, however, as more authors began studying the Networks' growing influence (e.g., Redding, 1995, 1996; Hamilton, 1996; Khanna and Palepu, 1997; Shigematsu, 1994). Some have said that emphasizing Confucianism is wrong, for more modern and specifically economic philosophical systems of behavior have replaced the old, traditional systems (e.g., Hamilton, 1996). Haley, Tan, and Haley (1998) pressed the argument for the continued relevancy of Confucianism as a dominant influence on the Networks' strategic planning and decision making because of its overriding importance in the development of the Chinese culture. In a 1985 speech to the World Management Congress Robert Kuok, Malaysia's great Overseas Chinese tycoon, discussed the importance of Confucianism to Chinese businessmen. He stated, "As children, we learned about moral values—mainly Confucian."

The focus of Confucian ethics and thought is the family. Confucianism's continuing importance stems from the continued preeminence of the family in Chinese life, its continued dominance over Chinese perceptions of the ideal in human behavior, and the creative tension and conflict between the influence of Confucianism on Chinese culture and human nature and the practical necessities and experiences of their lives on the other. Haley, Tan, and Haley (1998) point out that Confucianism and the other philosophies that influenced Chinese culture viewed economic nature as something either to deny or to control.

The Family

The one overwhelming constant in Confucianism is the family. The family dominates an individual's moral considerations and behaviors. It determines:

- the individual's relationships with other common individuals whom he meets in the course of a day;
- the individual's relationship with a sovereign or any other authority figure from outside his family circle;
- the individual's relationships with society at large; and
- the individual's relationships with family members.

The Confucian family is both immediate and unending. The individuals owe responsibility to their nuclear family, their extended family, and their ancestors. The family is the basis not only for an individual's place in society, but also for his or her relationships in society. The duty between a father and son supersedes even the duty between a man and his sovereign—a man's duty to his parents even exceeds his duty to his own person (Haley, Tan, and Haley, 1998). In addition, the Confucian view of loyalty is very personal. Loyalty is to the prince, not to the state—to the father and memory of the father, not to the friends and subordinates of the father. Loyalty and the subordinate's duty to his superior, or loyalty between two business associates, is just that and no more, it does not extend to the superior's or the business associate's company. Recognizing this factor is crucial to understanding the evolution of Chinese business relationships.

Confucianism's Influence on Business

According to Haley, Tan, and Haley (1998, p. 36), "The most immediate element of Confucianism's influence on the Chinese economic culture deals with its perception of the merchant class and the profit motive. In both instances, they were frowned upon." Confucian philosophers and mandarins viewed the merchant class with suspicion while exalting the peasantry. The peasant was exalted because he was tied to the land and thus needed of the central authority to maintain social and political stability. The peasant and the state were viewed as having mutual interests, and thus the peasantry could be depended upon to support the state.

The merchant was frowned upon because the merchant was mobile. The merchant's mobility allowed him to find surpluses of goods in one location and transport them to where those goods were scarce and earn his profit. However, mobility also made the merchant undependable as he could flee with his goods to areas more conducive to profitability when the situation called for it. In addition, Haley, Tan, and Haley (1998) note that Confucian mandarins may have viewed the merchant class as a threat to their power owing to their wealth and their ability, much like the princes and their mandarins, to provide the masses with the necessities of life.

Confucian economic and social theory maintained that a key part of good rule was to provide the masses with sufficient wealth to give themselves and their families the basic necessities. Unlike Western economic philosophy, the goal of traditional Chinese economics is not the creation of wealth but the maintenance of a minimum acceptable subsistence for all members of society. The excess over and above this subsistence level was the benefit earned by society's rulers as reward for providing a sufficiency of prosperity and stability. Lau in his translation of the *Tao Te Ching*, quotes Lao Tzu as saying: "Not to honor men of worth will keep the people from contention; not to value goods which are hard to come by will keep them from theft; not to display what is desirable will keep them from being unsettled of mind." Thus, the profit motive would create a situation in which the masses would demand a greater share of the nation's wealth, thereby increasing what would be considered an adequate subsistence level for the masses to be satisfied. The profit motive was viewed as corrupt. To have promoted the goal of wealth creation would have meant displaying desirable goods, causing "contention among the people."

A man in Confucian society also had to maintain his proper place and behavior in society. Confucians believe that a man must display behaviors that are specific and appropriate to each relationship and social interaction one faces in life. This does not mean that Confucian societies are static; they are not. Confucianism developed an authoritarian and hierarchical social structure but not a static one. All people are enjoined to advance themselves as far as their skills, talents, efforts, and luck will take them, but at every step of their advance, they must learn and display all the proper behaviors for their present position in society, at that particular time of their life, and for whatever particular social interaction they are engaged in. This factor is crucial in the display of "uprightness," which in Chinese relationships must be displayed for absolute trust to be earned in the building of a network.

Ethics and the Building of Trust

Confucian ethics, like all other aspects of Confucianism, focuses on relationships between individuals. Confucianism addresses ethical duty through five unidirectional relationships. They are unidirectional as the ethical duties owed between the two polar members of the relationship differ, with the lesser member (the second party listed) of the relationship owing a higher, more stringent ethical duty to the greater. The five relationships are:

- Sovereign–Minister
- Father–Son
- Husband–Wife
- Older–Younger (some maintain it should be Older brother—Younger brother)
- Friendship

When a relationship falls outside of these five relationships, Confucianism has a basic injunction that all members of society should strive to maintain social harmony. The requirement to maintain social harmony intrudes upon ethical concerns because it is expected that if someone is treated unethically, he will resent that unethical treatment and through his efforts to obtain retribution or justice will create in social disharmony. This desire for social harmony should not be underestimated. It is exemplified by a statement made by Cheung Kim Hung (editor of *Next* Magazine, Hong Kong): "In Chinese business circles, the emphasis is on harmony. People agree to compete or not to compete."

The Contextual Nature of Confucian Ethics

Confucian ethical standards are very high, but they are also contextual. It is important not to confuse the contextual nature of Confucian ethic with Western schools of situational ethics; nothing could be further from the truth. The factor that determines the precise ethical behavior and duty you owe another is the relationship you have with that person. Confucian ethical standards do vary to a much greater extent than do those within a single Western society or culture, but they are much less flexible. The variation in ethical duties Confucian standards impose has little to do with the situation you find yourself in and everything to do with the context imposed by the relationship for which the standards were set. Hence, rather than one ethical standard being promulgated, there are as many as seven standards. One standard is prescribed for each of the five relationships. For those who cannot accept the notion that all people fall into one of the five relationships but believe in the standard of social harmony, a sixth standard is prescribed to assure the maintenance of social harmony. Finally, for those who refuse to accept the idea that all men fall within one of the five relationships, and recognize that not all people can create a negative effect on social harmony, there is a seventh standard. In all instances, the effect of a particular situation on the prescribed duties is minimal, and the effect of the relational context is supreme.

The Prescriptive Nature of Confucian Ethics

Confucian ethics is prescriptive. Proper behaviors in all situations are established; behaviors based on the foundation of the family are prescribed for all human relationships. In Confucian societies, commercial relations are extensions of family relations. The basic principles of doing business in Western societies were unheard of or even frowned upon in Confucian business practices.

The prescriptive, familial nature of Confucianism is important because it is unethical to behave in a way that is not prescribed for an established relationship. Conversely, when dealing with behaviors that take place outside the contexts of the five relationships, virtually any behavior that does not cause significant social disharmony is ethical. Because of the extremely personal nature of Chinese ethics, one must usually have a personal relationship for a direct ethical duty to exist. In addition, because all Confucian relationships are extensions of familial relationships, something acceptable only within a family relationship in the West may be accepted in Chinese commercial relationships. Because of the very personal nature of Chinese business relationships, the Chinese created, and largely still depend on, the Network form of business.

WHAT IS A NETWORK?

The Overseas Chinese operate in Networks, but the Overseas Chinese Network system of doing business is merely an extension of the same business practices that the Chinese have used throughout their history to circumvent the isolationist policies of their various governments over the centuries. The only real difference is the further refinement of practices made possible by technological improvements and greater acceptance of the business classes in their new homelands.

A tremendous misperception about the Networks is that they must be exclusively clan or family based (Haley, Tan, and Haley, 1998), Haley (1999), Haley and Tan (1996, 1999), and Haley, Tan, and Haley (1998), however, have all emphasized trust as the key element in Network formation. Besides trust and family (or clan), there are three other bases for Network formation: the locality of origin, the dialect or subdialect spoken, and the traditional guilds. The rapid growth of Chinese companies, and the increased complexity of the various Asian economies and their growing interconnectedness with the world economy, have led Haley, Tan, and Haley (1998) to argue that trust has become the primary basis for Network formation and building. Table 15.1 presents the different bases for Chinese Network formation.

Whether you are speaking of a Network that is comprised of independent companies, or one that is comprised of executives within the same firm, a Network is a tool. A business Network, as defined in Charan (1991), is a tool created to:

- build trust;
- speed decision making;
- facilitate high-quality decision making;
- build customer satisfaction; and
- generate competitive advantages for network members.

Management theorists have created other tools to perform these same functions (e.g., market research, SWOT analysis, investment in information technology). What is it that makes the Network and Network-based strategic management worthy of being studied? More to the point of our discussion, why should we

Table 15.1
Bases for Chinese Networks

Network Type	Basis for Network
Clan grouping	By family surname
Locality grouping	By locality of origin in China
Dialect grouping	By dialect/sub-dialect spoken
Guild grouping	By craft practiced
Trust grouping	By prior experience/recommendation

Source: Haley, Tan, and Haley (1998), p. 14.

study the Chinese Networks and the strategic management that has evolved from this concept?

The simple answer to the first question is that the network is the most human and natural of strategic business practices. Wherever man has had to make crucial decisions under conditions of uncertainty, networks, and the strategies associated with them have arisen. Haley, Tan, and Haley (1998: 95) quote one of the Overseas Chinese millionaires as saying:

> Making decisions without feasibility studies is not a Chinese trait, it is a decision-making trait which is common to any who enter business under conditions of scarcity. If you take the risk, maybe you lose your money, but maybe you don't. If you invest in the research or feasibility study, you don't have any chance to win, you no longer have the money to invest.

The historic nature and diversity of Networks over time and geographic distance can be seen in Table 15.2. Whatever continent and time period you investigate, you will find Networks. The Chinese Networks have grown very influential in today's economy, and given the population of the world's Confucian cultures, they will gain even greater influence. In addition, developing an understanding of the Chinese Networks and strategic systems will help us understand other business network systems such as the Overseas Indian, the domestic South Asian and Indian Networks, and the Hispanic Grupos.

Business networks can be both intra- or supra-company, that is, made up of individuals or companies. Intra-company networks have historically been informal networks of individual executives or of blue-collar workers. These networks of friends and associates within a company can rival the company's own formal management in efficiency and influence. Because they are informal and are not recognized by senior management, they are generally of no direct benefit to the company. The key elements in developing a network are a perceived mutuality of interests, trust, and, if not friendship, a degree of respect for one another. Although a company may learn to use an employee network to its benefits and

Table 15.2
Networks over Time and Distance

- The Overseas Indian Networks
- The Hispanic Grupos
- The Old School Tie
- Japanese Inter- and Intra-Firm Networks
- Criminal Networks
- Secret Societies (e.g., the Masonic Order and Magnus Dei)
- The Islamic Clans
- The Feudal System
- The Scottish Familial Clans
- The Roman Republic's System of Political Patronage
- The Historic Tribal Nations of the American Indians and Africa

can create an environment conducive to network formation (Charan, 1991), a company cannot build a network simply because it cannot mandate the creation of the trust, friendship, or respect on which networks are based (Haley, Tan, and Haley, 1998).

The Chinese Networks represent a classic network structure, and like most business networks, they are comprised of both intra- and supra-company elements. Supra-company networks consist of independent companies and businesspeople who join together for their mutual profit and benefit. Because of the personal nature of Chinese relationships, the Chinese Networks are almost always between businesspeople who have established long-term ties, either through long-term experience in business dealings or through familial or friendship ties. Chinese Networks also extend inward to companies that are associated with each other—in one of the ways described by Haley, Tan, and Haley (1998). Most commonly, it will be by a senior industrialist sponsoring a former employee into ownership or control of their own company. In this fashion, Chinese Networks evolve into a web of intermingled intra- and supra-company networks. Examples of these webs abound and include such companies as Acer Computers, Wuthelam Group, CP Group, and Salim Group (Haley, Tan, and Haley, 1998).

This Network form of business organization, though not unique to the Chinese, has been developed to a high level of success and performance by the Overseas Chinese. They have also introduced unique elements to the Network system through the civilizational differences proven to exist between the philosophical underpinnings of Chinese and Western cultures (Fei, 1992). The growing size and importance of the Chinese business Networks, and of the Chinese economy generally, justify study of the Chinese form of network management as an alternative system of business management that is especially useful in emerging economies and business situations where managers are operating under conditions of scarcity.

THE NETWORKS' STRATEGIC PRACTICE

As Western MNCs have moved into Asian markets in recent decades, rights, among other things became a hot isue. Interestingly, reporting on these issues has gone beyond the immediate issues of the breaking of contracts and copyright/patent infringement to a discussion of the networks that dominate business in Asia. Both academics (Haley and Tan, 1996; Hofstede, 1994; Nakamura, 1992; Redding, 1995) and popular writers (Kohut and Cheng, 1996; Seagrave, 1996; Weidenbaum and Hughes, 1996) have published a great deal on the Networks' strategic management and planning. Many have argued that the Overseas Chinese do not conduct strategic planning. As Haley (1997), Haley and Haley (1997), Haley and Tan (1996), and Haley, Tan, and Haley (1998), have shown, however, this is patently false. The Networks do have their own strategic management style, and it can be understood in terms of Western economic and strategic theories.

Nakamura (1992), among others, has argued that strategic decision making in East Asia and many of the ASEAN countries was developing along the same lines as strategic decision making did in Japan. Haley (1997), Haley and Haley (1997), Haley and Tan (1996), and Haley, Tan, and Haley (1998) maintained that the similarities were superficial and that Western managers would be disadvantaged if they dealt with the Networks as if they were dealing with Japanese firms.

Chinese management throughout Southeast Asia, and increasingly when operating within China, have followed conglomerate diversification. Among the important characteristics that distinguish successful Overseas Chinese companies are the following:

- They are highly diversified, often undertaking unrelated diversification, and contravening mainstream, Western theoretical notions.
- Management has good relationships with the often enormous, public sectors in these countries.
- The companies are network based.

Subjective data and information are important inputs to decision making.

Chu and MacMurray (1993) attribute the rapid growth of the Networks in Southeast Asia to their speed in decision making. The Networks' speed and their control of information constitute major, competitive advantages (Haley and Tan, 1996; Redding, 1995). The Networks' management also tends to exhibit idiosyncratic rather than professional corporate characteristics. For example, Ghosh and Chan (1994), in their study of strategic-planning behaviors among firms in

Table 15.3
Planning Characteristics of Strategic Constructs

Strategic Theorists	Staff/Line Dependent	Data/Experience Dependent
Hofer & Schendel	Staff	Data
Porter	Staff	Data
Prahalad & Hamel	Staff/Line	Data/Experience
Mintzberg	Staff/Line	Data/Experience

Source: Haley (1997).

Singapore and Malaysia, classified their planning activities as idiosyncratic, ad hoc, and reactive. The only important market-related factor they found centered on the "CEO's personal knowledge of market," which was the fourth-most-important factor contributing to success in planning, and reflects the idiosyncratic nature of their planning—the "CEO's personal knowledge" of the market not the firm's or the marketing manager's, assumes importance.

STRATEGIC PLANNING AND THE NETWORKS

Western management revolves around the wealth of information available for anyone with the desire and wit to find and to use it. Table 15.3 summarizes some of the dominant characteristics of strategic systems propounded by prominent theorists with respect to the primary personnel responsible for planning activities and the kind of data/information that dominates analysis and decision making.

The Traditional School

Hofer and Schendel (1978) are among the earliest conceptualizers of a classic, strategic planning system, and Michael Porter's (1992) system is very similar. Both systems require large amounts of high-quality internal and external information. Both are analytical and rational, and both depend on largely sequential collection, analysis, and interpretation of data to generate the necessary information. Managers collect, analyze, and interpret the data within a fixed, perceptual world-view of the interactions between companies and their environments. They emphasize threats and opportunities in a company's external environments. The basic assumption underlying Hofer and Schendel, Porter, and similar theorists' systems is that the relationships between firms and their environments can be defined, measured, and analyzed through objective data within a positivist framework. Both systems rely on staff to perform the data collection and analysis required to develop recommended actions to senior management. The dependence on defined objective data without also including subjective experiential data creates a situation described by Mintzberg (1987, 1994) as one that separates minds and hands.

The Networks, with management decision making highly dependent on experience and on intuitive use of qualitative information, use many fewer staff than Western companies do. Consequently, the strategic management concepts proposed by Hofer and Schendel, and Porter do not explain Chinese strategic planning practices. The extensive high-quality, quantitative data required by Hofer and Schendel's strategic planning system does not exist in most Asian environments where the business environment has been described as an informational void (Haley and Tan, 1996).

Prahalad and Hamel's Core Competencies

Prahalad and Hamel (1990) emphasize a more internally focused strategic system that emphasizes knowledge of the company's strengths and capabilities. Successful strategies exploit core competencies to obtain success. This internal focus tends to favor line management with its greater knowledge of the company, its operations and markets. Strategic planning emphasizing core competencies may or may not depend on collecting quality objective data and staff. It permits the combination of Mintzberg's planning of the hands with planning of the mind. Prahalad and Hamel (1990) define a core competency as a characteristic that

1. provides potential access to various markets;
2. makes an important contribution to the perceived benefits a firm provides its customers; and
3. is difficult to imitate.

Prahalad and Hamel's strategic concepts are more user friendly for the Networks. While the Networks diversified, they also developed and perfected their core competency—their decision-making style. The Networks' decision-making style:

1. Provides potential access to various markets, as evidenced by their conglomerate diversification. Table 15.4 provides many examples of the diversity of markets which Network conglomerates serve.
2. Makes an important contribution to the perceived benefits a firm provides its customers. The Networks' ability to contribute to their customers' perceived benefits is evidenced by their market dominance and the degree to which foreign companies (a market also) seek them out as partners in the region.
3. Is difficult to imitate. Since the Network maintains secrecy on its sources of information, and Networks are based on trust and loyalty, it is difficult for potential competitors to imitate.

Table 15.4
Families and Businesses in the Overseas Chinese Networks

Family/Leader	Primary Businesses
Indonesia	
Liem Sioe Liong	Cement, processed foods, flour milling, steel, banking, real estate, investments
Eka Tjipta Widjaja	Diversified
Oei Hong Leong	Beer, tires, consumer products
Mochtar Riaddy	Property, banking, insurance
Suhargo Gondokusumo	Agri-industries, property
Prajogo Pangestu	Timber, car assembly
Malaysia	
Robert Kuok	Plantations, sugar and wood processing, media, hotels
Quek Leng Chan	Finance, diversified
Lim Goh Tong	Casinos, real estate
Vincent Tan	Leisure, manufacturing, investment
Philippines	
Lucio Tan	Beer, tobacco, banking, investments
Henry Sy	Retailing, cement, investments
Alfonso Yuchengco	Banking, insurance
Antonio Cojuangco	Telecommunications, real estate
John Gokongwei	Real estate, diversified investments
Thailand	
Chearavanont Family	Agri-business, real estate, telecommunications
Kanjanapas Family	Real estate, transport, finance
Ratanarak Family	Cement, Banking, telecommunications
Sophonpanich Family	Banking, real estate, investments
Lamsam Family	Banking, real estate

Sources: Compiled from Haley and Haley (1997); and East Asia Analytical Unit (1995).

Mintzberg and the Networks

Mintzberg's theoretical model seems be an even more appropriate model to describe the Networks' decision-making style than Prahalad and Hamel's. In Mintzberg's model, strategic plans are both directed and emergent. Emergent plans evolve from the collective, behavioral patterns of company personnel (Mintzberg, 1987, 1994; Mintzberg and Waters, 1985) in reaction to competitive and market events.

The Networks' strategic planning emphasizes emergent strategic planning. Haley and Tan (1996) described the low level of formal education possessed by the founders of most Network companies. This characteristic, together with the history, Confucian culture, and scarcity of resources, created decision-making perspectives and criteria different from those of most Western managers of MNCs. The Networks' managers considered data based on their experiences, advice from trusted friends, and their personal perceptions to be the only reliable market data acquirable.

Network executives interact with their environments to create strategies. News, rumors, what Westerners would consider insider information, and intuitive perceptions of market trends all create the output of interest. Confirming evidence is sought through the Network, and both necessary and available resources are estimated. The situation is analyzed using the above inputs, and decisions are made and implemented. Usually, plans retain maximum flexibility, and the decisions implemented do not require investments so large as to put the company at risk (Haley, Tan, and Haley, 1998). In the course of implementing the Network executive's decisions, additional information is acquired, the strategy is fleshed, out, and appropriate changes in strategic direction—from increased investment to withdrawal from the market—are made in reaction to results and external market events. Thus, the strategies emerge from the executive's and the firm's learned business behaviors, as well as from these factors' interaction with the market. If a strategic partner is needed, one will be sought out.

Although major Overseas Chinese firms are generally significant family-based conglomerates, potential partners are likely to be nonfamily. The partners invited to participate in the investment base their decisions on the potential profits of the project, but judgment of the risk or uncertainty involved in the investment is based on the partners' confidence and trust in the proposing executives' judgment and managerial abilities. Although this is a subjective judgment, it is no more subjective than risk factors built into Western net present value techniques (Haley and Goldberg, 1996). Therefore, strategies followed by the Networks as a whole bubble up from various Network companies—this is a key and unique element in the Networks' strategic planning. In Western management models, including Mintzberg's own strategic planning construct, this bubbling-up processes occurs on an intrafirm basis; within the Networks, it also occurs on both an intrafirm and *supra-firm* basis.

Wada (1992) presented an example of this supra-firm bubbling-up process when he noted how a Chinese businessman in Hong Kong decided on a multimillion dollar investment—fifteen minutes after he received a phone call offering him the opportunity. The time frame displays the qualitative analysis of subjective data, the role of trust in judging the soundness of the investment, and each executive's intimate knowledge of the business and markets. The entire process displays bubbling up of the strategy from an individual company into the Network. Wada indicated that this display of speed and action-based investment was among the primary reasons he moved Yaohan's (trading firm) headquarters from Japan to Hong Kong, leaving only management of Japanese operations in Japan. Although the entire process was internal, based on executive judgment, this process represents planning by the hands as it is based on the partners' experience in the industry, market, and with each other.

BUT IS IT A STRATEGIC PLANNING MODEL?

There are very few empirical studies of Asia's holistic/intuitive decision-making styles. Haley and Tan (1996) and Haley, Tan and Haley (1998), in their observations of managers, found that they rely on the following:

- *Hands-on Experience*: To make decisions quickly, managers must be experienced line managers who know the firm's work routines and processes, its product(s), market(s), business environment, and industry first hand. Senior Asian businessmen are involved in all aspects of their firms' activities and remain so throughout their careers.
- *Transfers of Knowledge across Businesses*: Asian companies often engage in unrelated diversification. Executives who succeed in unfamiliar industries possess intimate knowledge of the business environments in which they operate. This knowledge allows them to generalize from past experience, recognize patterns of similarities and dissimilarities in the different businesses they enter, and apply those generalizations in the new context.
- *Qualitative Information*: Asian executives process myriad bits of information and consider several alternatives in-depth before they act, but they do so almost entirely internally. Their decision making is highly articulated, but results are rarely presented in written, analytical form. Asian executives use qualitative, often subjective, information supplied by their Networks Their subjective data preferences, though not the choice of most Western managers, generally offer more accurate reflections of reality than quantitative data from the region would.
- *Holistic, Information Processing*: In an informational void, conventional, analytical problem solving that stresses sequential, systematic, and step-by-step approaches to decision making often proves unworkable. In the Networks' experience-based intuitive model, managers take a general approach to problems, define parameters intuitively, and explore solutions holistically.
- *Action-Driven Decision-Making*: Speed is a key characteristic of the Asians' business dealings. The Asian decision-making model reflects authoritative management, quick decision making, and senior executives' empowerment and accountability. Losses caused by considered action tend to be more acceptable than losses caused by inaction.

In his discussion of strategic planning, Mintzberg (1994) argued that strategic planning consists of the following four activities: (1) detecting discontinuities, (2) knowing the business, (3) managing patterns, and (4) reconciling change and continuity. Haley (1997) compared Haley and Tan's (1996) discussion of the Networks' decision making and commented at length on the similarity and overlap between the Network managers' decision making and Mintzberg's four activities. The following discussion leans heavily on his remarks and clearly shows that the two constructs are closely related.

- *Detecting discontinuities, or detecting basic changes that will require a significant change in how business is conducted* (he termed it the essence of strategic planning): Haley argued that Networks managers' use of contacts within local governments and communities was the Networks seeking to detect discontinuities. The Networks' web of associates is used to determine potential changes in government policy, in competitive situations, and in markets and other environments that can cause discontinuities.
- *Knowing the business*: Haley argued that this relates directly to Haley and Tan's (1996) hands-on experience. Network managers participate in all major aspects of their firm's activities both actively and intimately.
- *Managing patterns*: Haley detected the management of patterns in both Haley and Tan's (1996) holistic information processing and transfer of knowledge. In both instances, the strategists rely on experience and perceptions to translate holistic data, viewed as patterns, and similarities in patterns between industries to infer the firms' present and future relationships with its internal and external environments, as well as to manage resources appropriately in order to optimize present and future benefits.
- *Reconciling change and continuity, or the encouragement of some patterns, and the discouragement of others*: Haley (1997) noted that the Networks' use of their associates to obtain information, pursue preferential treatment, and lobby for or against the promulgation of laws, regulations, and privileged positions within desired markets and industries fits Mintzberg's activity precisely. The goal of the Network managers conducting these activities is to reconcile patterns of change and continuity to enhance the strengths and minimize the weaknesses of the Networks' companies.

Thus, when Haley and Tan (1996) described the decision-making style of the Chinese Networks, they were delineating what is clearly a strategic planning model when judged by Mintzberg's (1994) four activities of strategic planning. Haley and Tan's formulation performs all the required activities of strategic planning. The Networks' strategic planning also qualifies as an alternative to the classic Western model of strategic planning as it:

1. Performs its activities almost exclusively through what Mintzberg portrays as "planning by the hands," whereas the traditional Western models perform their activities almost exclusively through corporate staff and planning of the mind. Visiting any business school's MBA classes in strategic planning and observing what is taught would clear any doubt on this point.
2. The Networks' strategic planning construct was developed entirely independently of Western schools of thought, unlike the Japanese model which was heavily influenced by such Western scholars as Deming and Juran, and even by the post-World War II U.S. military government of Douglas MacArthur.

3. Performs all the activities of strategic planning as expounded upon by Henry Mintzberg.

COMPETITIVE IMPLICATIONS

The previous sections have highlighted the historical and cultural underpinnings of the Chinese Networks and the strategic planning style of the Networks. The strategic planning processes of the Overseas Chinese have been analyzed to gain a greater understanding of them and to justify calling those processes an alternative strategic planning model to the traditional Western models of strategic planning. This chapter concludes with a discussion of the competitive implications of the Network strategic planning model. Some of the major implications are listed below.

Strategic Competitiveness

- *Networks on the Defense*: The Networks seem to be extremely aggressive as evidenced by their speed of decision making and implementation, but their strategic strength is on the defensive side. Their strategies are to maintain competitive advantage—the informational void. Without the informational void, the Networks could face active challenges, especially from foreign MNCs which here competitive advantages in product and process technology, brand equity, R&D, advertising and promotional skills, distribution and finance. Through the fog of the informational void, the Networks compete with different foreign MNCs, often by joining forces with other MNCs in return for access to other MNCs' advantages. The informational void also reduces the Networks' local competition by reducing the effectiveness of non-Network businesses.
- *Networks on the Offense*: Few of the Networks' firms are well positioned to take the offensive against foreign MNCs in their home markets. The Networks' core competency is both their strength and weakness. Without developing a core competency (their decision making) less dependent on their competitive advantage (their home environments), most Network companies have failed when they have taken the field in markets that are as foreign to them as their home markets in Asia are to most Western companies. Fei's (1992) argument that the differences between the Western and Chinese cultures are civilizational, and not merely cultural, cuts both ways. Their core competency is much more environmentally dependent than the core competencies of most successful, large Western companies. Western MNCs willing to invest in research, data acquisition, and contacts, can attack Network competitors in their home bases, whereas Network managers, with their greater need for an intimate understanding of their product markets, will have difficulties retaliating against the MNCs in the MNCs' own home markets.

Strategic Planning

- *The Preeminence of Line Management in Asia*: Foreign MNCs in Asia should emphasize line management when seeking managers for their Asian operations, especially when they deal with Asian partners. Non-Asian line managers will encounter the same difficulties in adapting to their new environments as former non-Asian staff managers moved into senior positions in Asia. However, line managers will be better able to find common bases for personal relationships with the Networks' managers, for both will have lived through many of the same experiences and concerns in the course of their careers and be able to use their common experiences as a basis for establishing an initial rapport. The Networks' managers would also find the line managers' business experiences of greater interest and value than those of staff managers.

Human Resource Practices

- *The Practice of Rotating Managers*: The core competency of the Networks' firms, and intimate knowledge of their companies' operations, markets, and business environments, argue against the MNC practice of rotating executives in foreign postings every two or three years. First, the rotations diminish the MNCs' abilities to employ emergent strategies in Asia. Rotation makes it virtually impossible for the MNCs' managers to gain the intimate knowledge of Asian markets necessary to generate effective, Asia-based emergent strategies. In additional, firms do not build contacts; humans do. This is especially true in Asia where loyalties are very personal and nontransferable (Haley, Tan, and Haley, 1998) to another person or to the institution an individual represents. When MNCs rotate employees in Asia, they fail to recognize that relationship building in Asia takes time. After two or three years, executives are just beginning to form strong relationships to produce significant profits for their companies. What is more, the incipient contacts that they have formed will be lost due to the nontransferability of personal loyalties.
- *Managers' Characteristics for MNCs*: Without plentiful, high-quality, hard data that MNCs generally utilize, Asia-based MNC managers must face business problems without the normal analytical and informational tools they have grown to expect over their career. MNCs should select managers for their Asian operations who are able to operate effectively in environments with high levels of uncertainty.
- *Network Staff's Morale*: Bright nonfamily managers working in Network companies are often unhappy. Frequently, they are frozen out of significant contributions to policy making, and the top jobs are reserved for family members, providing raiding opportunities for MNCs. In 1996 *The Economist* reported that executives of Network companies in Hong Kong were dissatisfied with their employment and that most would prefer to work for MNCs. Their loyalties are bought and paid for through substantial annual performance bonuses and generous retirement schemes.

A General Warning

As Fei (1992) has stated, differences between Chinese and Western cultures are not merely cultural, they are civilizational. Nothing should be taken for granted. Intellectual property rights are a significant source of conflict between Western and Asian governments and companies not because the Chinese and Asians are more dishonest than Westerners, but because these rights have never existed in Asia (Haley, Tan, and Haley, 1998). The Chinese and other Asian cultures, economies, and governments never developed the concept of intellectual property rights. For the most part, even commercial law is a recent import from the West. Given the recent introduction of many Western concepts of commerce, as well as Asia's long history of trade and commerce, it is difficult to understand many Western managers doing business in Asian markets expect to practice business as usual in Asia. Instead, they have to practice, or at least recognize and adapt to, Asian business practice. The Chinese management practice of gaining an intimate working knowledge of their company's markets and business environments is a significant lesson that Western managers and management theorists should learn from Asia.

REFERENCES

Backman, M. (1999). *Asian Eclipse: The Dark Side of Business in Asia*. New York: John Wiley & Sons.

Charan, R. (1991). How Networks Reshape Organizations—For Results. *Harvard Business Review*, Reprint No. 91503.

Chu, T. C., and MacMurray, T. (1993). The Road Ahead for Asia's Leading Conglomerates. *McKinsey Quarterly*, no. 3, pp. 117–126.

East Asia Analytical Unit. (1995). *Overseas Chinese Business Networks*. Canberra, Australia: AGPS Press, Department of Foreign Affairs and Trade.

The Economist. (1996). The Limits of Family Values. Special Issue, "Survey of Business in Asia," March 9–15, pp. 12–22.

Fei, X. (1992). *From the Soil: The Foundation of Chinese Society*. Berkeley: University of California Press.

Ghosh, B. C., and C.-O. Chan. (1994). A Study of Strategic Planning Behavior among Emergent Businesses in Singapore and Malaysia. *International Journal of Management*, 11(2), pp. 697–706.

Haley, G. T. (1997). A Strategic Perspective on Overseas Chinese Networks' Decision-Making. *Management Decision*, 35(8), pp. 587–594.

Haley, G. T., and Goldberg, S. (1996). Net Present Value Techniques and Their Effects on New Product Research. *Industrial Marketing Management*, 24(3), pp. 177–190.

Haley, G. T., and Haley, U.C.V. (1997). Making Strategic Business Decisions in South and Southeast Asia. *Conference Proceedings of the First International Conference on Operations and Quantitative Management, Vol. 2*, Jaipur, India, pp. 597–604.

Haley, G. T., and Tan, C. T. (1996), The Black Hole of Southeast Asia: Strategic Decision-Making in an Informational Void. *Management Decision*, 34(9), pp. 37–48.

Haley, G. T., and Tan, C. T. (1999). East versus West: Strategic Marketing Management Meets the Asian Networks. *Journal of Business & Industrial Marketing*, 14(2), Special Issue on Business-to-Business Marketing in Asia.

Haley, G. T., Tan, C. T., and Haley, U.C.V. (1998). *New Asian Emperors: The Overseas Chinese, Their Strategies and Competitive Advantages*. Oxford, UK: Butterworth-Heinemann.

Haley, U.C.V. (1997). The Myers-Briggs Type Indicator and Decision-Making Styles: Identifying and Managing Cognitive Trails in Strategic Decision Making. In C. Fitzgerald and L. Kirby (eds.), *Leadership and the Myers-Briggs Type Indicator: Theory, Research and Applications*. Palo Alto, CA: Consulting Psychologists Press.

Haley, U.C.V., and Stumpf, S. A. (1989). Cognitive Trails in Strategic Decision-Making: Linking Theories of Personalities and Cognitions. *Journal of Management Studies*, 26(15), pp. 477–497.

Hamilton, G. G. (1996). The Theoretical Significance of Asian Business Networks. In G. G. Hamilton (ed.), *Asian Business Networks*. New York: Walter DeGruyter, pp. 283–298.

Hofer, C. W., and Schendel, D. (1978). *Strategy Formulation: Analytical Concepts*. St. Paul, MN: West Publishing Co.

Hofstede, G. (1994). Cultural Constraints in Management Theories. *International Review of Strategic Management*, 5, D. E. Hussey (ed.). West Sussex, UK: John Wiley & Sons, pp. 27–47.

Hsu, P.S.C. (1984). The Comparison of Family Structure and Values on Business Organizations in Oriental Cultures: A Comparison of China and Japan. *Proceedings of the 1984 AMA Conference, Singapore*, C. T. Tan (ed.), pp. 754–768.

Khanna, T., and Palepu, K. (1997). Why Focused Strategies May Be Wrong for Emerging Markets. *Harvard Business Review*, July–August, pp. 37–51.

Kohut, J., and Cheng, A. T. (1996). Return of the Merchant Mandarins. *Asia, Inc.*, March, pp. 22–31.

Lau, D. C. (1963). *Lau Tzu: Tao Te Ching*. London: Penguin Books.

Legge, J. (1970) *The Works of Mencius*. New York: Cover Publications.

Mintzberg, H. (1987). Crafting Strategy. *Harvard Business Review*, July–August, pp. 66–75.

Mintzberg, H. (1994). The Fall and Rise of Strategic Planning. *Harvard Business Review*, January–February, pp. 107–14.

Mintzberg, H., and Waters, J. (1985). Of Strategies, Deliberate and Emergent. *Strategic Management Journal*, 6, pp. 257–272.

Nakamura, G.-I. (1992). Development of Strategic Management in the Asia Pacific Region. *International Review of Strategic Management*, 3, D. E. Hussey (ed.). West Sussex, UK: John Wiley & Sons, pp. 3–18.

Pan, C.C.H. (1984). Confucian Philosophy: Implication to Management. *Proceedings of the 1984 AMA Conference, Singapore*, C. T. Tan (ed.), pp. 777–781.

Porter, M. (1992). *Competitive Advantage: Greating and Sustaining Superior Performance*. New York: Free Press.

Prahalad, C. K., and Hamel, G. (1990). The Core Competence of the Corporation. *Harvard Business Review*, May–June, pp. 79–91.

Redding, G. (1986). Entrepreneurship in Asia. *Euro-Asia Business Review*, 5(4), pp. 23–27.

Redding, G. (1995). Overseas Chinese Networks: Understanding the Enigma. *Long Range Planning*, 28(1), pp. 61–69.

Seagrave, S. (1996). *Lords of the Rim*. London: Bantam Press.

Shigematsu, S. (1994). The Study of Overseas South Asians: Retrospect and Prospect. Working Paper, Graduate School of International Development, Nagoya University, Japan.

Wada, K. (1992). *Yaohan' Global Strategy, the 21st Century Is the Era of Asia*. Hong Kong: Capital Communications Corporation, Ltd.

Waley, A. (1996). *Confucius: The Analects*. Ware, Hertfordshire, UK: Wordsworth Editions, Ltd.

Weidenbaum, M., and Hughes, S. (1996). *Bamboo Network*. New York: Martin Kessler Books.

Index

About the Editor and Contributors

ABOUT THE EDITOR

FRANK-JÜRGEN RICHTER has lived, worked, and traveled extensively throughout Asia. Fluent in Mandarin and Japanese as well as his native German, he holds a doctorate from Stuttgart (Germany) University, has studied business administration and mechanical engineering, and has done other postgraduate work at Tsukuba University, Tokyo. Dr. Richter has written articles for various professional and scholarly journals, authored two books, and is the editor of two previous books for Quorum, *Business Networks in Asia* (1999) and *The Dragon Millennium* (2000).

ABOUT THE CONTRIBUTORS

PARTHASARATHI BANERJEE is a scientist with the National Institute of Science, Technology and Development Studies (NISTADS), New Delhi. Earlier he was Visiting Professor to the L'École des hautes études en sciences sociales, Paris; Visiting Associate with the École Polytecnique, Paris; Japan Foundation Fellow to the Tokyo University; and Post Doctoral Fellow to the State University of New York at Albany. He has written several books and research papers. His areas of interest include industrial and social organizations, business networks, and strategic management.

FRANK L. BARTELS is Assistant Professor of International Business at the Nanyang Business School of Nanyang Technological University, Singapore. He has published widely on issues related to Asian business, technological cooperation, and global competition.

CAROLINE BENTON is a freelance consultant. She was formerly a director of a Japanese subsidiary of an European manufacturer and was chief consultant at a marketing consulting firm for foreign-affiliated companies in Japan over the last five years.

CHIPPER BOULAS is a partner of Booz-Allen & Hamilton, working out of its Hong Kong offices, with over nine years of consulting experience across many industrial and marketing-intensive industries. He has special expertise in strategy formulation. In Asia, he has pooled Booz-Allen's efforts to understand local conglomerates, the causes and outlook for the Asian economic crisis, and the implications—risks and opportunities—for both local and multinational corporations. Before joining Booz-Allen, he worked with McKinsey and Co. in both New York and Paris, and previously with Rockwell International as an engineer in fiber-optic telecommunications.

IAN C. BUCHANAN is a Singapore-based partner of the international management and technology consulting firm Booz-Allen & Hamilton. While the views expressed here are the author's own and do not necessarily reflect those of the firm, they do draw on the firm's ongoing research into the causes and likely direction of Asia's crisis. He has lived and worked in the region for 26 years.

BETTINA BÜCHEL is an Assistant Professor at the Asian Institute of Technology in Bangkok, Thailand, where she specializes in internal business management and organizational behavior. In addition to her teaching activities, she has served as consultant to public and private organizations such as ABB, Hewlett-Packard, WHO, and Telephone Organization of Thailand. Her research interests include organizational learning, knowledge management, and joint venture management.

BABU RAJ GOPI is a Senior Associate in the Operations Management Group of Booz-Allen & Hamilton. He worked for over two years out of the firm's Singapore office at the height of the Asian crisis. He specializes in operations strategy and delivery stream transformation and has worked with clients in several global engineering and consumer product companies.

GEORGE HALEY is Director of the Marketing and International Business Programs at the University of New Haven, Connecticut. His particular research interests are marketing and strategic decision making in the Asia Pacific region and Mexico, with an emphasis on business networks and groups. His award-winning book, *New Asian Emperors: The Overseas Chinese, Their Strategies and Competitive Advantages* (with Chin-Tiong Tan and U.C.V. Haley), was published in 1998. He has taught in executive-development programs for major universities in the United States, Australia, Mexico, Singapore, and India, and he has consulted on strategic and industrial marketing with companies in the Americas, Australia, and Asia.

HAROLD R. KERBO is a Professor of Sociology at California Polytechnic State University, San Luis Obispo. He has been a Fulbright Professor at Hiroshima University, Japan, a Fulbright-Hays grant recipient to study in Thailand, a visiting professor at two universities in Thailand, a visiting professor at Duisburg University, Germany, and most recently a visiting profesor at the University of Zurich, Switzerland. He is the author of several books and articles, including *Social Stratification and Inequality*, 4th ed., and co-author of *Who Rules Japan? The Inner-Circles of Economic and Political Power.*

MARKUS KHANNA is a research assistant at the Chair of International Management, University of Erlangen–Nürnberg, Germany. His interests include international strategy and management, formation and implementation of joint ventures, and strategies for corporate planning processes. He has written and advised widely in these subject areas.

JOHN KIDD worked in industry for about ten years before he moved to Birmingham University, and later still, to his present position at the Aston Business School. His publications include essays on Japanese management methods (funded by the Japan Foundation). This work has broadened to include all Asian managers following a period at the China Europe International Business School, Shanghai. Recently he was a member of a UK Overseas Science and Technology Expert Mission evaluating manufacturing in Japan and Korea from a cultural and technical perspective.

WOLFGANG KLENNER is Professor of East Asian Economics at the Ruhr-Universität, Bochum, Germany. He was a visiting professor at the University of Tokyo, University of Nagoya, University of International Business and Economics, Beijing, and at various American universities. His research projects focus on China's economic policy and reforms, Japan's industrial structure and organization, economic relations between Western and East Asian companies, and cooperation and competition in East and Southeast Asia.

BRIJ N. KUMAR is Professor and Chair of Business Economics and International Management at the University of Erlangen–Nürnberg, Germany. Previous Chairs include Munich and Hamburg. He has authored and co-authored over 100 publications (including ten books) on various subjects of international management in Germany, the United States, the United Kingdom, Japan, and China. In addition, he is a consultant to companies and ministries and is acting member of the editorial boards of various professional management journals.

HAFIZ R. MIRZA is Professor of International Business at the University of Bradford Management Centre, United Kingdom. His research interests include trade, investment, and development in East and Southeast Asia, and he has published a number of books, including *Global Competitive Strategies in the New World Economy* (1998).

KRIENGSAK NIRATPATTANASAI is currently a Vice President at Thai Dhanu Bank. He was Marketing Director of Kepner-Tregoe Thailand, where he worked with a number of leading corporations in Thailand, Cambodia, and Singapore. A second-generation Chinese immigrant native of Thailand, he is also a columnist for the Asia Pacific Management Forum's *Thailand Tales*, the monthly journal published on the Internet about Thai culture and implications for business.

STEFFEN P. RAUB is Assistant Professor at the School of Management, Asian Institute of Technology (AIT) in Bangkok, Thailand. His research and teaching focuses on organizational behavior and organization theory, organizational change, learning and knowledge management, and international business management. He has consulted with a variety of national and multinational corporations and is a co-founder and partner of the Geneva Knowledge Group.

ROBERT SLAGTER is Associate Professor of Political Science at Birmingham-Southern College in Birmingham, Alabama. For the last ten years he has pursued his interest in political and economic development in Asia and the role of culture in the success or failure of transplanted institutions, especially corporations. Along with Harold R. Kerbo he has recently completed a sociology text, *Modern Thailand*, to be published in Fall 2000.

LUCREZIA SONGINI is Assistant Professor of Management Accounting, Strategic Planning and Management Control Systems in Luigi Bocconi University, Italy. She is also Assistant Professor in the Scuola di Direzione Aziendale Bocconi Business School. Her research and teaching activities focus on management accounting, Japanese management, target costing, strategic planning and performance measurement, and evaluation and reporting systems.

YOSHIYA TERAMOTO is Professor of Social System Design at the Graduate School of Knowledge Science, JAIST (Japan Advanced Institute of Science and Technology). He is also Visiting Professor of Organization Theory at the Graduate School of Asia-Pacific Studies, Waseda University, and a visiting researcher at NISTEP (National Institute for Science and Technology Policy), the Science and Technology Agency, Japan. Professor Teramoto has written and lectured widely on organizational learning and knowledge management.